*Dedicated to my wife Joy,
and my sons Duncan,
Thomas, William and
their families.*

remember your heritage

Introduction

We live in an increasingly complex society, and Hunwick has undergone significant changes during the lifetimes of its oldest residents. Despite all of the changes, the community spirit has remained strong. It is our hope that we can nurture this spirit by sharing knowledge about the village's history. A sense of local identity and pride can boost people's sense of belonging, which can promote a greater desire for community engagement.

'History' is not just about wars, Kings, Queens, explorers and politicians; it is the story of our ancestors' lives, from the gentry to miners and other labourers. We inherit many of the traditions and values of the society and culture they developed and benefit from their learning and achievements. By exploring our heritage, we can better understand how the landscape around us took shape. This knowledge may encourage people to influence and shape our society and environment in the future. The History of Hunwick is a tale worth telling!

This book is my attempt to organise and presenting the information I have gathered during three years of extensive research. While my research has answered some questions, it has also raised many more. Rather than wait until I have found all the 'missing' information, I have decided that the best way to move forward is to print this edition now in the hope that it might inspire others and provide a starting point for further exploration.

We all have a part to play in recording the History of our Village.

Sources of Information

In 2004 Sue Smith, the Headteacher of Hunwick Primary School, secured funding for a Digital Community Project. The project's aim was to increase the level of IT awareness and competence within the village, while collecting information its history.

The project team recognised that they needed to capture the information from the diminishing pool of memories that were held by Villagers. An enthusiastic group of Villagers, led by Alan Edmundson, collected photographs and information about the village and life in the village. The project was supported by Steve Thompson from Middlesbrough University.

A website was created for the village. Unfortunately, it had a short lifespan as the funding required to host it, dried up. Fortunately, Alan had retained many of the photographs and printed materials that had been collected.

In July 2018 Ian Richardson Jnr and Alister Ruddick set up the Hunwickian Facebook page. Images collected by the Digital Village Project were frequently shared on the Hunwickian Page, consistently generating a lot of discussion. This discussion prompted me to explore the Village's history further.

I am not a historian but am simply a 'miner' of information. Over the past three years, I have compiled information from conversations, both in person and via social media, with over one hundred Villagers. I have searched the internet, all of the local the libraries of Bishop Auckland and the archives of Durham University's Palace Green Library, the Common Room in Newcastle, the Fitzhugh Library at Middleton-in-Teesdale, the Durham Mining Museum at Spennymoor and the Coal Board Mine Abandonment Plans stored at Mansfield. Unfortunately, throughout the period that I have been conducting my research, Durham County Council Records Office has been closed.

I have assembled the information I have gathered and present it here, in the hope that it might encourage others to explore and support further investigations into the social and industrial history of the village.

Acknowledgements

I am grateful to everyone who has supported me in my research. Assembling, validating, and interpreting the information presented in this book would not have been possible without the support and encouragement of the many Villagers who generously gave their time to talk and to guide me.

- The twelve Villagers who agreed to be interviewed and have their stories included in this book
- Tim Wellock, for his encouragement and for interviewing and writing up the Villager's Stories
- Wendy Sproates, for editing the images and preparing them for print
- Lorraine Stephens, for proof-reading and correcting my drafts
- Joan Mason, for proof-reading and technical support
- Donald White, for access to his notes and memory
- Olive Linge, for her encouragement for me to write this book
- The National Library of Scotland, for access to their maps archive
- Mike Harkness and Hannah Cartwright, Durham University Library Archives and Special Collections
- Derek Sims, Kath Maddison and Lorne Tallentire, the Fitzhugh Library, Middleton in Teesdale
- Peter Storey and Vivienne Lowe, the Brancepeth Archive
- Julian Harrop, Collections Resources Co-ordinator, Beamish Museum
- Nick Boldrini, Historic Environment Record Officer, DCC Archaeology Section
- Jennifer Hillyard, The Common Room of the Great North, Newcastle upon Tyne
- Roy Lambeth, Durham Mining Museum, Spennymoor
- David Coates, for allowing me to use photographs taken by his grandfather, Herbert Coates
- Northern Heartlands for their support with the Heritage Walks and Story Gathering Project
- Gavin Bake, for his original drawings and artists impression of Hunwick Colliery

The photographs in this document have been obtained from a variety of sources including those collected by the 2006 Hunwick Digital Village Project. Those obtained directly from the original photographer or from a particular publication, have been duly acknowledged. Some photographs, despite attempts to trace their origin, remain anonymous.

If photographs or images have been used without due credit or acknowledgement, I apologise. If anyone believes this to be the case, please let me know and the necessary credit will be added at the earliest opportunity.

Contents

Chapter 1. Hunwick, a Village

Hunwick, Centre of the Universe

Hunwick is a pretty small dot on any map, yet some would consider it the centre of the universe. For many of the 90+ year old Villagers, some of whose reminiscences feature in this book, Hunwick is their world. They have seen it emerge from the threat of Category D, under which some pit villages heard the death knell, to become a peaceful, prosperous, contented community.

Two Icelanders are so convinced of Hunwick's historic place as an important central hub that they have gone to astonishing lengths to prove it. None of the many factors they have unearthed provides concrete proof, but together they provide a convincing argument. They believe that the area on which football pitches and the cricket field stands was a regional hub in pre-Christian times and was the site of the Battle of Brunanburh in 937AD. There is no doubt that an important battle took place, but its location is the subject of various theories.

The Footprints of our Ancestors

Archaeological evidence helps us to find out what our ancestors 'did' and where they 'did' it. It provides some of the information that we need to reconstruct the story of the village. Durham's 'Keys To The Past', archaeological database, includes references to a stone axe of Neolithic or Bronze Age (2300 BC to 800 BC), found between Hunwick and Toronto, a possible iron-age enclosures between Pixley Hill and High Grange, a possible deserted Early Medieval village at Helmington Row and a Roman Fort at Binchester. (Keys_to_the_Past, D1788)

The Neolithic or Bronze Age stone axe which was recorded, in 1949, as having been found on an allotment near the river at Hunwick, was later amended to having been found at Toronto. (Hildyard, 1952,1) The Keys to the Past database, although reminding us that they are uncertain of the actual location, place a location 'pin' close to the Equestrian Centre. (Young R. , 1984)

Image 0383 – Bowes Museum

A newspaper article, in 1980, reported that George and Nancy Gowland, in the 1950s, had found two 'Anglo Saxon' axe heads on their ten-acre allotment between Hunwick and Toronto. This allotment was on the west side of Birtley Lane, half way between the Equestrian Centre and Newton Cap Colliery.

George worked for the Wear and Tees River Board (now Northumbria Water) as a site manager. He had a good local knowledge of the area and had access to the river. He was a member of Durham University's Archaeology group.

George found many Roman artefacts on the river banks and on the river bed, near Binchester Fort. (Gowland, 13 November 1980) A historian from Corbridge Museum visited George and Nancy and examined the artefacts. It was thought that his finds were held by Corbridge Museum but unfortunately, they have no record of the finds.

George and Nancy Gowland

Image 0424 – by kind permission of John Gowland

Although the location of the deserted, Early Medieval village at Helmington Row is unknown, Villagers' report having seen the remains of foundations in a field between West Farm and Rumby Hill. (keystothepast, Ref_D1812) Interestingly, the Holy Well and a field named 'castles', identified on the 1761 Enclosure Map, are in the same vicinity, quite close to Constantine Farm. A *"Neolithic Trancet Derived Arrow Head, two flakes and rough core"*, found at Water Gate, (Rumby Hill), are held by Bowes Museum. (Bowes_Museum, R1_RPM_9_12_76)

Aerial photographs taken in 1968 identified small circular cropmarks to the south-west of the Junction at the top of the village, where the road to North Bitchburn meets the B6286 and on the west side of the road, half-way down High Grange bank. Although there was nothing visible on the ground, the cropmarks were interpreted as suggesting that there might have been iron-age enclosures on these sites. (DCC_Archaeology, D410)

The archaeology confirms that people were living or moving through the area before the Romans arrived in 80 AD.

Extensive archaeological excavations at Binchester Fort have confirmed that it accommodated large numbers of Roman soldiers from 80 AD until 410 AD. Binchester Roman Fort is open to the public and provides visitors with a fascinating insight into life in one of the largest Roman military installations in northern Britain. The Fort is on the other side of the River Wear, less than two miles from Hunwick.

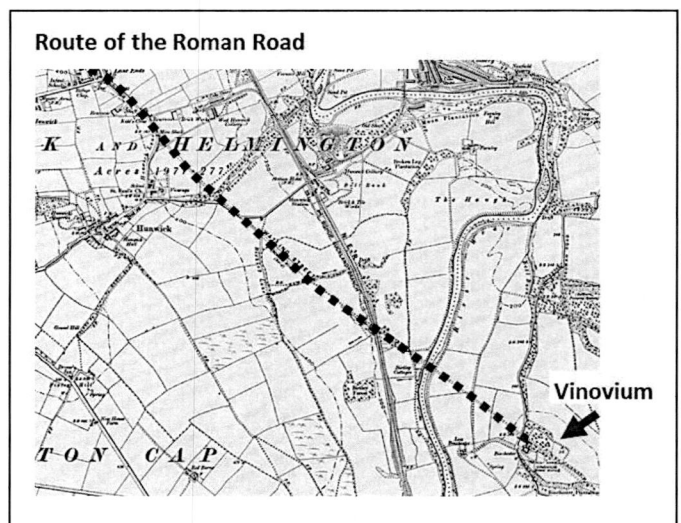

Route of the Roman Road

Vinovium

The Roman Fort, known as Vinovium (Vinovia), was built on high ground overlooking the River Wear. It was built to protect Dere Street, the main Roman Road linking York to Hadrian's Wall, as it crossed the River Wear.

The Fort provided accommodation and support for Roman soldiers as they moved through the region. It also controlled and influenced what happened in the region.

Excavations at Vinovium have uncovered evidence to confirm that it was a very busy Roman Fort capable of accommodating over 1000 soldiers. The Fort was initially built in 80 AD and rebuilt, on the same site, in 158 AD. It was refitted in 360 AD to provide accommodation for cavalry that would be able to respond more quickly than infantrymen to threats from the North.

For over three hundred years, large numbers of Roman soldiers and their families lived less than two miles from Hunwick. The Fort relied on the land around it for food and supplies, possibly using timber, coal and iron ore from around the village.

The Roman Road

When the Romans arrived in Britain, they imposed a structure and improved the quality of the roadways in the country. A section of a Roman road, Dere Street, ran from the Fort of Vinovium at Binchester, crossing the river below the Fort and running along the line of the existing road through Hunwick village before heading north, through Willington and onwards to Lanchester, Corbridge and Edinburgh. The Roman Road crossed the river close to the site of the current sewerage works at the Flatts, Bishop Auckland and then climbed up Birtley Lane and on through Hunwick

'The Roman Way continues visible as it ascends from the River Wear, and at the distance of about 1000 yards from it enters a blind lane, which it follows very obscurely for a short distance, and passes about 200 yards below the church at Hunwick. A little farther, it appears to enter the lane leading to Helmington Hall, and continues along it as far as the spot where it turns off to the westward. The cottage and garden on the west side are on it, and the traces are clearly to be seen down to the brook at Helmington Hall, both at the cottage and in the field at the back of it. At the Hall the line is somewhat on the western edge of the road, as it ascends from the bridge, and continues along the course of the road to Willington' (MacLauchlan, 1858)

A survey of the Roman Road between Bishop Auckland and Lanchester was undertaken by the Royal Commission on Historical Monuments (England) in 1959. Having found worked stones in the river bank, the survey suggested that the road crossed the River Wear using a bridge with stone piers and a timber superstructure. (Dymond, 1961)

Helmington Hall Cottages

Image 0003 – The Herbert Coates Collection

Roman river crossings

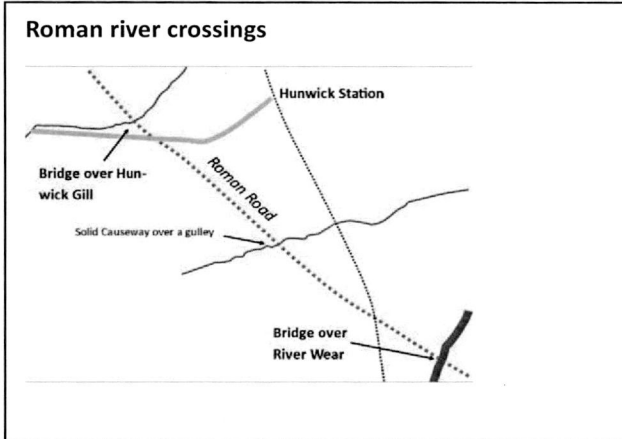

Roman Bridge over Hunwick Gill (artists impression)

Image 0005 - (Dymond, 1961) - J E Williams Illustrator

The artist's impression, originally published in the Archaeological Journal, shows what the bridge, that carried Dere Street across Hunwick Gill might have looked like.

The survey identified that the road would also need to negotiate the steep-sides of the Hunwick Gill, the stream that runs down from the Church and into the River Wear.

"This gill, 50 ft. wide from lip to lip and 20-25 ft. deep, is sharply riven in the surface of a plateau. It is therefore too steep and narrow to have been negotiated by a zig-zag. In addition, the road on each side leads to the very lip of the gill."

It also identified that between the bridge over the Wear and the bridge over Hunwick Gill, the road would need to cross another small stream that ran in a six-to-eight-feet wide gulley. They concluded that it was likely that a solid causeway would have been built, with the probable provision of a pipe or culvert for the stream to flow through.

In 2024, East Durham Detectors, uncovered Roman coins, a buckle, a stylus and a perfume bottle top that would have been used by a high-status lady, in a field north of the village, on the line of the Roman Road.

The Legionaries based at the Fort would have been supported by Auxiliary soldiers, men drawn into the army from across the Roman Empire, sometimes voluntarily, sometimes by force. Archaeological 'finds' confirm that soldiers from Spain and Holland had been based at Binchester.

After the Romans

Sometime around 410 AD, Britain ceased to be part of the Roman Empire. The Fort at Binchester was abandoned by the Roman Army. The Legionaries were withdrawn and re-deployed to other countries in the Roman Empire. Some of the Auxiliary soldiers were abandoned without pay. They became local petty warlords or were absorbed into neighbouring communities who were trying to resist attacks from Saxon pirates and other enemies.

When the Romans left Britain, the absence of a strong central government and a disciplined army left a vacuum that land-hungry Anglo Saxons, filled. Through invasions, trading or simply by being left behind by the Roman Army, people from northern Germany and Holland established themselves in the area.

Archaeological evidence, including finds from a 6th century, Anglo-Saxon cemetery, confirms that people continued to live at Binchester Fort, after the fort was abandoned by the Romans. The Fort is 1.4 miles from Hunwick

Escomb Church, one of the oldest Anglo-Saxon churches in England, was built, sometime around 675 AD, using stone 'robbed' from the Roman Fort at Binchester. Escomb is 1.5 miles away from Hunwick.

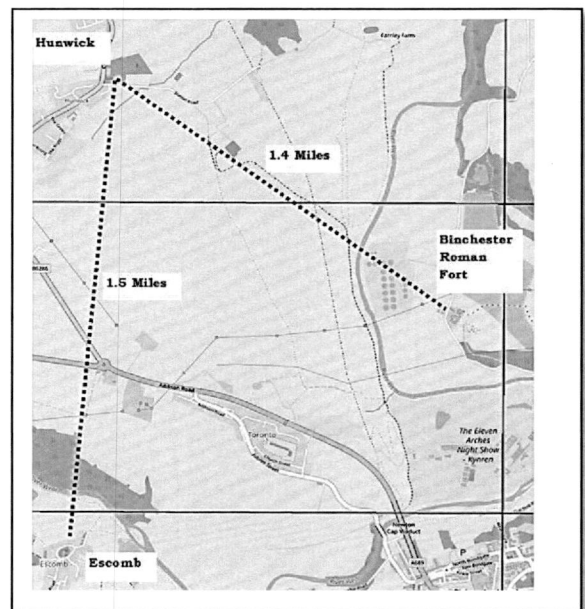

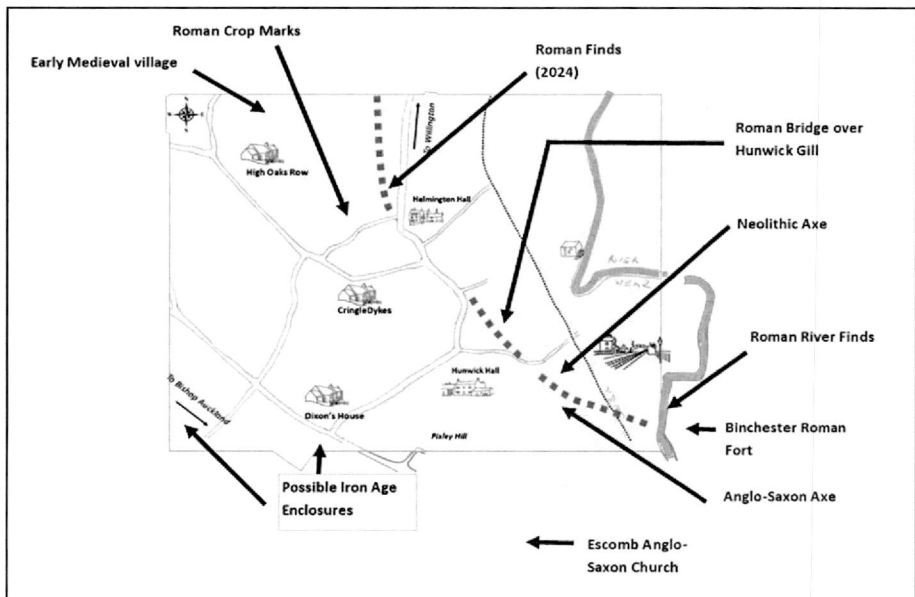

The map to the left, highlights the evidence 'finds' that confirm that people have lived or passed through Hunwick since early times.

Hunwick on the Map

'Hunwick' appears on Christopher Saxon's map which is the earliest map of County Durham, printed in 1576. (Saxon, 1576) It also appears on the 1662, 1768, and 1818 maps as well as the Ordnance Survey (OS) maps that were surveyed and printed after 1856.

Maps and contemporary documents spell 'Hunwick' in many different ways, including: Hunewyk, Hunwyk, Hunewye, Hunwyke, Honewyk and Honnewicke.

Why the village became known as 'Hunwick' attracts as many different theories. One theory is that it is derived from the Anglo-Saxon name 'Hunna', with 'Hunwick' being translated to mean the 'dairy farm of Hunna' (Surtees, The History of the Parishes of Hunwick, Helmington, Witton Park and Etherley, 1923) Another theory is that it was derived from the German 'Hune' suggesting a bold warrior. (Magazine)

Christopher Saxon's Map, 1576

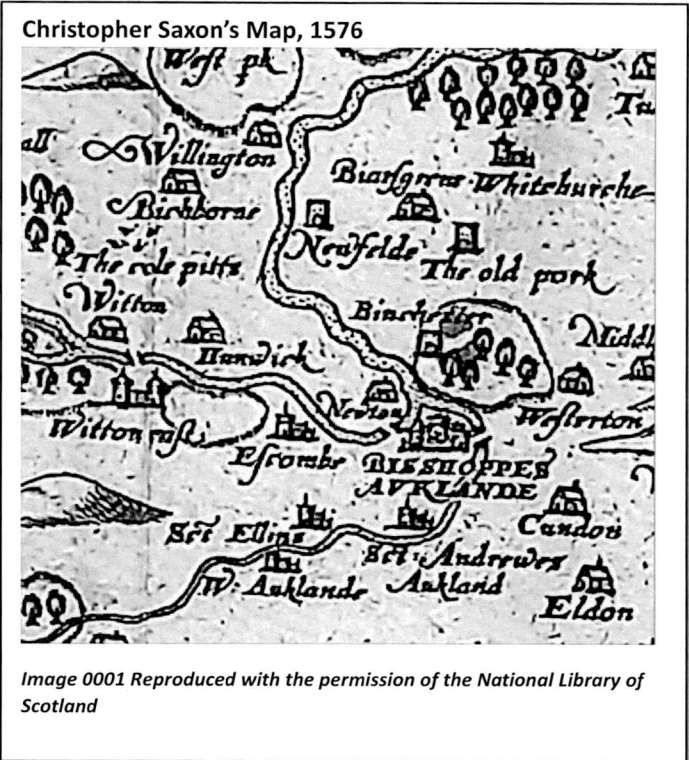

Image 0001 Reproduced with the permission of the National Library of Scotland

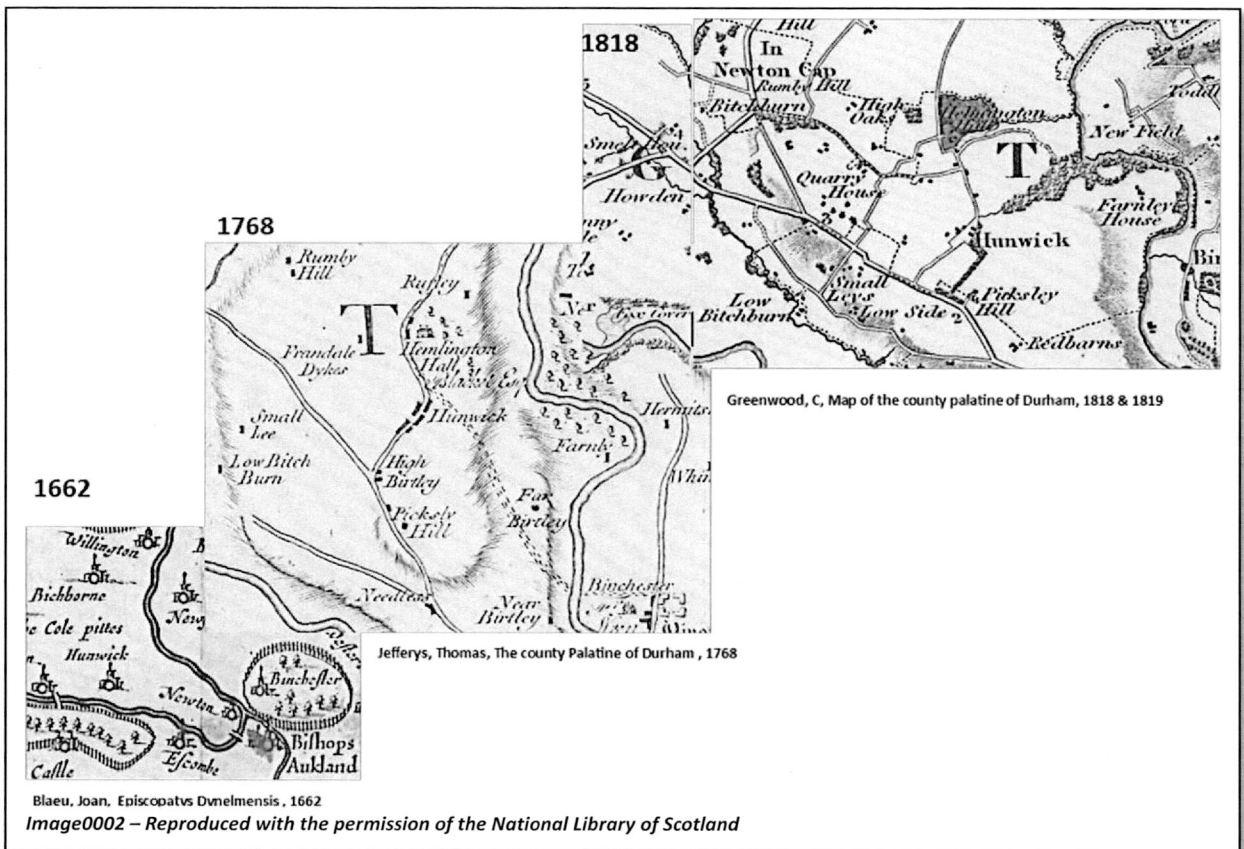

1818

Greenwood, C, Map of the county palatine of Durham, 1818 & 1819

1768

Jefferys, Thomas, The county Palatine of Durham , 1768

1662

Blaeu, Joan, Episcopatvs Dvnelmensis , 1662

Image0002 – Reproduced with the permission of the National Library of Scotland

Björn Vernharðsson's interpretation is that 'wick' implies much more than a dairy farm and that it is more likely that it is referring to it having been a 'thing' or a site. He considers that 'Hun' is often used to identify a finial, a capital or dome on flagpole, inferring that the name 'Hunwick', was used to describe an important site. Björn uses this explanation to support his hypothesis that Hunwick was a social centre of Anglo-Saxon Northumbria.

The Roads to Hunwick

Once built, the Roman Road and river crossing, would have been used by anyone wanting to move around or through the area. After 410 AD the Roman roads and bridges would have fallen into disrepair but the routes would have continued to be used by anyone who needed to move around the country.

The Anglo-Saxons were pagan. In 634 AD Oswald became King of Northumbria and requested St Aidan to come from Iona to convert Northumbria to Christianity. In 635 AD, St Aidan established a monastery at Lindisfarne and began his missionary work. St Cuthbert, became the Prior at Lindisfarne from around 665 AD.

After Cuthbert's death, pilgrims flocked to his shrine at Lindisfarne. The ordinary life of the monastery continued until 793 AD, when the Vikings raided the area. The Vikings captured York in 867, and established control over the area. In 875 AD, the monastery on Lindisfarne was abandoned and the body of St. Cuthbert, together with other relics, were taken to the mainland in the hope that they could be kept safe from the Vikings.

The relics of St Cuthbert, which included the head of St Oswald and the Lindisfarne Gospels, had been a major attraction for pilgrims. In 1104, the body and relics found a home in the new Norman cathedral at Durham.

Pilgrims travelled long distances to visit Durham to see the relics. Large numbers would have travelled along the Roman road to get to Durham Cathedral. Those travelling from the south, would have travelled along the Roman Road that passed through Hunwick. Perhaps they used the Roman Well that was north of what is currently the Quarry Tea Room?

Drovers' Roads

In addition to the network of Roman Roads, Drovers' roads criss-crossed the country connecting ancient market towns. Large herds of cattle, sheep and poultry were moved long distances, from Scotland and Ireland to southern markets along Drovers' roads. Scottish cattle were sold at Carlisle and Corbridge markets and were then herded down the country. Irish cattle were imported to ports on the west coast and were brought over the Pennines into Durham, Yorkshire and Northumberland.

Drovers picked up animals from markets and farms along the routes that they travelled. They had to be licenced as the animals that they took responsibility for were valuable and they handled large sums of money.

The Drovers moved their herds at a leisurely pace, providing opportunities for grazing as it was in their interest to maintain or even improve the condition of the herd before they delivered them to the market. They preferred to keep to the higher ground, away from local herds and where free grazing was more likely to be available. The visibility provided by the higher routes also made it more difficult for robbers to ambush them.

The Drovers' Roads would try to avoid going through the centre of a town or village and would seek out easy river crossings. Inns were established along the routes of the Drovers' Roads. Drovers' Inns provided food and drink and a small field called a 'pinfold', to keep their animals safe overnight. A pinfold was also used, in Open Field systems, to impound animals that had strayed onto land that they should not have been on.

For many years, wool underpinned the local economy. Salt was important to preserve meat for the winter months and coal was in demand to heat the large houses and ecclesiastical buildings in the wider area. Wool, lead, salt and coal were carried on packhorses using the Drovers' Roads or Pack Horse Roads.

Drovers, in addition to moving cattle long distances along Drovers' Roads, would also use the 'Green Lanes' that connected market towns with surrounding villages, to herd cattle, sheep and poultry to and from markets.

The industrial revolution and the development of large concentrations of people in the cities, meant that it was more profitable for local farmers to produce milk rather than to keep cows for meat. This increased the use of the long-distance Drovers' roads until the 1850s when it became possible, and more economic, to move cattle by rail. The historic animal fairs were replaced by Cattle Auction Marts sited beside railway stations. The Drovers' Roads would then only be used to move cattle short distances either to or from market or between summer and winter grazing.

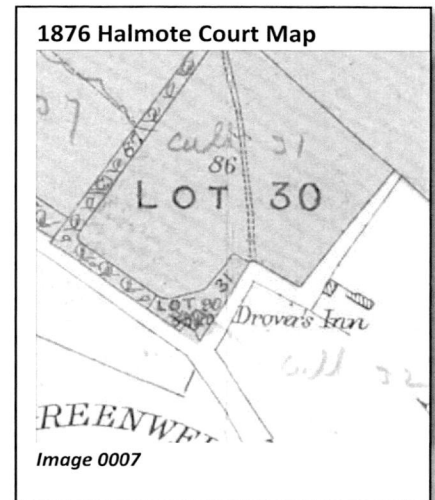

1876 Halmote Court Map

Image 0007

The 1761 Enclosure Map for Hunwick Moor, identifies 'Pinfold Lane' at Pixley Hill. The 1857 OS map identifies the 'Drovers Inn' at Pixley Hill. Maps show a small field on Pinfold Lane. The field had access to water from a spring and from the 'Rodding Burn' (a stream), that ran through an adjoining field.

Before the house that currently stands on the site of Drovers' Inn was redeveloped, it had stables attached. These stables would have been used to stable the pack horses or Drover's horses.

Villagers have shared stories of an ancient road running through Blakeley Hill Farm which lies between Pixley Hill and North Bitchburn.

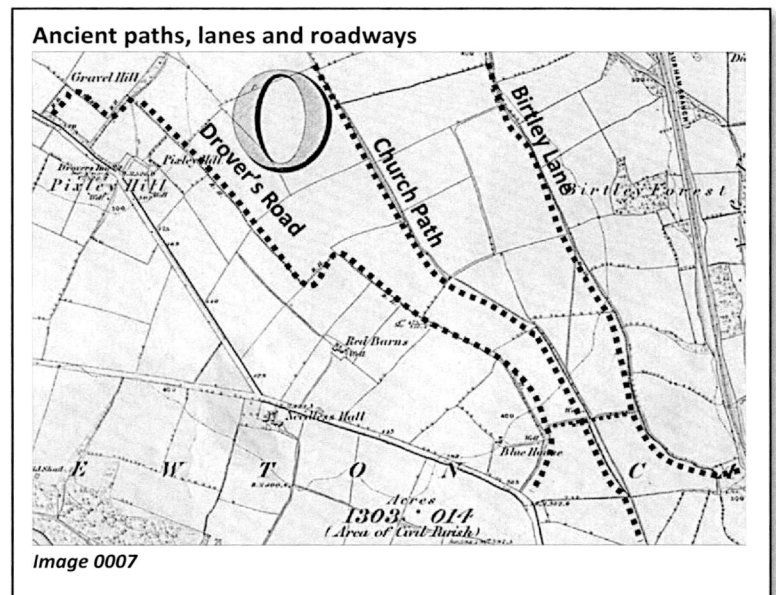

Ancient paths, lanes and roadways

Image 0007

The 1761 Enclosure Map shows the Drovers' Inn at Pixley Hill being adjacent to a number of *'ancient foot ways'*. For it to be economic to run an Inn in such an isolated location, there must have been sufficient passing trade.

A Drovers' Road ran from Corbridge to West Auckland passing by Helme Park with another connecting Fir Tree with Hamsterley. A number of different Drovers' and Packhorse roads ran through Wolsingham. Reputedly, Howden, North Bitchburn and Fir Tree were all on Drovers' Roads. (Surtees, The History of the Parishes of Helme Park etc) (Hutton, 2011) (Close)

The choice of name for the Inn, its proximity to a 'pinfold' and other, known, Drover's Roads, adds weight to the theory that a Drovers' Road ran past Hunwick. If there was an iron-age enclosure at Pixley Hill, perhaps the Drover's Road was a very early route? (DCC_Archaeology, D410)

The network of Roman Roads and Drovers' Roads connected the areas of the country that they passed through. Before the opening of the railways, the Drovers and the Carriers that operated the Packhorses, would engage with the communities that they encountered on their route. They would, in addition to supporting trade, be a 'communication channel' through which communities received and transmitted news, information and ideas.

Early Land Holders

We know that Hunwick Village existed in 882 AD, as it was included in the land that was identified as part of *'the lands between the rivers Tyne and Wear'* that was given to the Community of St. Cuthbert, to provide for its upkeep. (Historia de Sancto Cuthberto)

Before the Norman invasion, Northumbria was ruled by a group of Viking Earls. *'In a time of public calamity'*, Bishop Aldune (959 - 1018), looked to the Earls of Northumberland for protection. Hunwick was mentioned as one of the villages, given to the Earls of Northumberland, in return for their protection. (Hutchinson, 1785)

In 1066, William the Conqueror invaded England and effectively became the owner of all of the land in the country. He gave the Norman knights who had fought alongside him, rights to hold land. In return he required these new land holding tenants to provide him with income and support. Initially land was given for military service but later, it was also given to individuals who had assisted with administrative support and services. These tenants were required to maintain order in the area of the country that they had been given.

In 1066, William introduced taxes to collect the money that he needed to pay the continental mercenaries who had supported him at the Battle of Hastings. These taxes were unpopular and resulted in a rebellion amongst people who lived in the North of the country.

In 1069 he sent an army to put down the Northern Rebellion. His army adopted a scorched-earth policy destroying everything and everyone in their path. This 'Harrying of the North' is thought to have resulted in the death of 75% of the population in Yorkshire and the North East and the destruction of most towns and villages. As Hunwick lies so close to the Roman road, it is likely that the village was destroyed during this period.

After the Northern Rebellion, William needed someone to look after the northern region and protect England from invasions by the Scots. In 1071 he appointed William Walcher, from Liege, as the first non-English Bishop of Durham. Bishop Walcher acquired estates in Northumbria which, at that time, included County Durham. He was required, on behalf of the King, to administer large areas of land, including the land around Hunwick. He became the first of the 'Prince Bishops' who held political and military powers in addition to their religious responsibilities.

Northumberland and Durham were not included in the Domesday Book. However, in 1183, the Bishop of Durham conducted a survey of the land that the Church owned. This survey, recorded in the Boldon Book, showed that *'Ralph of Binchester holds Hunwick'* and that Roger Bernard held 48 acres in *'Helmygdene'*. (Morris, 1982)

It is quite difficult to untangle and explain who owned the individual parcels of land around Hunwick. For my purposes, I think it is best to assume that the Church, in the form of the Bishop or the Prior of the Monastery of St Cuthbert, 'held' all of the land in the area.

The community of St Cuthbert had established a Monastery in Durham in 995 AD. The Bishop of Durham gave the Prior of the Monastery, land so that it could sustain itself. By 1189, the Priory of Durham was well established with large land holdings. The Monastery, in addition to acquiring lands from the Bishop of Durham, acquired wealth from the donations of gold, silver or jewels from pilgrims who came to see the relics of St Cuthbert. The Prior and later the Dean and Chapter and then the Ecclesiastical Commission, who in the 1850s took over the Cathederal estates, managed the estates.

The Bishop leased his lands to his supporters including Ralph of Binchester (the Wrens), The Earl of Westmorland (the Nevilles of Brancepth and Raby Castle), Sir William Eure, Sir William Bowes, Lord

Strathmore, Viscount Boyne and Lady Barrington. These great landed families either managed the land themselves or leased them to sub-tenants.

The Bishop, the Dean and Chapter, the Ecclesiastical Commission and the great landed aristocratic families, all relied on trusted councillors including lawyers, stewards, foresters and high-ranking household and estate managers. These individuals worked for more than one estate. Members of this trusted, minor gentry, became sub-tenants of the Bishop, the Dean and Chapter or the major landowners that had actually employed them.

John Burdon and John Hoton, who held positions of responsibility for major land holders, both acquired land in Hunwick. In 1353, Bishop Hatfield appointed John Burdon of Helmington Hall, to be the keeper of Auckland Park for life. John Hoton, of Hunwick Hall, was one of John Neville's most valued retainers and *'held all of his estates because of the patronage of the Nevilles'.* (Hampton, John Hoton of Hunwick and Tudhoe, County Durham, esquire to Richard III, 1985)

A list of the Knights of the Bishopric of Durham, compiled in 1264, includes Sir Roger Bernard de Helmington. (Hutchinson, 1785) A lease dated 1285, confirms that Sir Roger Bernard held the Helmington Hall estate at that time. (Durham_Records_Office, D/Gr_57 For Bernard's estate, see HS, P. 16))

The Hatfield Survey, 1345-1381, recorded that Robert of Binchester held Hunwick and that the Bishop of Durham had given him Hunwick for 'service outside of his district'. John Burdon of Helmington Hall, had taken the surname of his wife, Alice. Alice was the daughter of Roger de Burdon who had died in 1357. On his death it was recorded that he held a *'messuage and 48 acres in Helmington and lands and tenements in Hunewyk – held of the Bishop and also of the lord (dominus de) Bynchester'.* (Surtees, The History of the Parishes of Hunwick, Helmington, Witton Park and Etherley, 1923)

In 1426, the Inquisition (post death enquiry), of the first Earl of Westmorland, recorded that his estate included *'Two houses and two bovates'*, two houses each with approximately 20 acres of land, in Hunwick. In 1429, Binchester and Hunwick were conveyed to Ralph, Earl of Westmorland (the Nevilles of Brancepeth and Raby). (Eneas Mackenzie, 1834) The Neville Family owned Brancepeth Castle until 1569, when it was confiscated following the family's involvement in the Rising of the North.

In 1534, Henry VIII took control of the land and property that had previously belonged to the Monasteries. This included some of the land around Hunwick.

The land and property were retained by the King until Durham Cathedral was re-founded as an Anglican Cathedral, in 1541. Some of the confiscated land, including land around Hunwick, was returned to the ownership of the Dean and Chapter for the upkeep of the cathedral. These lands were managed by the Dean and Chapter and later the Ecclesiastical Commission. At the same time, Henry VIII, also returned land to the Bishop of Durham.

Hunwick has been recognised as a village for more than a thousand years.

The Settlements

The proximity of Hunwick to the River Wear and to the Roman Road and the Drovers' Road, is likely to have influenced the decision of the people who settled in the area.

During the nineteenth century, this decision would have been influenced by the employment opportunities provided by coal mining and brickmaking.

The expansion of coal mining and brickmaking led to the opening of Hunwick Railway Station that connected the village to the national passenger and freight network.

In addition to the houses around the Village Green in Old Hunwick, Hunwick Village includes the settlements at Lane Ends, New Hunwick, Quarry Burn, Oaks Row, Rough Lea, Hunwick Station and Hunwick Lane.

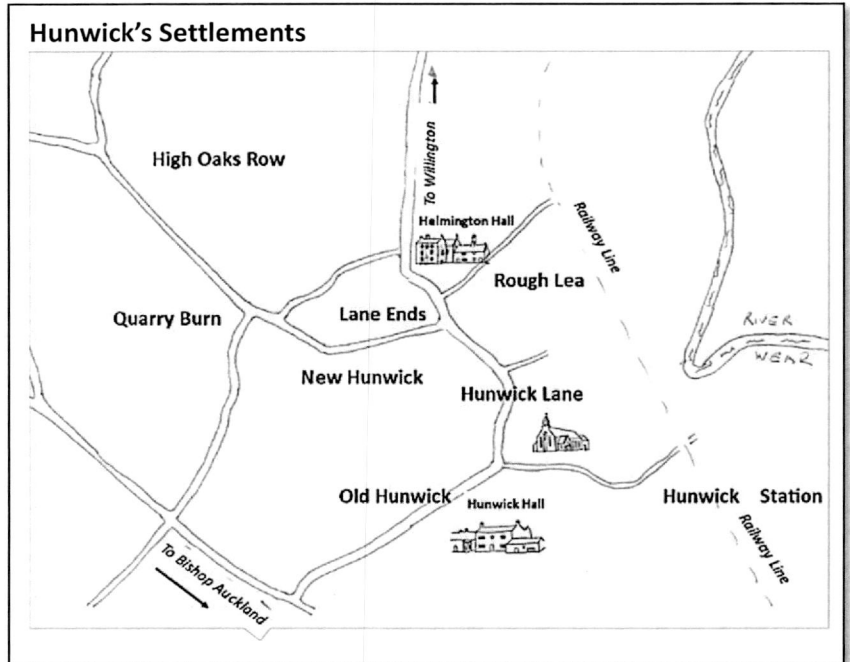

Hunwick's Settlements

These settlements developed alongside roadways. The 1761 Enclosure Act that enclosed Hunwick Moor, also defined and named the footpaths and 'lanes' in the village.

The paths were used by Villagers as they moved to and from the fields as well as to access the village wells and the mill. The roadways would have been used to move animals between grazing and pasture, and onto Common Land. The paths and roadways existed before today's farms were established.

Some of the lanes are now known by different names, but they are all still in use today.

In addition to the lanes and roadways that are shown on the 1761 Enclosure Map, others are marked on an 1876 Estate Map and on the 1857 OS map.

The routes link the village fields to the Village Green and to the barns, byres and

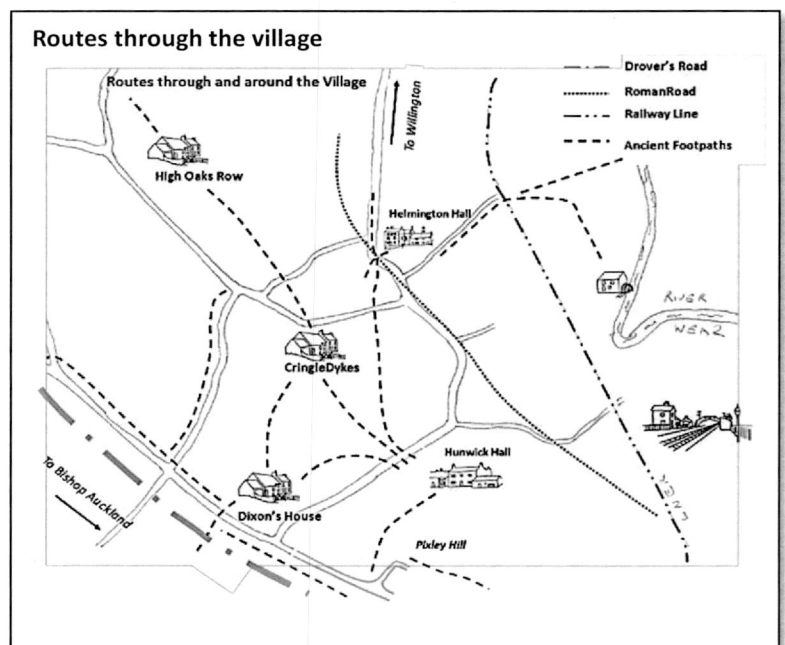

Routes through the village

blacksmiths that were around the Village Green. They also link the village to the Furnace Mill.

Many of the tracks and paths, shown on the 1876 Estate Map, that lead from the Village Green, are still in use today as public rights of way.

The Estate Map shows the Village Green, before North View and Woodbine House were built, extending down to the Quarry in which Raby House was built. The Green was much larger than it is today. All of the foot ways led to or from the Village Green. Hunwick Lane ran through the Village Green.

1876 Hunwick Estate Map

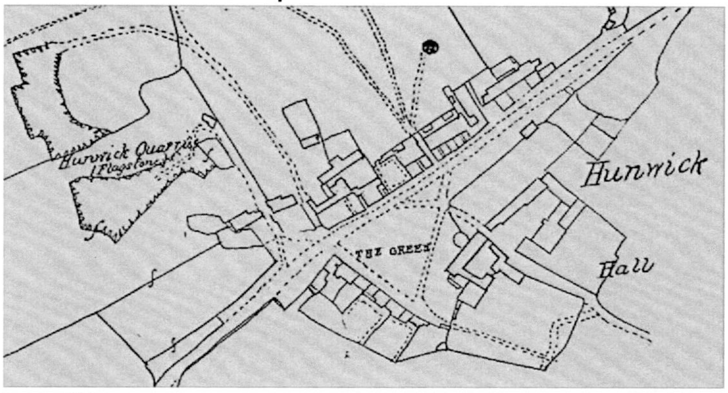

Image 0008

In 1555, the Highways Act made the upkeep of roadways the responsibility of local parishes or townships. The 1761 Enclosure Act gave the responsibility of maintaining the *'township roads'* in Hunwick to the landowners whose land bordered onto the roadway. In Hunwick and throughout the country, this led to a poorly maintained network of road. Before the eighteenth century, people would either travel on foot or horseback. In 1872, the roads were in *'a very imperfect state'* and would have only been suitable for pack horses. (Richley, 1872)

Horse-drawn stage coaches needed good roads. The Turnpike roads were introduced in the early 1700s to support the increasing commerce and communication between towns and villages, that the Industrial Revolution needed. The Turnpike roads were maintained to a higher standard with tolls having to be paid by those who used them. It was a road network that enabled long distance horse-drawn coach travel with connections to major towns and cities. Four miles per hour was considered to be a good speed for a coach using a good road, eight miles per hour was very fast! It took three days to travel from London to Newcastle by Stage Coach.

Wealthy Villagers from Hunwick would need to get to Bishop Auckland or West Auckland if they wanted to travel by Stage Coach. The *'Exmouth'*, the Lancaster to Newcastle stage coach, stopped overnight in Bishop Auckland and the London to Edinburgh stage coach passed through Bishop Auckland. One coach route between West Auckland and Alston, crossed the river at Witton-le-Wear, before passing through Fir Tree and travelling up Weardale.

The 1861 Hunwick Estate Map describes Wolsingham Road, the road that climbs Pixley Hill and goes onto North Bitchburn, as the *'Great Road leading to Wolsingham'*. This was the main road that carts and carriages would use to travel between Bishop Auckland and Wolsingham.

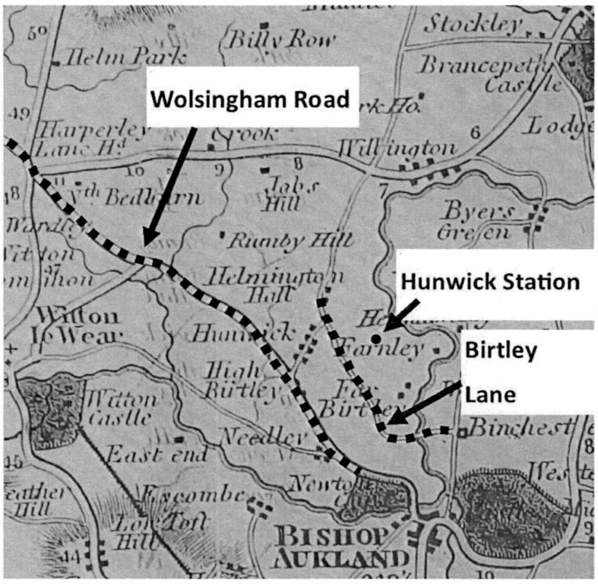

Henry Teesdale's 1833 map identifies Wolsingham Road as a Turnpike Road. It also shows Birtley Lane. Station Road does not exist in 1833.

The Turnpike roads tended to follow valley routes so did not take over the higher routes that had been used by the Drovers. This meant that many of the disused Drovers and Packhorse roads have survived as footpaths or rights of way.

Wolsingham Road

Hunwick Station

Birtley

Lane

Land Use- Agriculture

While our values and culture have evolved from the working and life experience of our ancestors, the landscape views that we enjoy today, are the result of the agricultural and industrial activity that has taken place in previous centuries.

To understand why the landscape around Hunwick, looks like it does today, we need to explore how the land has been used and how people have worked and lived in the past. We will need to use information that was recorded about events or transactions. This information will only be available if someone had thought that it was important enough to be recorded and kept. Information about births, deaths, marriages, wills and financial and legal transactions are 'things' that have been thought to be important enough to record.

We are fortunate to have two significant houses, Hunwick Hall and Helmington Hall, both of which have left financial and social 'footprints' for us to explore. The 'footprint' for Hunwick Hall begins in 1418 and for Helmington Hall, in 1285.

In addition, the Bishop of Durham, as the Lord of the Manor, kept records of transactions that were made by copyholders and of legal disputes. The 1761 Enclosure Act that divided the Common Land around the village, also provides valuable clues as to how the land was being used.

Using this information, I have attempted to build a model or a picture of how the land around the village was being used and how Villagers worked the land in the 1600 and 1700s.

The Open Field System

Typically, a village would have one large 'village-field' that would be used to grow crops and to feed animals. The poorer-quality, less productive land around the village-field, would be used as 'Common Land'.

I interpret the following as evidence that an Open-Field system was in operation in Hunwick before 1761:

- The 1761 Enclosure Act for the enclosure of Hunwick Edge Moor confirms, that the village did have Common Land on the periphery of the village.

- 1761 Enclosure Act identifies the location of 'ancient stiles' and 'ancient foot ways'. The stiles were openings or ways through a hedge or a fence that were typically found around a large village-field. The location of stiles suggests that there had been a fence between the village field and the surrounding Common Land. The 'ancient footways' were the paths that workers used when travelling to and from the different areas of the field in which they were working.

- 1761 Enclosure Act identifies a 'Pin-fold' at Pixley Hill. Stray animals would be moved into a 'pinfold' or pound.

- An inventory prepared for the sale of the Hunwick Hall Estate in 1635 tells us that the Estate had an Ox-Close, a pasture set aside to feed the plough teams. It also tells us that the 8 oxen that belonged to the Hall would graze alongside the 28 oxen that belonged to the three farms on the Estate.

The Common Land is highlighted on the sketch map. The position of 'stiles' identified on the 1761 Enclosure Map are also highlighted on the sketch map.

This suggests that there had been a fence between the village field and the surrounding Common Land.

The Open or Village Field, would have been farmed collectively by the residents of the village, albeit under the control of a 'superior' land holder. The system relied on relationships between the Lord of the Manor, the land holding tenants and the land workers.

The Lord of the Manor would have kept the 'demense land', the land that could be cultivated easily and was productive, to provide food, fuel and materials to support the Manor House.

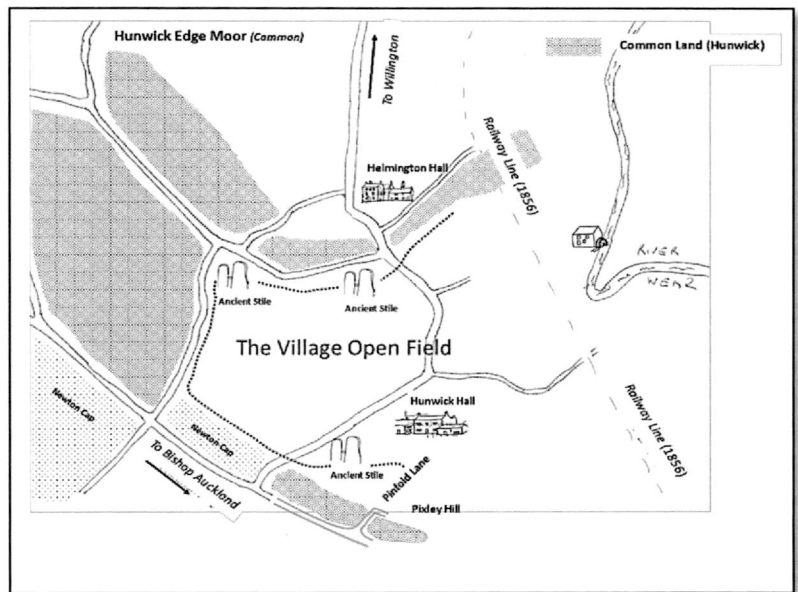

The Open Field would be divided into many narrow strips. Typically, Villagers would be allocated a number of strips that would be distributed across different areas of the field to ensure that individuals had a mixture of the better and poorer areas of the land in the field. Some of the demesne land would have been organised as strips in the same Open Field. The field would not have any internal hedges or walls but there would be a very narrow strip of turf between the strips so that it was clear what area of the allocated field, individuals were allowed to use.

Growing the same crops, year after year, on the same strips resulted in reduced soil fertility. Crop rotation was designed to allow the soil to recover its fertility following its use to grow a crop. To allow crop rotation to work, the strips in the 'village field' would be grouped together and worked as a separate field within the 'village field'. A crop rotation scheme for a field might have been to leave the field fallow for a year, grow wheat the next year and grow oats in the third year. Depending on what crops would be most useful and on the particular land conditions, peas or beans might be grown instead of oats in the crop cycle. (Bailey, 1810)

Cultivation of the arable land would have been labour intensive, requiring the land to be ploughed, planted, weeded and harvested. Within the village, land holders would be required to follow a rigid crop rotation scheme and a plan that specified when ploughing, seed sowing and harvesting would be done.

Villagers would be allowed to graze their animals on the arable strips after the grain had been harvested and in the meadows after the hay had been harvested. As well as providing grazing for the animals, the land benefited from their manure. Small landholders might have a single cow, a few sheep, a pig and a few hens. For everyone other than large landholders, it would have been subsistence farming where what was grown or the animals that they kept, was for their own consumption or to pay their tithes and rent.

At the end of the 18th century, farmers with many strips of land, would plough using their own teams of oxen while poorer farmers would work together to plough, often using their cows to pull the plough.

The arable strips would be ploughed using a single-share plough. The first furrow would turn the earth to the right. At the end of the strip the team of oxen would be turned around and the plough would be pulled back along the strip turning the earth back towards the 'mound' created by the first pass down the strip.

As this process is repeated a 'large mound' is created along the length of the strip. As this happens, so a low strip/ditch is created between the mounds. This working would create the ridge and furrows that can sometimes be seen in fields. The strips typically would be between seven and nine feet wide.

Before horses were used to pull the plough oxen were used. Oxen, castrated bulls, were more muscular and stronger than cows and were happy to eat grass. They did not need the expensive grains that horses did. Depending upon the ground conditions and the plough being used it could take up to 8 oxen to pull a plough but often a team of four would be used. The first four would be allowed to rest and graze while the second team of four took over and continued with the ploughing. The oxen would need to be fed during the winter, as without them ploughing could not be done.

Ridge and Furrow Working, Quarry Burn

Image 0700 – by kind permission of Thomas Pallister

Ridge and Furrow Working, Blakeley Hill Farm

Image 0356

In addition to the arable land, some land in the Village Field would be set aside as permanent pasture for animals to graze and some would be set aside as meadow land to grow the hay needed to feed the animals during the winter. An inventory prepared in 1635/36 for the sale of the Hunwick Hall Estate, tells us that the Estate had an Ox-Close which was a pasture set aside to feed the plough teams. In total, the Village had thirty-six oxen that they needed to feed during the winter.

Villagers were allowed to graze their animals on the 'common' land, the land that was difficult to work or that was less productive. To prevent over grazing of the Common Land, a limit was set on the number of animals that each individual could graze on the common.

With the Open Field system, it was difficult to ensure that animals were kept on the correct strips. Stray animals were impounded in the 'pinfold'. This inevitably led to disputes which would be resolved by the Bishop of Durham's Manorial Court, known as the Halmote Court. Maps show Hunwick's pinfold at Pixley Hill.

Hunwick's Open Field System

The sketch map below has been constructed using information from the 1761 Enclosure Act, the 1843 Tithe Map, Ordnance Survey maps showing field boundaries along with information provided by a DCC Archaeology

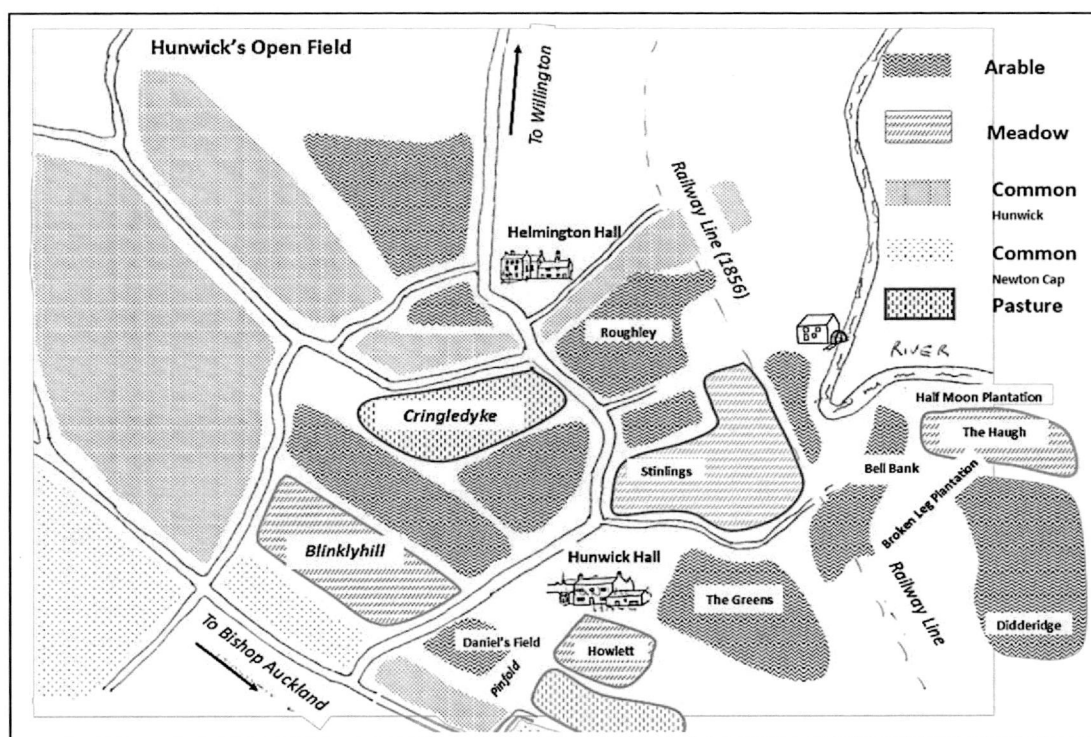

aerial survey. The map is simply a 'best guess' at what the village's Open Field might have looked like. Hopefully this map will be refined as a result of feedback and the discovery of further information that this book might stimulate.

Increasing demand for grazing land- The Woollen Industry

Sheep were kept for meat and for wool. From as early as the 13th century there are records of wool being bought and sold by the Church. Fleeces from Durham were considered to be of a quality only suitable for making course cloths (russet) generally used to make working clothes. Initially, raw wool (fleeces or fells, fleeces with the skin left on) were exported from Hartlepool, the port that belonged to the Bishop of Durham. They were shipped to Holland and Belgium where they were woven into material.

During the 14th century the volume of the raw wool that was exported went down and the volume of the woven material exported went up.

Much of the land around Hunwick would only have been suitable for grazing sheep. An inventory prepared for the sale of the Hunwick Hall Estate in 1663, confirms that sheep were being kept at that time, as it listed '8 oxen, 17 kyne, 3 bullocks, 7 cattle two years old, seven cattle one year old, 2 horses and 2 mares, 10 fatte weathers (castrated rams often used for wool), 22 store weathers, 60 ewes, 2 rams, 40 sheep and hoggs, 9 swyne'. (Durham_University_Special_Collections, D/X235/1, 1596)

Furnace Mill, a Fulling Mill, had operated at Rough Lea between 1687 and 1828. Fulling, the thickening and cleaning of woven cloth, is a process where woven material is immersed in boiling water and agitated by a mechanically driven paddle. The boiling water shrinks the woven yarn while the paddle, driven by the water wheel, pounds and compact the fibres. The process creates a smoother and more hard-wearing fabric.

Fullers earth (a clay), pigs' urine or potash was used as a detergent to help with the cleaning process. The potash was produced by burning bracken. After fulling, the cloth was hung, outside, on frames covered in tenter hooks so that the shrunken cloth dried out flat. (Aspin, 2006)

As well as Furnace Mill in Hunwick, there were Fulling Mills at Stanhope, Wolsingham, Witton-le-Wear, Bedburn and Bishop Auckland as well as many downstream, around Durham City. This would suggest that wool processing was a large-scale activity in the area.

Wool was a major export for England. The raw wool and later the woven material would have been sold at local market or fairs, or sold to travelling wool merchants. (Richley, 1872) The Guild of Weavers and Websters was established in Durham City in 1450. This group of craftsmen and merchants monitored and controlled the quality and marketing of woollen goods. (Freemen) As a quality control measure, the Guild required cloth workers to fix a seal/tag to the cloth that they produced confirming its dimensions and who had produced it. The cloth workers were also be expected to pay tax on the material that they produced. The material was inspected to confirm that it met the required standards and that the tax had been paid. At this stage a second tag was attached.

If it was viable to operate a Fulling Mill in Hunwick, there must have been a cottage industry in the area where wool was combed, spun and either woven or knitted. Apart from an entry in the 1828 Parsons Trade Directory listing John Beck as a Weaver at Pixley Hills, I have not been able to find any other evidence of wool being processed in the area.

Enclosure of Hunwick Moor (Common Land)

The Statute of Merton in 1236 provided a mechanism for landlords, under certain conditions, to enclose land so that they had exclusive access to it. This was driven, during the 1400s and 1500s by the increasing price that could be obtained for wool.

Arable farming was labour intensive, sheep farming required fewer people but more land. If a landlord wanted to graze more sheep, they needed to find additional land.

Before Enclosure, the only land that was enclosed by hedges or walls would be the 'garths' or 'closes' that were close to the farmer houses. All other land, with the possible exception of meadow land, would be 'open' and not fenced. The landscape would be very different from what we see today.

Originally, the enclosure of Common Land would take place by informal local agreements. An increasing population created the need for the land to be able to feed more people than it had previously. By enclosing the land, it was thought that overgrazing would be reduced and the land could be managed better.

By the 1700s a legal process had been established that required an Act of Parliament to enclose the Common Land. For a moor to be enclosed, three quarters (by area) of the land holders would need to agree to enclosure. They would also need the funds that would enable them to pay the legal and survey fees that would be required to get the Act passed by Parliament and the allocation made and fenced.

In 1760, the Bishop of Durham and *'several Freeholders and Copyholders within the Manor of Bondgate'* petitioned parliament to enclose Hunwick Edge. The argument that was put forward to support enclosure was that the 1200 acres on Hunwick Common *"at present yields little profit, but is very capable of improvement when inclosed"*. (Durham_University_Special+collections, 1761)

In 1761 the Enclosure Act was passed by Parliament which allowed this Hunwick Common land to be divided up and allocated to individuals who were thought to have held rights to the land. The 1761 Enclosure map is a little confusing as it includes Common Land for Hunwick as well as adjoining Common Land belonging to Newton Cap, Witton-le-Wear and Escomb. (University, Enclosure Act, 1761; Durham_University_Special+collections, 1761)

Nine hundred and fifty acres, of the twelve hundred acres that made up Hunwick Moor, were allocated to six people Joseph Reay (Hunwick Hall), William Blackett (Helmington Hall), Robert Shafto (Newton Cap and Escomb), John Bacon (Newton Cap), Martin Dunn (Newton Cap) and Margaret Wilson (Newton Cap).

The remaining two hundred and fifty acres were allocated to the twenty others who had claims on the moor.

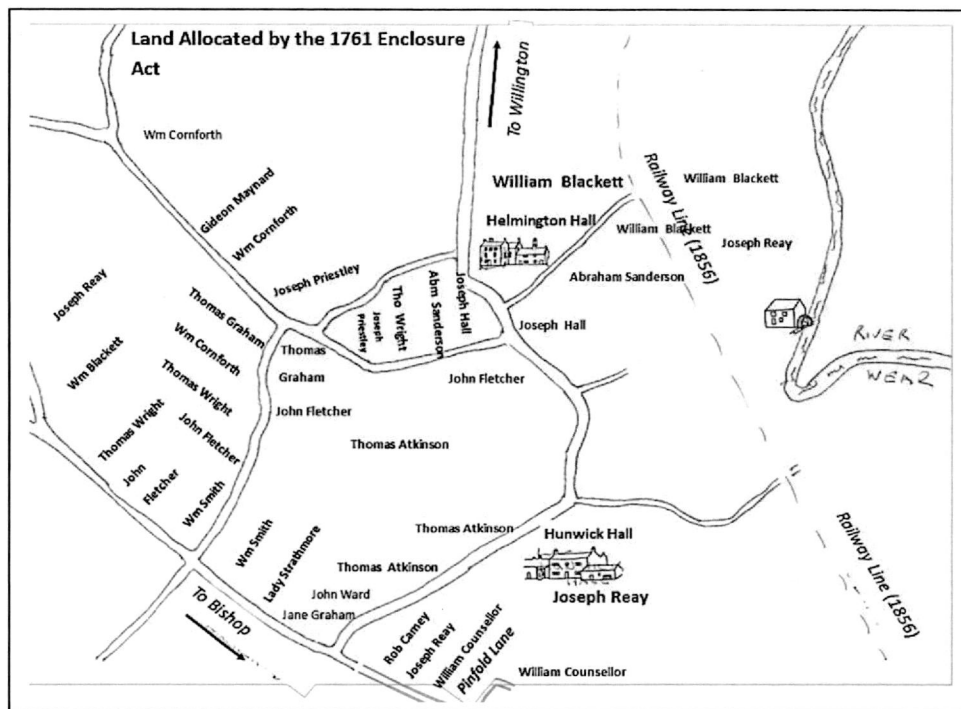

Land Allocated by the 1761 Enclosure Act

The 1761 Enclosure Act identified that the Bishop of Durham, as the Lord of the Manor, would receive the compensation of 6 pence per acre for the Common Land around the village that had been allocated and enclosed.

The enclosure of Hunwick Moor resulted in the people in the village losing their right to use the Common Land and being left with an area of land that was too small or of too poor quality for them to be able to eke out an existence. To survive, they either had to work for someone else or leave the village to find employment elsewhere. At the same time, agricultural machinery was being developed that reduced the reliance on manpower and made more efficient use of the land. Cutting and threshing machines meant that more grain and hay could be grown meaning that farmers could keep more livestock during the winter months; seed drills meant that seeds could be sown in rows, making weed control easier and reducing the wastage of the previous broadcast methods.

As well as developments in technology, farmers had begun to think more about how they maintained their soil quality. Early crop rotation systems meant that every fourth year the field/strip would be left fallow to recover its fertility. Instead of leaving a field/strip fallow either clover or ryegrass was grown. This introduced nitrogen back into the soil and along with increased use of manure, permitted more intensive use of the land.

Farmers also began to take more interest in the qualities that they needed in the cattle that they kept on their land. They engaged in selective breeding and began to maintain herd books and monitor milk yields, fat content and auction prices. The Shorthorn breed was developed in Durham to be a general-purpose cow that could be used both for meat, tallow and milk and that was suitable for the type of land available in the County. These developments were driven by local fairs and shows that encouraged farmers to breed better animals and to make them aware of more efficient ways of farming.

Land Management in Hunwick

The Church, in the form of either, the Bishop of Durham, the Prior of the Monastery of St Cuthbert, the Dean and Chapter of the Cathedral or the Ecclesiastical Commission, originally held all of the land in Hunwick. While references can be found to both Hunwick Manor and Helmington Manor, Hunwick does not appear to have been manor in its own right. It was part of the Manor of Bondgate in the Parish of St Andrew's, Bishop Auckland. The Bishop of Durham was the Lord of the Manor.

The term 'manor' can refer to both something physical, a house, a hall or a block of land, or a community controlled by a Lord of the Manor. Originally, the focus would be on working the land in the Manor to provide the food and fuel required to support the Manor House and Estate.

The Lord of the Manor would have leased the 'freehold' right to parcels of land to a number of larger land holder and have given individual Villagers the right to use strips of land in the village field. The details of their right to use the land was recorded on the Manorial Roll. They were called copyholders and had customary rights which meant that they could not be evicted unless they had failed to pay their rent or had committed some misdemeanour, perhaps failing to cultivate a strip or allowing livestock to trespass. The right of copyholders to their land was passed down through the family.

The Bishop of Durham managed his copyholders through the Halmote Court which kept records of all transactions. Fortunately, some these records have survived and provide a valuable insight into the management of the Estate.

Typically, the Lord of the Manor or his Steward lived in the Manor House. His 'freehold' tenants, who paid rent and could sell their land if they wished, lived in more modest farm houses. Some small fields or 'Closes' that were adjacent to the Manor House or the houses of the freehold tenants, would have been enclosed by walls or fences and retained for the exclusive use of the Lord of the Manor or freehold land holder.

The farm workers would live in a small cottage close to the Manor House or the house of a freehold tenant farmer. After having provided the required service to the Lord of the Manor, they would work on the strips of land that had been allocated to them and which provided the food that they needed for their own survival. They would be required to follow a cultivation plan that would be set down by the Lord of the Manor. They would also be allowed to graze their cow in the common pasture and their pigs in the wooded areas.

Over time the ownership of the land and property became separated and the manorial lord would not necessarily own the manor house or the land of the manor.

The Black Death in 1349 significantly reduced the population of the country. This would have resulted in vacant strips in the Village Field, where whole families had died. Some of the Villagers who survived would have prospered and have been able to buy or rent additional pieces of land. Large land holders would have found it very difficult to find workers to operate what was a very labour-intensive arable farming system. This further encouraged the move towards renting or leasing land. The Open Field system was forced to evolve quite rapidly.

By the end of the fourteenth century, the Bishop of Durham, the Dean and Chapter of the Cathedral and many of the major land-holders had decided that, rather than work their land themselves, it was easier and more profitable to rent out their land to others and to take an income from their land. This change of emphasis created a need for stewards, lawyers and administrators to organise the leases, collect the rents etc

The dispersal of the Monastic land in 1539 enabled those foresters, stewards and lawyers who had previously assisted with the administration of the manors, to acquire lands and aspire to become accepted as members of the 'gentry'.

Hunwick Hall Estate was rented directly from the Bishop of Durham. Helmington Hall Estate rented some land directly from the Bishop. The remainder of the estate was rented from the Neville family, who had rented it, as part of a larger bundle of land, directly from the Bishop.

The Burdon's of Helmington Hall and the Hutton's of Hunwick Hall were considered to be relatively minor landholders. In 1398, the 'manor' of the Burdon's of Helmington comprised of nothing more than a *'single messuage, 70 acres of arable land, 10 acres of woodland and a water mill'.* (Surtees, The History of the Parishes of Hunwick, Helmington, Witton Park and Etherley, 1923)

The development of the Farms

Over time, as the farms became larger and the Common Land was enclosed and no longer available for village use, the Village Field disappeared. A villager who had previously worked a few strips in the Village Field and kept a few animals on the Common Land, became a farm worker for someone else.

In 1635/36, an agreement for the sale of the freehold of Hunwick Hall Estate, listed five farms. Three of the farms had a house with one garth each. One farm had a house with two garths and one just had a house. (Durham_University_Special_Collections, D/CG 33/14) A garth is a field with a fence or wall around it. It would generally be close to the farm house and be used to keep livestock in.

An 1861 Estate map identifies seven farms on the Hunwick Hall Estate. (Durham_Records_Office, D/CG_33/14)

- Wright, Fidler, Gloy, Stevenson and Suerties, each had a House with two garths.

- Snaith, Young, and Forman, each had a House with one garth.

- Wilson, had a House without a garth.

I have not been able to find anything that would allow me to relate these farms to known farms. However, assuming that the number of oxen that a farm had was related to the size of the farm, it might be that Wright's Farm became Farnley Farm, Stephenson's farm became Constantine Farm and Gloy's Farm became Rough Lea Farm.

Unfortunately, I have not been able to find any records for the Helmington Estate.

The 1761 Enclosure map, in addition to Hunwick Hall and Helmington Hall, identifies twenty land holders, in and around the village.

These smaller land holders had the farms, that were located between the two large blocks of land 'owned' by either Hunwick Hall, (Mathew Bell), or Helmington Hall (Robert Spencer).

The sketch map, is based on an 1861 Hunwick Hall Estate map and Bell's 1852, map of Royalty owners, shows the landowners in the 1860s. (Bell, 1852)

Land Holders circa 1860

Hunwick Hall and Helmington Hall had, until the twentieth century, been the major land holders in the village. As 'freeholders', both estates had the option to either work the land themselves or sell the freehold to others who would manage and work it. By the end of the twentieth century, the two estates had been broken up and sold.

The Village Farms identified on the 1843 Tithe Map

An analysis of the 1821 census shows that, in the township of Hunwick and Helmington, out of the 33 families that were living in the township, 26 were chiefly employed in agriculture with 4 being employed in trade or manufacture. (Census_Office, 1821)

Tithes were originally a tax which land owners had to pay support the local church. The tax would be paid in the form of agricultural produce. By the early 19th century paying tithes 'in kind' was considered by tenants to be very inflexible and was unpopular. The 1836 Tithe Commutation Act required tithes in kind to be converted to more convenient monetary payments.

A Survey was conducted in 1843 to find out which land was subject to tithes, who owned it, how much was payable and to whom. The Tithe Map that was created shows that, in Hunwick, eleven farms paid tithes to the Church. (Durham_University_Special_Collections, Tithe Map, Hunwick and Helmington township (Auckland St Andrew parish) (DDR/EA/TTH/1/135) Award with plan, 1843)

Quarry Burn Farm [Brewery] (15 acres)	Hunwick Farm (26 acres)	Lane Ends Farm, (18 acres)
Dixon's House [Blakeley Hill], (15 acres)	Oaks Row, (7 acres)	Rough Lea Farm, [owned by Helmington Hall], (280 acres)
Farnley Mill [Furnace Mill], (17 acres);	Kate's Close [The Poplars], (13 acres);	New Hunwick, (3 acres).
Helmington Row, (20 acres)	High House, [Dairy Barn], (20 acres)	

The farms that belonged to Hunwick Hall Estate are **not identified** on the map and would **not** have to pay tithes as the Estate would pay rent to the Bishop of Durham for the land.

Village Farms belonging to Hunwick Hall Estate in 1861

An 1861 Estate map for Hunwick Hall identifies seven farms on the estate. In 1871, an Estate Schedule listed the acreages that each farm on the estate had at that time. While Rough Lea Farm was shown on the Tithe Map in 1843 as comprising of 280 acres and belonging to the Helmington Estate, by 1861 it is included as part of Hunwick Hall Estate. By 1871, its acreage is shown as 80 acres.

Hunwick Hall Farm, (400 acres) Including Quarry Farm	Blue House [Toronto]	Farnley House, (195 acres)
Constantine Farm [Rumby Hill], (180 acres)	Rough Lea Farm, (80 acres)	Woodlands (Wadsworth? [High Grange]), (70 acres)
Cringle Dykes [New Hunwick], Farm] (3 acres)		

Before the coal mines opened, Hunwick was made up of scattered settlements centred around the farms at Lane Ends (Helmington Hall Farm and Lane Ends Farm), Hunwick Green (Hunwick Hall Farm and Quarry Farm/South View Farm), Hunwick Station (Farnley House Farm), Quarry Burn (Quarry Burn Farm), Oaks Row (High Oaks Row Farm), Rough Lea (Rough Lea Farm and Furnace Mill Farm), Blakeley Hill (Dixon's House Farm) and The Poplars (Kate's House (Close) Farm).

The settlements were based around the farm and included, the farm house, farm buildings and the cottages that accommodated the farm workers. (**Note:** New Hunwick Farm is shown on the 1843 map as a 3-acre farm while the 1861 and 1871 Estate maps identify the 3-acre farm as Cringle Dyke)

Until the 1950s, all of the village farms would have at least one cow to provide milk and butter for the family. Some farms kept additional cows so that they could sell milk and butter to other Villagers.

They would also keep pigs, ducks, geese and hens, as well as growing crops. Some farms also kept beef cows which they would sell to local butchers.

The butchers generally had their own fields and slaughter houses. They would buy beef cattle from local farmers or

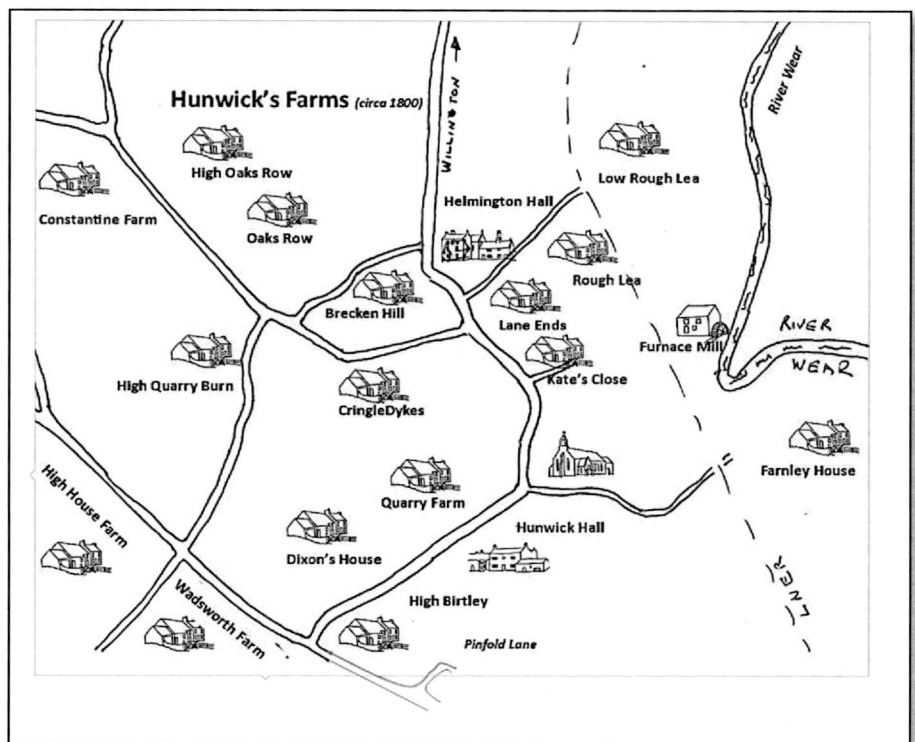

from the cattle mart and would keep them in their own fields until they needed to slaughter and butcher them ready for sale in their butcher's shop.

Heslop's ran a butcher's shop and slaughter house at Lane Ends. Bishop Auckland Cooperative Society ran a butcher's shop and slaughter house at Kates's Close. Thompsons had a slaughter house at Lane Ends and John Tulip ran a butcher's shop at Quarry Burn. There was also a butcher's shop in an outbuilding between Lilac House and the Two Bay Horses and another ran from Number 7 the Green.

During the Second World War, food was rationed as the merchant ships, that had previously carried imported foodstuffs, were being sunk at an alarming rate.

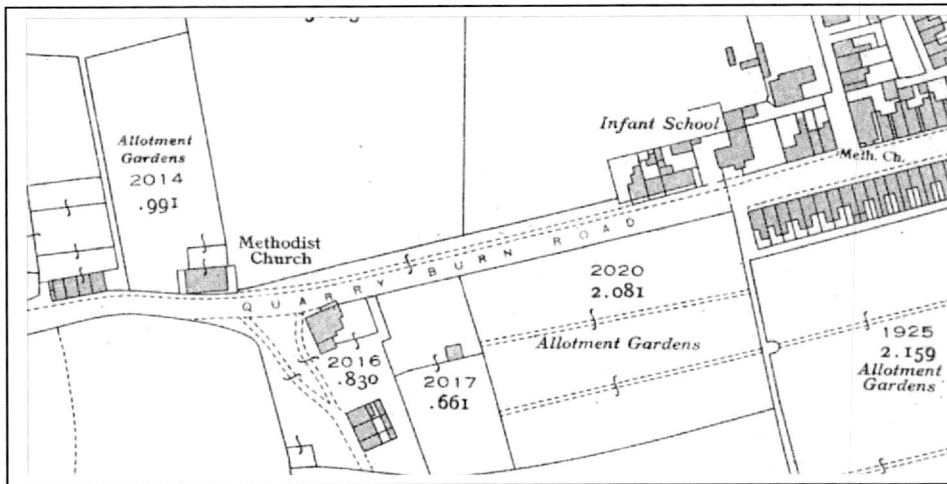

Everyone in the country was encouraged to cultivate every available piece of land to feed the population.

There were allotment gardens at New Hunwick, to the rear of West View and Helmington Terrace, and to the rear of North View,

Villagers remember the large range of fruit and vegetables that their families grew and on which they relied.

They also remember the competition between Villagers as they grew leeks and other vegetables, not just to eat, but to enter into local fruit and vegetable competitions.

Allotments to the rear of West View

Image 0357 – (Alma Edmundson, 2006 Digital Village Project)

Many Villagers who were lucky enough to have a garden or allotment, kept pigs or hens.

Before the widespread use of the glass milk bottle in the 1930s, the farmer or more often his wife, would take the fresh milk, in 'milk churns' around the village and sell the raw milk directly to Villagers.

They would dip 'pint' or 'quart' measures (containers), into the churn and ladle the milk out into containers that were provided by the customer. As there was no safe way to store milk, it would be delivered, fresh from the farm, twice a day.

Hunwick Hall Farm delivered milk to houses in Old Hunwick. Villagers remember Mrs Holborn using a yoke across her shoulders to balance two containers full of milk and later, Dick Shaw from Toronto carrying a container of milk from door to door.

Shoulder Yoke

Image 0700

Milk Churns

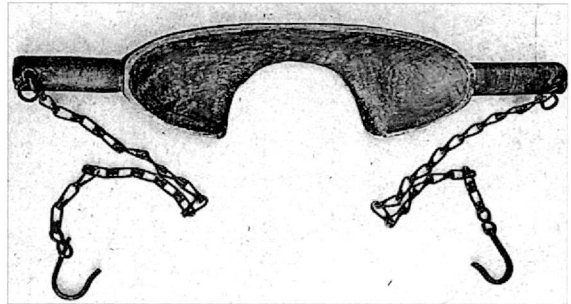

Milk Measure, half pint

Jimmy Johnson and Ann Newton (nee Johnson)

Image 0378 – by kind permission of Harold Newton

Villagers remember Jimmy Johnson, who ran a small holding to the rear of his house at 3 West End, having a milk round during the 1930s and 1940s. He used a yoke across his shoulders to carry two containers of milk as he visited customers at Lane Ends. Ena Lawrence, his daughter, remembers him sitting on a stool and singing while milking the cows in a byer in a field below the Chapel at West End.

If a farm's horse and cart was available, they would be used to deliver the milk. Villagers have shared stories of Mrs Horner from Low Rough Lea Farm, Sarah Hedley from Cringle Dykes, Dickie and Valerie Temby from South View Farm and William Burdon from Hunwick Station, using horse drawn carts, until the 1950s, to deliver milk.

Richard and Jane Temby ran South View Farm in the late 1950s with their son and daughter, Dickie and Valerie.

As well as delivering milk in the village, they also delivered to Sunnybrow and Toronto. Mandy Temby remembers her grandmother, Jane, talking about how they used to sell milk and veg from the back of a horse and cart, in the *"good old days"*.

Mandy also remembered her nana's story about her grandad's horse, having finished delivering to their last customer in Toronto, always got home before him. *"It must have known it was home time and grandad had to walk home".*

Dickie Temby's milk float with Agnes Smith (nee Bourne) and Betty Dunn (ne Pratt) in the Village Parade, 1950.

Image 0011 - (Wally Smith, Digital Village Project 2006)

Beginning in 1942 and until 1954, milk was rationed to 3 pints per person per week. The Milk Marketing Board was established in 1933, to buy, advertise and sell milk. This guaranteed that farmers got a reasonable price for their milk and that excess milk was made into cheese or butter. Farms sold their milk to the Milk Marketing Board or the Cooperative Society who would process and bottle the milk. Farmers would take their churns, each holding twelve gallons of milk, to Hunwick Station where it would be put onto goods trains and taken to Durham for processing and bottling. The bottled milk was distributed by the railway network to stations from where the bottled milk would be collected by milkmen.

The risk of contracting tuberculosis from raw milk led to the requirement in the 1950s, that milk had to be pasteurised to kill the dangerous bacteria and make milk safe to drink. Herds had to be tested for TB and farmers had to update their cow byres and procedure. This led to many of the smaller milk producers selling their herds of milking cows.

By the 1950s road transport had taken over from rail. The farmers no longer had to take the churns to the station. They were collected by waggons, from milk stands that were positioned at the end of the farm tracks. The crates of full milk bottles would be delivered to the milkmen, early every morning, by waggon. The milkmen would deliver bottles of milk to customers early each morning. The glass milk bottles had to be collected back by the milkmen and returned so that they could be reused.

In the 1950s there were five milkmen delivering in the village, Arthur Farrow and then Kathleen Linsley delivered from Rough Lea Farm. Dickie and Valerie Temby delivered from South View Farm. Denzil Moreland delivered from Willington Cooperative Society from its shop in Cooperative Terrace. Reg and Cyril Parkinson from Cooperative Terrace and Fred Williamson from Helmington Terrace also operated milk rounds from the village.

The movement of cows in and through the village caused quite a lot of disruption. Every morning, John Johnson walked his herd of cows from his byre at Kate's Close up to graze in the fields at Quarry Farm. Every evening he walked them back down to be milked. Albert Temby had a similar daily routine walking his cows from South View Farm, up through the village to graze in the fields behind Numbers 28, 29 and 30 South View and back down again at the end of the day. Things got even more complicated every Thursday, when Frank Tinkler from Helmington Hall, herded cows though the village on their way to Bishop Auckland Cattle Mart.

In the 1930s, in addition to selling milk locally, farms would make butter and cheese on their farms. Villagers remember going to Hunwick Hall Farm when they needed more milk and being encouraged to help to make butter while they were there.

During the Second World War and until 1954, eggs, butter, meat and cheese were all rationed and local farmers were not allowed to sell directly to the public. Eggs would be collected, by a merchant who would have to be licenced by the egg marketing board.

Thomas Hedley, who lived at Raby House, was a licenced egg, butter and cheese merchant. He bought eggs, butter and cheese from the farmers and sold them to local shops who would then sell them to the general public. The eggs, butter etc could then be sold by the shops on 'ration', an individual being allowed one fresh egg, 2 oz of butter and 2 oz cheese per week.

Chapter 2 - The Landscape

The contours of the landscape that we see around us today have been broadly shaped by the underlying geology. Humans settled in the valleys, on the hills and on the moors. They cleared the woodland to create meadows and fields that they could cultivate. Our ancestors gradually changed the landscape as they moved from an open or village field cultivation system towards the individual farms that we have today.

Through their activities they created the mosaic of fields, hedgerows and walls that we see around us today.

Landscape today

A requirement of the 1761 Enclosure Act was that the new owner would: *"make and erect and forever here after uphold maintain good and efficient bounder fences and hedges"*. (Durham_University_Special_Collections, CCB/D/1956/12/32857, 1956) The easiest and quickest way to enclose a section of land was to dig a trench and pile the spoil that had been excavated as a mound parallel to the trench. A hawthorn hedge would be planted on top of the mound.

The boundaries hedges or walls that were established in 1761 were laid out by surveyors. This resulted in walls or hedges that followed a straight line while the pre-enclosure boundaries followed the roadways, natural features or ridge and furrow working which resulted in more curved boundary lines.

The hedgerows form an important component of the landscape. It is in the hedgerows that the trees become established and grow to provide the 'height' to the landscape that we value.

Some of the hedgerows that we see around the village will have been planted before 1761 but the majority will have been planted following the 1761 enclosure.

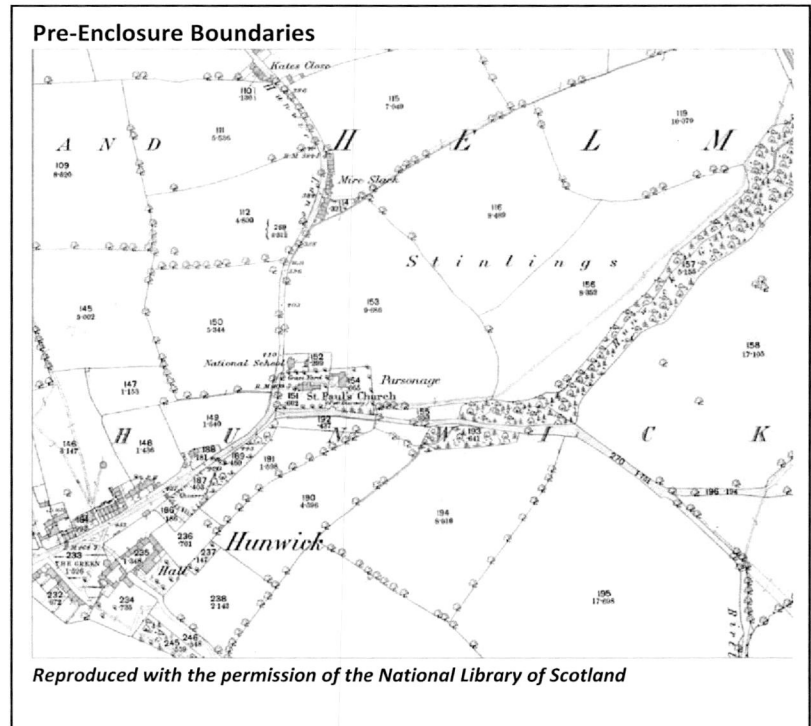

Pre-Enclosure Boundaries

Reproduced with the permission of the National Library of Scotland

The drive for increased food production during the Second World War and for 'efficiencies of scale' during the 1950s, resulted in the removal of some of the enclosure hedges as farmers created larger fields to allow larger machines to be used.

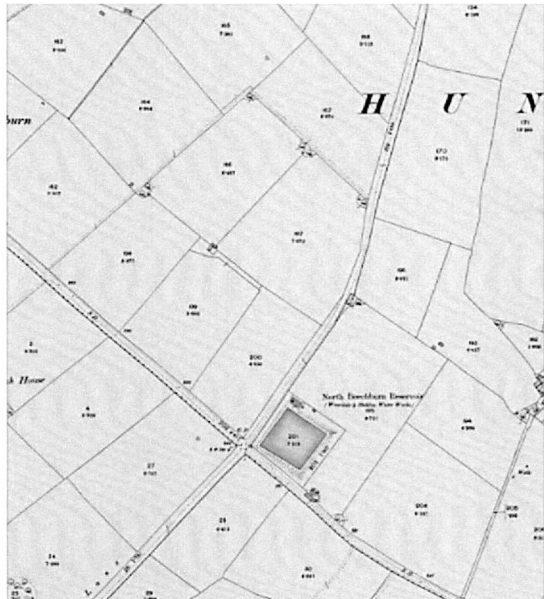

Reproduced with the permission of the National Library of Scotland

It is recognised that there is a strong correlation between the number of 'woody', tree and shrub species in a hedge and its age in centuries. One extra species becomes established for every one hundred years of existence, typical species being hawthorn, holly, elder, ash and blackberry.

It is possible to estimate the age of a hedge by counting, in a 30-yard stretch of hedge, the number of different tree and shrub species that are established.

An Enclosure Act (1761) hedge would typically have three species whereas a hedge with ten or more species, is likely to be pre-1066.

Farmsteads, made up of the farmhouse, barns, byres and garths, are scattered around the village. As land passed down from one generation to the next, it was often divided amongst a number of beneficiaries. If land had become vacant it was often bought by neighbouring farms and merged into their existing farm. The size and composition of the farmsteads have evolved over the years as landholdings have been merged or fallen into disuse. The drive to increase the productivity of the land during the Second World War brought more land into use which also impacted on the landscape.

The development of more powerful tractors meant that the agricultural implements that they could pull, also increased in size. It was easier and more efficient to operate large machinery in large fields so a lot of hedgerows were grubbed out and the fields got bigger.

Architecture of the Farms

Whether still being used or derelict, farm houses and farm buildings form part of the man-made landscape.

In the 1800s, all of the village farms were mixed farms. They managed arable, pasture and meadow land. Typically, they would have a range of byres, haylofts, granaries, stables, pigsties, cattle sheds and barns, close to the farm house. Several of the farms had 'ginn gangs' attached which harnessed the power of a horse walking around a central axle to provide the power to drive agricultural machinery.

All of the surviving Farm Houses and the traditional barns and buildings that surround them were built in the late

Rough Lea Farm

Image 0013 – by kind permission of Amanda Adamson

1700s or early 1800s. They used local stone and originally had flag-stone roofs or clay, pantile roofs. The walls were built using lime mortar and random stones with a rubble infill.

The house and buildings have evolved and expanded over the years to meet the changing demands and developments in agricultural practice.

As fields increased in size so did the size and functionality of the harvesting machinery. Byres and barns had to be modified or new ones built to accommodate or allow access to the larger machinery and mechanical handling equipment.

Breckon Hill

Image 0018 - by kind permission Margorie Tait

Breckon Hill

Image 0017 - by kind permission Margorie Tait

Furnace Mill

Quarry Farm

Image 0016

Hunwick Hall Barn

Kate's Close Farm

Hunwick – A Tourist Destination

Many claims have been made for a village that:

> 'occupies a romantic situation on the north side of the Wear' and that contains 'a spring of water, *called Furnival well, said to have possessed some medicinal virtue'*. A Well that was "*much resorted to by the people of Bishop Auckland and the surrounding district*".
>
> 'From Brancepeth the tourist may profitably continue his journey to Hunwick, where he will find considerable remains of a medieval house' and that 'little more than half a mile north of the village of Hunwick is a fine old seventeenth century house, known as Helmington Hall'. (Boyle, 1892)

In 1820, Peter Fair, when describing the *'Gentlemen's seats of Hunwick Hall and Helmington Hall'*, recognised the potential of the improvements that had been made to Helmington Hall, to create a *'delightful place'*.

He recognised the 'romantic scenery' and considered that the quality of water of the Furnace Spring was not quite as good as the *"Harrowgate waters".*

> "the residence and property of the Rev. Robert Spencer, is pleasantly situated on the banks of the Wear, has been considerably enlarged by the present owner, by the addition of two handsome Gothic rooms. The gardens are laid out with great taste, and are delightfully situated. A new stone bridge has been lately built over the rivulet which runs close by the Hall and garden; and from the great quantity of wood lately planted, Helmington in a short time will be a most delightful place. Along the banks of the river, where the scenery is most romantic, you come to a corn - mill, near which is a spring bursting from the side of the hill, (close by the river side) strongly impregnated with sulphur, & c. little inferior to the Harrowgate waters. H. U, Reay, Esq. the proprietor, has lately inclosed it with a building, and made a good road to it down the hill, by an easy descent of a flight of stairs". (Fair, 1820)

An article in Volume 1, Society of Antiquaries of Newcastle upon Tyne, 1855-1857, describing the challenges that the engineers and contractors had encountered when building the North Eastern Railway line from Durham to Bishop Auckland concluded that:

> "in the bosom of the earth there is nourishment, and on its face, there is written "I promise to pay". Mineral traffic will be enormous, and travellers will flock to the beautiful branch of the North Eastern – which might seem to have been constructed for the very purpose of pleasing a tourist's eye." (Tyne)

And then the Collieries arrived!

In 1864, after the collieries had begun production and railways had opened up to passengers, John Murray, in a 'Handbook for Travellers in Durham and Northumberland', describes a pleasant rail journey from Durham but, after 7 miles into the journey, thought little of Willington station and after a further 8 ¾ miles, thought the same about Hunwick Station! (Murray, 1864)

9 m. *Willington* Stat., in the midst of a hideous colliery.
13½ m. *Bishops Auckland Stat.* See Rte. 3.

BISHOP AUCKLAND, DURHAM, SUNDERLAND, NEWCASTLE, & SOUTH SHIELDS.

LEAVE														SATURDAYS		SUNDAYS		
Bp. Auckland	...	8 10	10 20	...	1 30	3 55	...	6 50	7 10	...	...	...	...	...	8 0	...	8 15	7 45
Hunwick	...	8 16	10 26	...	1 36	4 1	...	6 56	7 16	...	...	...	...	...	8 6	...	8 21	7 51
Willington	...	8 22	10 32	...	1 42	4 7	...	7 2	7 22	...	2 10	...	8 12	...	8 27	7 57
Brancepeth	...	8 30	10 40	...	1 50	4 15	...	7 10	7 30	...	2 18	...	8 20	...	8 35	8 5
Brandon	...	8 36	10 46	...	1 56	4 21	...	7 16	7 36	...	2 24	...	8 26	...	8 42	8 11
Durham arr		8 45	10 55		2 4	4 30		7 25	7 45			2 33			8 35		8 50	8 20
Durham dep	5 33	8 55	11 5	11 35	2 5	4 40	5 0	7 36	8 45	10 25	12 8	Stop	7 20	10 25	5 15	5 15	7 45
Leamside arr	5 43	9 5	11 13	...	2 14	4 49	...	7 45	...	10 35	...	7 29	10 35	5 25	8 5
Leamside dep	5 45	9 15	11 15	...	2 15	4 50	...	7 55	...	10 42	12 16	7 30	10 42	5 35	8 55
Fence Houses	5 51	9 22	11 21	...	2 21	4 56	...	8 1	...	10 48	...	7 38	10 48	5 41	9 1
Pensher	5 56	9 27	11 26	...	2 26	5 1	...	8 6	...	10 53	...	7 44	10 53	5 47	9 7
Coxgreen	6 0	9 31	11 30	...	2 30	5 5	...	8 10	...	10 57	...	7 49	10 57	5 52	9 12
Hylton	6 5	9 36	11 35	...	2 35	5 10	...	8 15	9 11	2	...	7 54	11 2	5 58	9 15
Pallion	6 10	9 41	11 40	...	2 40	5 15	...	8 20	...	11 7	...	7 59	11 7	6 3	9 20
Millfield	6 13	9 43	11 43	...	2 43	5 18	...	8 23	...	11 10	...	8 3	11 10	6 6	9 23
Sunderland (Central)	6 20	9 50	11 50	12 3	2 50	5 25	5 30	8 30	9 20	11 17	12 35	8 10	11 17	6 10	9 30
Newcastle	...	9 48	11 30	...	2 55	5 0	...	8 0	...	...	8 25	...	10 0	9 35
South Shields	...	10 40	12 20	...	6 35	...	8 55	10 15	11 45	...	8 55	11 45	...	10 20	10 10

Short trains between Leamside dep 1.40, 2.55 p.m.—Sundays, 5.36, 9.5 a.m. 6.35, 7.36, 8.28, 8.50 and 11.40 p.m
Leamside & Durham } Durham, dep 5.45, 10.44 a.m, 2.35, 5.25 p.m. Sundays, 7.0 a.m, 5.50, 9.20, 7.30, 8.10, 11.20 p.m

LEAVE	a.m	a.m	a.m	a.m	a.m	p.m	p.m	p.m	p.m	p.m					
Newcastle	5 10	7 15	...	9 30	10 25	...	1 17	4 55	7 8	9 25	11 10	...	3 30	6 30	8 20	5 20
South Shields	4 55	7 0	8 5	9 10	10 15	12 30	...	4 25	6 20	9 30	...	...	3 15	6 15	9 5	5 0
Sunderland (Cent'l)	...	7 20	8 30	9 35	10 30	12 55	1 30	5 0	6 40	10 10	10 45	...	3 50	6 35	8 35	5 20
Millfield	...	7 25	8 35	9 40	10 35	1 0	...	5 5	6 45	10 15	...	3 55	6 40	8 40	5 25
Pallion	...	7 29	8 39	9 44	10 39	1 4	...	5 9	6 49	10 19	...	3 59	6 44	8 44	5 29
Hylton	...	7 33	8 43	9 48	10 43	1 8	...	5 13	6 53	10 23	...	4 3	6 48	8 48	5 35
Coxgreen	...	7 37	8 47	...	10 45	1 12	...	5 17	6 57	10 27	...	4 7	6 52	8 52	5 40
Pensher	...	7 41	8 51	9 55	10 51	1 16	...	5 21	7 1	10 31	...	4 11	6 55	8 59	5 45
Fence Houses	...	7 46	8 56	10 0	10 56	1 21	...	5 26	7 6	10 36	...	4 16	7 1	9 5	5 52
Leamside arr	...	7 52	9 3	10 6	11 2	...	5 33	7 12	10 43	11 8	...	4 23	7 8	9 11	5 59
Leamside dep	6 10	8 1	9 20	10 7	11 12	1 28	...	5 42	7 13	10 45	11 10	...	4 38	7 16	9 15	6 5
Durham arr	6 20	8 11	9 30	10 17	11 21	1 38	1 55	5 52	7 25	10 55	11 20	...	4 48	7 26	9 25	6 20
Durham dep	6 22	8 25	...	10 35	11 32	...	2 15	6 8	...	...	...	1 40	4 51	7 28	...	6 22
Brandon	6 31	8 34	...	10 44	11 41	...	2 24	6 17	...	...	...	1 50	5 0	7 37	...	6 31
Brancepeth	6 37	8 40	...	10 50	11 47	...	2 30	6 23	...	...	...	5 6	7 43	...	6 37
Willington	6 45	8 48	...	10 58	11 55	...	2 38	6 31	...	...	...	2 5	5 14	7 51	...	6 45
Hunwick	6 50	8 53	...	11 3	12 0	...	2 43	6 36	...	...	...	5 19	7 56	...	6 50
Bp. Auckland	6 57	9 0	...	11 10	12 7	...	2 50	6 43	...	...	...	5 26	8 3	...	6 57

(Catherine Finlinson, Digital Village Project 2006)

Chapter 3 – Quarrying and Mining

The stone, coal, clay and iron ore that was found under Hunwick resulted in the rapid growth of Hunwick's population in the nineteenth century. The value of what lies beneath the ground was recognised before mining became widespread. The Bishop of Durham, when agreeing tenancies, reserved the rights to whatever was under the ground along with rights to sink and access any mines.

Stone Quarrying

The quality of the Flagstone in Hunwick was such that in 1663, it was specified that either Hunwick Flagstone or Flagstone from Brusselton Quarry was to be used in the Bishop's Chapel at Auckland Castle. Bishopric accounts record that in 1640, rent had been paid for a stone mine in Hunwick and notes that *'mines had been exploited continuously from the early 16th century'*. (Extracts from 'correspondence of John Cosin', 1663)

There were three quarries in the village, two behind the Joiner's Arms and one opposite the entrance to Quarry Farm Close.

The quarry, nearest to the road, beside Quarry Farm, was a Flagstone Quarry owned by the Hunwick Estate. In 1828 Joseph Robson was identified as a stone mason (Parsons_and_White Trade Directory, 1828) and in 1856, his son, John Robson was listed as Stone and Flag merchant. (Whellan, 1856)

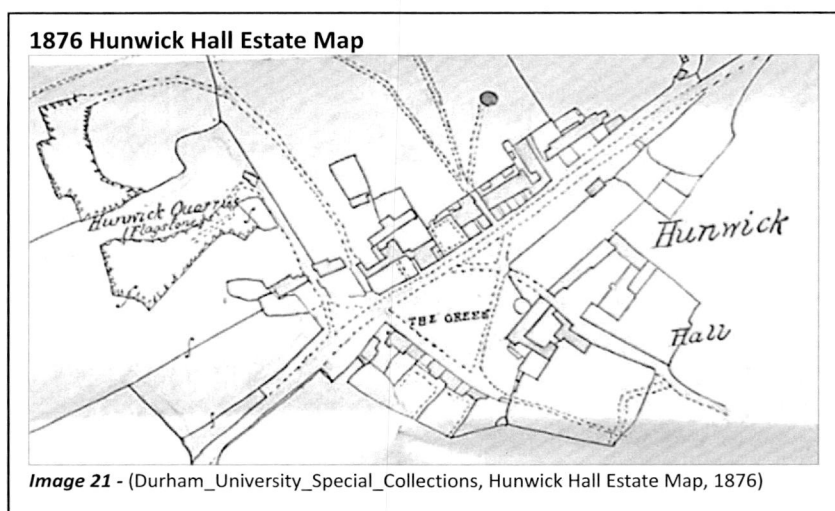

1876 Hunwick Hall Estate Map

Image 21 - (Durham_University_Special_Collections, Hunwick Hall Estate Map, 1876)

To confuse matters, the 1841 census shows another John Robson, also aged 15, as an agricultural labourer living in the household of John Young. The 1871 census records John Robson, aged 46, farming 40 acres along with his wife Ellen and his son, three daughters and a servant. The position on the census enumerator's walk route, the acreage and the link to John Young, suggests that they were living on Quarry Farm.

Business must have been booming in 1854, when John Robson advertised in the Durham Chronicle, for six quarrymen to start work immediately at 'Flagg Quarry'. Quarry Row was built to accommodate these quarry workers.

The second quarry, which was beyond Flagg Quarry, was a sandstone quarry that was operated in 1858 by John Fletcher who was described as a farmer and quarry man. The Will of Thomas Robson who died in 1804, mentions Margaret and John Fletcher as beneficiaries. The 1841 Census records John Fletcher, a farmer, aged 35 living with Margaret Fletcher aged 60, perhaps this was his mother who had inherited the farm? The 1843 Tithe Map lists Hunwick Farm (26 Acres), as belonging to the Heirs of Robson, and being occupied by John Fletcher. This was probably South View Farm.

Stone from these quarries was still being used in the 1890s, to build houses in the village.

The disused quarries were used as adventure playgrounds by the village children who remember an air-raid shelter in the 'back hollows', the quarry that was furthest from the main road.

The sandstone quarry was filled-in with the 'night soil' collected by the 'midden-man' from the earth toilets around the village. The flagstone quarry was filled-in when the foundations were dug in 1955, for the new council estate.

The third quarry was towards the bottom of the original Village Green, opposite Lilac House. Raby House was built in this quarry.

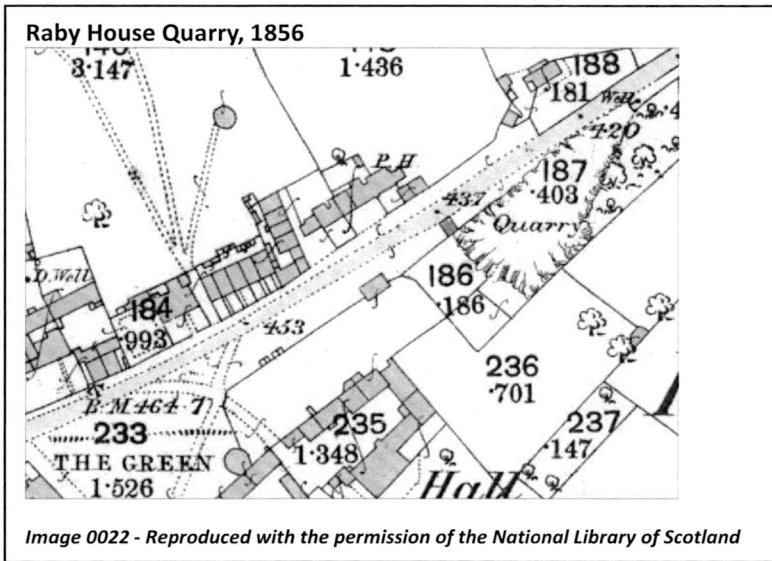

Raby House Quarry, 1856

Image 0022 - Reproduced with the permission of the National Library of Scotland

The 1761 Enclosure Map shows the 'Quarry Well', close to Quarry Burn Beck, to the west of Helmington bridge

Maps show a quarry at Brecken Hill and a gravel pit behind New Hunwick/Cringle Dykes.

Gravel Hill lies between Pixley Hill and the Green Rising Nursery.

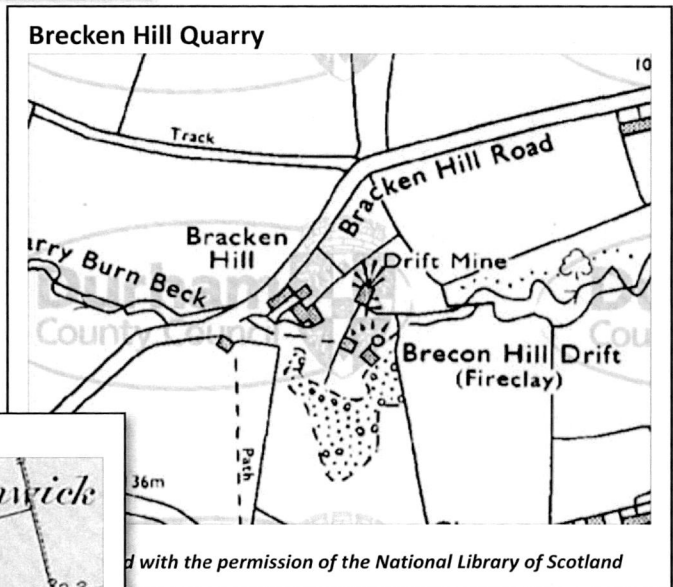

Brecken Hill Quarry

...d with the permission of the National Library of Scotland

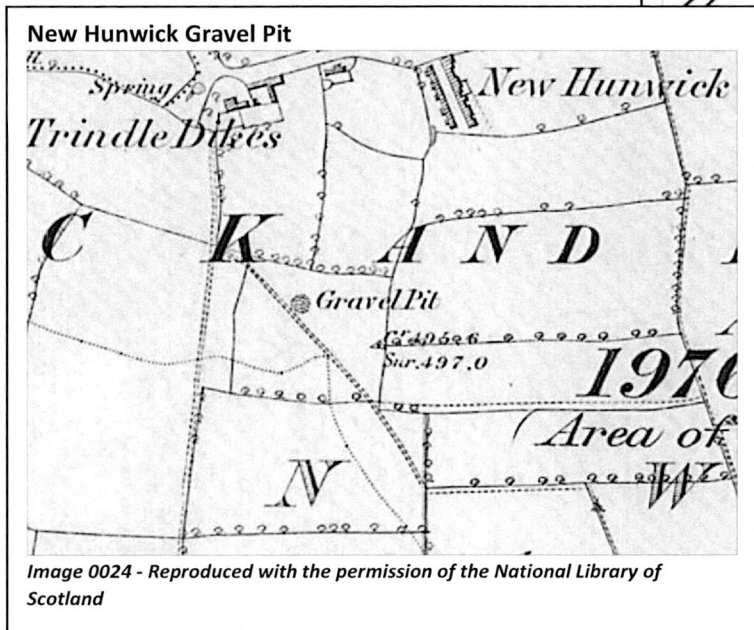

New Hunwick Gravel Pit

Image 0024 - Reproduced with the permission of the National Library of Scotland

Following the Agricultural Land Classification site survey in 1992, the Wear Valley Local Plan confirmed that there was evidence of gravel extraction around the centre of the site.

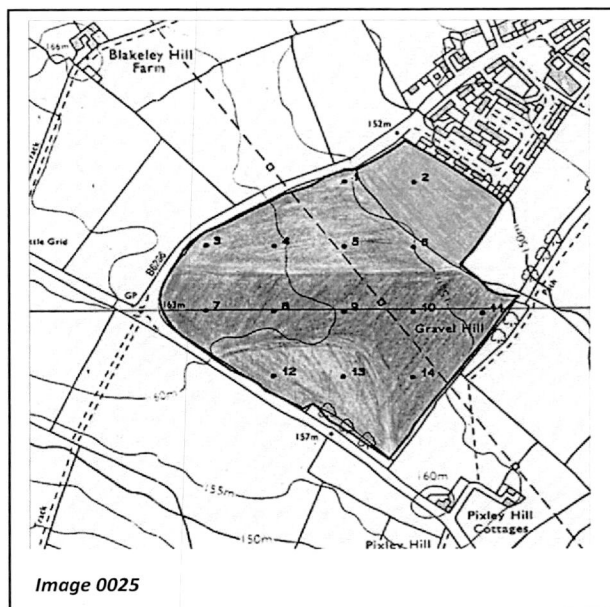

Image 0025

Iron Stone Mining

There is evidence, in the 1664 records of the Bishopric, that ironstone was being mined on 'Hunwicke Moor', very probably at Constantine Farm, and of iron being smelted at Furnace mill. (Durham eThesis)

The water power provided by the River Wear has been harnessed since at least 1632 but it is likely that a Water Mill was in use much earlier. The Hatfield Survey in 1345 makes reference to a 'stagno molendini' a mill pond or dam in Helmington. Surtees (1923) highlights that in 1398: *"John de Byrden the elder died in possession of ..... and the site of a water mill in Helmeden".* (Surtees, The History of the Parishes of Hunwick, Helmington, Witton Park and Etherley, 1923)

A furnace, to smelt iron, was built in or before 1632 at what is now Furnace Mill Farm. The ironstone was transported from surface workings at Constantine Farm and smelted using a water powered blast furnace. The water wheel would operate the bellows that would provide the airflow for the furnace. The charcoal for the furnace was either coppiced locally from Birtley Wood or transported from Helm Park or Bedburn. (Gates, 2015)

A legal conveyance, which identifies a parcel of ground *"whereupon is a furnace for iron works in Hunwick"*, confirms that the Furnace was still in existence in 1649 (Surtees, The History of the Parishes of Hunwick, Helmington, Witton Park and Etherley, 1923)

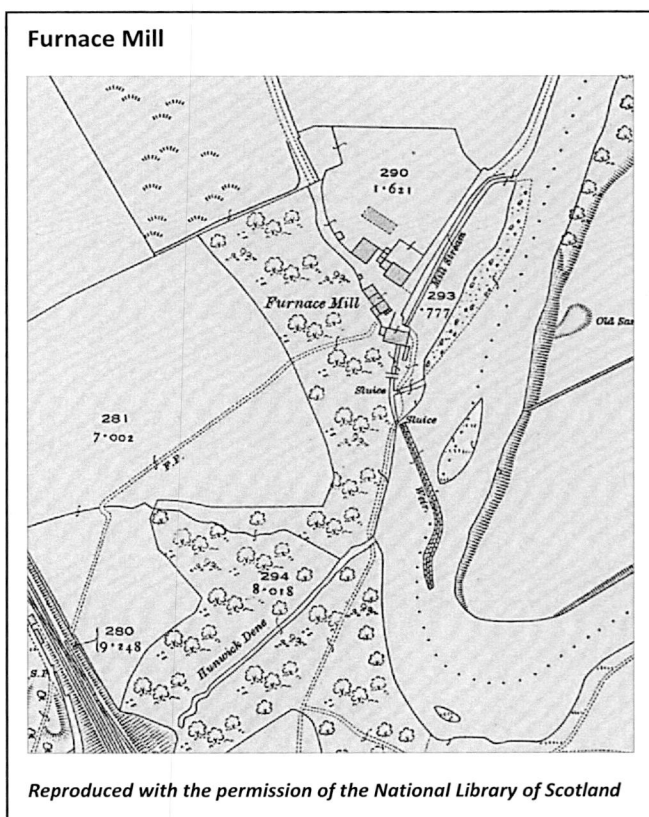

Furnace Mill

Reproduced with the permission of the National Library of Scotland

Although a 'smelt mill' is shown on a Herman Moll map in 1724, it is believed that the iron furnace was replaced by a Fulling Mill in 1687.

Perhaps the furnace that had previously been used by the smelt mill might have been adapted to use the wood/charcoal from the surrounding area, to heat the water which would be required by the fulling process?

Furnace Mill was converted into a Corn Mill. In 1828, William Dixon was described as a 'Corn Miller'. The 1841 census shows Mary Dixon (60) and James Dixon (20) at 'Furnish' Mill. The Tithe Map shows that the Mill was occupied by James Dixon in 1843. The 1851 Census records Robert Marr as being 15 years old and an Apprentice blacksmith. In 1858, Robert was the Miller at Furnace Mill. In 1890 William Wetherell was listed as being a Baker and Miller at Furnace Mill but by 1894 and again in 1902, Mrs Mary Wetherall was listed as the Farmer at the Mill. John Hanson is listed at the Mill in both 1914 and 1938.

The Development of the Collieries

Coal was formed, over millions of years, as vegetation died and was covered by sediment. This process resulted in layers or seams of coal being formed in the ground beneath us. The seams vary in thickness and all have different names such as 'Harvey', 'Beaumont', 'Victoria' and the 'Five-Quarter'. The seams cover quite a large area, some continuing out under the sea. In Hunwick, the seams are relatively close to the surface.

Maps drawn in 1611 and 1662, identify 'cole pitts' in and around Hunwick.

These 'pitts' would have accessed the coal by either surface workings, or by using a 'bell' pit. With a bell pit, a shaft was dug down to a shallow seam. The coal from the seam, around the bottom of the shaft, was dug out and lifted to the surface in a basket by using a simple windless. Both techniques left scars on the landscape whether in the form of spoil heaps or hollows in the ground caused by the collapse of a shaft.

Although its actual location is unknown, a 'land sale' colliery, a colliery where coal was only sold locally, operated on Hunwick Moor between 1551 and 1810. Records show that Bishop of Durham was receiving rent from coal mines in Hunwick from as early as 1640. (Hodgson, 1990)

John Speed, 1611

Image 0026 - Reproduced with the permission of the National Library of Scotland'

The development of steam pumps that could keep the mines dry and steam locomotives capable of hauling the coal to the sea ports, meant that by 1840 it had become viable to sink coal shafts in Hunwick. Prior to this, employment in the area would have been predominately land-based.

Coal Royalties

Landowners, owned the coal that was under their land. If a landowner leased out their land to a tenant, they would either retain the right to mine the coal under the land or would allow the lessee to mine the coal beneath the land.

Whoever held the right to mine the coal, would enter into agreements with colliery owners. The colliery owners would develop the colliery and then mine the coal. They would pay 'royalties' to the land owners or tenant.

The area outlined on the map shows the 'royalties' of the Hunwick Estate that were leased to Bolckow and Vaughan Ltd, in 1916. (The_Common_Room, NEIMME/WAT/101/2/6)

Coal mining offered big rewards for both the landowner, through income from royalties, and the colliery owners through the sale of the coal and fireclay that they mined. The colliery

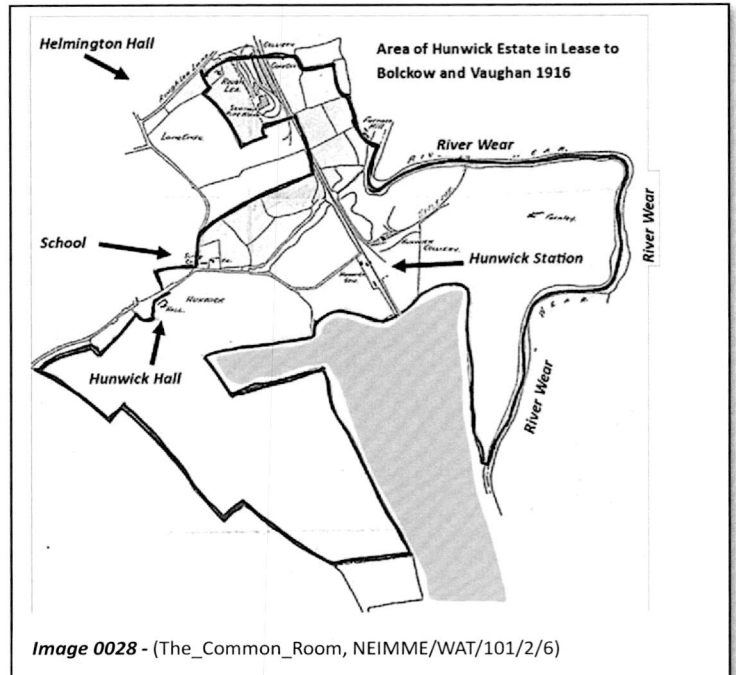

Image 0028 - (The_Common_Room, NEIMME/WAT/101/2/6)

owners had to be prepared to take the financial risks involved with the search for coal and the development of the colliery infrastructure.

The sketch map shows the landowners who, in the 1840s, would receive Royalty income from land in Hunwick.

Names include: Matthew Bell MP (owner of Hunwick Hall); the Bishop of Durham; the Dean and Chapter; Rev G Fielding (Vicar of St Andrew's and owner of Cringle Dykes); Executors of Spencer (owners of Helmington Hall); Lady Barrington (Birtley); Messers Fletcher; Capt R Ramshay; T Graham; Lowen Hall and A Booth

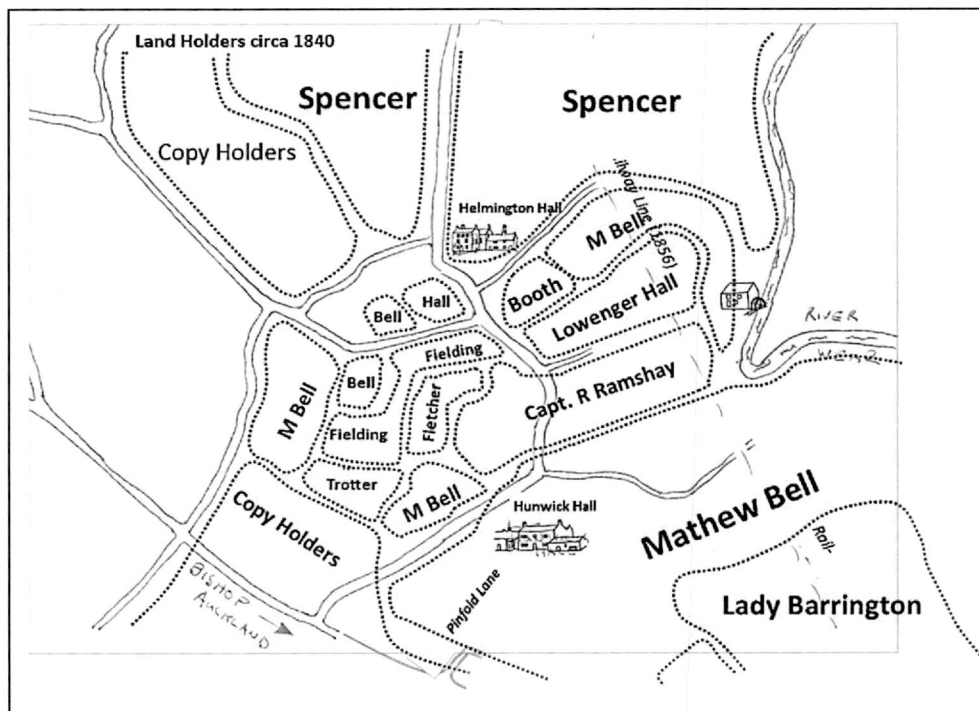

Mining Methods

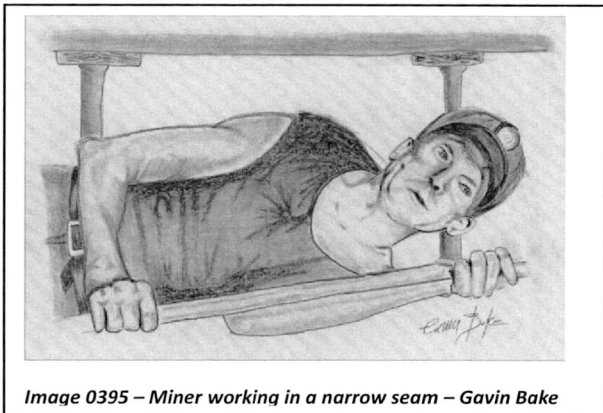

Image 0395 – Miner working in a narrow seam – Gavin Bake

To access the seams of coal a colliery would either have a 'drift', a tunnel that is dug down at an angle into the ground, or a 'shaft' that is sunk vertically into the ground. When a shaft or drift is dug down into the earth, it will pass through several different seams of coal, at different depths below the surface.

Once the shaft had been sunk or the drift had been driven from the surface, roadways were established which were tall and wide enough for men and material to be moved to the coal face where the coal was dug out from the seam. Normally there would be two roadways, one either side of the coal face, one being connected to an upcast air shaft and the other to the downcast air shaft.

A fan in the upcast shaft (or a fire basket hung in the shaft) drew air up the upcast shaft. This in turn, would draw air out of the mine workings and draw in fresh air down the downcast shaft and into the workings. This provided the ventilation that allowed men to work beneath the ground.

The coal was dug out from a coal face, the horizontal seam of coal between the roadways. The coal face effectively moved forward leaving a void. After a calculated distance, working on that face would be stopped. This would leave an area of the coal seam in place, it would be left as a 'pillar' so that the roof, the layers of rock above the seam in that 'room' was supported and would not collapse.

Miners would move forward to the other side of the supporting pillar and open up a new coal face in another 'room'. This meant that although the layer of coal had been removed, the pillars would support the ground and there should be no disturbance to land above. This void would be filled with waste, rather than take it to the surface. The roof might be allowed to collapse into the void after it had ceased to be mined.

As the mine workings expanded and became more complex, systems had to be developed to ensure that the air was forced to circulate around all of the mine workings where men were working. Doors were positioned in the roadways to direct the air flow. These doors were opened and closed by a 'trapper', often a young boy, as miners moved along roadway.

The Royalty map shows the complicated arrangement of royalties that followed the pattern of the field and estate boundaries above ground. Colliery owners, when working below ground, had to make sure that they did not encroach upon the coal reserves of a neighbouring Royalty. A dispute in 1872 between Newton Cap Colliery and Hunwick Colliery illustrates how close, underground, the different collieries were working to each other.

To help with this, there was an agreement that mining would not take place within 40 yards of the boundary of a Royalty. This meant that after being mined, in addition to the pillars of coal within the workings that had been left, there was also a barrier or fence of coal left around the Royalty. This was often seen as a waste and there was a temptation for the pillars and the barrier to be 'robbed'. This was a dangerous practice resulting in roof collapses.

Dust, poor light, poor ventilation, dangerous gases and low seams made working conditions very poor.

A Durham Mining Museum record of the death, in Jan 1912, of Thomas Clennell at Hunwick Colliery, cites miners using naked candles for light to work by, as the cause of the explosion that killed him. The report explains that miners had previously been using safety lamps but after testing had shown no dangerous gas was present, candles, which provided better light for the miners to work by, were being used.

The 1856 OS map identifies a 'Gin Shaft', behind what is now Wear View.

Miners would have been lowered down the shaft on a rope by a hand or horse operated windlass. They sat in a basket or just on a cross piece of timber at the end of the rope, as they were lowered down the shaft.

The miners worked by candle light and used picks to release the coal from the seam before shovelling it into a basket (corves) that was hauled up the shaft by the windlass. The coal would have been used locally, probably by the large houses.

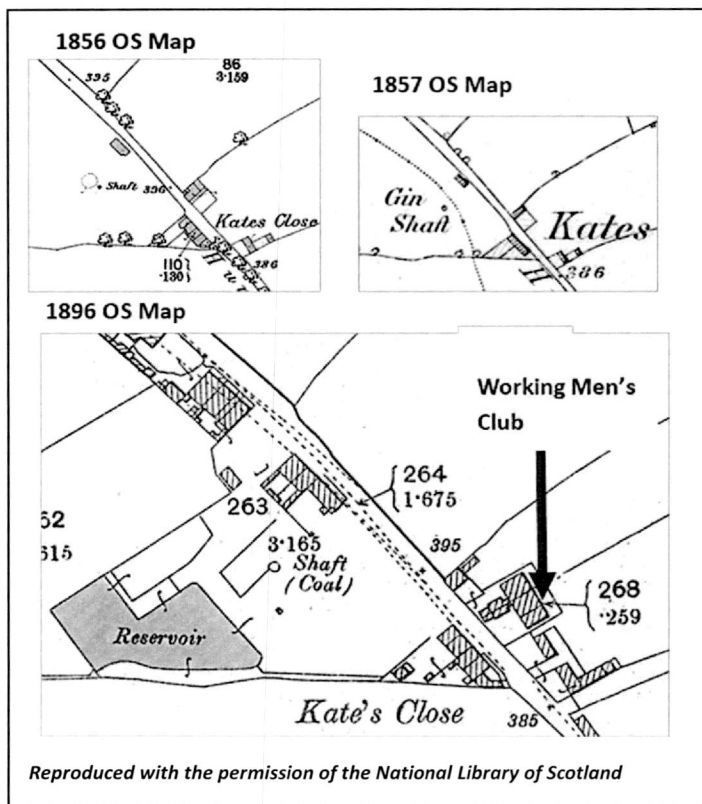

Reproduced with the permission of the National Library of Scotland

Coke Making

Coke was used in blast furnaces as well as to generate the steam that powered ships, railway locomotives etc. It is produced by the controlled burning or baking of coal in coke ovens. The coal mined in Hunwick had a high carbon content making it ideal for making coke. The quality of the coal is mentioned in an advertisement for coke that appeared in Bradshaw's, 1845 Railway Gazette, Volume 2.

'Mr T C Gibson, owner of Hunwick Colliery, and manufacturer of a very superior quality of OVEN-BURNT COKE for Locomotive, Steamboat, or Stationary Engines, Iron and Brass -founders, ... is ready to CONTRACT for any quantity of COKE, or COALS, of the best quality, for making COKE, and will undertake the delivery of the same at any port or place in England, Scotland, Ireland, or the Continent'

Coking coal tends to crumble easily into small pieces and ends up as dust. While this is useful in the coke making process, it makes it difficult to transport. It is therefore less attractive as a fuel for heating houses. It also has a high bitumen content, which makes burning it, without a good chimney to remove the gases, dangerous.

Coke ovens were generally built close to mine workings. Typically, they would be 10 feet in diameter and 7 feet high, lined with firebricks and having a short chimney in a domed roof with a damper that could be used to control the air flow. There would be a large doorway in the side through which the coal could be loaded and out of which the hot coke could be raked out before being sprayed with water to cool it and prevent further burning.

While the oven is still hot, another load of coal would be shovelled in, the doorway would be temporarily bricked up but would include some air holes. The Coke Burner used these air holes to control the burning process. As the coal burnt, flammable gases would be emitted through the top of the oven. The ovens would be left to burn for between seventy-two to ninety-six hours.

A series of coke ovens would be organised in rows, with railway sidings running parallel to the rows of ovens to make the loading and emptying of the ovens 'easier'. The Coke Burner, as well as constantly checking the burning process, would also need to shovel something like 6 ton of coal into, and shovel 6 ton of hot coke out of each oven. (Fordyce, 1860)

Hunwick's Collieries

There were five collieries in Hunwick, Hunwick Colliery, West Hunwick, Rough Lea, Brecken Hill and the Bell Pit. On some documents, the Bell Pit, is referred to as the Bridge of Hunwick Pit.

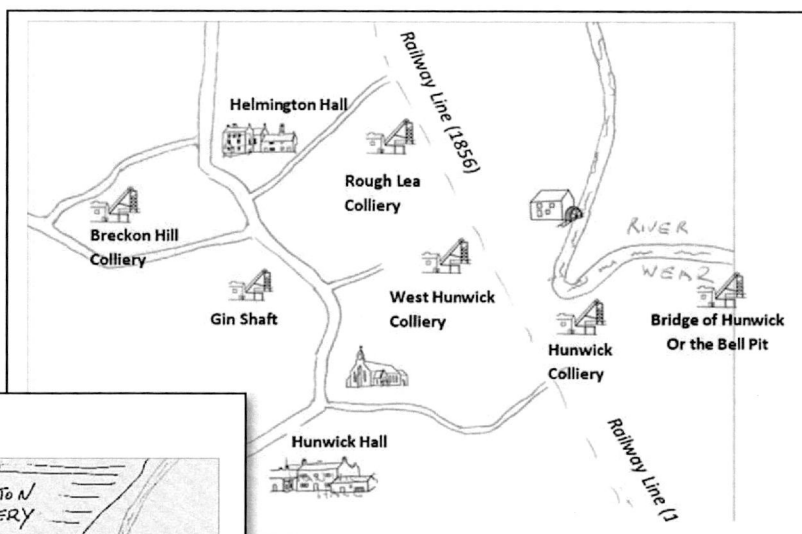

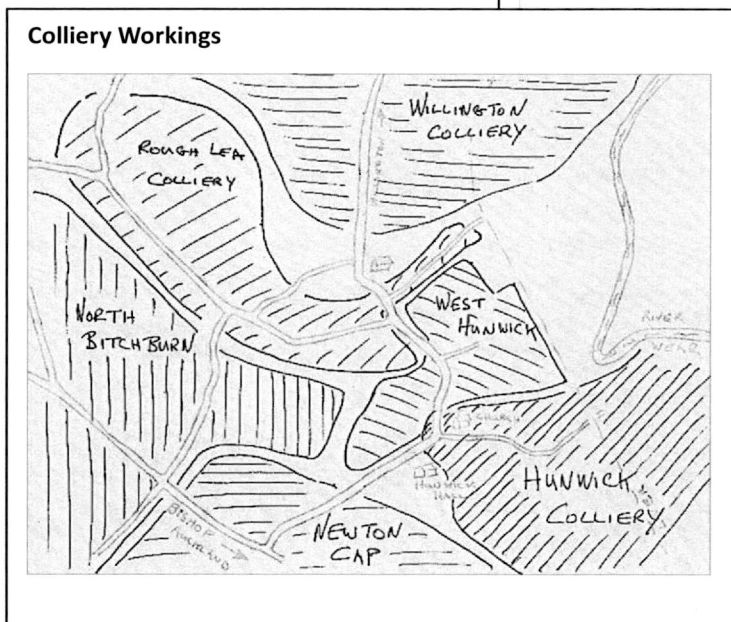

Colliery Workings

The sketch map identifies the general areas in which the collieries were mining coal around the village.

Although North Bitchburn and Newton Cap collieries were not in the village, some of their workings were.

Hunwick Colliery

Developing collieries was very expensive. However, the potential financial return, encouraged many investors to take the risk, and fund developments. In Jan 1837, two years before the shaft for Hunwick Colliery was sunk, a detailed viability and profitability study was completed. It calculated that the annual profit from operating the colliery would be £9,639. That would be equivalent to something like £900,000 today. (The_Common_Room, NEIMME/WAT/3/50/457)

On 30th January 1837, Mathew Bell leased the rights to the coal that belonged to Hunwick Hall Estate, to George Allison. (Room, Johnson material (John-9-429) The lease covered the 712 acres of coal that laid beneath the Hunwick Estate. On 11th March 1839, George Allison transferred ten-per-cent of his interest in

Hunwick Colliery to Barnard Spindler of London, on the understanding that he provided the funding to open up the colliery, sinking the shafts and providing all of the machinery. (The_Common_Room, NEIMME/WAT/3/50/008)

Records kept by The North of England Institute of Mining Engineers at the Common Room, Newcastle, show that there were two shafts sunk at Hunwick Colliery.

The first shaft, the Gibson Pit, was sunk at Hunwick Station in 1839. It was 192 feet (58m) deep and the top 75 feet of the shaft were lined with firebricks. This shaft had a diameter of 12 feet and was divided vertically, into two sections. One section was used for pumping water out of the workings using an 80HP, high pressure steam pump with the other section used for raising and lowering men and materials. The second shaft, which was 9.5 foot in diameter, was used exclusively for raising coal and fireclay. There were two 25 HP, high pressure, steam winding engines on the site, housed in an engine house. (The_Common_Room, NEIMME/WAT/3/50)

There are no photographs of Hunwick Colliery. Gavin Bake has created this artist impression of what the colliery might have looked like, in the early 1900s, when viewed from the Station Hotel (the 'Monkey'), looking towards Newfield.

Image 0600 - Artist's impression of Hunwick Colliery by Gavin Bake, 2024

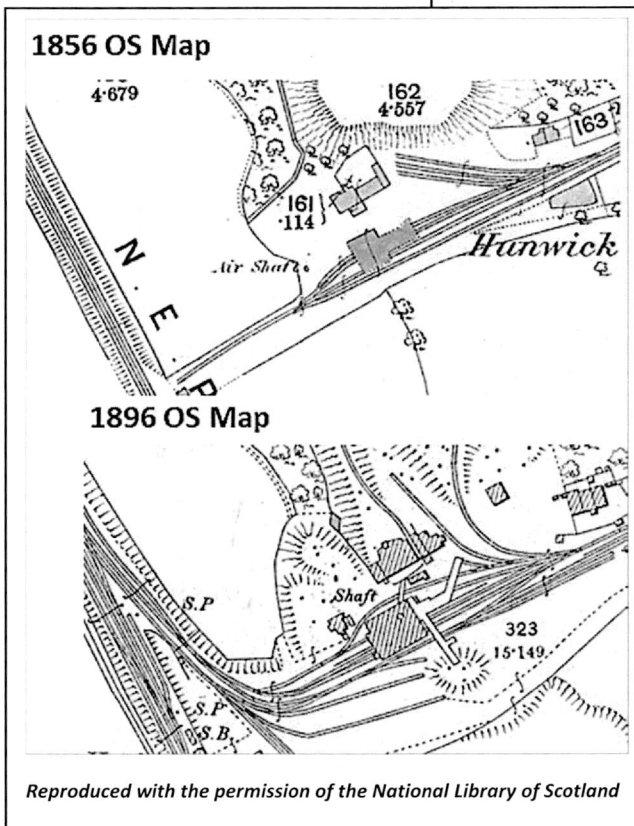

1856 OS Map

1896 OS Map

Reproduced with the permission of the National Library of Scotland

Thomas Cumming Gibson, bought Hunwick and Newfield Collieries, at a public auction in January 1842. The collieries were bought from the Sheriff under a 'writ of Poigne'.

Hunwick Colliery was advertised as *'consisting of 712 Acres .. with certain engines, & c., a railway and 119 coal-waggons'.* T C Gibson also owned Woodifield Colliery.

In addition to the two shafts at Hunwick Colliery there were two drifts, one to access the Busty seam and another to access the Victoria seam.

In January 1843 Hunwick Colliery was transporting 1023 tons of coal per month along the West Durham Railway to Port Clarence at Hartlepool.

Interestingly, the colliery owner, was also the owner of a three masted, iron steam propelled schooner that he named the SS Hunwick.

It carried coal out of Hartlepool. Unfortunately, SS Hunwick left West Hartlepool for London with a cargo of coal on the 11th November 1858, and sprang a leak and foundered in a gale on 15th November 1858 in Yarmouth. The crew saved themselves in their own lifeboat. (Hartlepool)

In 1856 the colliery was leased by the Hunwick Estate, to John Robson and Ralph Ward Jackson. The Spectator, August 15th 1857, records that the partnership of Robson and Watson as brick manufacturers had been dissolved. Shortly afterwards, Ralph Ward Jackson, became *'solely entitled to the colliery'* and by 1860, the West Hartlepool Harbour & Railway Company was running the colliery.

The 1856 OS map shows the colliery to be well established. Two bridges had been constructed to enable coal and coke to be transported across the river to Newfield and then on to the West Durham Railway line. The same map shows a significant spoil heap covering quite a large area of previously wooded land. By 1896 further rail sidings had been created along with a connection to the North Eastern Railway line.

An 1864 advertisement, offering Hunwick Colliery for sale, lists two houses for 'agents' (Hunwick Cottages, now November Cottage), 44 coke ovens, a blacksmith's shop, a joiner's shop, a store house, an office, stables as well as 300 coal waggons, being on the colliery site.

The same advertisement identifies eight double and thirty-one single cottages, on the Newfield side of the river, being included in the sale of Hunwick Colliery. It would appear that the majority of the men that worked at Hunwick Colliery, lived in Newfield.

The 1864 advertisement, by highlighting it as a 'Coking Colliery' and listing the 44 coke ovens, confirms that coke was being produced at the colliery from more or less the beginning of the mining operation.

In 1864, Lancaster and Brogden bought the colliery, at a public auction for, £25,000, from the West Hartlepool Harbour & Railway Co. That would equate to approximately £4,000,000 today.

In 1865, by an Act of Parliament, the North Eastern Railway Company took on the interests of West Hartlepool Railway Company and by 1870, Bolckow, Vaughan & Co were operating the colliery.

Bridges to Newfield, 1856

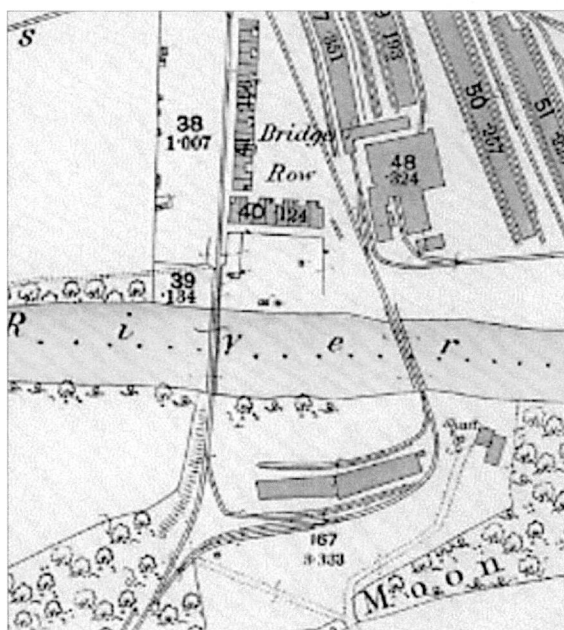

Image 0032 - Reproduced with the permission of the National Library of Scotland

The 1896 OS map shows the colliery as quite a large concern with several railway sidings. It is not clear where the 44 coke ovens were on the site. They might have been the Beehive ovens that were on the riverside beside the Bell Pit? Or perhaps between AdaVille and November Cottage as suggested by the layout of the railway lines and recent excavations?

Water was needed to wash the coal and to cool the coke after it had been fired. Advertisements for the sale of the colliery, highlighted the availability of a good supply of water on the colliery site. The 1856 OS Map show a reservoir close to the Colliery Offices that became November Cottage. The flooded clay pit on the site of the brickworks might also have been used as a reservoir.

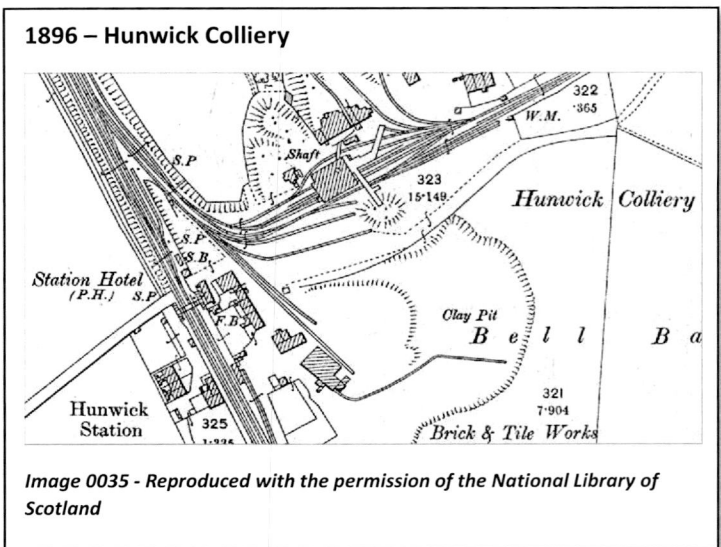

1896 – Hunwick Colliery

Image 0035 - Reproduced with the permission of the National Library of Scotland

At its peak in 1884, four-hundred and nineteen men and boys were working at the mine. Ref Mineral Statistics UK report Durham Mining Museum records show that in 1894, the workforce had contracted with one-hundred and seventeen men and boys working below ground and twenty-one working on the surface.

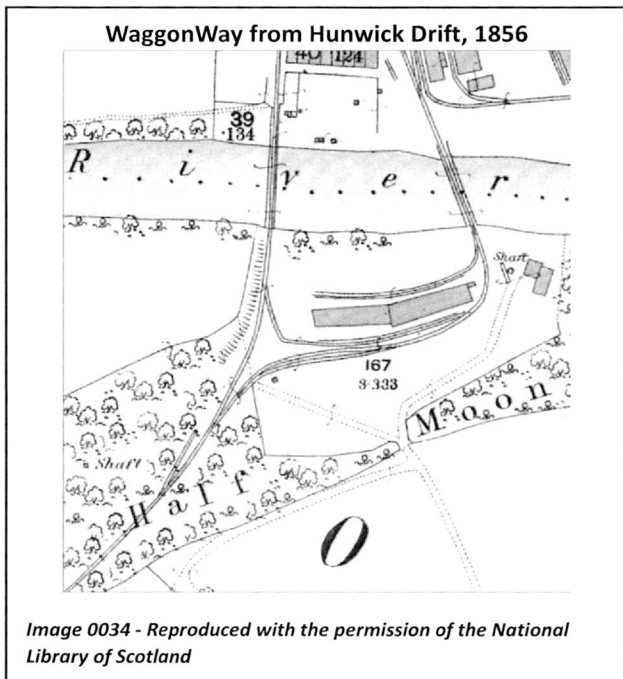

WaggonWay from Hunwick Drift, 1856

Image 0034 - Reproduced with the permission of the National Library of Scotland

The 1856 Map shows a shaft, possibly boring Number 1201, in the Half Moon Plantation. A siding is shown leading to this shaft, from the 'waggonway', that connected Hunwick Colliery to Newfield on the other side of the River Wear. By 1896 this shaft was described as an *"Old Shaft (coal)"*.

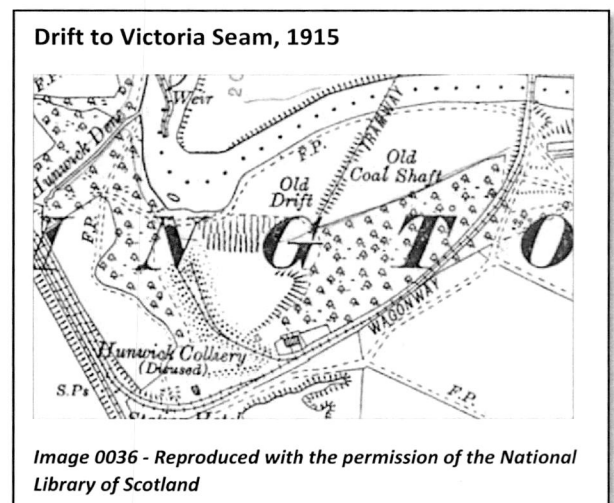

Drift to Victoria Seam, 1915

Image 0036 - Reproduced with the permission of the National Library of Scotland

The 1915 map shows an 'Old Drift' mine, below Hunwick Colliery, connected by a 'tramway' and a third bridge, to Newfield. The Durham Mining Museum record of the death in Jan 1912, of Thomas Clennell, at Hunwick Colliery when the *'Victoria Seam was being opened up by means of a 'dip-drift'*. This, along with the Coal Authority abandonment maps, confirms that this drift was being opened up in 1912.

The coal reserves must have been significant enough to justify a new bridge to be constructed to connect the drift to Newfield.

> *"the pit was accessed via a low wooden bridge, the stumps of which were visible in the 1950s, across the river from Newfield and into the base of the very steep river bank, a drift which was brick arched ... about a hundred yards, at just before the point the roadway turned to the east and cut through solid rock with no brick lining".* (Donald White's notes)

Coal seams

The Gibson shaft was 192 feet deep and allowed coal to be mined from the Brockwell or Main Coal seam, which was 156 feet below ground level.

There was also a drift from the surface, to the Busty and to the Brockwell seams, this was to improve the ventilation in the workings. The main shaft was not deep enough to allow the Victoria seam, 220 feet below ground level, to be worked so in 1912, a drift was driven down to the Victoria seam.

The other seams were worked from the roadways in the Brockwell seam, along with 'Stone Drifts', that allowed men and materials to travel between the seams, and 'Staple shafts' which allowed coal, segger (fireclay) and waste to be dropped down to the Brockwell seam so that it could be taken to the shaft to be hauled to the surface.

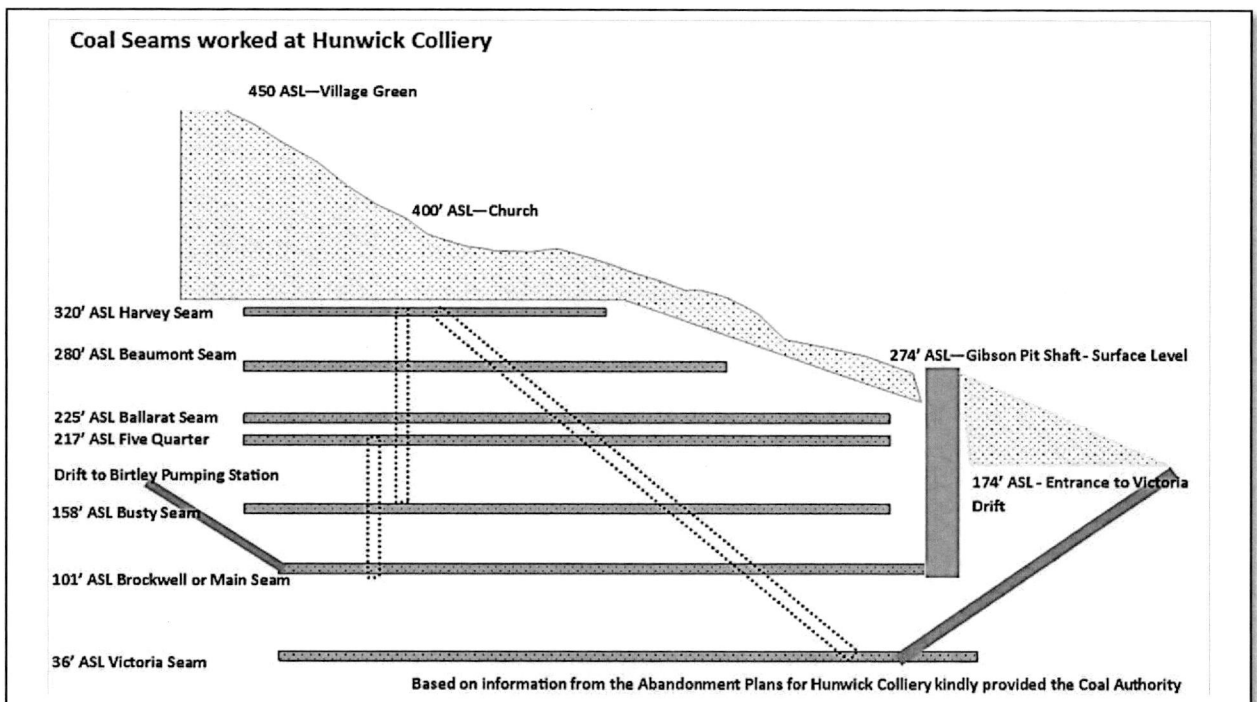

Coal Seams worked at Hunwick Colliery

450 ASL—Village Green

400' ASL—Church

320' ASL Harvey Seam

280' ASL Beaumont Seam

274' ASL—Gibson Pit Shaft - Surface Level

225' ASL Ballarat Seam
217' ASL Five Quarter

Drift to Birtley Pumping Station

174' ASL - Entrance to Victoria Drift

158' ASL Busty Seam

101' ASL Brockwell or Main Seam

36' ASL Victoria Seam

Based on information from the Abandonment Plans for Hunwick Colliery kindly provided the Coal Authority

Durham Mining Museum records identify twenty-one miners who were killed while working at the Gibson Pit. One fatality, William Howden, a 13-year-old Horse Driver, was killed in November 1859 when his head was crushed between the cage and the shaft. The report explains that 9 boys were in the cage at the time.

Hunwick Colliery closed in 1921.

The Bell Pit (Bridge of Hunwick)

In 1839, a waggon way (railway) bridge, was built across the River Wear to connect Hunwick Colliery, the new colliery that was to be established at Hunwick Station, to Newfield. From Newfield the coal was transported on the West Durham Railway.

An 1839 early Estate map, shows a bridge across the River Wear, connecting the Bell Pit, on the riverside, close to Farnley Farm, to railway lines on the Newfield side of the river.

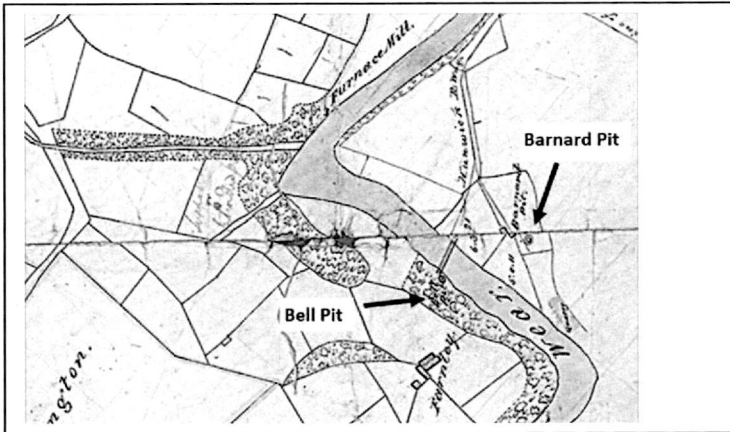

Bell Pit (Bridge of Hunwick)

The Common Room NEIMME/Wat/32/8

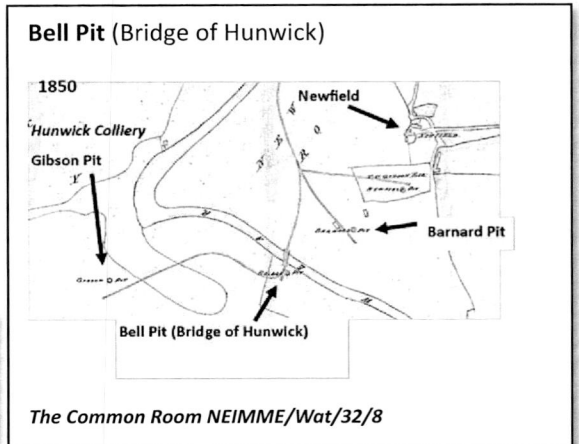

The Gibson Pit at Hunwick colliery is not shown on the map, suggesting that the Bell Pit, sometimes referred to as the Bridge of Hunwick Pit, might have been Hunwick's first, recorded pit? (The_Common_Room, NEIMME/Wat/32/33) The earliest record of the Bell Pit producing coal, is in the 1842 Estate accounts.

The Barnard Pit was sunk, on the Newfield side of the river, before 1841.

The shaft for the Bell Pit, was 9 feet in diameter and 22 fathoms (132 feet) down. Unfortunately, a 'Dip Dyke' was discovered in the coalfield. This meant that the seam of coal (the five-quarter seam) rose very sharply, by 23 feet. The result being that the Bell pit, the engine pit (main coal shaft used for raising coal) for the colliery, was 23 feet below the Barnard Pit shaft. This had implications for the water level in the pit and the volume of water that needed to be pumped out of the workings.

A stone drift was driven between the two shafts which were also connected, via the workings, to the shaft at Birtley. Birtley was used as a pumping station to lift the water out of the mine workings and into the river. (Room, WAT_3_50)

The 1856 OS map shows the bridge to the Bell Pit and a second bridge, a short distance downstream. The downstream bridge connected the 'Gibson' Pit at Hunwick Colliery, to Newfield Colliery.

The same map shows the shaft for the Bell Pit, to the east of the upstream bridge and very close to

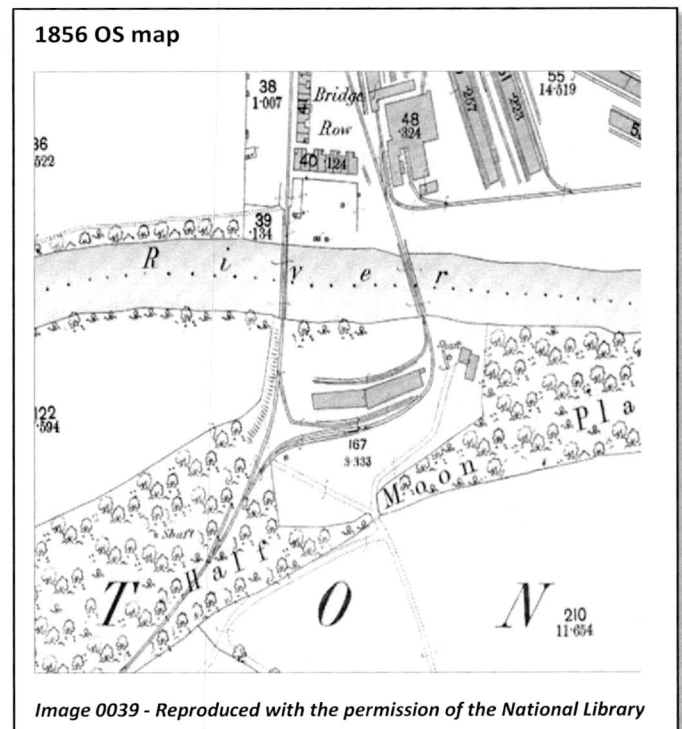

1856 OS map

Image 0039 - Reproduced with the permission of the National Library

the outline of 'Gibson's', Beehive coke ovens. The ovens had railway tracks on both sides of them that connected them to the collieries on both sides of the river.

Coke would have been discharged from the bottom of the ovens and would need to be cooled before being loaded onto railway waggons. The position of coke ovens at the Bell Pit, close to the river, makes sense considering the appetite that the coke making process had for water.

Looking towards the coke ovens at ground level

Image 0402

Frank Atkinson described the ovens as they were in 1974:

"A long line of beehive-shaped coke ovens *once stood overgrown and almost lost in rough land close to the river. This is an early range of ovens, mostly in quite good condition. They were built in the 19th century. They run in two lines, back-to-back with space for rails both above and between the ovens. Most are circular, but there are one or two small square ones with domed tops similar to the circular ones".* (Atkinson, 1974)

Looking along the top of the two lines of ovens

Image 0404

There is very little information available about the Bell Pit. Reputedly, it had a short working life.

The upstream bridge and the railway lines to the coke ovens, are shown on an 1876 Estate map, but are not shown on the 1896 OS map.

The 'Bell Pit' is at the bottom of 'Bell Bank', on the Hunwick side of the river, with maps showing 'Bell Hill', 'Bell Burn', 'Bellburn Wood' and 'Bellburn' pumping station, on the Newfield side of the river. It was also on land which was owned, after 1828, by Mathew Bell.

To add to the confusion, the disturbance shown on the Lidar Digital Terrain Map of the land upstream of the Bell Pit, suggests that 'Bell' pits might have previously been worked on the site. With a 'Bell Pit', miners dig a shaft down to the coal seam and dig out the coal from the area around bottom of the shaft.

Lidar Map – Bell Pit

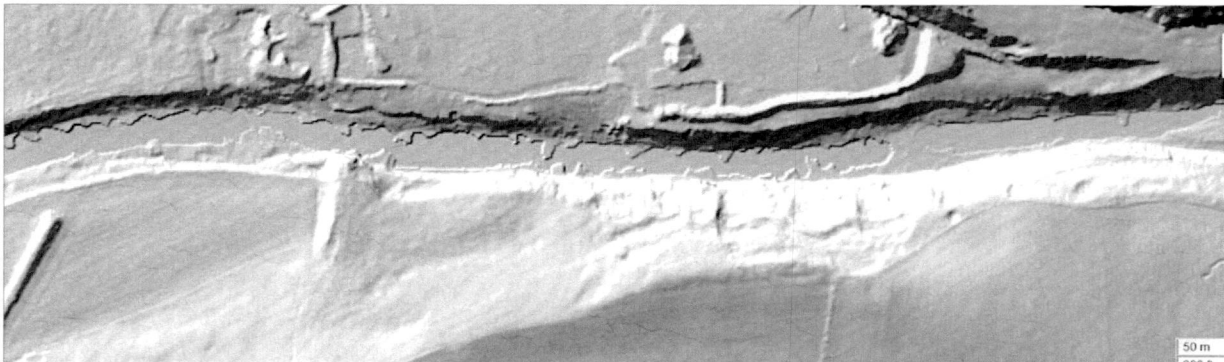

Image 0041 - Lidar

The unsupported area around the shaft would soon collapse. When this happened, the miners would attempt to follow the coal seam by digging another shaft, close to the first shaft. The waste from the newly opened shaft would be thrown into the hollow created by the collapsed bell-pit.

The Lidar Map also shows the location of the river crossings, the bridges and the 'tram way' that connected Hunwick Colliery Drift to Newfield and for one of the railway lines that connected the Bell Pit to Newfield.

Birtley Pumping Station

On the 1896 OS map, approximately half a mile south from Hunwick Colliery, towards Birtley, a drift is shown. This 'adit', a near horizontal drift, drained water from the workings that ran along the Hunwick side of the river.

A little further to the south, at Birtley Cottages, the Coal Authority abandonment plans, show a shaft that is connected to the workings of the Bell Pit and to the workings of Newfield Colliery.

It is marked as 'Birtley Pumping Pit' and is close to the river. Water was pumped up from the Five-Quarter coal seam, 180 feet below the surface, and into the River Wear.

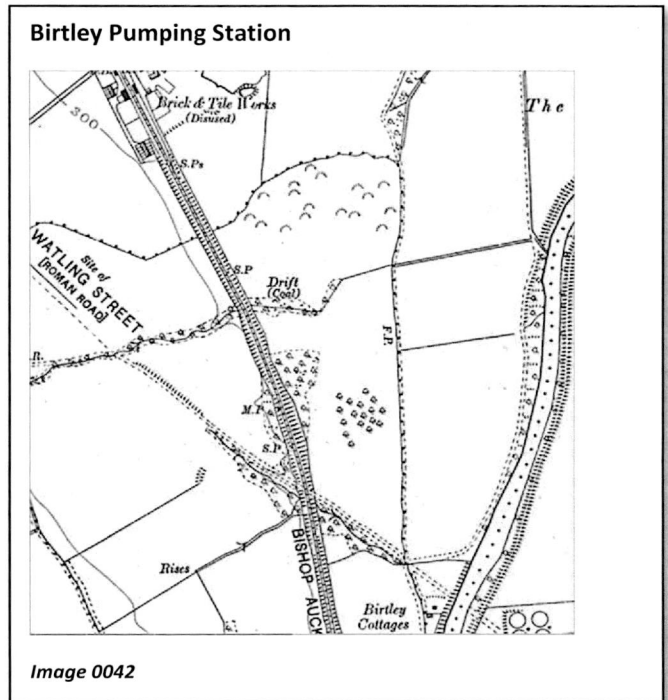

Birtley Pumping Station

Image 0042

West Hunwick Colliery

Some references to 'New' Hunwick Colliery are confusing. An advertisement in the Newcastle Guardian and Tyne Mercury on 29th August 1857, offered 'New' Hunwick Colliery for sale.

It offers *'All the SEAMS of COAL and FIRE-CLAY lying under CRINGLE DYKES FARM, and other CLOSES of LAND in the Township of Hunwick, in the county of Durham, to the extent of about 93 Acres'.*

West Hunwick Colliery

Image 0043

It explains that

'the shaft has been sunk down to the main coal seam without any water having been met with in the sinking. The five-quarter seam is believed to extend over the larger portion of the Royalty." They will also convey a *"STRIP of LAND for the purposes of a railway from the colliery, forming a junction at a short distance with the North-Eastern Railway, by which the produce of the colliery will be vended.'*

Borings were made around the village in attempt to find viable coal seams. Details of the borings include Shaft Number 1203, which was identified as the *'New Hunwick Shaft'*. The grid reference for the boring, locates it on the site of what became *'West Hunwick Colliery'*.

The advertisement claims that *'the North Eastern Railway is only a short distance away from the colliery"*. This would confirm that the *"New Hunwick Colliery"* that they are describing, was really the colliery that became known as *"West Hunwick Colliery'*.

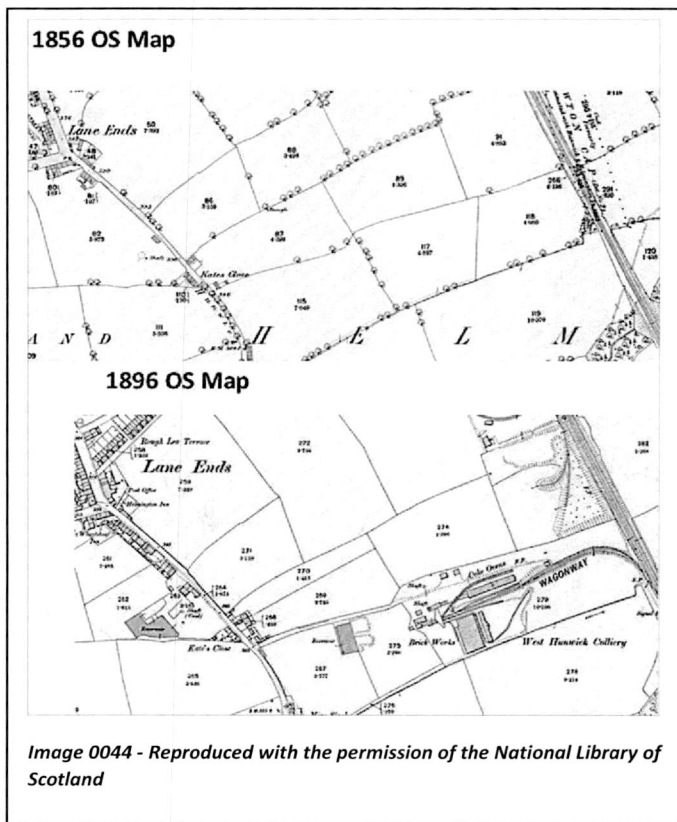

1856 OS Map

1896 OS Map

Image 0044 - Reproduced with the permission of the National Library of Scotland

Newcastle Guardian - August 1857

New Hunwick Colliery, Near Bishop Auckland

To Be Sold By Private Contract

All the SEAMS of COAL and FIRE-CLAY lying under CRINGLE DYKES FARM, and other CLOSES of LAND in the Township of Hunwick, in the county of Durham, to the extent of about 93 Acres, excepting barrier.

The Coal and Fire-clay are held under a lease for the term of 21 years, commencing from the 1st day of July, determinable by the lessees at the end of the third or any succeeding year of the term.

The certain rent for the first year is £100, and for the residue of the term £280, with power to make up short workings at any time during the term. The tental rent is 17s 6d per ten of 52 tons, and 16 cwt. each ten. The fire-clay rent is 6d the long ton of 22 cwt. and a half. The certain rents have all been paid up by the present lessees.

The lessees have the usual powers to use common brick-clay and freestone for colliery purposes, with a power of outstroke to work adjoining royalties, at a rent of 4s 6d per ten for outstroke, wayleave, shaft, air and watercourse rent.

The lease contains other usual clauses,

The shaft has been sunk down to the main coal seam with out any water having been met with in the sinking. The five-quarter seam is believed to extend over the larger portion of the royalty.

The present lessees will sell, if required, ONE UNDIVIDED SIXTH-PART of the SEAMS of COAL, under the adjoining lands of **Mr. John Fletcher**, containing about 20 acres.

They will also convey a STRIP of LAND for the purposes of a railway from the colliery, forming a junction at a short distance with the North-Eastern Railway, by which the produce of the colliery will be vended.

The Coal is believed to be Coking Coal of a superior quality.

Image 0047 – Durham Mining Museum

West Hunwick Colliery operated on the site of the current Dyson's Brick Works. The 1857 advertisement was for a shaft, possibly sunk in 1845, and for a site for a colliery. Maps show that between 1856 and 1896 the green-field site had been developed into a large colliery and brickworks.

An advert in the Durham Chronicle on 16th October 1857 for four, newly developed dwelling houses describes them as being *'situated in one of the largest and most flourishing Colliery Districts in the neighbourhood, adjoining the New Hunwick Sinking, which had recently been purchased by North Bitchburn Coal Company'*.

If the North Bitchburn Coal Company had bought the colliery in 1857, it is likely that the colliery would have opened in 1858. Durham Mining Museum Records show that by the 1870s it was owned by the Lackenby Iron Co.

The colliery and brickworks were offered for sale in 1877 and again in June 1879. It was described as *'the Colliery, brickworks together with the valuable coal Royalty … together with buildings, railways, coke ovens and brick kilns complete in every respect for producing large output of coal and fireclay … the drawing and ventilation shafts are sunk to the 5/4 and Busty seams'*. (Midlands and Northern Coal and Iron Trade Gazette, 17 October 1877)

In July 1879, it was reported that the colliery was the property of Messer's Lloyd and Company, and that it had been offered for sale by public auction and that not a single bid had been received. (Engineering, 1879) It appears that Lloyd and Co went bankrupt in 1879.

A report of a fatal accident at the colliery in 1898 reveals that Joseph Torbeck and Co were the owners at that time.

In 1896 the colliery employed seventeen men and boys below ground and five on the surface. Employment peaked in 1900 with one hundred and thirty-nine working below ground and twenty-two on the surface. Ted Bowes, who worked at the colliery after the First World War, explained in a newspaper article, that West Hunwick was a *'small colliery with 20 Hewers'*.

The colliery was not working in 1910 but was back in production by 1915 employing thirty-seven men and boys. (Durham_Mining_Museum, 2024)

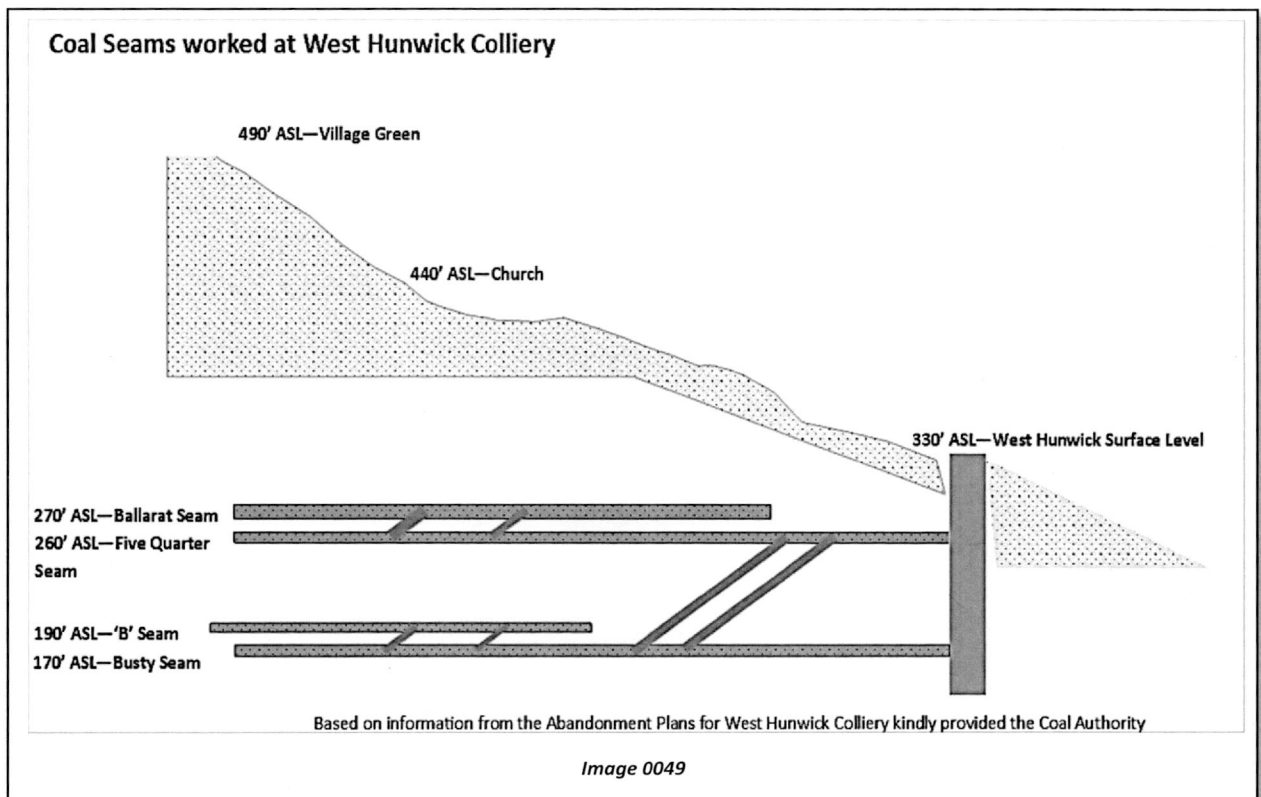

Coal Seams worked at West Hunwick Colliery

490' ASL—Village Green

440' ASL—Church

330' ASL—West Hunwick Surface Level

270' ASL—Ballarat Seam
260' ASL—Five Quarter Seam

190' ASL—'B' Seam
170' ASL—Busty Seam

Based on information from the Abandonment Plans for West Hunwick Colliery kindly provided the Coal Authority

Image 0049

The colliery mined coking coal and fireclay. A newspaper advertisement confirms that the Coking Plant at the colliery was in operation in 1879. The 1896 map identifies some coke ovens as 'disused'. It also shows the newer ovens, with railway tracks on both sides.

The hot coke needed to be cooled before being loaded on to railway waggons. The colliery had its own large reservoir on site to store water, as well as one behind what is now Wear View.

In 1910 the colliery was owned by The West Witton Ganister Firebrick Company. and from 1924 until 1935, by the West Hunwick Silica & Firebrick Company Ltd. During this period, in addition to manufacturing firebricks, most of the fireclay was either sold in the form of 'pugged' or dry ground fireclay.

There is some confusion about when the colliery closed. It was either 1938 (Blackett, 1980) or 1942 (NCB). Reputedly, an attempt was made in 1936 to develop the Busty Seam to the East of the railway line, but it was abandoned because of the poor section and poor quality of the coal and segger.

Rough Lea Colliery

Henry Stobart & Company sunk the shaft for Rough Lea in 1858. Henry Stobart was a partner in the North Bitchburn Coal Company who owned the colliery from 1880 until 1920.

The 1857 OS map shows Open Fields which were developed to create the large colliery and pipework's complex shown on the 1915 OS map.

The shaft was sunk to the Brockwell seam which was 180 feet below the surface. Coal Board abandonment plans show that quite a small area of this seam was worked under the Rough Lea Colliery site. The other seams were worked via a drift that was driven from the Rough Lea Colliery site, up beyond Quarry Burn Row. This allowed the seams, under quite a large area, to be worked. The Durham Mining Museum records that the coal seams were abandoned in 1925.

A day-drift and air-shaft at Breckon Hill allowed miners to access the workings and assist the mine ventilation. The site also included a lamp cabin, a fan-house and stables for the pit ponies.

At its peak, in 1910, it employed three-hundred and six men and boys underground and eighty-five on the surface. In 1925 the Colliery only employed three surface workers suggesting that the mine was being run down until it eventually closed in 1931. (Durham_Mining_Museum, 2024)

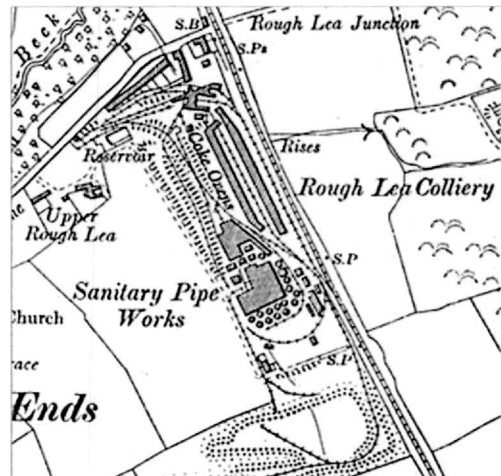

Image 0051 - Reproduced with the permission of the National Library of Scotland

Rough Lea Colliery - 1907

Image 0050

In addition to mining coal, the colliery mined fireclay which was used in the manufacture of fire bricks and pipes. The colliery had coke ovens and a sanitary Pipe Works on its site.

The Pipe Works continued to operate after the colliery closed.

Rough Lea Tub Token

Image 0389 - By kind permission of Martin Rowley

In 1920, the North Bitchburn Coal Company became a subsidiary of Pease and Partners, who operated Rough Lea Colliery until 1931/2.

Coal Seams worked at Rough Lea Colliery

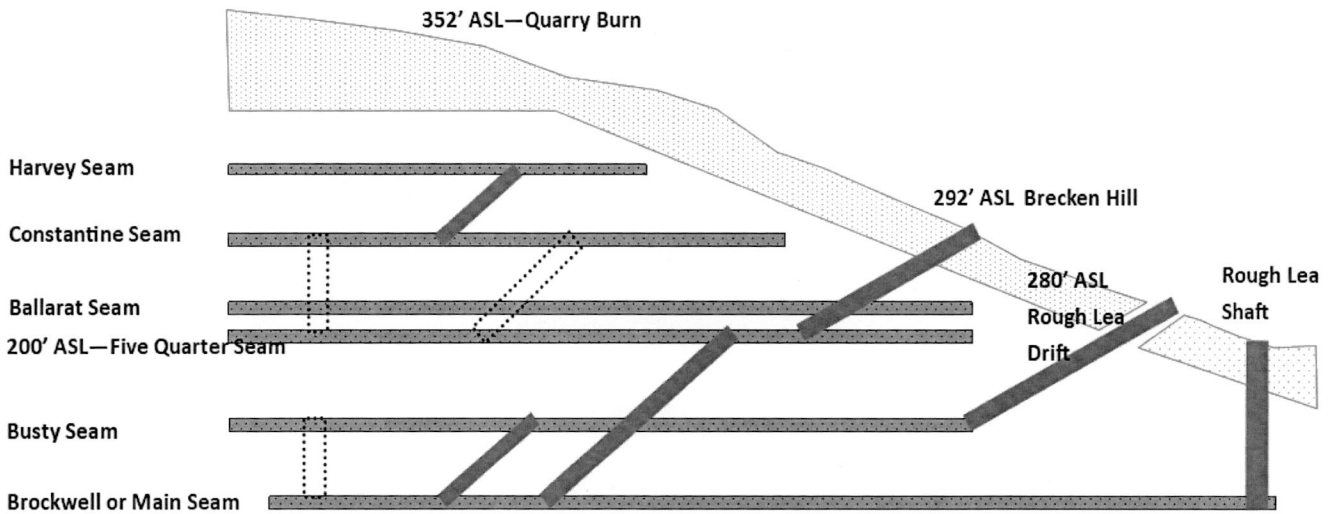

Harvey Seam

352' ASL—Quarry Burn

Constantine Seam

292' ASL Brecken Hill

Ballarat Seam

280' ASL
Rough Lea
Drift

Rough Lea
Shaft

200' ASL—Five Quarter Seam

Busty Seam

Brockwell or Main Seam

Based on information from the Abandonment Plans for Rough Lea Colliery kindly provided the Coal Authority

Image 0054

The photograph below shows the site in the late 1940s after the colliery had closed.

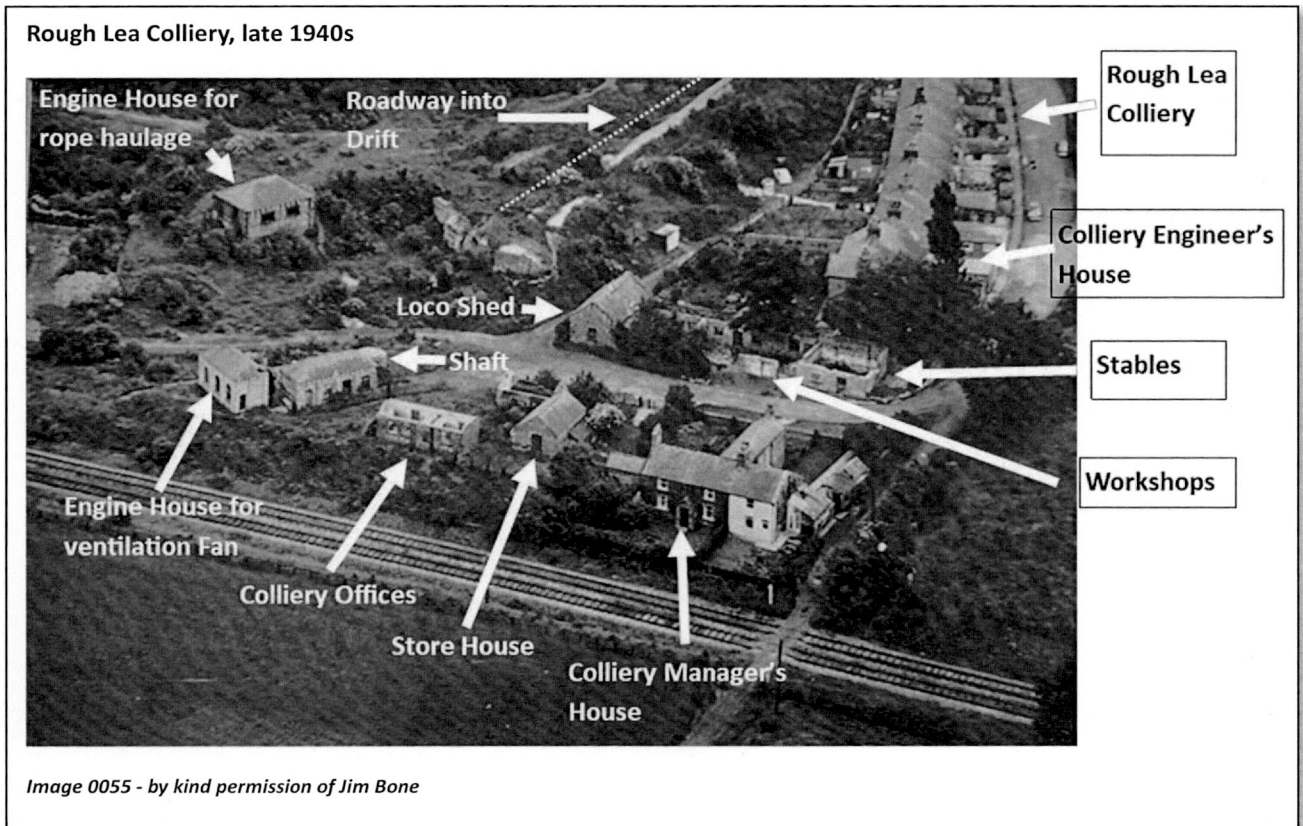

Rough Lea Colliery, late 1940s

Engine House for rope haulage

Roadway into Drift

Rough Lea Colliery

Colliery Engineer's House

Loco Shed

Shaft

Stables

Workshops

Engine House for ventilation Fan

Colliery Offices

Store House

Colliery Manager's House

Image 0055 - by kind permission of Jim Bone

A large ventilation fan, driven by a steam engine, pulled the stale air up the shaft and out of the mine workings. Large diameter steel pipes also ran down the shaft. A steam driven pump, used these pipes to pump the water out of the mine workings.

A steam driven rope haulage system pulled 'tubs', along the underground rail tracks and out of the drift. The coal was screened by size, and crushed if required, into different piles depending upon what it was to be used for.

A newspaper cutting, discovered by Kathleen Johnson in the bottom of a drawer, reports that during the demolition of the colliery in February 1932, an engine that was reported to be 120-year-old at the time the article was written, had been found.

Rough Lea Rope Haulage Engine House

Image 0416 - By kind permission of Donald White

The engine had been brought to the colliery in 1848 and had been used as a winding engine for 40 years, lifting 360 tons of coal up the mine shaft, every day, for 40 years.

After being decommissioned as a winding engine, it was redeployed into the Coke Works to power the coal crushing and washing plant. It worked for a further 36 years, until the colliery closed in 1924.

The engine was a single cylinder, eighty horse-power, Scots-Russel beam engine, with a flywheel which was twelve feet in diameter, was built in Chester le Street. It was built sometime around, 1812 and was used at another County Durham colliery, before being moved to Rough Lea in 1848.

The Colonel, 1867

Image 0363

The colliery had its own steam locomotive to move coal, pipes and fireclay around the site. They assembled the trains of waggons in the sidings which were then collected by a mainline locomotive.

There was a signal box and an engine shed on the site. Arrow, Lilly, The Colonel, Crossfield and Comet were all locomotives that were known to have worked on the site. (C_Mountford, 1977)

Rough Lea Fan House

Image 0415 – By kind permission of Donald White

Brecken Hill Colliery

Brecken Hill colliery is not shown on the 1857 OS map.

In 1861, Brecken Hill Farm, along with the coal royalties, were advertised for sale in the Durham County Advertiser.

The 1896 OS map shows two drifts and an Air Shaft on the colliery site. The Air Shaft and one of the drifts, were connected to the five-quarter coal seam, that was worked by Rough Lea Colliery. The drift was classed as a day-drift, which allowed miners to enter and exit the Rough Lea workings which extended up to and beyond Quarry Burn Row.

The five-quarter seam was eighty-four feet below the surface at Brecken Hill.

The colliery closed down when Rough Lea Colliery closed in 1924.

1896 OS Map

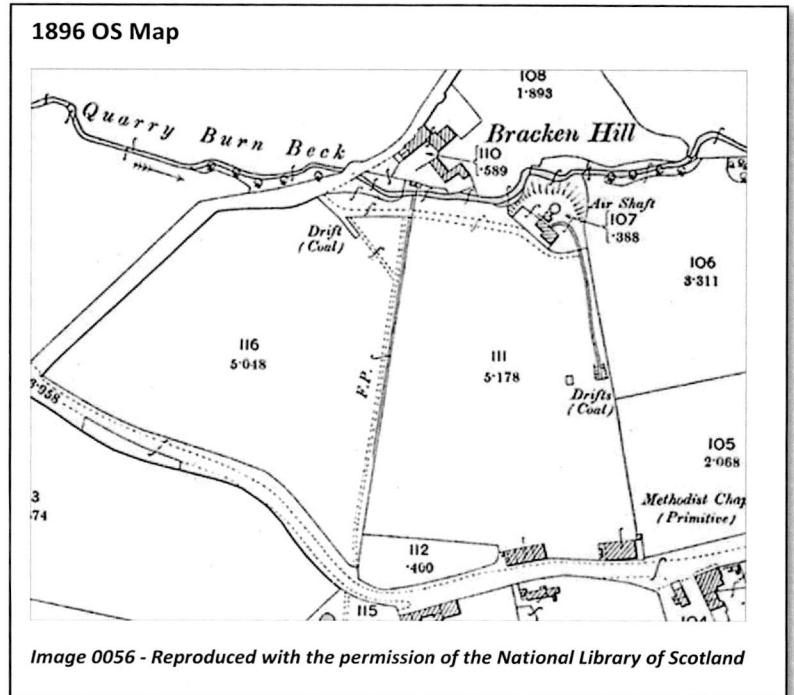

Image 0056 - Reproduced with the permission of the National Library of Scotland

In 1963, the North Bitchburn Fireclay Company opened up a new drift mine on the site. Coal and fireclay were mined until the colliery closed in 1972. The coal and fireclay were transported by road. The coal was delivered to Darlington Power Station and the fireclay to North Bitchburn Pipe Works.

One of the colliery buildings that still exists, was the Lamp Cabin from where miners would collect their pit lamps and tokens before entering the mine. At one time, a room in this building was used as a band practice room for the Rough Lea Silver Band. This building has now been converted into a holiday cottage. The other building on the site was used to stable the pit ponies.

Chapter 4 - Brick and Tile Making

Bricks have been used for building since Roman times. Clay was dug from clay pits. Before the Industrial revolution clay would be dug near to the site where the bricks were needed and the bricks would be made on the site. Brick workers would move and work close to the sites where the bricks were required.

The clay was usually dug in the autumn and left to weather over the winter. During the winter, the clay would be turned occasionally and any stones would be removed. The clay would be worked again in spring with any remaining stones being removed before it would be combined with sand and water and 'kneaded' into a consistency that could be moulded. The mixture was pressed into a wooden brick-shaped mould before being turned out and stacked ready for drying.

The moulded clay would then need to be heated either in a simple 'clamp' where charcoal would be placed underneath and around the bricks and covered in earth after the charcoal had been lit. The advantage of using a simple 'clamp' was that they could be built anywhere, as no permanent structure was required, but it was difficult to control the temperature. Brick kilns, allowed the brickmakers to control the temperature and produced more consistent bricks with less wastage in terms of poor-quality bricks or tiles.

The Industrial Revolution highlighted the need to increase the productivity of land and the need to bring wet land in to production.

The enclosure of Hunwick Moor in 1761 will have focussed the attention of land owners on drainage. They will have been keen to drain any wet land. Farmers had been draining land since Roman times. Clay pipes or tiles had been used.

In 1783, following the American War of Independence, the government had introduced a brick tax to help it to repay its war debts. The tax was based on the number of bricks that were put into the kilns before they were 'fired'. Any losses or breakages that happened during the manufacturing stage resulted in the brickmaker losing money. The tax increased if bricks were above a standard size or if the pipe or tile had a polished finish.

Farmers were unhappy with the tax as it increased the cost of draining land and industrialists were unhappy that the tax made it more expensive for them to build mills, collieries, houses for their workers etc. Councils were unhappy because road building required a lot of bricks and pipes to create culverts and drains. In 1826 the importance of reclaiming wet land using hollow clay pipes was recognised and so bricks and tiles that were solely used for drainage were exempt from the brick tax.

In 1850, the tax was removed from all brick products. By this time, the demand for coal was beginning to have an impact on the village. The need for colliery buildings and housing for the workers, created a demand for building materials. Stone was relatively expensive to quarry and took more skill and time to build with than bricks.

Hunwick was well placed as the local clay was considered to be of a *'superior quality'*. (Ashby, 2005) A newspaper advertisement in February 1853, that offered a 'Drain Tile Manufactory' To Let, confirms that clay was being moulded and fired at Hunwick Station, before the colliery brickworks had opened in 1856. The 1841 census recorded that a brick maker was living in the village so bricks were possibly being manufactured as early as the 1830s.

There were three Brick Works operating in Hunwick: one at Hunwick Station, one at West Hunwick Colliery and one at Rough Lea Colliery. All three manufactured firebricks but West Hunwick went on to concentrate on specialist furnace bricks, sinks etc, while Rough Lea concentrated on salt-glazed pipes and high-quality sanitary ware.

Hunwick Bricks

G L W - G L Watson, Hunwick Station

T C Gibson – Hunwick Station

N B C C Ld - North Bitchburn Coal Company, Rough Lea

N B C C Ld - North Bitchburn Coal Company, Rough Lea

W H C - West Hunwick Colliery

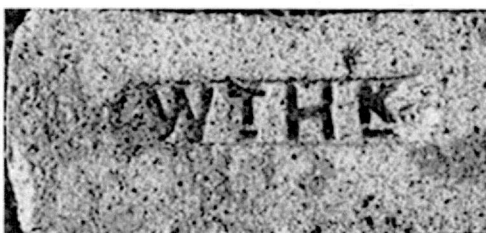

H & N – Hunwick and Newfield, Hunwick Station

H & N – Hunwick and Newfield, Hunwick Station

Image 0060 – by kind permission of Chris Tilney

Ordnance Survey Maps show that both Hunwick Colliery and West Hunwick Colliery had clay pits on their sites. The clay from these pits would have been used to produce ordinary bricks that could be used for building. When the shafts were sunk for the collieries in the village, fireclay was discovered in between the coal seams. The fireclay or segger, had a high silica content which meant that it could be used to make fire bricks. Firebricks could withstand the high temperatures used in furnaces. Ganister, a sandstone with an even higher silica content than the fireclay was available locally, and could be used to make bricks and components that can be used in really high temperature furnaces.

Hunwick Colliery Brick Works

In 1839, Hunwick Cottages (now November Cottage) and the colliery engine house were being built using stone. In February 1853, a *"Drain Tile Manufactory"* was advertised to be Let on the Hunwick Estate, *"immediately contiguous to the proposed Durham to Auckland railway"*.

The 1856 OS Map identifies a Brick and Tile Works at Hunwick Station with a building close to the main railway line. Perhaps 'drain tiles', used for field drainage, were being manufactured on the site at Hunwick Station, before the colliery opened? This would explain the substantial clay pit that is shown on the 1896 map. The map also shows that the Works had its own railway siding along with an increased range of buildings.

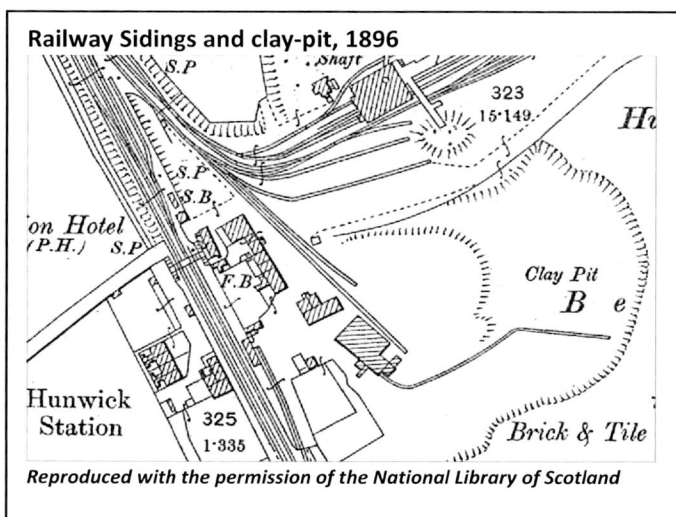

Brick and Tile Works, Hunwick Station, 1856

Reproduced with the permission of the National Library of Scotland

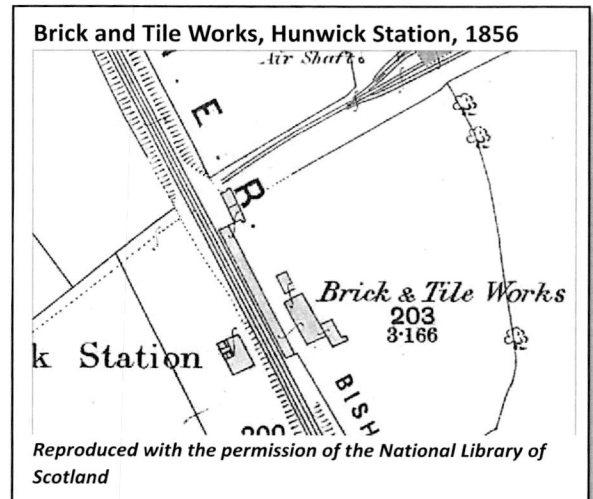

Railway Sidings and clay-pit, 1896

Reproduced with the permission of the National Library of Scotland

There is some confusion as to when the Brick Works first opened. Davison lists T C Gibson & Co as manufacturers of firebricks at Hunwick Station in 1855. He also records John Robson, the owner of Hunwick Colliery (Hunwick Station), as having opened a Brick Works in 1856. However, the 1853 advertisement offering 'To Let' the *'Drain Tile Manufactory'* would imply that the Works had begun operating earlier.

Durham Mining Museum records show that fireclay was not mined at the colliery until 1896. So where did the fireclay come from if they were manufacturing firebricks 1855? (Davison, 2022)

The Spectator, August 15th 1857, records that the partnership of Robson and Watson as brick manufacturers was dissolved in August 1857. Might it be related to the article in the Jurist in 1849 that recorded that John Robson was in *'the Goal of Durham'* as an insolvent debtor?

The LNER railway line opened in August 1856. By 1896, the Station Hotel, a Ball Alley and Station Cottages had been built at Hunwick Station.

The 1861 census records George Lindsay Watson at the 'Tile shed' employing 3 labourers. Davison records that G L Watson was operating the Works in 1868. (Davison, 2022) The 1871 census records that John Richardson was the Inn Keeper at Hunwick Station, living with his wife Mary L Richardson (nee Watson), and daughters including Jane Ann Watson and Mary Lindsay Watson. When John Richardson died in 1872, his daughter, Jane Watson, operated the Brick Works until 1880, when they were bought by her sister Mary Lindsay Richardson.

George Hall, a brick manufacturer, who was living in the Station Hotel, went into liquidation in February 1882. In the same year, Mary Lindsay Hall, took out a mortgage on the Brick Works. Davison lists M L Hall as working the Brick Works in 1884. The 1901 Directory of Clay workers, lists Mrs. Mary L. Hall, as working at Hunwick Station Brick Works

Davison lists the Hunwick Brick and Tile Company as operating at Hunwick Station in 1902. Hunwick Brick and Tile Works, announced in the Durham Advertiser on 1st July 1904, that *'Best Common Bricks'* were available from the Works. On the 29 July 1904, an advertisement in the same newspaper claimed that *'a good face is to be found on our bricks'* and highlighted that they were also *'metal and machinery brokers'* having stocks of *'engines, shafting and pipes'*. They reinforced this in an advertisement on 5th August by claiming that they manufactured a *'regular brick, unequalled for strength, colour and uniformity'*. This confirmed that common bricks were being manufactured as well as firebricks. A 1907 advertisement for the Works claims that it has a *'very extensive bed of excellent brick clay at a depth of 70 feet'*.

The Brick Works were described in a for sale advertisement in the Durham County Advertiser, on 25th October 1907, 'as a complete and up to date brick making plant capable of manufacturing 60,000 bricks per week'.

The sale included 4 kilns, a brick drying shed, a six roomed house and two cottages on a 6-acre site. The reason given for the sale was the dissolution of a partnership and that interested parties should contact Mr G Trotter, who the Directory of Clay Workers had listed as operating the Works in 1906. (Clayworkers, 1901)

It would appear that the Gibson family, throughout various marriages and partnerships, had run the Brick Works from the 1850s until 1901, when the Works passed through the ownership of Henry Curry, James Hunter and in 1904, to G Trotter who offered the Works for sale in 1907.

Maps show that by 1920 the Brick Works had closed and the sidings had been lifted.

One of the kilns survived until 2013. One end had been used as a garage and the other end as a cow byre.

A Garage, 2013

Image 0401

The last kiln being demolished, 2013

Image 0402

West Hunwick Brick Works

Hunwick Colliery and Brickworks

Image 0066

A Brick Works was opened on the West Hunwick Colliery site in 1879. It used the segger, that was mined at West Hunwick Colliery, to make firebricks for the Blast Furnaces at Teesside.

In 1902 the West Hunwick Colliery Company was established and traded until 1914 when the West Witton Gannister Firebrick Company was established and traded until 1921. During this period the Works split its production between firebricks and ganister bricks. Ganister, a sandstone with a higher silica content than fireclay, was discovered on Knitsley Fell (between Hamsterley and Wolsingham) and was used to make silica bricks.

Silica bricks can survive very high temperatures and are used in furnaces and kilns. In 1925, Hunwick Silica and Firebrick Company was established and a new yard was built to be used solely for the production of silica bricks. The old yard continued to produce fireclay bricks. Silica bricks were very fragile and needed special railway waggons with shock absorbers to carry them. The bricks were packed into the waggons using straw or heather to protect them.

West Hunwick Colliery closed in 1937. Before the colliery closed the Brick Works had stock piled fireclay. This stock pile allowed production of firebricks to continue until 1939.

During the Second World War the new yard was kept busy making silica bricks for the steel works, gasworks and coke works.

Image 0068 - by kind permission of Dyson Technical Ceramics Limited

In 1946 the old Newcastle kilns were replaced by twenty-four double-ended, coal fired Newcastle Kilns. At this time two-hundred and thirty men were employed at the Works.

The Works had its own steam locomotive that moved the railway waggons around the site and into the railway sidings.

In 1952 an oil-fired tunnel kiln was built. The production of silica bricks ceased in 1957 and the Works then concentrated on the production of basic refractory bricks using raw materials imported from around the world.

In 1983 the Works employed sixty-seven people. (Davison, 2022)

Double ended Kilns under construction, 1946 Hunwick Station in the background

Image 0067 - by kind permission of Dyson Technical Ceramics Limited

The Works were taken over by Price-Pearson in 1960 and then J &J Dyson in 1967. The Newcastle kilns were demolished in 1970 with production then relying on the gas and oil-fired kilns.

Owners

1875 - Lackenby Iron Co.
1879 - Lloyd and Company
1880 - Joseph Torbock
1890 - 1895 Torbock & Co.
1900 - 1910 Owners of West Hunwick
1914 - West Witton Ganister Firebrick Co
1925 - Hunwick Silica and Firebrick Company
1927 - West Hunwick Silica & Firebrick Co Ltd

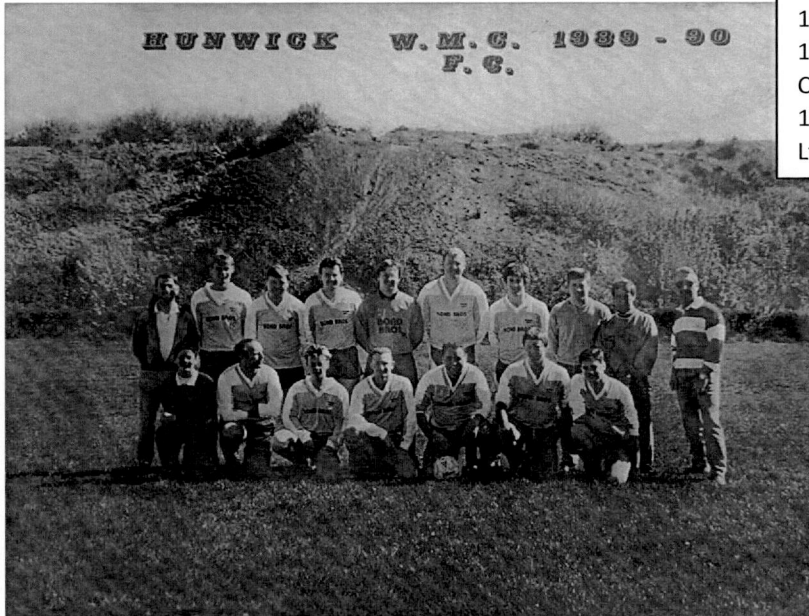

West Hunwick Colliery Heap, the 'Westy'

Image 0385 – by kind permission of Kevin Dunnett

The heap, that was to the north of the Brick Works and at the bottom of the Recreation Ground, was a magnet for all of the village youngsters.

It was a practice ground for motor cycle experimentation, camping, sledging and a whole range of adventures. The heap was shared by West Hunwick and Rough Lea Colliery sites.

The photograph below, was taken when the Rough Lea Works were being reclaimed. It shows the heap between the West Hunwick Brick Works and Rough Lea.

West Hunwick Brick Works, derelict Rough Lea Pipe Works in the background

Image 0403

Image 0065

The Works had their own railway sidings and shunting locomotive that assembled the 'trains' of waggons ready for collection by main-line locomotives.

The sidings were controlled by a signal box that was manned by the Signal Man at Hunwick Station, who had to walk along and operate the points when waggons were being collected or returned

Rough Lea Fireclay and Pipe Works

Fireclay, which was referred to locally as segger, was the grey clay that was found above coal seams. Rough Lea Fireclay Works was established in 1879 at Rough Lea Colliery. The colliery, until it closed in 1924, supplied the fireclay used to make the sewerage and drainage pipes, as well as the coal which fired the kilns.

The segger was also used to make high quality, glazed sanitary ware, garden fancy ware, chimney pots and gravestones. The gravestones, which were cheaper than marble or stone headstones can be found in Hunwick as well many other local graveyards.

"Over the fields was piled the excrement of the mine. The blue shale enclosing the Harvey seam had been found suitable for the production of fireclay bricks and high-class sanitary ware, and so those fields which had once produced the food of man now lay groaning beneath an ever-increasing mound of rotting blue shale rock. There in the winds and rains it decomposed. It is curious how the harsh and unforgiving strata when mined should act with such rapidity when in the open air.

Alongside this ever-increasing shale tip were spread-eagled the brick kilns of the new industry. Here men bore a new art, at rolling mills, brick-making tables, sanitary slabs and kiln, upon foundations so truly laid.

Nearby the brick kilns was erected the coking plant. The coke-ovens were like gigantic bee skeps. Filled with coal dust and waste from the screening plant. All the by-products by virtue of this process of coke making went into the air in belching clouds of smoke and in flames that leaped upwards like coronae of so many suns. Only the coke was left, and huge blocks of red salt, which were discarded as useless".
(Heslop Harold)

When the segger arrived at the Works, it was left to weather in a big heap on the site. Donald White explains: the process:

"Large amounts of segger were taken out from [Coal] seams which were close together. It was ground to a fine powder in the Rough Lea works mill and made into clay.

At Rough Lea works the segger (heaped at Rough Lea and near the West Hunwick works) was brought from the Westy heap in 5 or 6 pit tubs, filled by hand, along a narrow rail track and drawn by Charlie, a small white horse, -- ill-tempered if you got on the wrong side of him. At the works it went up a slight slope and was tipped into the building at the mill and shovelled into the mill by hand.

The segger, ground and made clay, was used for making Drainage pipes, Toilets and Belfast sinks on the Rough Lea site. My father, working there for many years, was an expert moulder in fire clay. The moulded clay objects were set to dry, before being glazed in the Painting Shed, (pipes not glazed here), in 'flats', ground floor long rooms heated by underfloor by 2 flues each flat running the length of the building to a chimney with a coal fire outside at the end, in a shallow pit, and stoked regularly by the fireman. The kilns for the drainage pipes etc were circular approximately 15ft or more in diameter with a shallow domed brick roof (beehive kilns) with about half a dozen fire holes round the outside regularly stoked. Pipes were stacked vertically about 3 or 4 high. The floors of the kilns were of slabs pierced with holes all over, holes about 1 and a half inches in diameter, and leading below to a tunnel and to a huge square chimney about 60ft high, serving several kilns. The door of the kiln was dry bricked up and daubsealed with clay with a small brick sized hole near the top from which the brick could be removed to see into the kiln. Just inside this was a protruding brick on which sat a small piece of clay about 5 inches by 2 inches by 2 inches into the top of which was inserted a short stick of silica. When the fireman saw this silica had melted and leaned over, it indicated that the pipes were fired and he could shovel rock salt onto all of the fires. This salt glazed the pipes inside and out making them water proof, brown and shiny." (Donald White's notes)

From the 1890s, the Works used fifteen circular, coal fired, down draught kilns until 1960s when they were replaced by oil-fired German designed kilns.

The Pipe Works looking from West Hunwick Colliery Heap

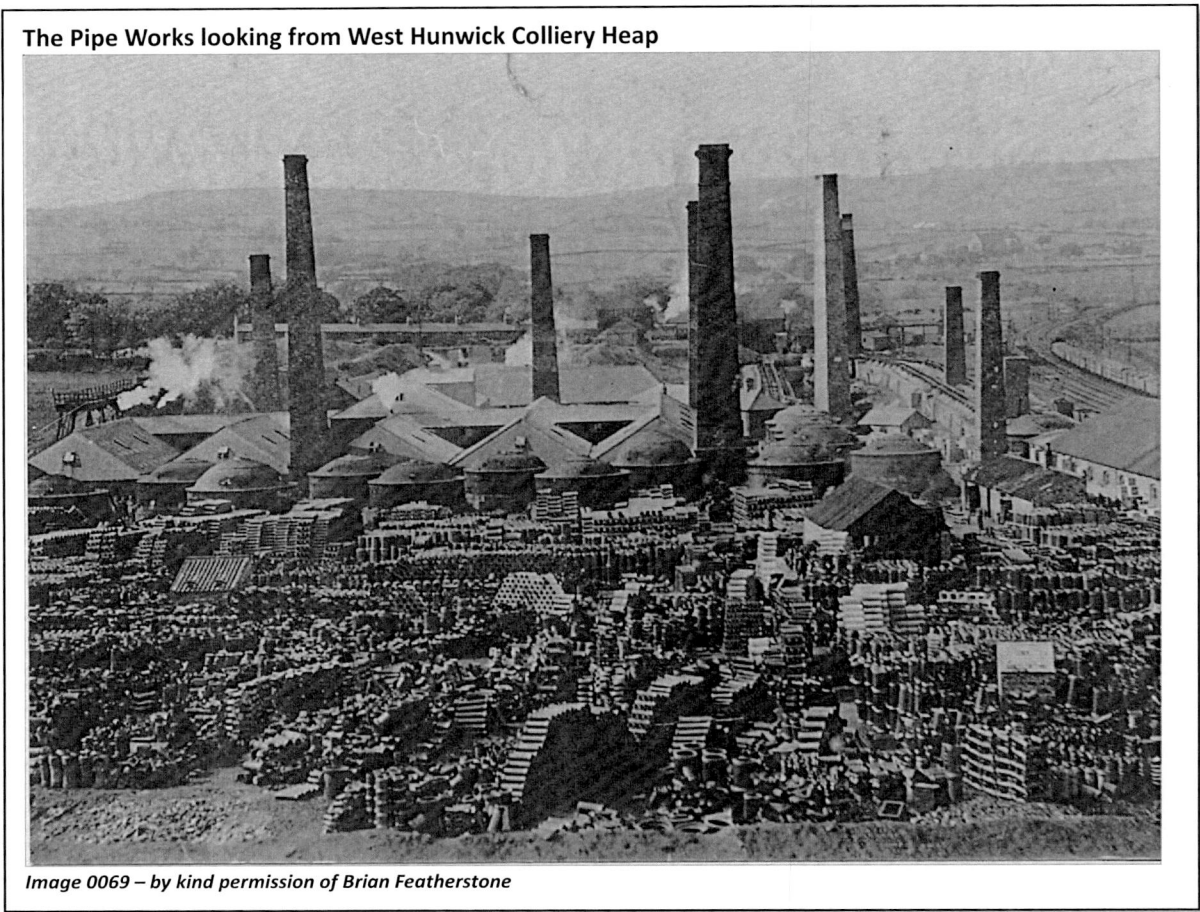

Image 0069 – by kind permission of Brian Featherstone

In 1927 the Works employed ninety men and was divided into two sections, the Pipe Works and the Sink Works.

The Pipe Works manufactured clay pipes used for water, sewerage and field drains. It also made sanitary pipes, garden fancy ware and chimney pots.

The Sink Works manufactured enamel glazed sinks, water closets and glazed bricks.

After 1924 the fireclay and coal were brought, by rail, from Newton Cap Colliery until the freight line at Hunwick Station was closed in 1958. After that, road transport was used to deliver the fireclay and coal from Newton Cap Colliery.

Rough Lea Sink Works, 1895

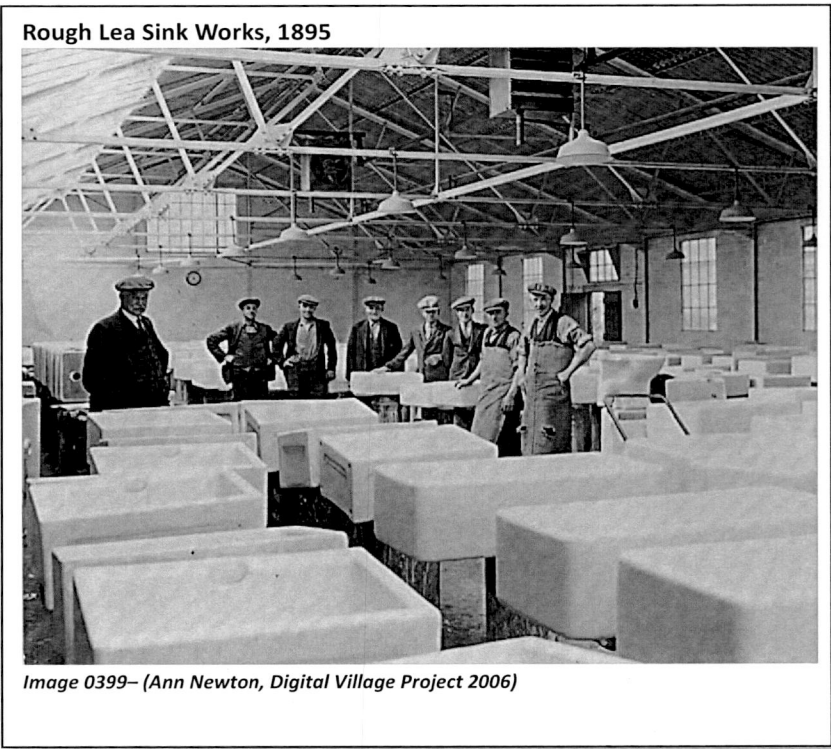

Image 0399– (Ann Newton, Digital Village Project 2006)

The Pipe Works looking from the railway line

Image 0362, (Jeff Race, 2006 Digital Village)

Pipe Works looking from the Rough Lea heap, West Hunwick heap in the background

Image 0322 – by kind permission of Donald White

During the Second World War a skeleton work force kept the Sink Works operating while the Army took over most of the building in the Pipe Works.

In 1920 the North Bitchburn Coal Company became a subsidiary of Pease and Partners, and operated until 1932 when it was put into the hands of the receiver. When a buyer could not be found, a new company was formed to run the North Bitchburn and Rough Lea Brick Works.

In 1952 North Bitchburn Fireclay Company that owned the Works decided to end the manufacture of white enamel ware at Rough Lea.   (Davison, 2022) In the early 1960s Hepworths took over the Works. They introduced the Hepseal pipe seal, which when fitted to clay pipes, provided a water tight joint between pipes.

John Cunningham explains that the Works were organised on two levels with the machines that made the 4-inch, 6-inch and 9-inch pipes, the Junction Stickers, the Manchester top machine, the fitting and blacksmith's shop on the ground floor. On the upper level you had the 'flats' for the hand moulders along with the mixers dust riddles and the dryer. The clay from the mill was moved along a conveyor belt that ran along the upper floor before it was fed down to the moulding machines on the ground floor.

Beginning in the early 1970s, plastic drainage pipes began to take over from the traditional clay pipes that were manufactured at Rough Lea.

A newspaper article written in 1972 entitled *"Gnomes to the rescue"* acknowledged that a recession in the building trade and competition from the recently introduced plastic pipes, was making trading very difficult.

The article went on to report that rather than introduce short-time working, the Pipe Works had diversified into the production of garden fancy goods that they had last manufactured in Victorian times. They began to manufacture garden edging, gnomes, urns etc.

Butter Barrel

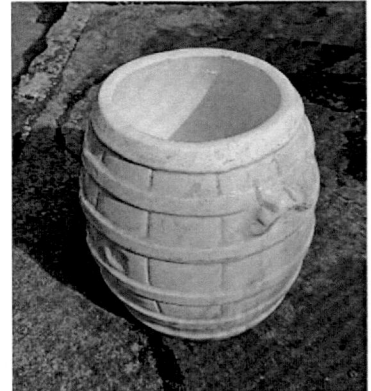

Image 0070 by kind permission Harold Newton

A Rough Lea Gnome

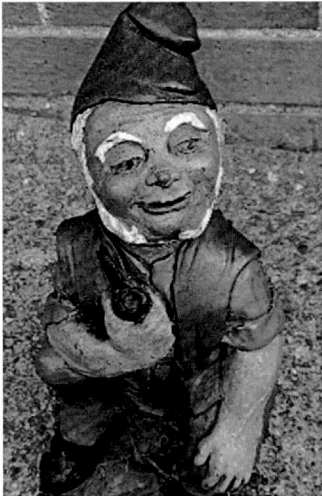

Image 0072 by kind permission John Cunningham

Garden Urn

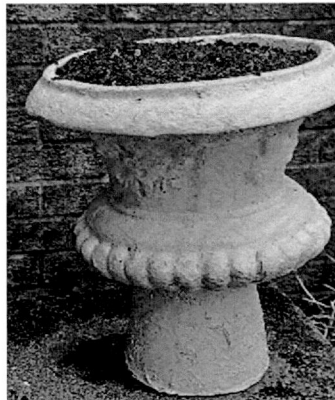

Image 0071 – by kind permission John Cunningham

The gnomes were painted by Villagers who were usually pensioners who had previously been employed at the Works.

The Works at one time were owned by the Pease Company and were managed by George William Johnson (1860 - 1911) who had started work as a brickmaker on Tyneside before coming to Rough Lea. When he returned to Tyneside in the early 1900s, his brother, James Johnson (1868 - 1959) became the manager. In 1939, the youngest of the three brothers, Thomas became manager. James and Thomas were responsible for developing the high-quality glazes for which Rough Lea became known.

In 1970, the North Bitchburn Fireclay Company, who owned the Pipe Works, opened a new drift at Brecken Hill where they mined coal and fireclay for use at the Rough Lea. Brecken Hill colliery closed in 1974. The sanitary ware and pipes were manufactured on the site until 1975 when the buildings were demolished.

Rough Lea Gravestone

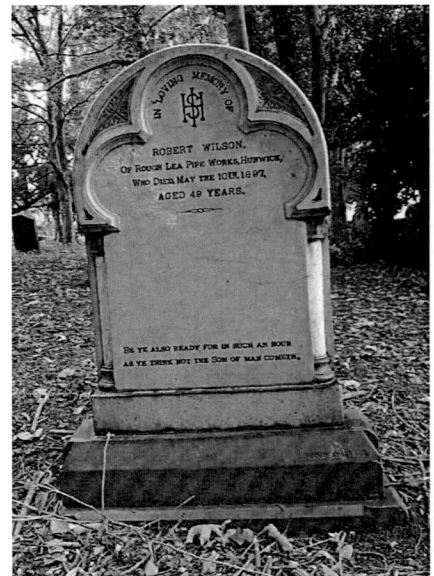

Image 0073

The Rough Lea Yard had its own railway sidings that were connected to the main line with access being controlled by its own signal box. The Works had its own locomotive that shunted the trucks around the sidings as they were loaded or unloaded. In an attempt to reduce breakages of the salt glazed pipes, from 1936 local road haulage contractors, including John Wragg and Dougie Gowland, transported the pipes to the customers.

The Rough Lea site was used as a depot for pipes that were manufactured by North Bitchburn Fireclay Company at their other sites until it eventually closed in the late 1970s.

Villagers remember John and Gordon Wragg removing sections of the brickwork at the bottom of one of the chimneys and replaced the brickwork, temporarily, with wooden pit-props. They then piled wood and tyres in the base of the chimney and set it on fire. The pit-props that were supporting the chimney, burnt away and the chimney toppled over.

Demolition of Pipe Works Chimney

Image 0414 – by kind permission of Robert Cunningham

Demolition of the Pipe Works, looking from West Hunwick Pit Heap

Image 0413

Chapter 5 - Population Growth and Houses for the Workers

Before 1800, the houses for agricultural workers were clustered around the Village Green and around farms at Lane Ends, Kate's Close, Rough Lea and Helmington Hall. After 1800, mining, quarrying, and brick and pipe making, influenced where houses have been built. These settlements have resulted in the current, spread-out structure up of the Village.

To understand how the settlement has developed, we need to examine the available maps.

The 1768 Thomas Jeffrey map and the 1818 Christopher Greenwood map show only a handful of houses and buildings in the village at that time.

Census data shows that in 1801, there were only 122 people living in the settlements that make up Hunwick Village.

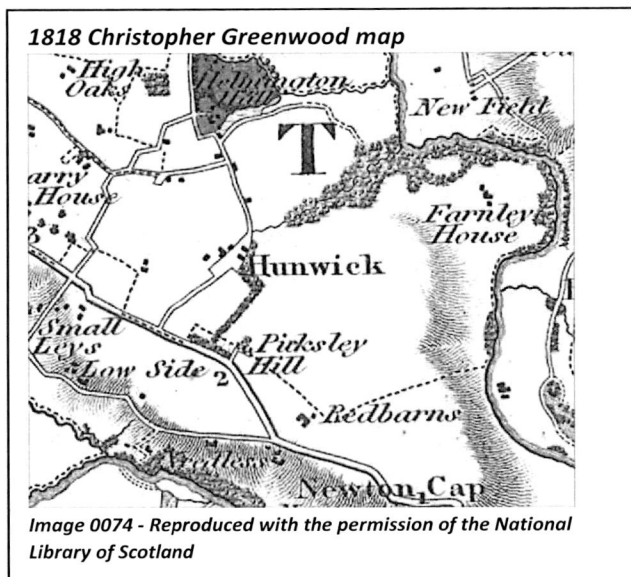

1768 – Thomas Jeffery

Image 0075 - Reproduced with the permission of the National Library of Scotland

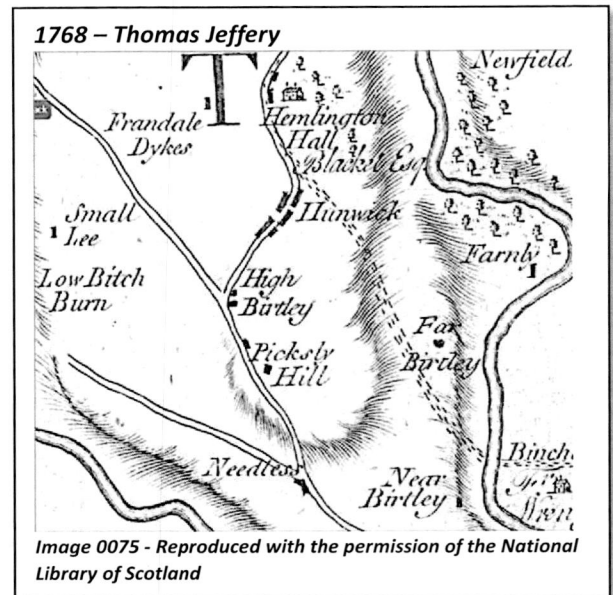

1818 Christopher Greenwood map

Image 0074 - Reproduced with the permission of the National Library of Scotland

Early maps show Hunwick Hall to the south of a long Village Green with other buildings, parallel to the Hall, on the north side of the Green.

Helmington Hall stands on its own without accommodation for agricultural workers. It is probable that, by the 1800s, the Helmington Hall Estate had found it more lucrative to rent out land to tenants rather that cultivate it themselves. It is likely that the accommodation for the workers would have been built beside the tenanted farms. Rough Lea Farm was owned by the Helmington Hall Estate and maps show building on its site that could have accommodated workers.

It is possible, on these maps, to identify:

• Hunwick Hall	• Lane Ends Farm	• Farnley House
• Quarry Farm	• Something on the site of the Helmington Inn (it is not on 1857 map)	• Dixon's House Farm (Blakeley Hill)
• Houses around the Joiners Arms on South View		• Furnace Mill
• Kate's Close Farm and Cottages (The Poplars)	• Helmington Hall	• Quarry Burn brewery
	• Brecken Hill Farm	• Cringle Dykes Farm
	• Quarry House Farm	• High Birtley Farm (1771)
	• High Oaks Farm	

The opening of the collieries, that began in 1839 with the development of Hunwick Colliery, created the need for more houses to accommodate the rapidly expanding workforce. The site for Hunwick Colliery, was developed at what was to become Hunwick Station.

In 1839, the main railway line from Bishop Auckland to Durham opened. The coal from the colliery was transported across the river to Newfield and onto Hartlepool via the West Durham Railway. As a bridge had been built across the river for the railway and as the colliery owner also owned Newfield Colliery, cottages for the miners that worked at Hunwick Colliery were built at Newfield.

The first detailed maps, the Ordnance Survey maps, began to be surveyed in the 1850s. The 1856 OS map, shows, in addition to the farms and houses shown on the 1818 map, the following:

• Church Lane	• the Church; the Vicarage	• house end of Wear View – along from the Club
• Stewarts Buildings	• School house	
• South View, houses below Joiners and Cross Row	• the National School	• Something around Jean's shop
	• Front Street, Lane Ends	• The Wheatsheaf
• Lilac House	• Additional building at Lane Ends	• Houses alongside of the Wheatsheaf

Census data shows a steady rise in the population of the village from 122 in 1801, to 164 in 1831. After 1831 the rate of increase began to accelerate. By 1841 the population had risen to 338 and to 486 by 1851.

In 1821, when the population was 160, there were thirty-one houses in the village. By 1851 the population had risen to 486 and there were eighty-nine houses in the Village. (Blackett, 1980) So, between 1821 and 1851, fifty-eight houses had been built in the wider Village.

The Fire of London in 1666 discouraged builders from using thatched roofs. Stone was used for roofing but its weight meant that it required heavy timber roof structures. Residents remember that Land Ends Farm, Tom Watson's Cobbler's Shop, Number 1 The Green and the outhouses behind Number 8 The Green having stone roofs. A 1911 photograph confirms that the Joiner's Arms also had a stone roof.

All of the houses shown on the 1857 map were built using stone that had been quarried in the village. Local builders report that when doing groundworks in the village, they often encounter layers of flagstone. The availability of these thin layers of stone, either from the village quarries, or simply from excavations on sites, might explain the characteristics of a lot of the early stonework in the village where walls often include a larger percentage than 'normal' of thin slabs of flagstone mixed in with sandstone 'rubble' blocks.

Early houses in the village either had stone roofs or red clay pantile roofs. Clay, 'S' shaped pantiles were lighter than stone slabs. This meant that lighter roof timbers could be used resulting in savings in both material and labour costs. Pantiles were originally manufactured in Holland and Belgium and were thought to have been brought back into the ports at Newcastle and Hartlepool, as ballast on ships that had carried coal on their outward voyage.

Records show that bricks were being manufactured in the village from 1856 at Hunwick Station and from 1879 at West Hunwick Colliery. The availability of fireclay, a by-product of coal mining, meant that both Brick Works concentrated on the manufacture of fire bricks that were used in steel making furnaces.

However, large number of red bricks were used in the village before the railway line was opened. It is very likely, that the Brick Works at Hunwick Station, was making red bricks, using clay from surface clay-pits, before 1856.

Bricks became the main construction medium by 1880 although some stone was still used for the construction of houses in the village until the 1920s.

'Old Hunwick'

Hunwick Old Hall, is a listed late medieval Manor house with its own chapel. It is built around a courtyard with many of the buildings, previously used for agricultural storage, now converted for residential use.

The evidence provided by architectural details of the surviving buildings and tree-ring analysis of some of the timbers, suggests the Hall would have been built around 1500 AD with the current house being built around 1700 AD. It has a chapel at the end of the north-east range of buildings.

Among later farm buildings that face onto the Village Green, is an octagonal Ginn house that allowed a horse to power farm machinery.

The 1761 enclosure map shows blocks of houses or buildings to the south of the Green, presumably including Hunwick Hall, and another row to the north of the Green. (Durham_University_Special+collections, 1761)

This outline map does not identify any buildings to the west of the Green although Villagers believe that some of the houses that are shown on the 1856 map to the west of the Village Green, were built in the 1600s.

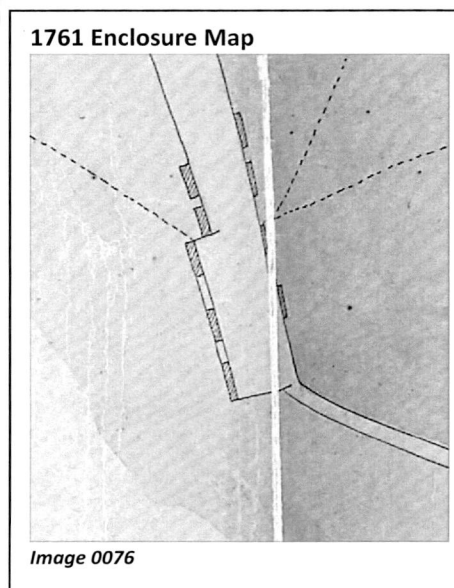

1761 Enclosure Map

Image 0076

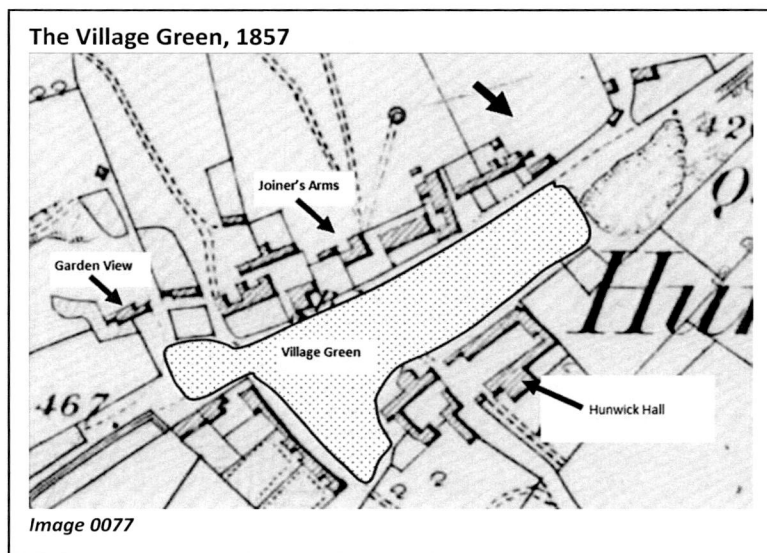

The Village Green, 1857

Image 0077

The 1856 OS map and an 1876 advertisement for the sale of the Hunwick Hall Estate, confirms that the Village Green extended down to the Quarry in which Raby House is built.

The maps show a wooded area towards the eastern end of the Green, below the quarry in which Raby House is now built. It also shows a triangular, open Green, in front of Quarry Farm's farmhouse. Woodbine House and Myrtle House were built on this Green in the late 1800s. North View was built on land that had previously been part of the original Village Green.

A stream collected water from the fields behind what is now Number 28 to 30 South View, and took it across the road to run down the side of the road in front of Stewart's Buildings. The stream then ran diagonally across the Village Green before making its way down to join Hunwick Gill.

The stream was culverted in 1955/6 when the new Council Houses were built. At the same time the Village Green was levelled creating the embankment that today runs along the northern and eastern sides of the Green. Residents talk of playing football on the Green in the 1940s and having to jump over the stream during the course of a game as well as having to contend with a sloping pitch.

There was a large sycamore tree on the Village Green as well as a Maypole and a sand pitch for quoits. John Pratt remembers being in the Joiner's Arms one night in 1987, during a power-cut. A storm was raging outside and George Maddison ran into the candle-lit pub, in tears, to report that the sycamore tree had been struck by lightning and had fallen down.

The Village Green has always been used for gatherings and celebrations.

Boer War Celebrations, 1900

Image 0386 - Beamish Museum - Peoples Collection

Cavalry assembling on the Village Green, 1900

Image 0411 – by kind permission of John Cunningham

Hunwick Ian attempt at recreating Boer War Celebration, 2014

Northern Echo, August 2014

Village Fayre, 2019

Image 0398 - by kind permission of Peter James Hughes

The 1856 OS map and the 1876 Hunwick Estate Maps both show, what was reputed to be one of the oldest houses in the village, Number 1 The Green. Its gable-end can be seen on the postcard behind the Maypole. It faces onto the main road and has been described as *'an old, double fronted, 2 storey, stone cottage that stood back from the road. It had a stone flagged staircase inside the house and a garden in front with a low stone wall around it'*.

The Village Green, Early 1900s

Image 0079 – The Herbert Coates Collection

Number 2 The Green, a very small house, is also shown on the postcard, facing the Green. Villagers remember a well-stocked garden, including productive pear trees, behind Number 1 and Number 2 The Green.

The first school was built in the village in 1635. It was thought to have been on the edge of the Village Green. (Gowland, 13 November 1980)

A House of Lords Education Return in 1833, reported that the Daily School was attended by ten males and six females. One theory is that, during the 18th and 19th century, this 'Daily' school operated in Number 1, The Green.

The 1841 census records William Robinson (50yrs) and Joseph Robinson (20yrs) as School Masters. Their relative position on the census enumerator's 'walk route', suggests that they were living somewhere around the Village Green. Perhaps they were living in Number 2 and using Number 1 The Green, as the school room?

Residents remember that before Number 1 and Number 2 The Green were demolished in the 1960s, Number 1 was owned by Billy Holborn, who frequently played the piano in the village pubs. Number 1 The Green, and the houses above in Stewart's Buildings, had bridges to their front gardens, over the stream that ran alongside the main road.

The postcard (Image 0079), confirms that Number 2 and Number 3, The Green were single-storey cottages in the early 1900s. They are shown on the 1856 OS map but it has not been possible to find any evidence which would establish when they were built or explain anything about their earlier life.

There are many stories about tunnels in the village. The Kennett family papers confirmed that William Kennett who acquired Hunwick Hall in 1637, was a Roman Catholic at a time when, although it was not an offence to be a catholic, refusal to attend Church of England services was (Durham_university_Special_Collections, 1297) So maybe they did dig a few tunnels to allow a Priest to hide or escape?

In 1964, two cottages had to be demolished so that Number 8 The Green could be built. The builders discovered a tunnel beneath the cottages. It is reputed that archivists from Durham University visited the site and although the tunnel wasn't accessible, they suggested that it might have been connected to the Chapel at Hunwick Hall Farm.

Houses in 'The Green', 1876

Image 0078

Maypole

Image 0351

Houses to the north of the Village Green, 1990s

Image 0387 – by kind permission of Verna Rutter

Stewart's Buildings were built in 1852 by the Blacksmith John Turnbull who had bought part of 'John Young's garth' from John Robson. John Young's garth is shown on deeds, to be to the rear of Stewart's Buildings and behind Number 1 to Number 8 the Green.

There were three quarries in the village, one opposite the entrance to what is now, Quarry Farm Close and two behind Garden View. 'Flagg Quarry', which was nearest to the main road, was a Flagstone Quarry. The second quarry, which was beyond Flagg Quarry, was a sandstone quarry. Raby House was built in what was the third quarry.

The Farm House for Quarry Farm, along with a collection of agricultural buildings, are shown on the 1857 OS map. From the public footpath, you can see one building with external steps providing access to the upper floor and stabling on the ground floor. This style of 'byre-house' was common until the early 1900s.

In 1894, the Joiner's Arms, 13 South View, along with the adjoining cottage, 14 South View and a 25-acre farm, including farmhouse and buildings, occupied by George Lindsay Jnr, was auctioned. (Star, 20 April 1894) The Farm House for South View Farm was for many years, 15 South View. It was reputedly, the saddle room, for Quarry Farm.

The 1857 map shows the barns for Quarry Farm and South View Farm are connected.

The map highlights the fields which were worked by Quarry Farm and those worked by South View Farm. The layout of the farm buildings and the layout of the fields would support the theory that at one time, they were operated as one farm.

Deeds for the Joiner's Arms include an 1874 plan that shows that the land to the rear was owned by John Robson.

In 1894 the Joiner's Arms, along with the adjoining cottage, occupied by Thomas Sunter, and a 25-acre farm, including farmhouse and buildings, was offered for sale. This suggests that the Joiner's Arms, the two cottages above and South View Farm, were part of the same estate.

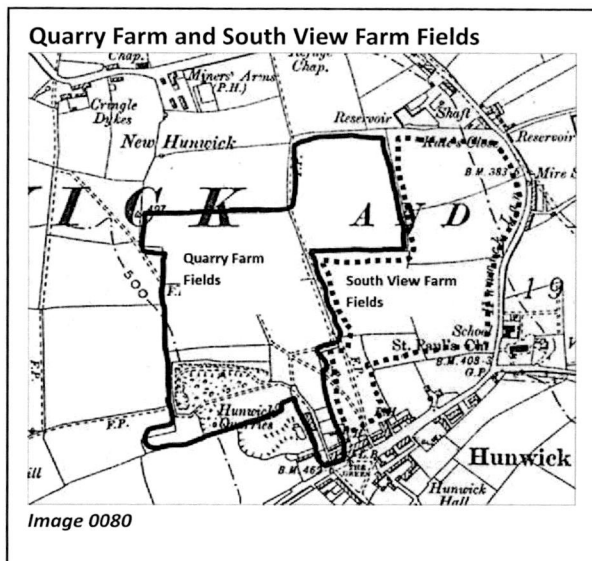

Quarry Farm and South View Farm Fields

Image 0080

The 1896 OS map shows six cottages in Quarry Row and four cottages and a house in Garden View. Quarry Row was known, in the 1950s, to be owned by Jayne Raw (nee Sunter) who had owned Quarry Farm. The houses, built for the quarry workers, had one bedroom, a living room and a pantry. Some had an extra bedroom, but all of the houses had earth closets.

Garden View was demolished in the 1960s. Residents moved out of Quarry Row in 1956 after which the houses stood empty for many years. When Norman Basey retired from Furnace Mill Farm in the 1980s, he built a bungalow beside the derelict houses. The houses were used to store agricultural equipment before being demolished in 2007.

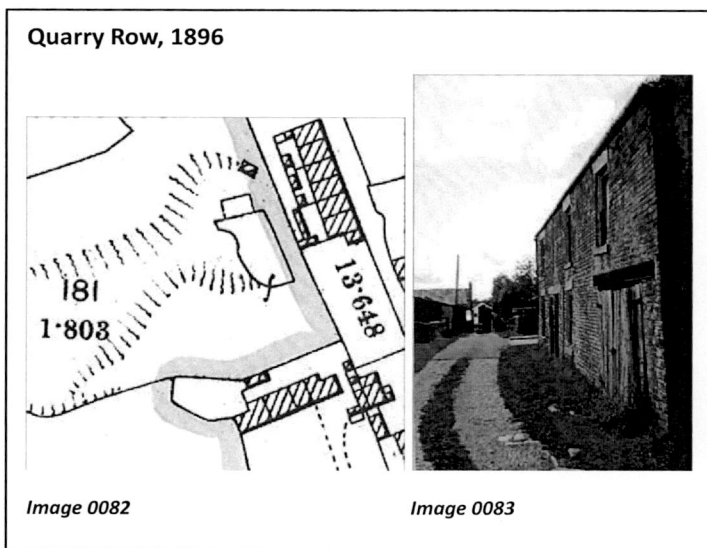

Quarry Row, 1896

Image 0082   *Image 0083*

Before they were filled in the 1950s, the two disused quarries behind Garden View were popular playgrounds for the village children. The quarry furthest from the main road, was known as the 'back hollows'.

Many residents remember visiting Joe Tyerman in Number 1 Garden View to have their watches repaired. They talk of a room with a large table strewn with small watch parts. Joe worked as a chauffeur for Ernest Craddock MBE, who was the Director and General Manager of West Hunwick Brick Works in the 1950s and 1960s.

1896 - Garden View

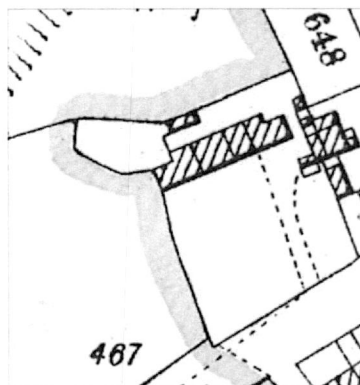

Image 0084

Garden View

Image 0081 - by kind permission of Paul Surtees

Christine Atkinson recalls living in number 3, Garden View in the late1940s. She remembers that the house had a pantry/kitchen and a front room downstairs and two bedrooms upstairs. It had one tap in the kitchen with all water having to be heated on the range.

Having a bath was a weekly event that meant that the tin bath had to be brought inside and filled.

The houses had no back door, which meant that residents had to walk past the house next door, then under an arch to go to the outside toilet that was behind the houses.

Russell Johnson, a local builder, lived in Number 1 Garden View which was larger than the other houses in the street. It had a small field attached in which he kept pigs and livestock. Christine Atkinson, after 70 years, still has a vivid memory of getting ready for school one day and hearing the screeching of the pigs as they were being slaughtered.

Number 1 Garden View was bought by Thomas Lawes in the late 1930s when he retired from running Hunwick Hall Farm.

Garden View and South View

Image 0378 – by kind permission of Joanne Boucher

While still a tenant on Hunwick Hall Farm, Thomas Lawes had bought a parcel of land above Stewart's Buildings and a parcel of land to the rear of North View

In 1936, he sold the land above Stewart's Buildings, to Russell Johnson, a local builder who built the first two, two-bedroomed houses that became St Paul's Way, on the plot. In 1937, a further two, three bedroomed houses were built.

St Paul's Way

Image 0086 – The Herbert Coates Collection

The fourth house, Prospect House, which became number 4 St Paul's Way, was owned between 1936 and 1952 by the Blacksmith, John Hodgson Johnson who had previously lived in Number 1 Garden View.

During 1955 and 1956, Crook and Willington Urban District Council built a further eight, two bedroomed houses in the same style as the first four, to complete St Paul's Way. They also built The Riggs, Green Rising and Holme Dene during the same period. Residents who had previously lived in sub-standard housing at Lane Ends, Quarry Row, Quarry Burn, Hunwick Station and Oakenshaw were relocated, by the Council, into the new houses.

The first four houses in the Riggs were two storey houses, the others were bungalows. The photograph shows the keys being handed over to Ray and Doris Blackburn who were the first occupants of Number 2, the Riggs on 28th June 1956.

Fred and Gertie Smith from Number 1 The Riggs, and William (Billy) and Elizabeth (Bessie) Cobb from Number 3, and Tom and Lottie Heslop from Number 4, look on as the keys are handed over.

Image 0330 - Beamish Museum -Peoples Collection

The first house, coming into the village from Bishop Auckland, Number 33 South View, was built in 1951 by Johnson's. It was built for Jeff Smith who owned the Austin/ Morris garage in Willington. His son, Oliver Smith used his father's large double garage as well as a detached garage in the field behind the Hollies, to build two light aircraft.

The bungalow next door down, was also built by Johnson's, for Jeff Smith's mother. The 'Hollies', Number 31 South View, was built by Fred Harker when he retired from High Wadsworth Farm. He did all of the building work himself. At that time, the plot onto which the small bungalow, Number 30A South View, was built, was a small garth used by South View Farm.

Numbers 28, 29 and 30 South View, the three large terraced houses that stand in an elevated position on the northern side of the main road, above Garden View, were built in 1909. They were originally known as Numbers 6 to 8 The Hill, Garden View, before being re-named in 1961, as South View.

Woodbine House, 22 South View, was built in 1893 as house with an integrated shop.

The 1881 census shows Richard Wood running a Grocery store and a 1906 Trade Directory lists him as running a Grocery and Drapery store.

At some point the shop was converted into a house with the 1911 Census recording that Woodbine House was occupied by two families, the Wood family and the Dobinson family. The same census records Will and Annie Snowdon along with a servant, living with Richard Wood who was 75 at that time.

Woodbine House, R Wood Grocers and Drapery store

Image 0171 – by kind permission of Verna Rutter

Looking from the Village Green, towards Woodbine House.

Image 0089 - the Herbert Coates Collection

Myrtle House, the detached, double fronted house, that stands below Woodbine House, was not on 1856 OS map but had been built by 1896.

It was reputedly built by the Sunter family who were farming Quarry Farm at that time. The 1911 Census lists John and Elizabeth Ann Sunter and their son Thomas (14yrs) living in the house.

Myrtle House and South View Farm House

Image 0344 - the Herbert Coates Collection

The 1856 and 1896 OS maps show two houses, Numbers 17 and 16 South View, standing closer to the road than Quarry Farm farmhouse, and the other houses in South View. It has not been possible to determine when these two houses were built, however, their position suggests that they would be built later than the farmhouse and later than 13 South View, the house that became the Joiner's Arms.

Houses around the Village Green, 1857

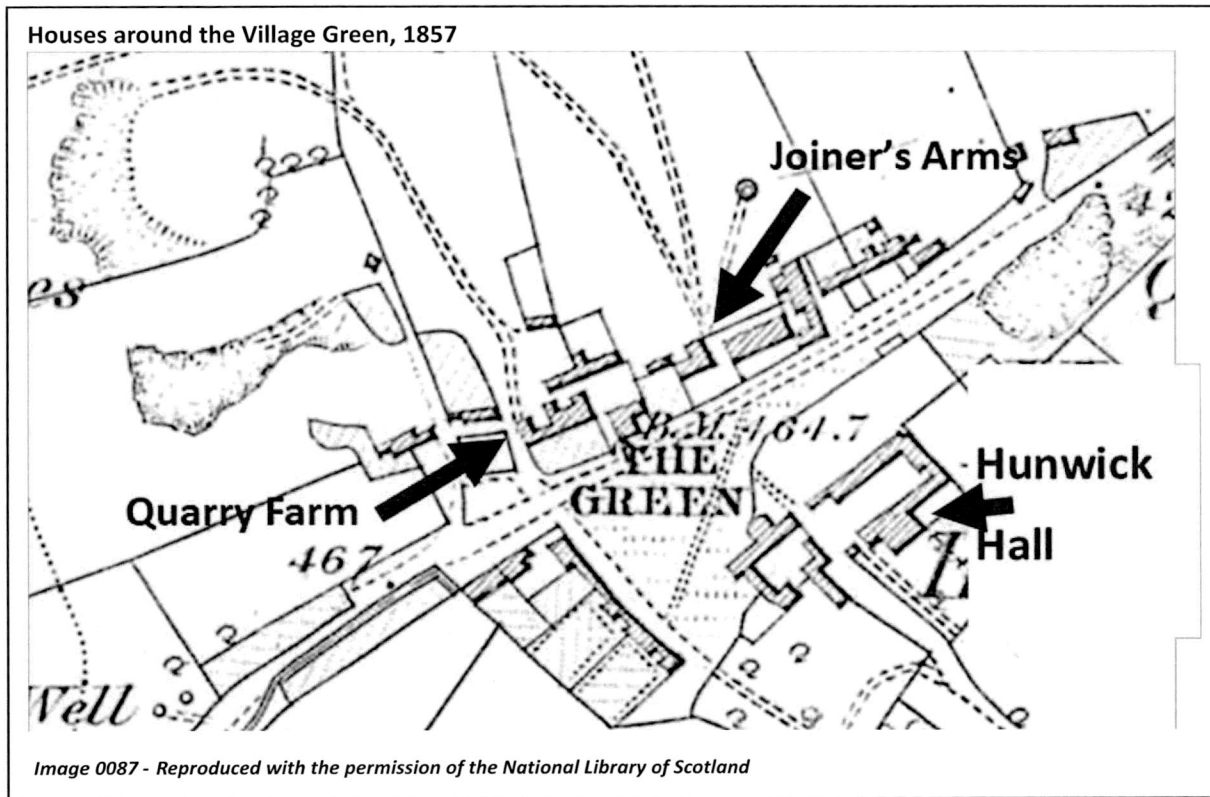

Image 0087 - Reproduced with the permission of the National Library of Scotland

Numbers 15 and 14 South View, the two cottages above the Joiner's Arms, are not shown on the 1857 map but they are shown on the 1896 map. Number 15 South View was used as the Farm House for South View Farm. In the 1950s, Dickie and Valerie Temby delivered milk and groceries from the farm.

The Joiner's Arms and South View looking down from the Green

Image 0090 - (Mary Alderson, 2006 Digital Village Project)

I have not established the actual date that the Joiner's Arms was built, other than it was before the 1856 OS map was surveyed. The building is shown on the map but it is not identified as a Public House. However, Whellan's Trade Directory, identifies James Gibbons as the landlord in 1856. (Whellan, 1856)

1856

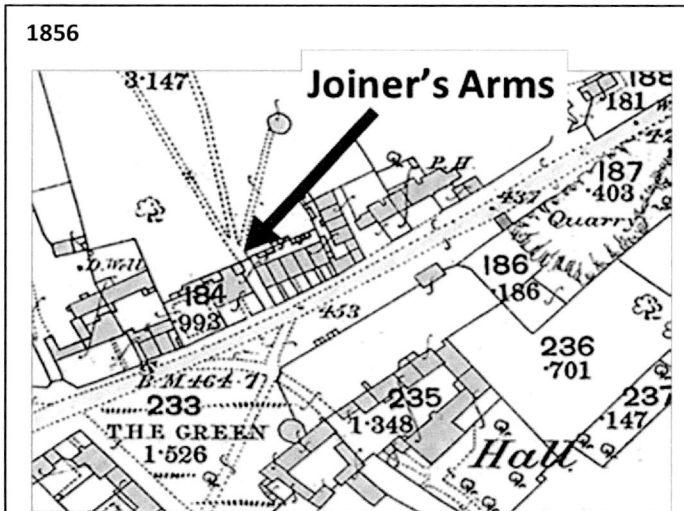

Joiner's Arms

1896

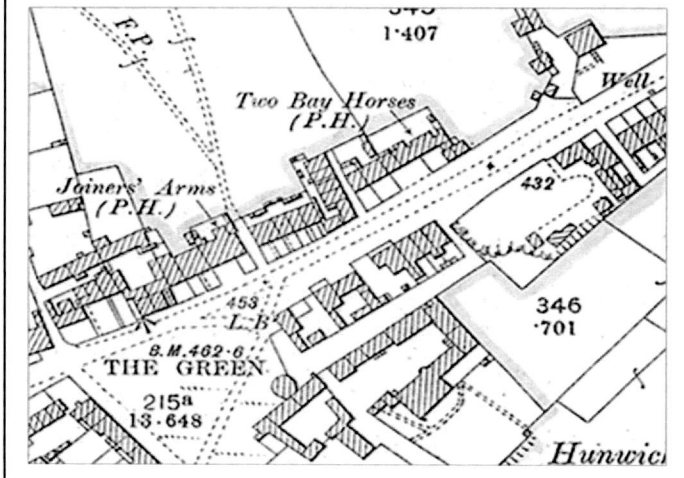

In 1894, the Joiner's Arms was bought by Blackhill Breweries and the farm by a Mr Wrexford. (Star, Friday 20 April 1894)

An 1874 deed shows that the Joiner's Arms had a stable, where the gent's toilets are now.

There is stonework in the Joiners Arms where thin layers of stone have been used to build a wall rather than larger stones as is the normal practice. This method of construction is often found in 16th century or earlier stonework. However, it might simply be because flagstone, thin slabs of stone, was being quarried 150 yards from the site. A photograph, taken in 1911, of the Joiner's Arms, shows that it had a stone roof.

The land upon which Numbers 11 to 8 South View, the five cottages below the Joiner's Arms that were built, was sold by John Robson to John Turnbull in 1852.

The cottages are shown on the 1856 map. The same map shows that 6 cottages in Cross Row and three cottages, now Numbers 2 -5 South View, above the Two Hunters Public House, had been built. A conveyance relating to Number 5, was made in 1852, suggesting that a lot of building was going on around the Green at that time.

The 1911 census provides information about the families that were living in 'Plew's Buildings'. I have not managed to establish where these houses were. However, the position in the enumerators walk route and that the Two Hunters Public House had been owned by Plew's Brewery, suggests that these cottages might have been 'Plew's Buildings'?

Plew's Brewery was taken over by Cameron's Brewery in 1923 who operated the Public House until it closed in the 1960s.

Looking down South View towards the Two Hunters

Image 0342 – the Herbert Coates Collection

The Two Hunters is listed as a public house in an 1828 trade directory and is shown on the 1856 map. It was built as a public house with a cellar. It was built in the style of a Coaching Inn and had stables to the rear. At some time, its name changed to 'The Two Bay Horses'.

Looking up North View circa 1900

Image 0096 - the Herbert Coates Collection

Lilac House is shown on the 1856 map but it is not clear when it was built.

There are references to land transfers of the site dating from 1808. In 1876 the house along with 3 Acres, the land upon which Quarry Farm Close was built, and a butcher's shop was known to be occupied by John Turnbull, a blacksmith.

The building that can be seen on an early 1900s postcard having a pantile roof, and a building that was attached to the Two Hunters, were both used as a butcher's shop.

The house, land and butcher's shop belonged to Simpson Heslop Snr, when he died in 1895.

Oliver Smith, a senior partner in the West Hunwick Silica & Firebrick Company, lived in the house in the 1930s and in the 1950s the house was occupied by Wilfred Turnbull who was the Manager of Rough Lea Pipe Works.

Looking down South View, towards Lilac House

Image 0097 -

Aerial view of Lilac House and Raby House, 1971

Image 0098 By kind permission of Chris Pratt

The aerial photograph shows that the stone wall that ran down from the Two Bay Horses to the stone out building/butcher's shop, had been demolished, to allow access to what is now Quarry Farm Close.

Thomas Hedley operated a butter, cheese and egg wholesaler business from an outbuilding in the old quarry behind Raby House.

Villagers remember playing tennis on the red-ash court that had been built in the Quarry. Linda Paley explains how Raby House acquired its name. Margaret Bowes (nee

Willens), who was born on the Raby Estate and married Robert Bowes in 1869, was living in Raby House in 1911. She named the house 'Raby House' and lived in it until her death in 1929.

The photograph also shows the tennis court in the grounds of Raby House that was developed and used by Helmington Hall Youth Club. Villagers also remember 'skin a cheese' competitions being held by the Youth Club at Raby House. Youngsters were timed as they removed the cheese cloth from the round of cheese.

Number 13 North View was built in 1877 by Edward Wilson, who had bought the land for the house from the Hunwick Estate in 1876.

1876 Estate Map – showing the Lots

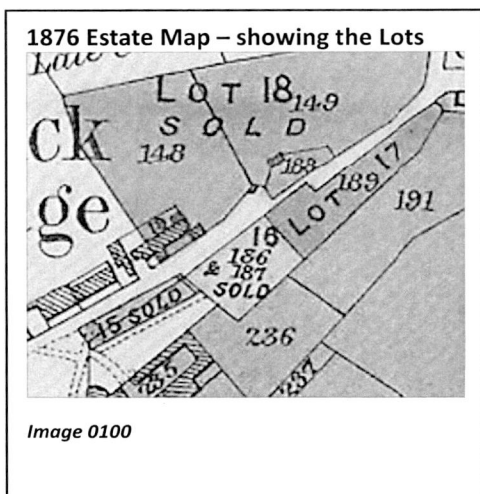

Image 0100

An 1876 estate map identifies Lot 17, the land that numbers 3 to 14 North View were built on. It is not clear whether Edward Wilson bought the Lot or whether he had just bought a plot of land from the Lot. Edward Wilson is identified in the 1841 census, as a joiner living in Old Hunwick.

Early documents identify Number 13 North View as 13 Hunwick Village. Other documents identify Number 10 North View as Argyle Crescent. This is a strange name for an individual house. Perhaps the whole street was named Argyle Crescent? With '13 Argyle Crescent' becoming '13 Hunwick Village', and finally '13 North View'?

In 1933, the land behind North View was sold to David Dodds. During the Second World War, this land was used as allotment gardens and had an air-raid shelter built on it.

Looking down North View from the Two Bay Horses

Image 369 – by kind permission of Harold Newton

By comparing the 1856 and 1896 maps we know that the following houses had been built in the intervening 40 years:

- Number 24 North View, Agnes Jane Taylor's (Bourne's) general dealers and grocery shop. This was thought to be a purpose-built shop with storage buildings to side and rear. The shop was not listed in the 1894 Directory but was listed in Kelly's Directory in 1902 and 1924
- Number 22 North View, a stone-built house
- Number 21 North View is now a brick-built house with a stone-built garage attached to it
- Number 19 North View, a stone-built house
- Numbers 16, 17 and 18 North View, stone-built houses
- Raby House and the attached house, Number 14 North View
- Numbers 11 and 12 North View were built at different times between 1856 and 1896. Probably built after Number 10?
- Number 10 North View, was built sometime between 1892 and 1896. This single storey, stone cottage known as 'The Well' was occupied by Miss Milne, the headteacher
- Number 1 and 2 North View at the junction with Station Road

The 1856 OS Map shows a building, probably a blacksmith's workshop, standing on its own on the Village Green close to Hunwick Hall's agricultural buildings. The forge in the blacksmith's workshop would mean that the workshop would be kept away from the farm's buildings because of the risk of fire.

The 1828 Parson and White Directory lists Joseph Turnbull as a blacksmith. John Turnbull, a blacksmith from Hetton, was recorded on the 1841 Census as being 60 years old and living with his son, also named John, aged 25. In 1861, John Jnr appears along with his son Anthony, who was also a blacksmith. By 1871, John had retired and Anthony was listed as a blacksmith with Henry Appley as his apprentice.

Looking down North View from the Joiner's Arms

Hunwick Village.

Image 0099 – The Herbert Coates Collection

By 1881 William Johnson had taken over the workshop. In 1879 and 1906, Trade Directories list John William Johnson as a Blacksmith.

Pat Hunt (nee Johnson) confirms that John William Johnson, her great grandfather, had moved to Hunwick, to be a blacksmith for Hunwick Hall Farm. At that time, Hunwick Hall Farm bred horses for the army. Alan Johnson, John William Johnson's grandson, worked with him as an apprentice. Interestingly, later in life, Alan owned the Two Bay Horses public house and built Orchard House, the bungalow behind North View very close to this Blacksmiths Shop

The workshop was relocated when North View was built. An early 1900s postcard shows the jib of a crane, protruding from the houses in North View. The crane looks to be attached to a stone-built workshop. The workshop is shown attached, on the down-hill side, to a stone-built house that no longer exists.

There is a gap on the up-hill side of the workshop that would have allowed access to Hunwick Hall Farm. The stone-built workshop still exists but is now used as a garage attached, on the up-hill side, to Number 21 North View, a brick-built house.

A well or horse trough, in front of Number 9 North View, is marked on both the 1856 and the 1896 OS maps. It is a Grade 2 Listed Building that is described as a 'fountain in wall'.

It is positioned just before the road begins to climb up from the Church towards the Village Green. Villagers remember the Rington's Tea and Coop Delivery cart horses stopping to drink from the well, before they tackled the hill.

When North View was being built, between 1892 and 1896, the well or trough was repositioned. Donald White, who represented the village on Crook & Willington Council and Wear Valley Council, from 1970 until 1991, remembers:

The Well

Image 0408 - (Wally Smith, 2006 Digital Village Project)

'when work was being done on the footpath in the later part of the 1970s or 1980s, there was revealed a similar looking trough, with arch like the well, in the bankside just to the right of the well. It is now earthed over.'

The three brick-built houses, that stand in a slightly elevated position at the bottom of North View were built circa 1910 and, reputedly, were originally known as Field View. These houses are now known as Numbers 3, 4 and 5 North View. Two of the double fronted houses, have decorative brickwork below the eaves, around the window and door reveals and on the chimneys. The brick work is very similar to that used on Number 6 to 8 West End, Number 6 to 9 Helmington Square and Number 39 to 41 Wear View. Possibly the trade mark of a local builder?

The 1915 map shows that the remaining houses in North View had been built, a few using stone but the majority using brick.

Hunwick Lane

The 1761 Enclosure map and the 1856 OS map identifies the lane that runs through the village from the Village Green at Old Hunwick down to Lane Ends, as 'Hunwick Lane'. Early post cards and indeed one street sign locates Church Lane, to be between the Church and Lane Ends.

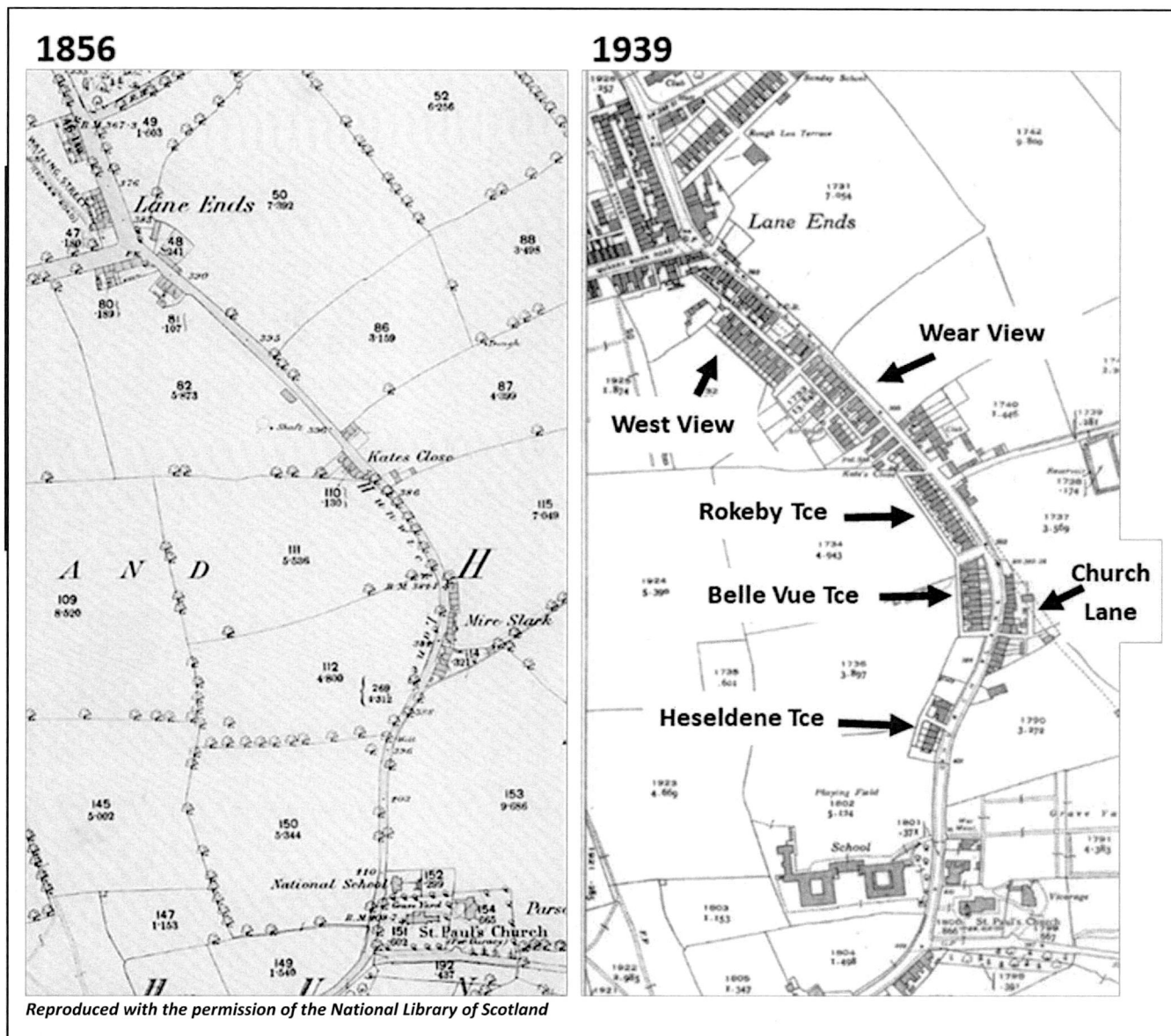

1856

1939

Reproduced with the permission of the National Library of Scotland

The 1856 map shows the Church, the Vicarage, the National School, the fourteen cottages in Church Lane, houses at Kate's Close and then houses at Lane Ends, on 'Hunwick Lane'.

The Church was built 1844 and consecrated in 1845. The National School (St. Paul's Church School) was built in 1848 and it was enlarged 1860 to create a large room and 3 classrooms.

Later it became the Church Hall and is now two private houses. School House was built in 1865 to accommodate the School Master.

St. Paul's Church

Image 0104 – The Herbert Coates Collection

The school on today's site, was officially opened on the 1st of September 1924. It consisted of a Senior School, called Hunwick Modern School, and a Primary School called Hunwick County School.

Hunwick Secondary School closed in 1976 but the Primary school continued to operate on the site. Parts of the old Secondary School were condemned and boarded up. Some rooms were later reopened and used as a Community Centre until 2014 when it was demolished.

In 1980 the Primary School was burnt down and was completely rebuilt.

School Fire, 1980

Junior School (left hand side) and Modern School 1924

Image 0106 (Sue Smith, 2006 Digital Village Project)

The 1856 OS Map shows Church Lane, a street of houses on the eastern side of the main road through the village.

Church Lane

Image 0107 – The Herbert Coates Collection

An early postcard shows several different styles of houses in the street with maps showing a group of five houses, closest to the Church, followed by a second group of five houses and then a group of four houses.

An advert in the Durham Chronicle on 16th October 1857, for four, newly developed dwelling houses describes them as being 'situated in one of the largest and most flourishing Colliery Districts in the neighbourhood, adjoining the New Hunwick Sinking'.

The advertisement is referring to West Hunwick Colliery so it is likely that the houses are the four that were nearest to the colliery. The four houses are described as having 2 rooms each with one house having four rooms. They are described as being occupied by William Gaines, John Robson, William Davison and Thomas Husband.

In the group of four houses that were closest to the Brick Works, one house was larger than the other three.

In the 1930s and 1940s, Joe Wood operated a motor haulage business from Number 11 Belle Vue Terrace. He had a petrol pump in a garden, at the end of Belle Vue Terrace that he used to fuel his waggons. He kept his waggons in a large garage on the opposite side of the road, at the end of Church Lane.

Belle Vue Terrace was built in 1912 by Charles Delve, a builder from the village who also built Helmington Terrace.

The choice of name, 'Belle Vue Terrace' is interesting, as in 1912 the view over the Valley would have been interrupted by Church Lane, on the opposite side of the road and the smoke and pollution generated by West Hunwick and Hunwick Collieries, Coke Works and Brick Works. These houses were relatively big, 3 bedroomed houses with gardens and good fittings, (deep pitch pine coving; fancy hallway corbels, etc.)

Church Lane

Reproduced with the permission of the National Library of Scotland

Rokeby Terrace was also built in 1912. The houses originally had two bedrooms with a front room and a scullery downstairs, and a small single storey kitchen to the rear.

It is interesting that a well is shown on the 1856 map, at what would be the bottom corner of the existing school playing field, where during periods of excessive rain, water still flows across the road.

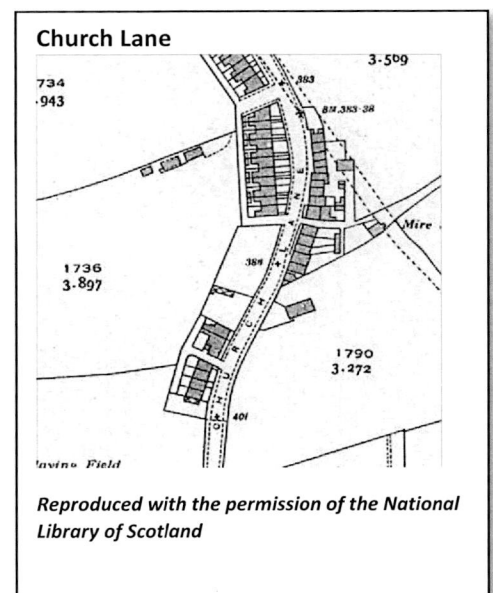

Rokeby Terrace 1939 – The Poplars on the right

Image 0122 – The Herbert Coates Collection

Heseldene Terrace, looking down from the school, 1922

Image 0359 - by kind permission of Linda Paley

Sometime between 1896 and 1915, Charles Delve, built the four houses in Heseldene Terrace, Ash-Ville, a larger, double fronted house and Belgrave House. Heseldene Terrace is show to the left on the photograph below with Belle Vue Terrace and Church Lane in the background. Heseldene Terrace overlooks a 'dene' that joins Hunwick Gill. Perhaps this influenced the choice of name?

Kate's Close

The 1856 map shows Kate's Close Farm, The Poplars, and the 4 small cottages on the opposite side of the road.

It was a working farm from the late eighteenth century until 1948, when the last of the farm land was sold. The land to the rear of the Poplar's, has been used as the Recreation Ground, since that time.

The Poplars, 1956

Image 0114

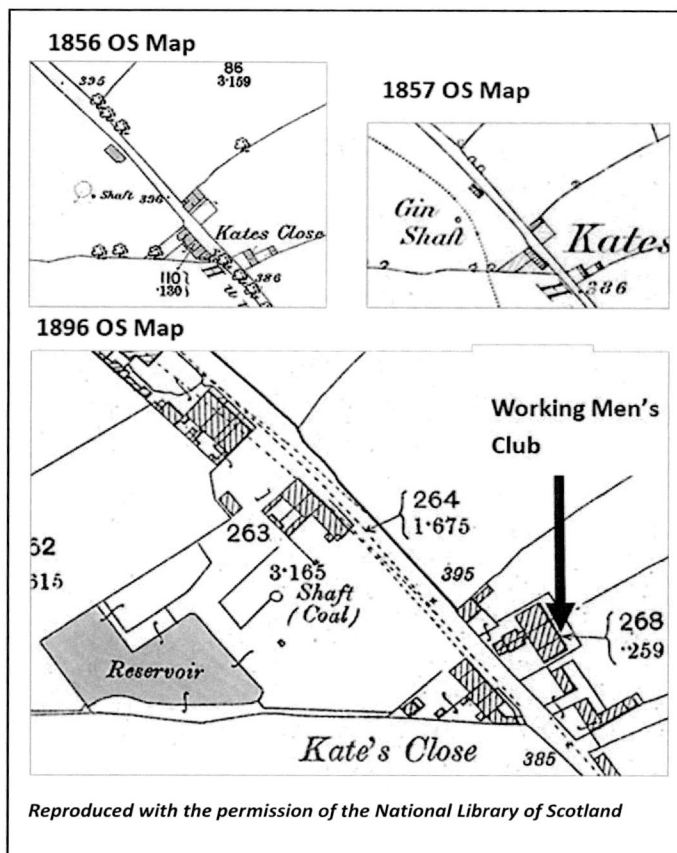

1856 OS Map

1857 OS Map

1896 OS Map

Working Men's Club

264
1·675

263

3·165
Shaft
(Coal)

395

268
·259

Reservoir

Kate's Close   385

Reproduced with the permission of the National Library of Scotland

From the 1860s the farm also operated a butcher's shop, complete with a slaughter house behind, from the single storey house next door to the Working Men's Club. By this time some of the land had been sold to allow West Hunwick Colliery to be developed.

In 1887, the farm and shop were bought, by William Raine who owned a shop at Lane Ends. In 1897 the farm and butcher's shop were sold to the Bishop Auckland Cooperative Society who continued to operate the butcher's shop and the farm. In the early 1970s, Norman and Freda Swann bought the shop and operated it as Grocers and General Dealers until the early 1980s.

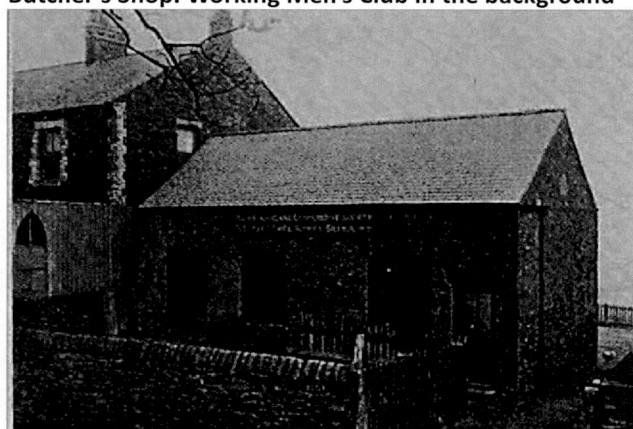

Butcher's Shop. Working Men's Club in the background

Image 0113

It is likely that the cottages at Kate's Close were originally built to house the farm workers or perhaps to house the miners that worked at an early mine, identified on maps, in the field behind Kate's Close cottages. The 1856 OS map shows a building, between the main road and the Ginn Shaft, that might have been a colliery building?

Meadow View, now Wear View was a street of three houses, which was built after 1856, but before 1896. Two were large, double fronted houses with the third being a single fronted house. All three houses have a decorative style of brickwork. Similar brickwork can be seen on houses at Helmington Square (1903), North View (circa 1910), and West End.

The 1915 OS map shows that a further three houses had been built in Meadow View. These houses were built in a slightly different style. A wall plate on number 42 Wear View, displays '1897'.

Hunwick Working Men's Club purchased the first two houses in Meadow View in 1908. The ground floor of these houses was believed to be the workshop of Joseph Turnbull who was a Joiner and coffin maker. The Club opened in February 1908 using money that twenty-five members had personally borrowed to purchase the building. Meadow View was re-named Wear View, in 1961. In 1954 the house next door, that became 40 Wear View, was acquired and the Steward's accommodation, the lounge and concert hall were created.

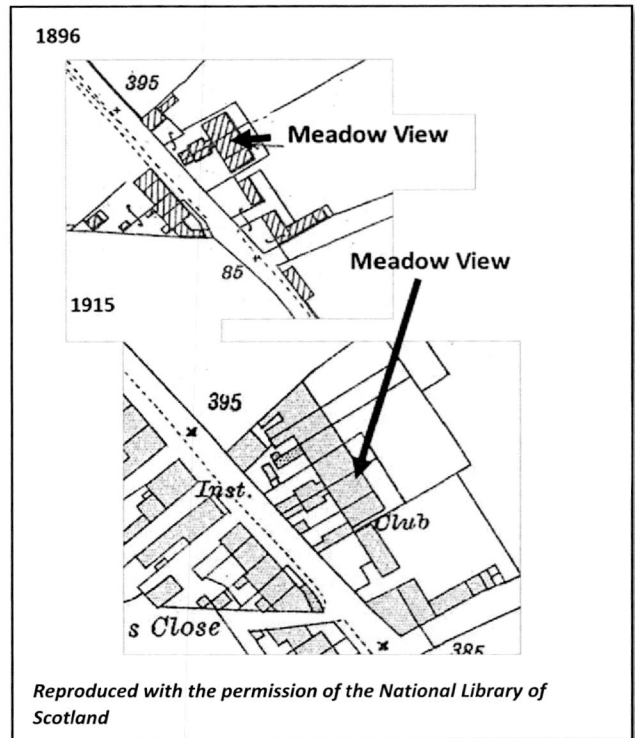

Reproduced with the permission of the National Library of Scotland

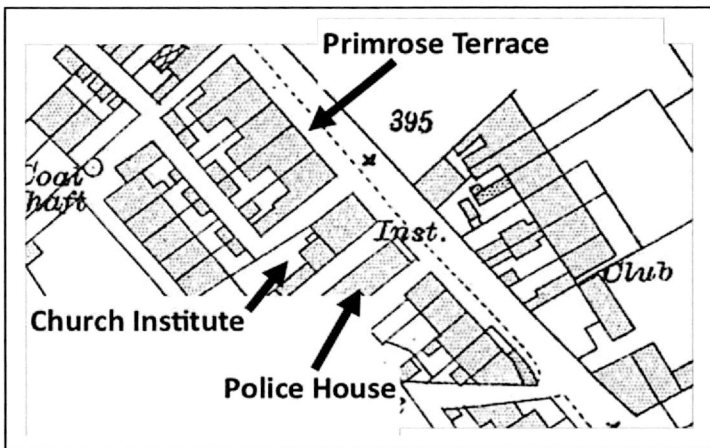

Number 32 Wear View, Highbury House, was the police house for the village. The Police and Constabulary Almanack identified the village as having a police sergeant and 2 constables during 1945, 1950 and 1955.

It is not clear when the village was first allocated its own police constable. The 1861 census identifies William Hopps, a police constable, living in the village. This might suggest that the population explosion in the 1850s, resulted in a police presence in the village.

St Paul's Church Wardens bought the land at Kate's Close, now Number 31 Wear View, to build the Church Institute Reading Room which opened in 1900. The Church Army Captain lived in the house behind the Church Institute. The Reading Room was upstairs and there was a large hut in the garden behind where dances were held. The Institute had closed by 1935 and the property was administrated by the Charity Commission until 1973 when it was sold and converted for residential use. Although the Reading Room on the first floor was closed between 1935 and 1973, the ground floor was used by Bishop Auckland Coop Society as a store and later as a doctor's surgery for the Crook Doctors. It was then used by Ann Belton and later Pauline, as a lady's hairdressers.

A street of five houses, known as Primrose Terrace, was built in 1897 alongside the main road through the village.

However, a street sign still exists, on the gable end of 26 Wear View, that suggests Primrose Terrace was also behind the houses that front onto the main road. The mystery was solved when residents remembered that the gable end of 1 Primrose Terrace (30 Wear View) had to be rebuilt and that the sign had been moved onto the gable end of house at the other end of the terrace. The 1911 census records that James Johnson, a worker at the sanitary sink Works, was living in 1 Primrose Terrace (30 Wear View), a six-roomed house, with a servant.

When Jean and Maurice Little bought the newsagents shop in 1961, it was known as Number 2 Primrose Terrace. Later in 1961, when the road through the village was widened, Primrose Terrace, along with, Kate's Close, Valley View, Wear Valley View, Meadow View and Hunwick Lane, were renamed Wear View.

Until the main road was widened in 1961, there was a very narrow section of road between the Wheatsheaf Inn and Kate's Close. This made it difficult for buses and large vehicles to pass each other. The postcard images show how narrow the road was. The triangular road sign warns motorists of the potential problem.

Looking along Wear View from Lane Ends- Tom Watson's Cobblers Shop on the Lefthand side of photo

Image 0340 - the R Alder Collection

At the top of Cooperative Terrace, opposite the Wheatsheaf Public House, there was a very old, stone-roofed, detached house with a single storey building attached.

Tom Watson lived in the house and ran a cobblers' shop from the single storey shop. The house and shop were very close to the main road and had to be demolished in 1955 in preparation for the road to be widened.

When the road was widened, the wall that ran on the field side of the road, was taken down and rebuilt in the field in the position that it is today. A footpath was also added on the field side of the road.

Looking along Wear View from Lane Ends

Image 0157.2

In preparation for the road to be widened, Durham County Council bought strips of land, from each of the properties in Meadow view and Kates Close. They also acquired a strip of land from the field on the eastern side of the main road.

Relocated stone wall

Image 0383

Looking back along Wear View towards Lane Ends

Image 0341 – the Lilywhite Collection

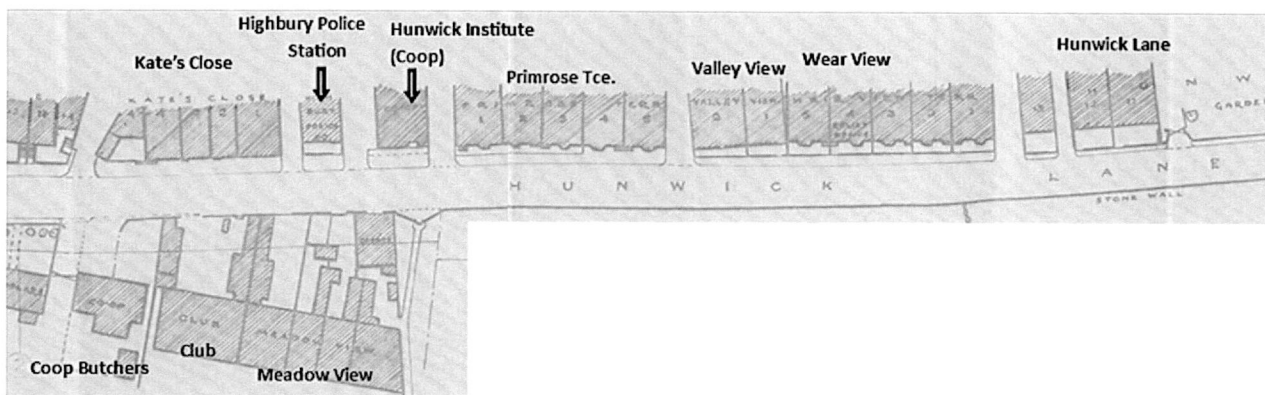

Kate's Close | Highbury Police Station | Hunwick Institute (Coop) | Primrose Tce. | Valley View | Wear View | Hunwick Lane

Coop Butchers | Club | Meadow View

A wall plaque, 'Established 1872', can be found on 'Helmington House', Number 11 and Number 12 Wear View although it is believed that the houses were built in 1867. Number 11 Wear View was at one point, the village post office.

By 1896, maps show that houses had been built to in-fill the gaps on west side of the road. It also shows the Orchard behind what was J W Wood's (later Wager's then Morralee's) fruit and green grocery shop on Hunwick Lane. West View, a street of 20 houses behind Hunwick Lane was built in 1910.

Lane Ends

Before the collieries were opened, a few houses were clustered around Lane Ends Farm. The farm appears on the 1843 Tithe Map as an 18-acre farm, owned by John Booth and occupied by Ralph Hutchinson. An 1861 Estate map identifies the farms three fields as belonging to, 'late Booth and afterwards Cutter, Nyle and North Bitchburn Coal Company'.

The farm is shown on Christopher Greenwood's 1818 map and on the 1856 OS map. The last reference to the farm was in Kelly's 1921 Trade Directory, that listed William Thomas Thompson as the farmer.

The parcel of land at Lane Ends, on which the high-density housing was built, had been part of the village's Common Land until 1761 when it was allocated, by an Enclosure Act, to Robert Thompson.

Rough Lea Colliery opened in 1858 and created the need for houses for its workers. It is likely

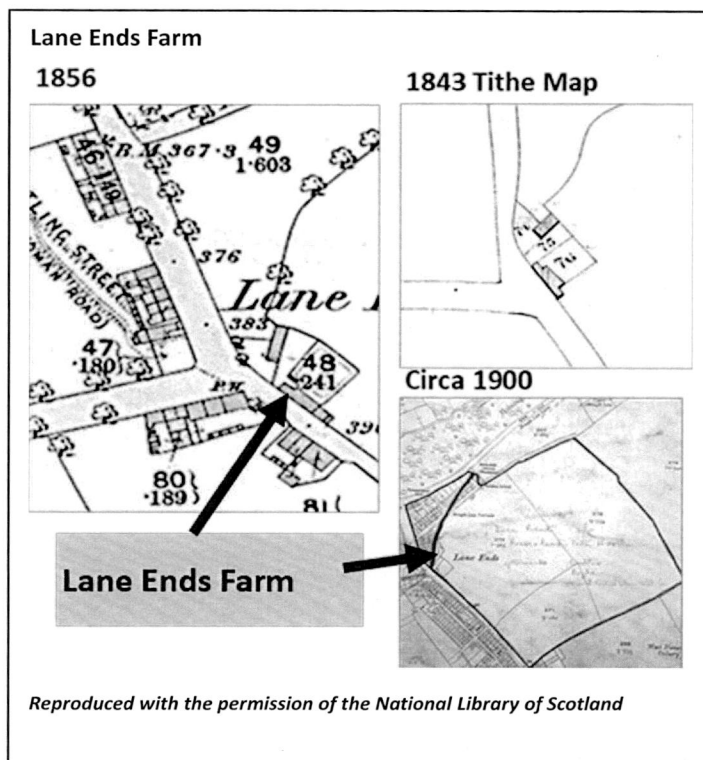

Lane Ends Farm

1856

1843 Tithe Map

Circa 1900

Lane Ends Farm

Reproduced with the permission of the National Library of Scotland

that the land was chosen for housing as it was north-facing and had little value for arable use. A ready supply of water was provided by the Roman Well and Helmington Beck would have been useful for drainage/waste disposal.

The trees in Helmington Hall's rookery shielded the high-density housing and the activities of the residents, from the view of Helmington Hall. Straker and Love, who owned the Helmington Hall Estate, built a five-foot-high wall around Helmington Hall, running up Hall Bank, along in front of Rough Lea Terrace and down to Rough Lea Farm. They used bricks from the Brick Works that they owned at Brancepeth Colliery in Willington.

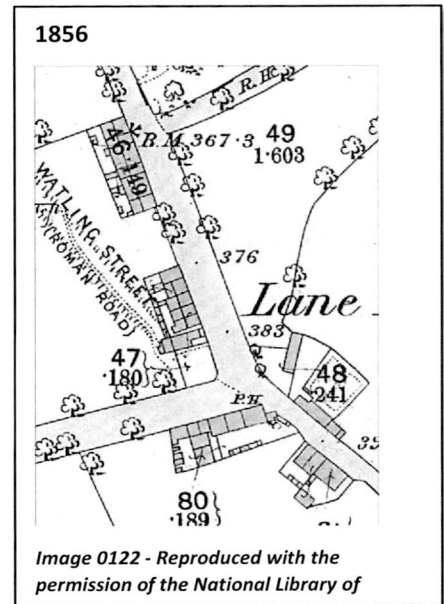

1856

Image 0122 - Reproduced with the permission of the National Library of

The 1856 OS map shows Lane Ends Farm and six houses at the top of Front Street and five houses at the bottom of the street. It shows three houses on, what was originally known as Church Lane, later as Hunwick Lane before becoming Wear View. It shows the Wheatsheaf Inn, Number 1 Helmington Square, with two buildings attached to it.

The New Connections Chapel was built in 1862 and the Infants school was built in 1878. Chapel Street, a mixture of two and three bedroomed houses, was built in 1879.

By 1896, Thompson Terrace, Back Thompson Terrace, Cooperative Terrace, Oxford Street had been built. Coronation Terrace was built in 1911, to celebrate the Coronation of George V.

The development of Lane Ends

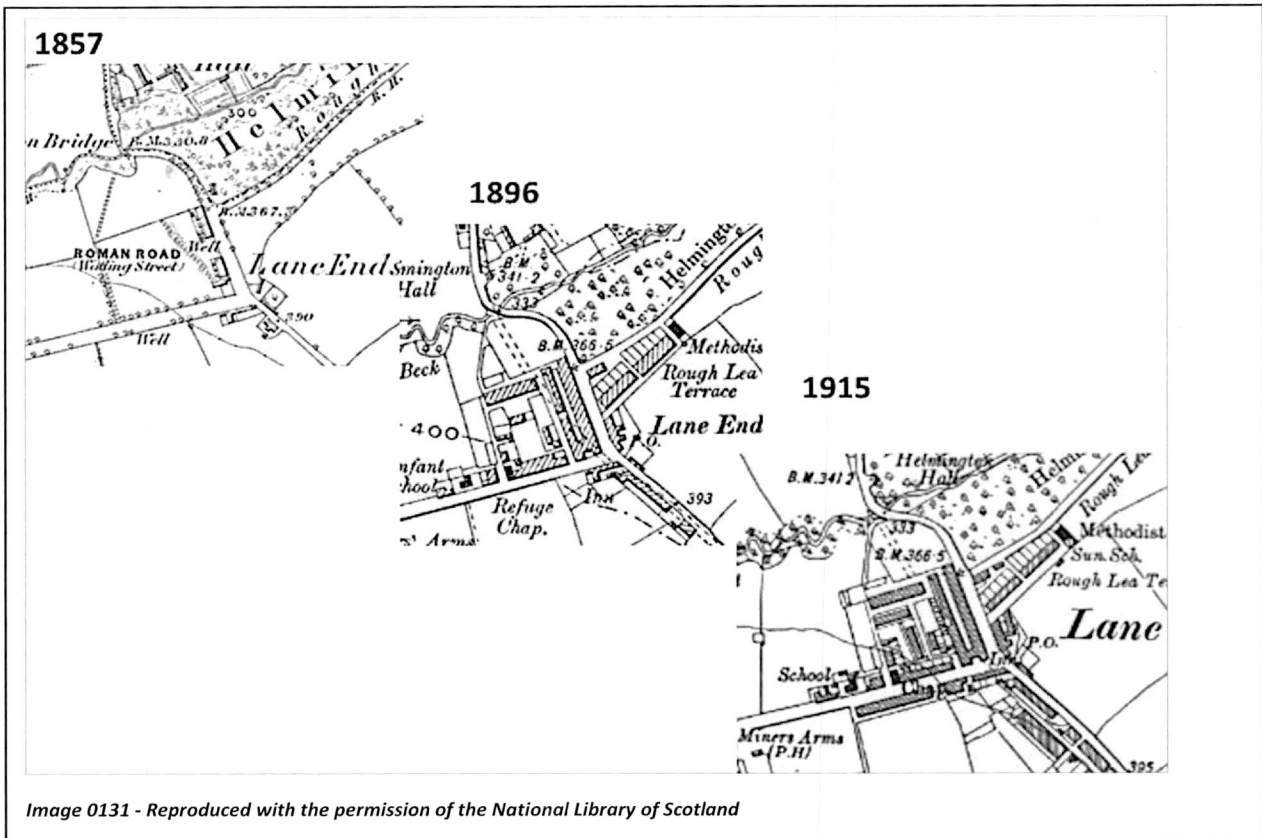

Image 0131 - Reproduced with the permission of the National Library of Scotland

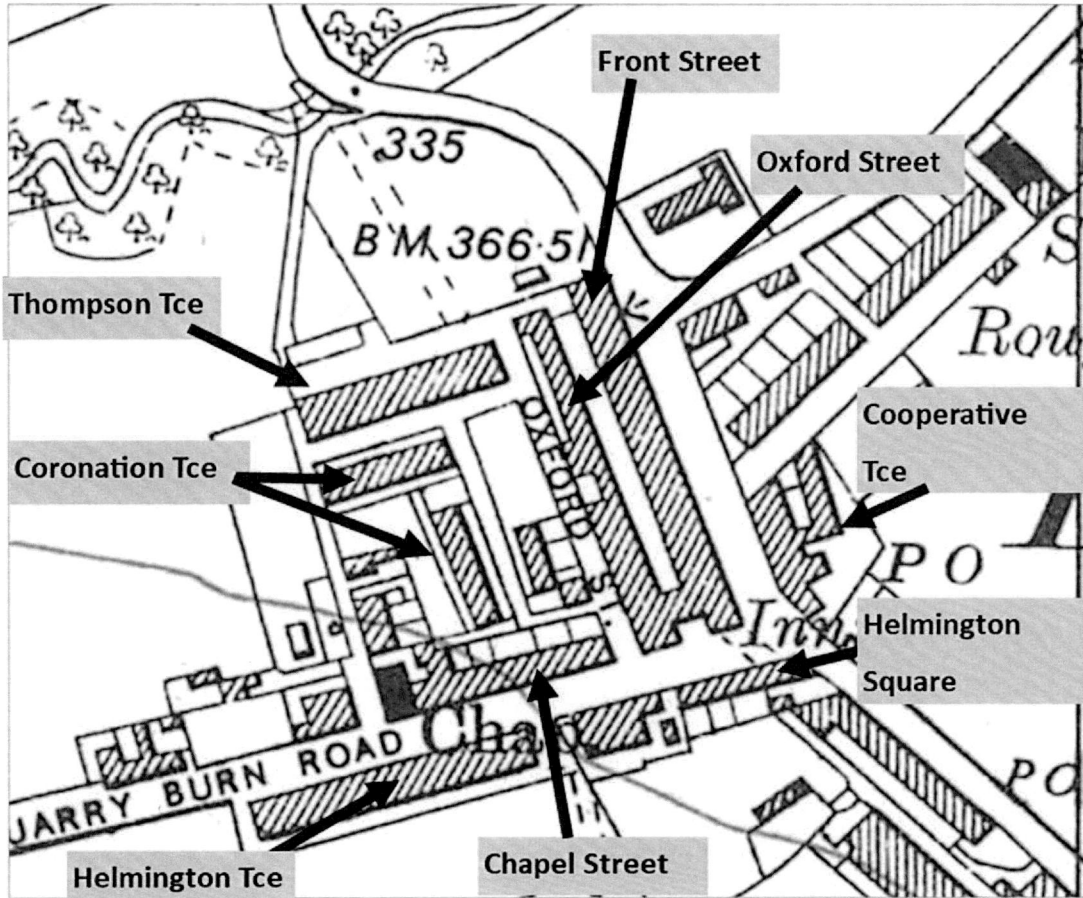

Lane Ends

Front Street

Oxford Street

Thompson Tce

Cooperative Tce

Coronation Tce

Helmington Square

Helmington Tce

Chapel Street

335

B M 366·5

QUARRY BURN ROAD

Thompson Terrace

Helmington Terrace, Coronation Terrace and West End, circa 1990

by kind permission of Paul Goundry

Looking down Chapel Street, towards Cooperative Terrace

Image 0198 – The Herbert Coates Collection

Front Street, looking up Hall Bank

Image 0153 - the Herbert Coates Collection

Cooperative Terrace, looking towards the Wheatsheaf

Image 0156 - Beamish Museum -Peoples Collection

An advertisement for the sale of four freehold cottages in the Daily Gazette for Middlesbrough 12 April 1939 provides us with some information about the houses. It explains that each of the back-to-back houses (numbers 3 and 4), *'contains a kitchen, pantry and one bedroom'.* To the rear is a large common yard with newly-erected WC's and coal houses. Details for number 5 and number 5-back were: *'each house contains a kitchen, pantry and two bedrooms yard with newly-erected WC's and coal houses'.* There was a passage from the front of the houses, that allowed access to the 'backs', the houses at the back of the street.

Harold Heslop, writing in the early 1900s, when Rough Lea Colliery was working wrote *'Taken on the whole. Old Hunwick was ancient and New Hunwick was merely a clutter of houses which had been hastily assembled to house the families of the men who broached the shallows of the earth wherein lay seams of the finest quality coal.'* (Heslop, 1987)

In the same document, Heslop describes the houses that had been built:

'Few of the houses had more than two bedrooms. All had a kitchen, and some a front room. In the kitchen all the chores were performed, despite the fact that most held a double bed always occupied by the father and mother of the family. Here the miners reproduced themselves. Here the progeny crawled and dunged until they picked up and sent off to school' (Heslop, 1987)

Although he referred to 'New Hunwick', it is likely that, as well as the two streets of houses in New Hunwick, he was also talking about Thompson Terrace and Oxford Street as the houses that had been hastily built. These houses were owned by the Colliery and rented out to their workers. This relationship, during times when workers withdrew their labour, raised the real fear that if a miner did not work, their family would be evicted from their house.

The houses in Thompson Terrace were built, 'back-to-back', and had one room upstairs and one room downstairs. One family lived in the rooms at the 'front' and another lived in the rooms at 'back' of the building.

Villagers who had lived in the houses in the 1940s, explained how some of the 'front' houses had been 'knocked through' (middle wall removed), into the 'back(s)' house. This created a larger house and explains the memories that some residents had of houses in Thompson Terrace:

"we had a living room and front room down stairs and upstairs there were two bedrooms, four of us were in the back bedroom.... I remember meat hooks in the ceiling where they used to hang the meat years before. The stairs were very steep. There was a long back kitchen leading from the living room that had a bath at the end but only cold water the hot was supplied by the Burco boiler in the living room. The toilet was outside at the very end of the yard. They were rented by Edkins".

The houses at Lane Ends were built on a hill meaning that neighbouring houses, gardens and yards were all at different levels. John Cunningham remembers a wall that separated Coronation Terrace from Chapel Street and how the land on one side of the wall was 6 feet below the level on the other side.

Coronation Street Party. Oxford Street and Thompson Terrace, May 1953

Image 0132 – (George Brown, Digital Village Project 2006)

Lane Ends celebrating Coronation Day, 1911

Image 0354 - by kind permission of Dave Calcutt

A Trade Directory printed in 1861 confirms that the Helmington Inn and the Wheat Sheaf were both in business in 1861. The 1896 OS map shows that Cooperative Terrace, Rough Lea Terrace and Norman's Buildings had been built.

The parcel of land upon which they were built, had been part of Joseph Hall's freehold allotment from the 1761 Enclosure of Hunwick Moor.

Before 1761, this north facing parcel of land, was Common Land. Later, it was bought by the North Bitchburn Coal Company, from George Norman who had acquired it from Henry Smith Stobart.

The Helmington Inn, looking towards Norman's Buildings

Image 0125 – The Herbert Coates Collection

Enclosure Map, 1761

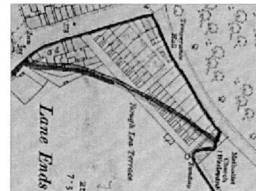

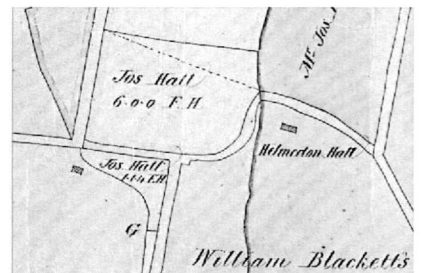

In 1868, Rough Lea Terrace was also built on this land. The tenants were colliery 'officials' who were employed by, and 'tied' to, the colliery. The Colliery Engineer for Newton Cap Colliery, lived in Number 3 Rough Lea Terrace which was the only double house in the terrace.

Rough Lea Terrace, looking towards Front Street

Image 0333 – The Herbert Coates Collection

Rough Lea Terrace, looking towards Rough Lea Chapel

Image 0404 – The Herbert Coates Collection

The The Wesleyan Chapel was built at Rough Lea in 1881. In 1984, Stephen and Wendy Spooner bought the Chapel, Vestry and School Rooms. They converted the chapel into a textiles factory and the Vestry and School Rooms into a house.

The factory traded as Wendeva, employing twenty machinists who made pocket linings, shoulder pads and general accessories for garments. They supplied local garment manufacturers including Varahwear, Raymars and Claremont Garments.

Rough Lea, Wesleyan Chapel

Image 0201– The Herbert Coates Collection

The factory operated until 1993 when it closed and was converted, in 1994, into a house.

In 1935, the foundations were dug for Helmington Hall Club, the 'Green Hut', on a plot of land on Hall bank at the top of Rough Lea Lane and in the Rookery of Helmington Hall.

Helmington Hall Social Club, looking up Hall Bank

Image 0211 – The Herbert Coates Collection

Maps show that the Temperance Hall (Pink Shed) had been built, on a plot of land between Rough Lea Terrace and Norman's Buildings, by 1915.

Reputedly, the shop on the corner of Norman's Buildings, at the bottom of Cooperative Terrace, had been the Rough Lea Colliery shop. The colliery would have operated a 'truck' system where miners were paid in tokens that could only be spent in the colliery shop. Although an Act of Parliament made the Truck System illegal some collieries continued to operate the system until 1887 when the Act was amended.

In the 1940s, the Pipework's Doctor lived in Number 1 Norman's Buildings and the Pipework's foreman lived in Number 4.

The Temperance Hall with Norman's Buildings in the background

Image 0317 – by kind permission of Donald White

Lane Ends Farm was at the top of Cooperative Terrace on the opposite side of the road to the Wheatsheaf. The buildings and the garth that had belonged to the farm, was used after 1921, by Tom Watson who was described as a boot and shoe dealer.

The house and shop were very close to the main road and had to be demolished in 1955, so that the road could be widened.

Tom Watson's Cobblers Shop (left), looking towards Church Lane

Image 0340 – The R Alder Collection

The general dealers' shop that was attached to the Wheatsheaf Inn was in business until the early 1970s, when it and the adjoining buildings, were demolished.

The land stood idle for many years, during which time, it was used as an adventure playground by local youngsters. It was developed to provide access to Oakfields and later to accommodate a single storey extension to the Wheatsheaf.

The Wheatsheaf, and a Welly Throwing Competition

Image 0124 – by kind permission of Robert Cunningham

In the 1960s, a prize bingo hall, operated in a temporary showground building, in the field above Chapel Street and behind the Infant School at West End.

Numbers 7 to 9 Helmington Square were built in 1903, on land that had been bought by William Raine from the widow of Henry Johnes Fielding, who owned Cringle Dykes Farm. These were larger, three bedroomed, better built houses with ceiling architraves etc. that were built for tradesmen or mining officials.

Looking from The Wheatsheaf, up Quarry Burn Road

Image 0126 – by kind permission of Robert Cunningham

William Raine had been a shop keeper at Lane Ends in the late nineteenth century, and had managed to acquire a lot of property in the village.

Looking down Chapel Street

Image 0198 – The Herbert Coates Collection

Number 6 Helmington Square, a large double fronted house, belonged to the butcher, Simpson Heslop. He ran the shop further down the street and had an abattoir behind the shop. All of the houses in Helmington Square share brickwork details that can also be seen on houses in Meadow View, North View and in West End.

Helmington Terrace, a street of twelve, 3 bedroomed houses, was built by Charles Delve in 1910 on land whichpreviously belonged to Cringle Dykes Farm. Trade Directories for 1906, 1910 and 1924 confirm that Charles Delve was a mason based in Hunwick.

Children Playing 'down the Dog Loupe' – looking towards Helmington Hall

Image 0376 – by kind permission of Harold Newton

Lane ends had numerous shops ranging from those selling groceries to hardware shops.

Residents who grew up at Lane Ends in the 1940s, report that they seldom needed to move out of the settlement as everything, including their favourite play areas, were at Lane Ends.

John Cunningham remembers the tall brick walls that surrounded the houses at Lane Ends. He describes a wall running along the northern edge of the settlement, separating the houses from an area of grass on Hall Bank that ran down to the beck.

In the 1960s, youngsters used to play on a piece of land at the bottom of Hall Bank. For some reason, it was known as the *"Dog Loupe"*.

All that is left of the houses at Lane Ends is Coronation Terrace along with one house from Chapel Street. The open land that is currently used as a community space, is where Front Street and Oxford Street had been.

Thompson Terrace was demolished in 1968, followed by Oxford Street. Front Street and Chapel Street were demolished in the 1970s.

Hall View was built in 1973 on what had been part of Thompson Terrace. The current Chapel Street was built on what had been part of the original Chapel Street.

'Shed-built' toys

Image 0381 – by kind permission of Harold Newton

Rough Lea

Looking down Rough Lea Lane, towards Rough Lea Colliery

Image 0335 – The Herbert Coates Collection

The 1857 OS map shows Upper Rough Lea Farm, Low Rough Lea Farm and Lane Ends Farm. Apart from these farms, there was nothing, other than open fields, at Rough Lea.

Rough Lea Colliery opened in 1858. The 1915, OS map, shows a large colliery site with Coke Works, Sanitary Pipe Works and extensive railway sidings, on what had previously been open farmland.

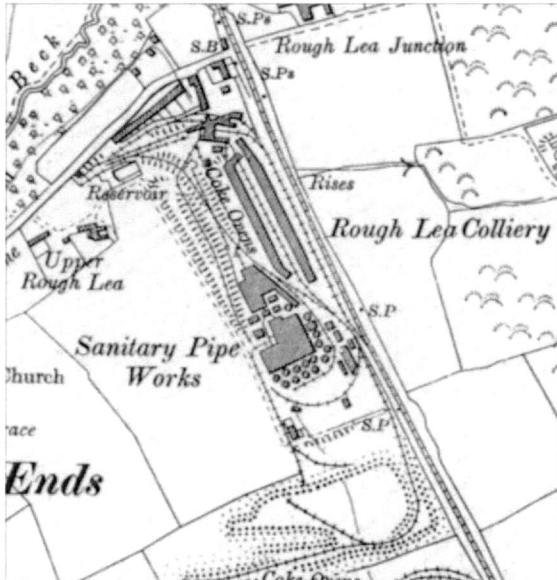

Rough Lea Colliery, 1915

Reproduced with the permission of the National Library of Scotland

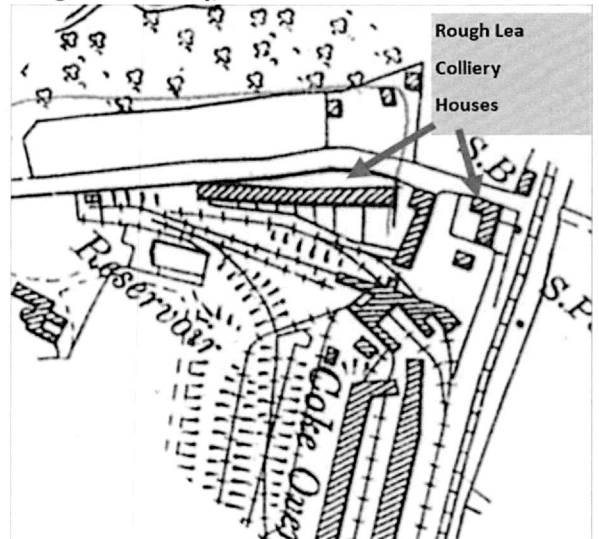

Rough Lea Colliery, 1915

Rough Lea Colliery Houses

Reproduced with the permission of the National Library of Scotland

'Rough Lea Colliery', a street of nineteen houses, ran up from the colliery yard and parallel to Rough Lea Lane.

Number 1 Rough Lea Colliery, the manager's house and Number 2, the under managers house, stood at the bottom of the street, parallel to railway line.

Rough Lea Colliery, the street

Image 0145 - by kind permission of Jim Bone

Number 3. was at the bottom of the street and was the colliery engineer's house. It was a large house with an office attached and a walled garden. The other houses in the street were two bedroomed houses. Number 19 Rough Lea Colliery was the colliery 'reading room'. It had a library and was used for meetings.

Rough Lea Colliery

Image 0412 -by kind permission of Donald White

Number 3 to Number 7 Rough Lea Colliery are still in use. Number 8 to Number 19 were demolished in the 1950s. Residents were relocated to new Council Estates either in Hunwick or at Hall Lane, in Willington.

Donald White, who grew up at Rough Lea, explains:

"At the top of the street [Rough Lea Colliery] was an open space where the Rough Lea Works had sand dumped for repairs. It was known as the Sand Heap. Lime was sometimes dumped there also. The lime was in sizes from road chippings size to smaller. It was riddled on a wire mesh 5ft high leaning at an angle. What went through was slaked by tipping water on it, this produced great heat, and mixed with sand to make mortar. This was before cement was widely used.

There was a brick-lined pit pond further over from the sand, about 6ft deep and sides lined steeply with fireclay bricks. Sometimes it was full others almost empty." (Ref Donald White's notes)

New Hunwick

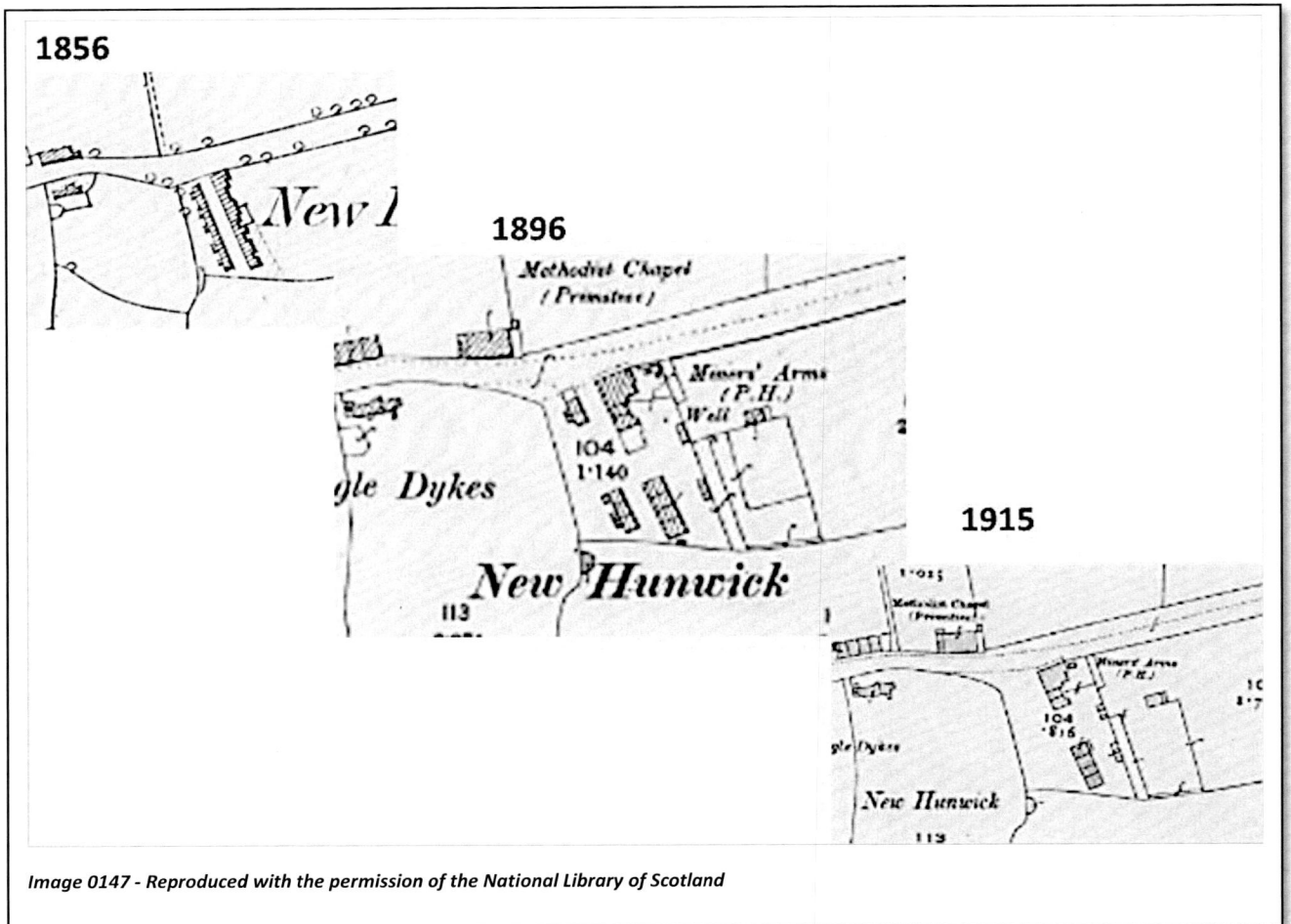

1856

New 1

1896

Methodist Chapel (Primitive)

Miners' Arms (P.H.)

Well

104
1.140

gle Dykes

113

New Hunwick

1915

Methodist Chapel (Primitive)

Miners' Arms (P.H.)

104

New Hunwick

113

Image 0147 - Reproduced with the permission of the National Library of Scotland

Coppice Wood is built at what was known as New Hunwick.

The 1843 Tithe Map shows two rows of houses at New Hunwick. The 1856 OS Map provides more detail showing two rows, with with approximately twenty houses in each row. Villagers confirm that the houses were built out of stone.

By 1896, the Miner's Arms is shown on the map but there are gaps in the two rows of houses with only twelve houses remaining.

The 1915 map shows the Miner's Arms with two houses attached, then a gap and a further four houses. Apart from the Chapel and two farms, New Hunwick Farm and Cringle Dykes Farm, there was nothing else at New Hunwick

The houses were built before 1843. The shaft for Hunwick Colliery, at Hunwick Station, was sunk in 1839. None of the other collieries in the village were in operation at that time. It is difficult to understand why the houses were built at New Hunwick in the first place and then why they were demolished when other houses were being built at Lane Ends to meet the demand created by the boom in mining at Rough Lea, West Hunwick and Hunwick Colliery?

We know that miners, employed by Rough Lea Colliery, used the 'day-drifts' at Brecken Hill and Quarry Burn that were connected to the workings of Rough Lea Colliery. The day-drifts were a short walk from New Hunwick. However, as Rough Lea Colliery had not begun working until 1858, there must have been some other reason for building so many houses in New Hunwick?

The Primitaive Methodist Chapel had opened in 1875 and the Miner's Arms and the Brewery Arms, a short walk from New Hunwick, were both trading in 1879.

For it to be viable for there to be two public houses and a Chapel, in an area where there were only sixty houses, forty at New Hunwick and twenty at Quarry Burn Row, would suggest that there must have been some other employment in the area? It is not clear how many people the Brewery employed.

The compulsory Purchase Order for the demolition of Quarry Burn Row explained that the houses had been built for miners who worked at Rough Lea Colliery.

The name 'Quarry Burn', adds to the confusion as, apart from a gravel quarry between New Hunwick and Blakeley Hill, I cannot find a quarry in the area. The 1761 Estate version of the Enclosure Map, shows Quarry Well, close to Quarry Burn Beck, at Lane Ends.

In addition to these two streets, known as 'New Hunwick' there were 4 houses above the Chapel shown on the 1856 map. These houses were originally known as Wallace Terrace and later as Number 5 to 8, New Hunwick and now Number 14 to 17, West End. Reputedly, they were built by a local mine owner as a dowery for his daughter, who would receive income from their rental. (Ref sold by William and George Dover to NBCC in 1921) The Street sign for 'New Hunwick' is on display in the Joiner's Arms.

In the mid-1950s, John Wragg, starting with a converted removal van, set up a haulage business that operated from the building that had previously been the Miner's Arms.

The Miner's Arms and John Wragg's Yard

Image 0148 – by kind permission of Steven Wragg

He operated their tipper waggons and articulated waggons from the site along with his pallet making and timber business until he retired in the mid-1980s.

He built a large garage onto the side of the Miner's Arm's Ball Alley. The garage was heated by scrap wood burnt in an old ship's boiler.

At one time Tony Nicholson, trading as Mercury Guitars manufactured guitars on the site.

In 2003 a housing estate, Coppice Wood, was built on the site that had previously been the Miner's Arms and Wragg's Haulage Yard.

The choice of name was reported as nothing to do with local woodland but simply a nod to the fact that a saw-mill had operated on the site.

The allotment gardens at West End/New Hunwick, that were owned by the North Bitchburn Fireclay Company, were relocated and Birch Meadow was built on the site in 2002 - 2004.

The Chapel, with Wallace Terrace in the background

Image 0361 – the Herbert Coates Collection

West End

The 1896 OS map shows a street of two houses, below the Primitive Methodist Chapel, and above the Infants School. By 1915, there were three houses in the street.

The large, double fronted houses with decorative brickwork, are now known as Number 6, 7 and 8 West End. The design and brick work are very similar to that on houses in North View, Helmington Square and Meadow View.

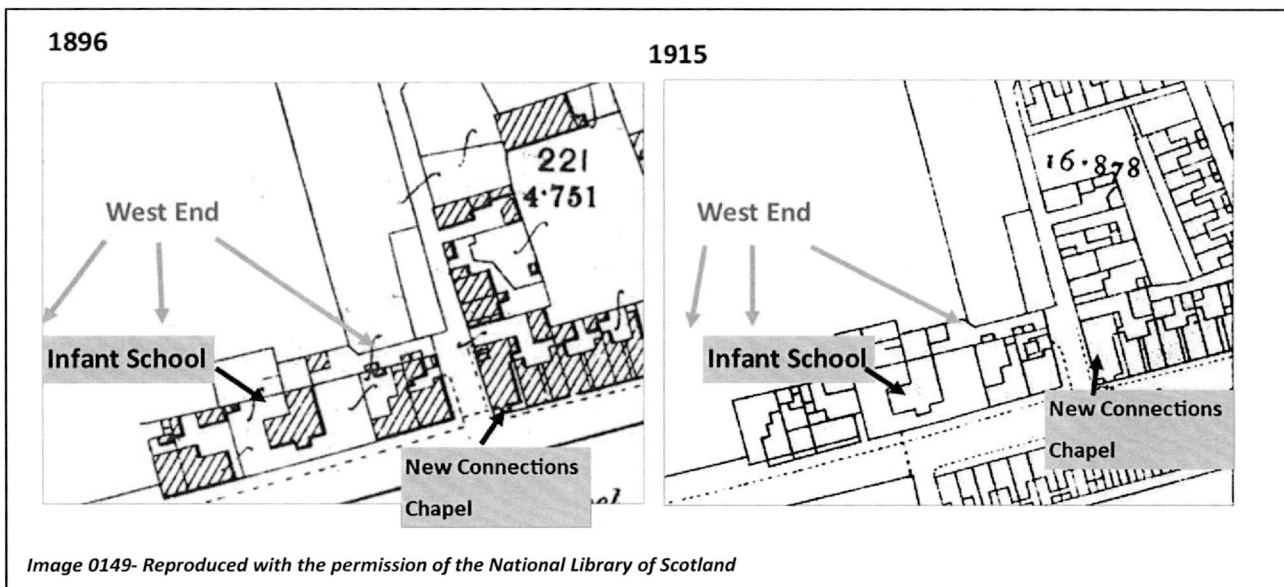

Image 0149- Reproduced with the permission of the National Library of Scotland

The land for Number 8 was bought by Ethel Raw in December 1909 from the sons of the Butcher, Simpson Heslop. Depending how quickly Mr and Mrs Raw managed to find a builder, the house was probably built in 1910.

Plans show it as a substantial, three-bedroomed house with an upstairs bathroom, a bay window and gated access to land to the side and rear, attached to the existing two houses.

Number 1, 2 and 3, West End, were above the Methodist Chapel that was on Chapel Street, but below the Infants School.

Number 3 West End is a larger, double fronted house from which, in the 1940s, Jimmy Johnson ran a small-holding. He had a barn and cow shed in the fields behind the house.

The new houses, Number 4 and 5 West End, were built on the site of the Infant's School that had been built in 1879.

School photographs show that the school was still operating on the site in 1921. In September 1924, the Infant's School was relocated into a new building on the site of the current school.

The rear of 3 West End

Image 0377 – by kind permission of Harold Newton

Quarry Burn Row, Primrose Hill and Oaks Row

An advertisement, for High Quarry Burn Farm, in the Durham Chronical, 29th May 1857, explained that the farm was in an area *'where there is demand for building sites'.*

Quarry Burn Row, Primrose Hill and Oaks Row are all marked on the 1957 OS map.

Quarry Burn consisted of a Brewery, a Public House, a row of twenty houses and a row of five houses.

Primrose Hill, which was a little further along Quarry Burn Lane, towards Rumby Hill, consisted of a row of three houses.

Quarry Burn Row did not have running water piped to the houses. Residents had to walk over two fields to Jinny's Well and carry water back to the house.

Quarry Burn Row was built in 1854 for miners working at Rough Lea Colliery. In 1939, Crook and Willington Urban District Council argued that the houses were 'old, damp, worn out and unfit for human occupation'. They were demolished shortly after this assessment.

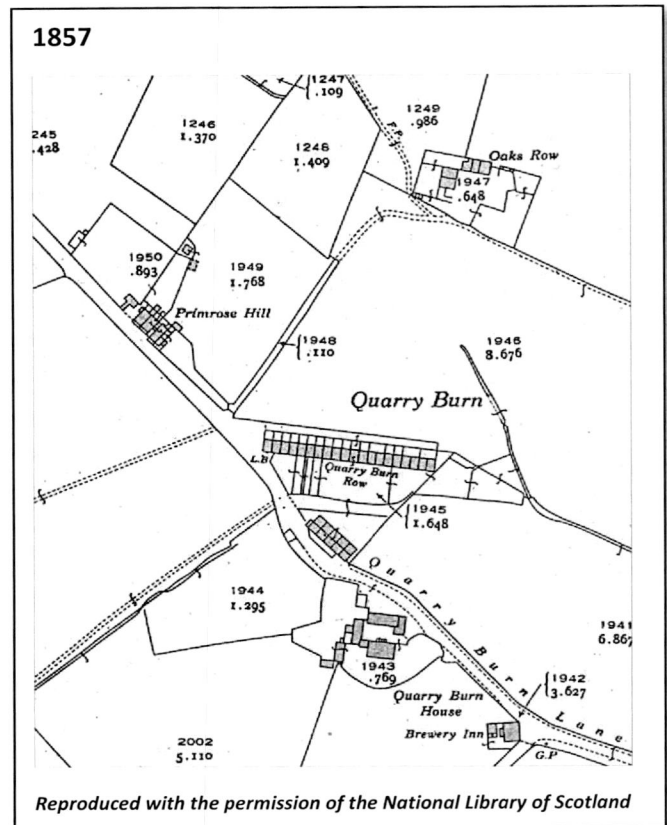

1857

Reproduced with the permission of the National Library of Scotland

Looking up Quarry Burn Lane towards the Brewery Inn - Quarry Burn Row on the right-hand side

Image 0343 - the Herbert Coates Collection

There were five houses at Oaks Row. Donald White remembers, *'there were houses round three sides of a sort of Green. Built of stone, some 3 storeys - ie low rooms under the roof with windows at floor level, some stone roofed, slabs held on with mutton bone through each.'*

The 1761 Enclosure Map, identified fields belonging to Thomas Graham. Quarry Burn Farm, when advertised to let in 1894 by the Brewery, listed, a farm house, farm buildings, stack yard and 25 acres comprising 4 fields and a garth of rich grass land.

Quarry Burn Row

Image 0150 - the Herbert Coates Collection

Quarry Burn Row

Image 0151 - the Herbert Coates Collection

A bore hole was drilled in 1844, on land south-east of Quarry Burn Brewery, to establish whether it was worth sinking a shaft and developing a colliery. The 'boring', number 201 - Bitchburn, found that there was a 2-foot seam of coal with water at 60ft, a 1-foot seam at 66ft and 2-foot seam at 90 feet below the ground level. The bore hole was in fields belonging to Quarry Burn Farm, a 25-acre farm that belonged to the Brewery and that was owned by George Stott and tenanted by John Young.

The coal seams under Quarry Burn were close to the surface and had been extensively mined. Villagers' share accounts of numerous mine collapses in the area. On one occasion, after a collapse, Pit-Ponies, belonging to Bitchburn Colliery, found their way into fields behind Quarry Burn Brewery. Reputedly, a 'Day Drift' to the west of the Brewery, enabled miners to access the workings of Bitchburn Colliery.

Hunwick Station

In 1856, the North Eastern Railway opened a railway line that ran through Hunwick Station. This line, now part of the Brandon to Bishop Auckland footpath, ran from Bishop Auckland to Sunderland and South Shields.

The 1856 OS map shows that the platforms and the Station Masters house had been built. The 1876 Estate map shows Numbers 6 to 10 Railway Terrace, the group of houses furthest away from the main road, had been built. Numbers 1 to 4 Railway Terrace are shown on the 1896 OS map. Numbers 1 to 4 had two bedrooms and were built out of stone. Number 6 to 10 had three bedrooms and were built out of brick.

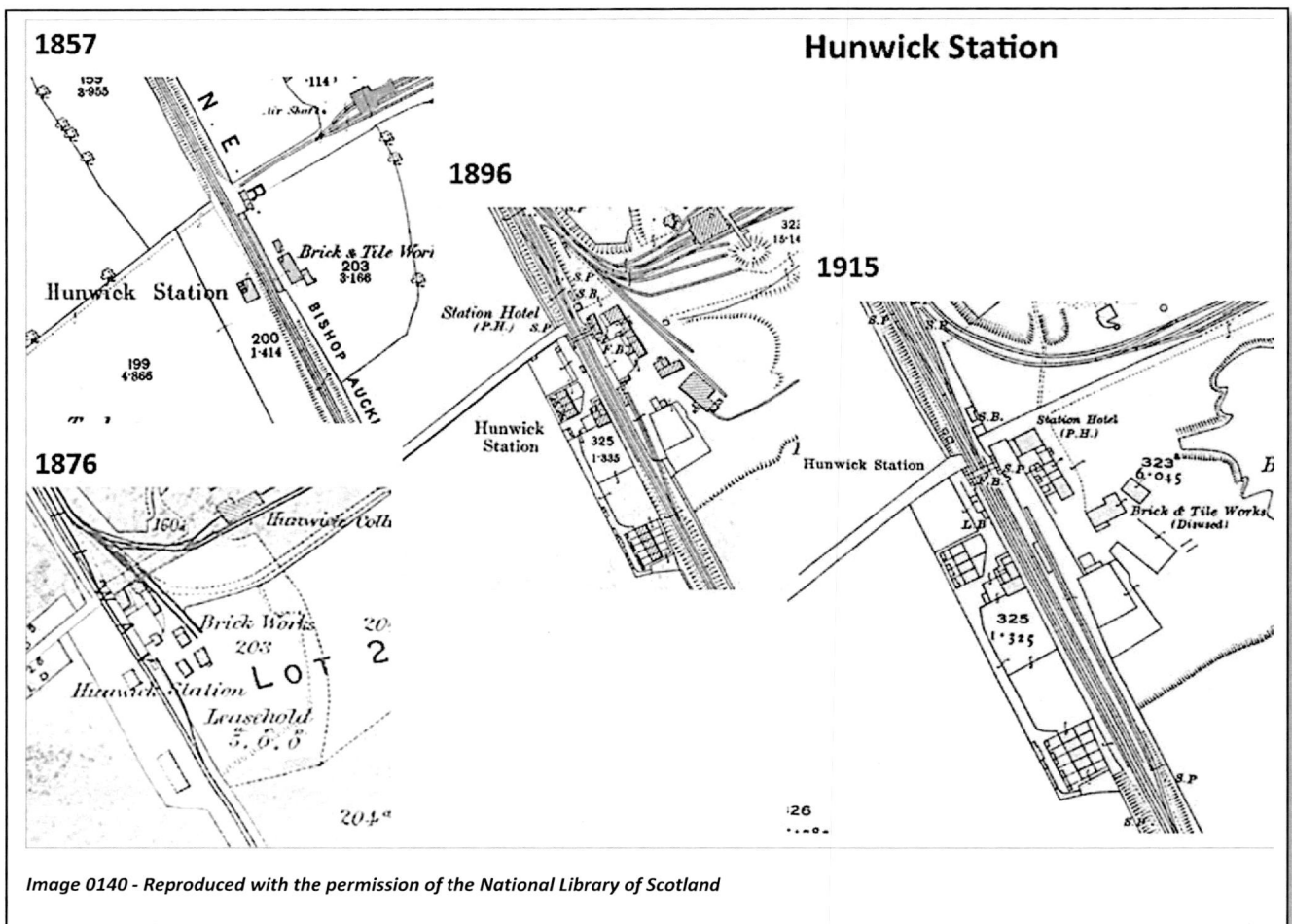

Image 0140 - Reproduced with the permission of the National Library of Scotland

Railway Terrace was built for railway workers or retired railway workers. In the 1950s, in addition to retired workers, the houses were occupied by a ganger, a signal man, a porter and a chef on the express trains.

Sometime between 1856 and 1876 the Station Hotel and the attached four cottages, Railway Cottages, and the Ball Alley had been built. The 1871 census, records John Richardson as living in the Station Hotel suggesting that these buildings might have been in use before 1871.

When the colliery opened at Hunwick Station, in 1839, the coal that was mined, was transported across a wooden bridge that had been built over the River Wear, to Newfield. At that time, the mine workers, lived in colliery houses that had been built for them at Newfield and used the same bridge to get to and from the colliery.

Hunwick Station

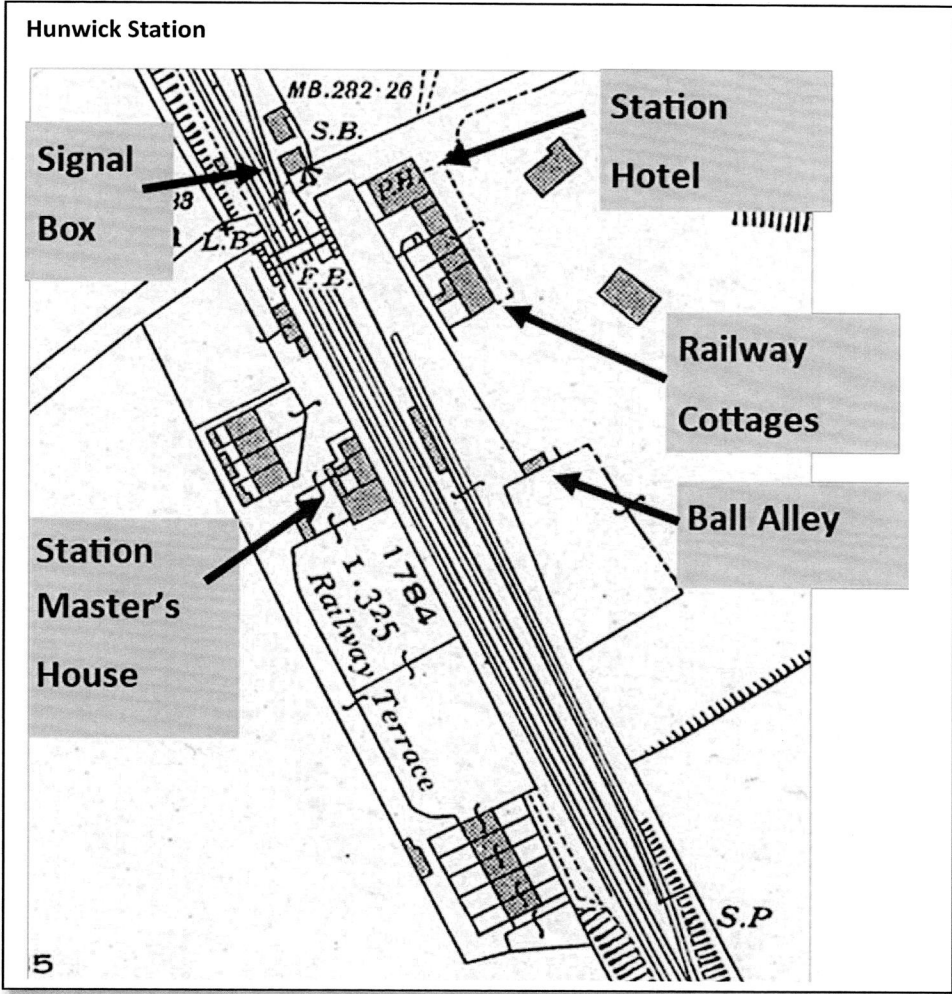

MB.282·26

S.B.

Signal Box

Station Hotel

P.H.

L.B.

F.B.

Railway Cottages

Ball Alley

Station Master's House

1784
I·325
Railway Terrace

S.P

Station Ticket Office

Image 0436 – Beamish Museum, Peoples Collection

Platform Waiting Room

HUNWICK

Image 0437 – Beamish Museum, Peoples Collection

BRUMWELL'S

Nurserymen
. Seedsmen .
and Florists

Newgate St,, Bishop Auckland

Farm, Vegetable & Flower Seeds
Fertilisers, Potatoes, Sundries, etc.

Head Office : 159 NEWGATE STREET
BISHOP AUCKLAND, Co. DURHAM
Phone: Bishop Auckland 434
Nurseries: HUNWICK STATION, WILLINGTON,
Co. DURHAM
Telegrams: HORTUS, Bishop Auckland

In 1839, Hunwick Colliery built two cottages and an office for their colliery agent. The cottages were originally known as Hunwick Cottages until the 1940s, when Sid Bramwell combined the two cottages and created November Cottage. He was a seedsman who specialised in growing fuchsias. He acquired land that had previously belonged to the colliery, and developed a nursery. (Directory, November 1949)

William Burdon, circa 1945, looking towards Hunwick Cottages. Clay Pit (pond) fenced with barbed wire. November Cottage in the background

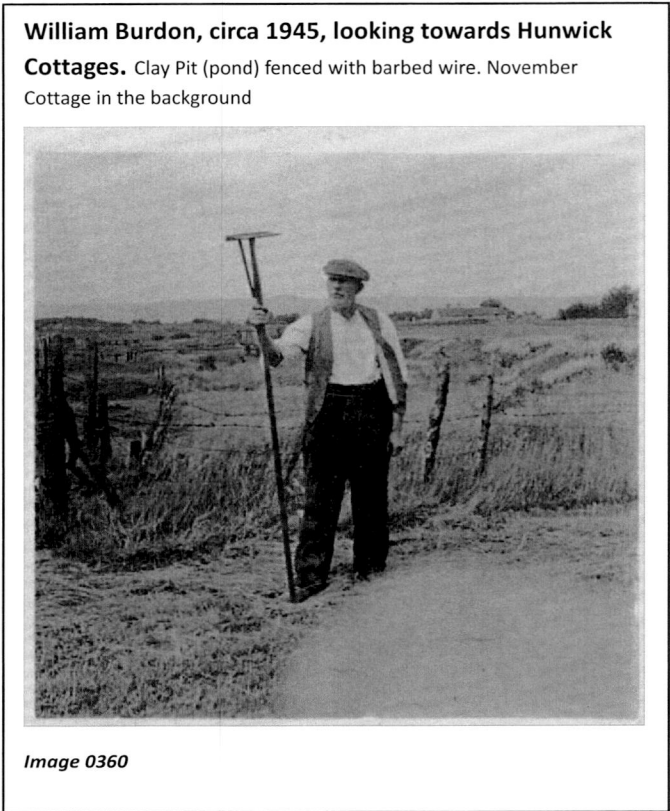

Image 0360

RyWell Grange, the bungalow on the small holding beside the Station Hotel, was built on the site of the former Brick and Tile Works at Hunwick Station.

John Raw, who after working in the South Africa goldmines, became an official at Rough Lea Colliery. He married Jayne Sunter, who's family farmed Quarry Farm, and together they built RyWell Grange.

The smallholding was bought in 1937, by William Burdon, when he retired from the police force. He was called back to police duties in 1939 until 1945 but continued to run the smallholding. He supplied and delivered milk at Hunwick Station. He retired in 1952 and moved into the Poplars in Wear View.

Foot bridge at Hunwick Station

Image 0350

There are several newspaper reports of accidents involving trains and pedestrians at Hunwick Station. Despite the obvious danger presented by a very busy railway line, a report in the Daily Gazette for Middlesbrough, on 16 Jan 1911, described the concerns of locals who, *'because the pedestrian gates were being locked, were having to use a recently constructed footbridge across the railway line rather that walk across the line'.*

In 1989, Rosie and Elsie Humble who lived in 28 South View, received a letter from a Gwen Skelton, a friend from their time at Hunwick School.

Gwen was born at Number 2 Railway Terrace in 1932 and lived there until 1944 when the family moved into Number 7 Railway Terrace because it had an extra bedroom.

She had lived at Hunwick Station until she was married in 1953, when she moved to Number 5 Stewart's Buildings. Her letter paints an interesting and very detailed 'pen-picture' of life at Hunwick Station. Gwen explains that the two blocks of houses in Railway Terrace were separated by the Station Masters House which was quite a posh house with an orchard, a big garden and a *"real WC"* noting that the other houses only had earth closets.

The road to Hunwick Station, from the village, was loose stone cobbles until the early 1950s when it was tarmacked.

In the Newcastle Evening Chronical of the 12th February 1973, nine houses, described as Hunwick Station Cottages, five of which had vacant possession, were advertised for sale. It would be safe to assume these were the nine houses in Railway Terrace. Reputedly, these houses including the Station Master's House and all associated land was bought and then sold on to private buyers.

Gwen Skelton also remembers *'a retired and rich couple, who had a car, moving into a new bungalow'*. This was probably AidaVille Cottage that had been built in 1933 and at one point was owned by G W Cable who had a Taxi business and then Mildred and Donald Newton who were coal merchants.

"On the other side of the line was the pub, some cottages and a large house at the end. There was a bungalow, a comparatively new rambling farm house owned by the Burdon's with a small farm … the ball alley and a railway docking area overgrown and hardly used was between the level crossing and the pub".

She remembered Number 2 Railway Terrace: *"it only had a small back kitchen with an earthenware slab-stone low sink (for washing and bathing), a 'copper' for boiling clothes, a high coal fire with set-pot, fired oven and a grate which took 3 buckets of coal at a time. We had cold water only. When hot water was needed for any use, it had to be kettle boiled or copper boiled. A walk-in stone larder with stone shelves was as good as a fridge."*

"The front room was sacrosanct. It had a semi tiled fireplace. A hardly sat in suite, a high bureaux bookcase and a mahogany piano. ….. Up a steep twisty staircase were 2 bedrooms. Ours looked up the field, our parents overlooked the front and the railway. When the midnight express rattled through nightly the wardrobes used to dance a jig with the vibration."

Gwen explained that bath night was the same every Friday night until she got married at twenty-one. *"First we girls went into the room. The tin bath, several kettles and ladle tin at the ready for top-ups. Rose refused to be washed in nothing but 'first water', for which privilege she paid the price of being first to bed, there being nowhere else to go! Then me, then Mam. All females up aloft, my brother next, and finally Dad who was the muckiest from his work and therefore the 5th in line for re-used water! He and Ron's job was to tidy up, empty the bath outside and rehousing the bath on its nail in the yard. 'Waste not want not' the water was not tipped out any old how, it was used to clean the whole yard before it finally got swept to the drain!"*

Chapter 6 - Village Shops and Businesses

The shaft for Hunwick Colliery was sunk in 1839, West Hunwick Colliery opened in 1854 and Rough Lea Colliery in 1858. In 1831, before the collieries opened, the village had a population of 164. A trade directory published in 1828, in addition to farmers, identified a corn miller, a brewer, a tailor, a stone mason, a vicar, a blacksmith, a victualler and a cartwright as trading in Hunwick. (William Parson, 1828) At this time, the economy was based on agriculture, with Villagers relying on the land and their own skills to find the food, clothes and anything that they needed to survive. The population of the village increased from 164 in 1831, to 2362 in 1891. It was this population explosion that created the need for the shops that would supply the food, clothes and 'things' that Villagers needed to work and survive.

In 1894, the number of different trades/occupations listed in Kelly's Trade Directory had increased to include draper and grocer, boot maker, shop keeper, librarian, lamp oil dealer, butcher, station master, blacksmith, dress maker, provisions dealer, beer retailer, coke burner, post office, butter factor, fruiter, china, glass and earthen ware dealer, joiner and engineer. Villagers could buy the majority of the everyday goods and services that they needed without moving out of the village. Except for an occasional visit to Bishop Auckland, Hunwick was more or less self-sufficient.

The opening of the mines attracted people from many areas of the country to move to Hunwick. Reduced employment opportunities in agriculture in Yorkshire and in the Cornish Tin Mines, encouraged a lot of families from those areas to move to Hunwick. They brought with them their own experience and ideas. They were all looking for a better life that they hoped employment in the coal mines would provide.

The majority of the shops were clustered around the high-density housing that had been built for miners at Lane Ends.

Inspection of census and Trade Directory entries suggest that often miners or their wives with entrepreneurial skills, opened shops or public houses as well as working in the mines. Detailed plans are not available, but it is likely that a few shops had been purpose-built to be shops, but the majority of the shops were simply larger houses that had been converted by miners who had identified an opportunity.

The Temby family is an interesting illustration of the migration of labour and entrepreneurship. James Temby, who had been born in Cambourne, was listed in trade directories, between 1894 and 1914, as running a Fruiterers at Lane Ends. He ran the shop with his wife Mary Ann Rogers, nee Condon. The 1881 census shows that James and Mary Ann shared their home with Mary Ann's mother and stepfather, Ann and Richard Condon and their sons, William James Temby (13 years), Albert (11 years) and Richard (9 years) and their daughter Matilda Jane (4 years).

William James Temby and Albert were born in Guernsey, Richard was born in Cornwall and Mary Ann was born after they moved to Hunwick. The ages and birth places of his children, shows that James Temby had lived in Guernsey before moving to Liskeard in Cornwall and then to Hunwick. Copper, tin, lead and silver were mined in Cornwall. The decline in mining in Cornwall coupled with the expansion of coal mining in Durham probably prompted James and Mary Ann's decision to move to Hunwick in the late 1870s.

James worked as a miner, while at the same time running a shop in Chapel Street with his wife Mary Ann.

When Mary Ann died in 1907, James passed the shop onto his daughter, Mary Emma Temby and her husband Thomas Fleming. Mary Emma had been born in Hunwick. They ran shop until they retired in 1945.

James's son, William James Temby, worked as a miner at Old Hunwick, West Hunwick, Rough Lea Bowden Close and in later years was a firewood dealer. His brother Albert Temby, farmed 'South View' Farm behind the Joiner's Arms. One of Albert's sons, Edward (Tiddler) was the landlord of the Joiner's Arms while his other son,

Richard, took over South View Farm. His youngest son, Richard, was recognised in his father's death notice as *'conducting a most successful business in New Zealand'.*

The list below includes over thirty shops that Villagers have identified, at some point in their 'lifetime', 1930 and later, have operated in the village. Trade Directories that were published frequently between 1850 and 1939 listed shop owners in the village. Information from these Directories has been used to confirm the information provided by Villagers and has provided information on shops that had operated before the 'living memory', of Villagers, that is before 1930.

	Owner	Business/Activity
34	Bishop Auckland Coop	Grocer
36	Police Station	
37	Hunwick Working Men's Club	
38	Edward Wilson	Joiner and Cartwright
39	Bishop Auckland Coop Butchers	Butchers, Slaughter house, General Dealer
40	Elizabeth Mary Pratt	Sweet shop
41	Joe Woods	Haulage
42	Lily Wood	Hairdresser
43	Harry Newby	Painter and decorator
44	Lilac house butchers	Butcher
45	The Two Hunters	Public House
46	Whites	General Dealer and Grocer
47	Thomas Hedley	Egg and Butter Factor
48	Hazel Robson	General Dealer then Dentist
49	John William Johnson	Blacksmith
50	A J Taylor	General Dealer
51	The Joiner's Arms	Public House
52	Ted Steele	Convenience Store and Off Licence
53	Richard Wood.	Grocers and Drapery store
54	St Paul's Church	Church
56	The Station Hotel	Public House

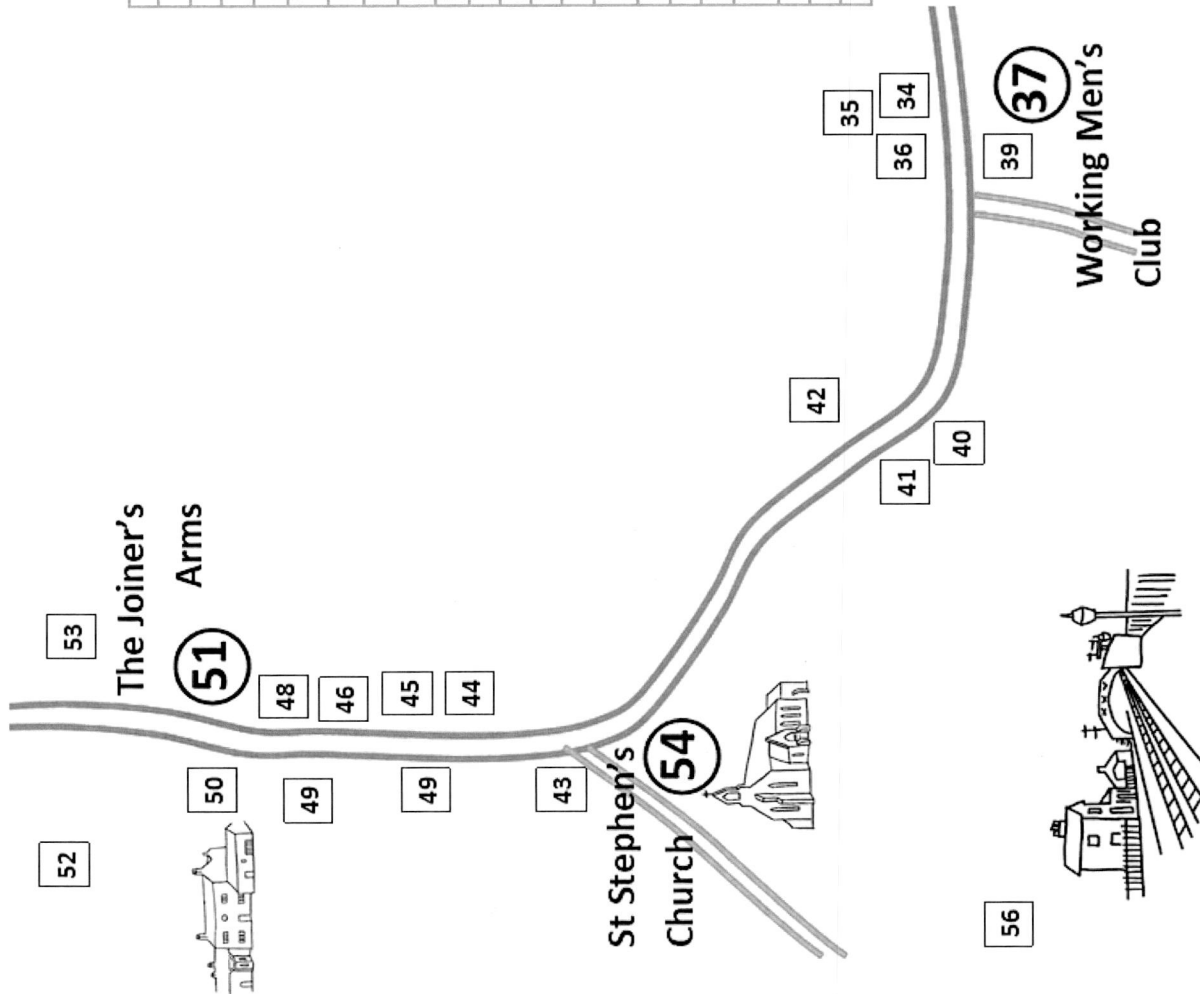

The Joiner's Arms

51

St Stephen's Church

54

Working Men's Club

37

53

52

50

49

49

48

46

45

44

43

42

41

40

39

36

35

34

56

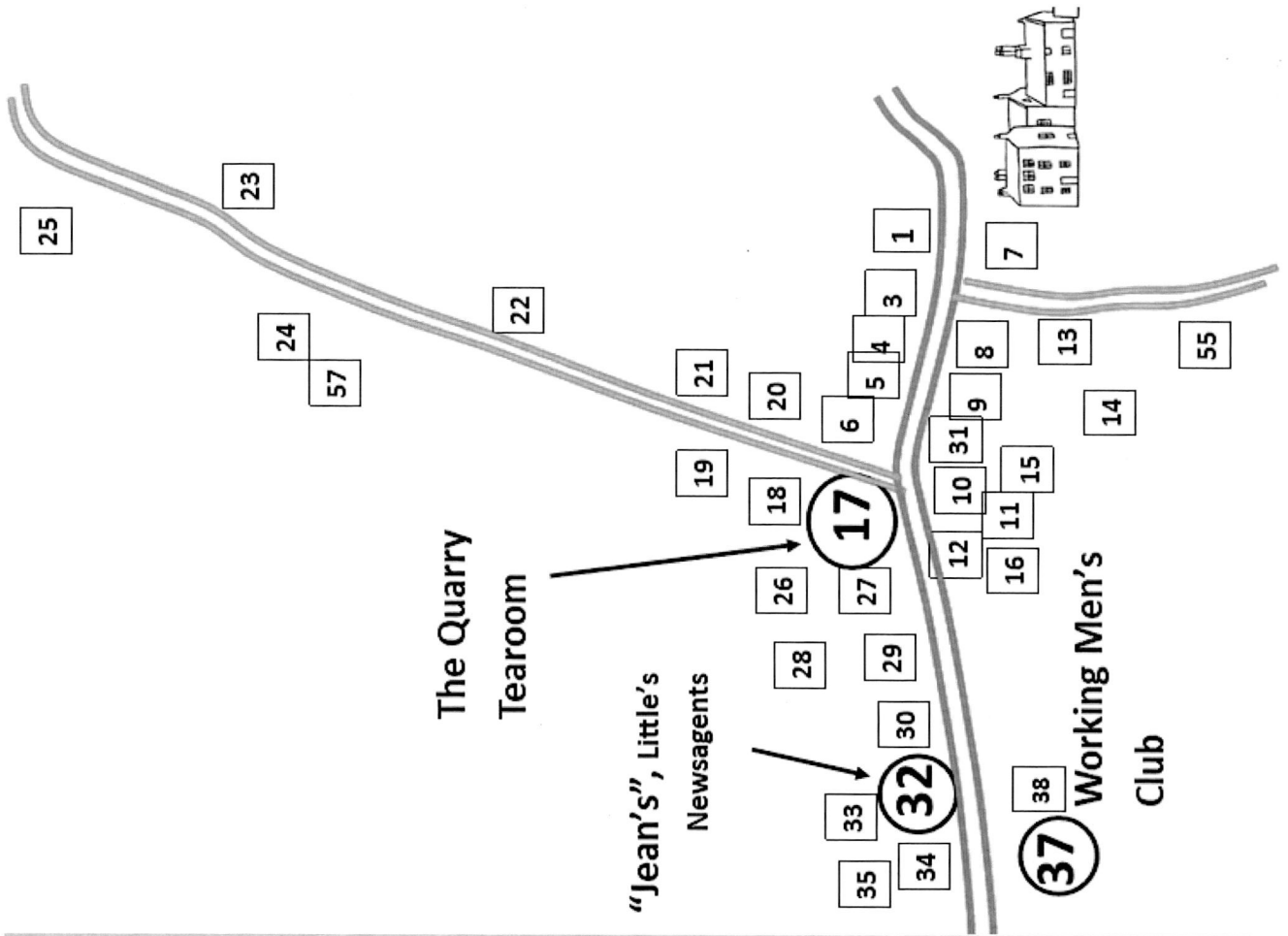

The Quarry Tearoom

"Jean's", Little's Newsagents

Working Men's Club

	Owner	Business/Activity
1	Mary Poate	Bread, Ham, Sweets & sweets
3	Mr &Mrs Barraclough	Groceries, sweets and cakes
4	Tommy Nicholson's	Hardware Store
5	William Fryer	Cobbler
6	The Helmington Inn	Public House
7	Helmington Hall Social Club	Social Club, (Green Hut)
8	Rough Lea Colliery Shop	General Store, later a Café
9	Mrs Evans	General Dealer
10	Willington Coop	General Dealers
11	Reg and Cyril Parkinson	Milkmen
12	Tom Watson	Cobbler
13	The Temperance Hall	Social Club, (Pink Hut)
14	Frank Wilson	Bus Company
15	Miss DeBurton	Wool Shop
16	George Thompson	Slaughter House
17	Wheatsheaf	Public House
18	Fred and Jean Williamson	Groceries
19	Simpson Heslop	Butcher and Slaughter house
20	Ted Sleath	Grocery and General Dealer
21	Thomas and Mary Fleming	General Dealer
22	New Connections Methodist Chapel	Chapel
23	New Hunwick Methodist Chapel	Chapel
24	The Miners Arms	Public House
25	The Brewery Inn	Public House
26	Phil Patterson	Fish and Chips
27	Robert Wood	Fruit and Veg
28	Tommy Wardle	Barber
29	Thomas Lumley,	Post Office
30	Les and Doreen Barker	Post Office
31	Mrs Raine	Post Office
32	Jean and Maurice Little	Newsagent and General Dealer
33	Stephen Whitfield	Chemist
34	Bishop Auckland Coop	Groceries
37	Hunwick Working Men's Club	
55	Rough Lea Chapel	Wesleyan Chapel
57	John Wragg	Haulage Contractor

I will attempt here to pull together the information that residents have shared with me about these shops. I will start at Lane Ends and move through the village towards the Village Green at Old Hunwick.

When coming into the village from Willington, the street that was on the right-hand side of the road as you climbed Hall Bank, was Front Street. The first shop that you would have seen was at Number 16 Front Street, opposite the turning for Rough Lea Lane. Mrs Fishlock [1], sold bread, ham, tinned fruit and sweets from this shop that had been run, in the 1930s by Miss Mary Poate.

Mrs Fishlock's son, Jack, was a Dental Technician who made dentures. Before moving back into his mother's shop, he worked from a shop towards the top of Cooperative Terrace. Villagers share memories of watching through the shop window as he fitted the teeth to the dentures.

Fishlock's, Poate's shop in Front Street

Image 0312 – by kind permission of Donald White

The Helmington Inn was at the top of Front Street [6]. After it closed as a public house in 1965, Dave Calcutt operated a Barber's Shop from the premises until 1966 when Margaret Bruce and Gretel took it over and manufactured and sold perfume. Dave Calcutt's customers were entertained by a well-spoken miner bird which enjoyed saying *"I am the Greatest"*, *"short back and sides"*

Front Street looking up to Wheatsheaf

Image 0153 - the Herbert Coates Collection

The Helmington Inn, Front Street and Cooperative Terrace looking towards Norman's Buildings

Image 0155 - the Herbert Coates Collection

and *"next please"*. It was also quite good at wolf-whistling!

Next door down, in Number 2 Front Street, William and Gwendoline Fryer [5] ran a cobblers' shop.

Below Fryer's, was Tommy Nicholson's hardware shop that also sold paraffin that would be used as lamp oil. Villagers remember the shop being referred to as *"Jane Nich's"* and that they could get the batteries from their wireless radios recharged at the shop.

Page 123

Dorothy Bromley (nee Brown) remembers, as a ten-year-old, along with friends, buying the small squares of carbide that the miners would use in their carbide miners' lamps. The miner's lamp would drip water onto the carbide. The reaction of the water on the carbide, generated the gas, that when ignited, produced an intense flame that the miners relied on to illuminate their work place.

The village children would place the carbide squares on the pavement and spit on them or drop them into puddles. They would light a 'tarry string' and use it to ignite the gas. Quite a dangerous activity!

During the war years when all metal was in short supply, Villagers remember buying repair kits from Nicholson's [4] shop that allowed them to repair holes in pots and pans.

On Front Street, between Nicholson's shop and Fishlock's shop, Mr & Mrs Barraclough [3] sold groceries, sweets and cakes. After their retirement, the shop was taken over by Mr & Mrs Kell.

Cooperative Terrace was opposite Front Street, running up from Norman's Buildings to Tom Watson's Cobblers shop [12]. William Raine and later Willington Cooperative ran a large store at the top of the Terrace [10], opposite the Helmington Inn. In the 1861 census and through until the 1911 census, William Raine was recorded as a Grocer and draper at Lane Ends.

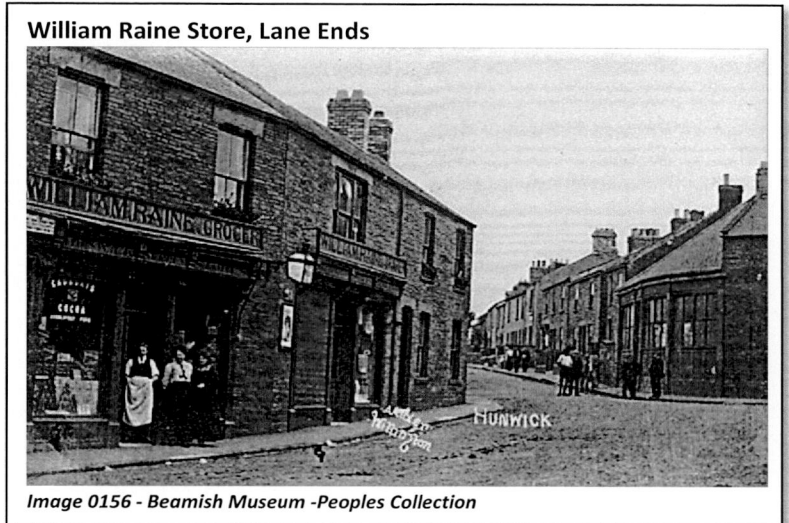

William Raine Store, Lane Ends

Image 0156 - Beamish Museum -Peoples Collection

It was listed in the 1925 and 1938 editions of Kelly's Trade Directories as the Willington Cooperative grocery store. The store must have changed ownership sometime after 1911 but before 1925.

Kelly's 1925 Directory lists Mrs William Raine as a Draper and running a post office at Lane Ends.

Willington Cooperative Store, Lane Ends

Image 0306 - Beamish Museum -Peoples Collection

This suggests that she continued to run the Post Office and Drapery after the Cooperative took over the store.

The store was double fronted with large shop windows and stables behind the store. They used a covered, horse drawn cart, with a barrel of vinegar fastened to its side, to deliver groceries.

Villagers remember Denzil Morland, the Co-op delivery man, being followed by youngsters who would compete to collect the manure that the horse deposited onto the streets.

Don White remembers Denzil explaining to him that his last delivery would be at Hunwick Station and that the horse knew it. As soon as they had delivered to the last house at Hunwick Station, the horse shot off up the road and back along to the stables as he knew he would be let out to graze.

At one time, Miss de Burton, the vicar's daughter, sold wool from part of the disused Cooperative Store [15]. At the top of Cooperative Terrace, in a building that was attached to Number 1 Cooperative Terrace was an abattoir that was operated by George Thompson [16]. Later, Reg and Cyril Parkinson ran a milk business from Number 1 Cooperative Terrace. Being regular attenders at local horse and dog race tracks, they also assisted Villagers who enjoyed a bet.

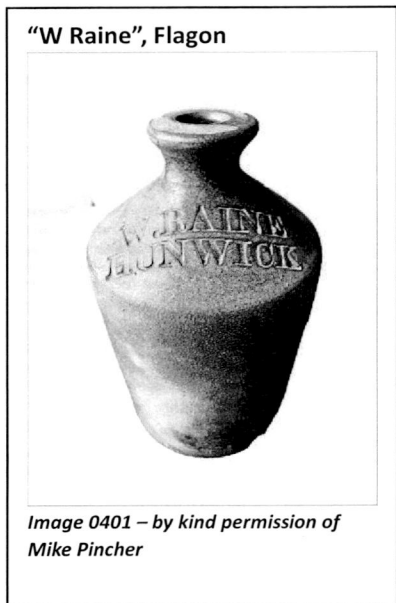

"W Raine", Flagon

Image 0401 – by kind permission of Mike Pincher

Towards the bottom of Cooperative Terrace, Mrs Evans [9] had a general dealer's shop that sold a wide range of items including sweets. Villagers remember its large shop windows and the quality of the "black Spanish" sweets. Dorothy Bromley (nee Brown), has a vivid memory of standing on the bus stand and looking up to see a calf looking down at her from an upstairs room in the shop!

Norman's Buildings, a block of four houses, are on the left, just above the road that ran down to Rough Lea. At one-point, Rough Lea Colliery shop [8] was based in Norman's Buildings. Miners, who were paid in tokens, could exchange the tokens for goods. Between 1956 and 1962, Mason's Café, Hunwick's version of an American Diner, operated in Norman's Buildings. It was close enough to Helmington Hall Community Club [7] to attract the younger Hunwickians. Number 1 Norman's Buildings was used, at one time, as a doctor's surgery.

Beyond Cooperative Terrace, opposite the Wheatsheaf Public House [17], there was a very old, stone-roofed, detached house with a single storey building attached.

Tom Watson [12] lived in the house and ran a cobblers' shop from the single storey shop. The house and shop were very close to the main road and had to be demolished in 1955 in preparation for the road to be widened.

Looking along Wear View from Lane Ends- Tom Watson's Cobblers Shop on the Left

Image 0340 - the R Alder Collection

Looking along Wear View, towards Lane Ends

Image 0341 – the Lilywhite Collection

Quarry Burn Road runs from the Quarry Tea room up to Quarry Burn.

There was general dealers' shop and a house, attached to the Wheatsheaf Inn **[18].** The shop was run by Jonti and Betty Alderson in the early 1950s. Bobby and Ellen Newell then ran it until 1959 when Annie and John Evans took over the shop. In 1969 Fred and Jean Williamson took over the shop and ran it until the early 1970s when it was demolished to allow the Oakfields site to be developed.

Number 6 Helmington Square **[19]** still exists and in 1938, was occupied by Simpson Heslop who was a butcher who operated a butcher's shop in one room of the house. He had a slaughter house to the side of the house. The slaughter house can be seen on the righthand side as you enter Oakfields Estate. Dixon Heslop took over the shop and ran it until 1964, when Doughie Barnes took over and ran it until 1974.

Heslop Butchers, Helmington Square. Pictured, Joe Heslop & Douglas Watson

Image 0159

Directly opposite, at the top of Oxford Street, Ted and Lily Sleath **[20]** ran a Grocery and general dealers shop until the early 1970s. Villagers remember in their youth, visiting the shop to buy a *'ha'penny ice lolly and blackjacks at 4 for a ha'penny.'*

They also recall Tot Sleath, Ted and Lily's son and Ozzy Rae, entertaining the village during the 1940s, 50s and 60s as DelRoy and Za Rainer. They had a mind reading, fortune telling and hypnotist act that they performed at carnivals, always travelling in a large American Buick or Jaguar car.

Moving further up Quarry Burn Road, in Number 7 Chapel Street **[21]**, was Fleming's general dealers. A double fronted shop run by Thomas and Mary Fleming along with Thomas's mother and his grandmother who was known locally as 'Little Gran'.

Thomas and Mary Fleming along with his mother and grandmother 1903

Image 0163 - by kind permission of Karen Hellens (nee Herbert)

Patterson's fish and chip shop **[26]**, of which it was said *"fed Hunwick during the second world war"*, was up a passage between the Wheatsheaf and the first house in what is now Wear View.

Villagers remember the queue extending down the passage and along the main road. They also remember the big, blue range in which the fish and chips were cooked. The fish was delivered from North Shields and was the last stop on the van's route. When the village was snow-bound the fish could not get through which caused a lot of disappointment in the village. The shop was demolished and when it was rebuilt, the passage was built over.

A few houses further along, at 4 Hunwick Lane (now Wear View), was Robert Wood's **[27]** fruiterers and green grocer shop. There was a walled garden and an orchard behind the shop which extended up behind Helmington Square.

Robert Wood's was mentioned in the 1871 and 1881 census as a Fruiter and Gardiner. The 1891 census lists William Wood, possibly his brother, as Grocer at Lane Ends.

Thomas and Mary Fleming in 1930

Image 0162 - by kind permission of Karen Hellens (nee Herbert)

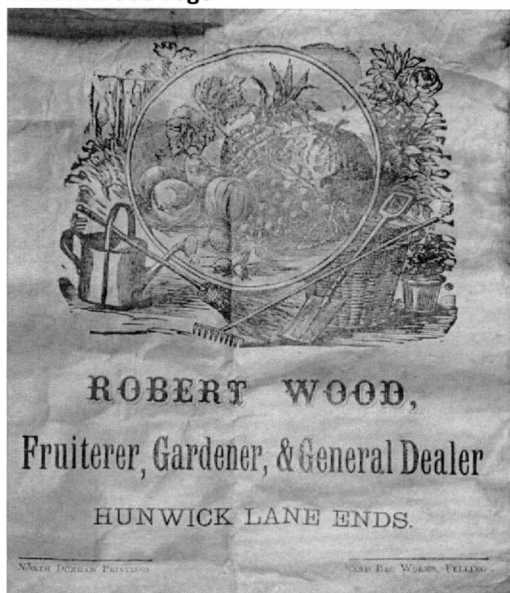

Robert Wood Logo

ROBERT WOOD,
Fruiterer, Gardener, & General Dealer
HUNWICK LANE ENDS.

Image 0165 – by kind permission of Susan Liddell

A paper bag discovered in an attic has 'Robert Wood, Fruiter, Gardener and General Dealer, Lane Ends', printed on it. Kelly's 1938 Directory lists William Wood at 4 Hunwick Lane. The orchard provided apples, cherry apples, pears, raspberries etc that were sold in the shop. Many Villagers, who in their youth had raided the orchard, still feel guilty about their actions. During the 1950s the shop and garden were run by Moralee's and in the 1960s by Mr Wager and then Mr Scott.

Tommy Wardle's barber shop [28] was in a tin or wooden shed, ahead of the gap in Wear View that allows access to West View. Villagers comment on the hairstyles of the day being determined by the size of the pudding bowl that Mr Wardle chose to use. His wife, Nurse Wardle was the district Nurse and Midwife.

A few houses further along at Number 10 Hunwick Lane,

now Wear View, was Helmington House which at one point was a Post Office [29] run by Thomas Lumley (1938) and then Mr Ford and Robert Hume-Cookson in the 1950s

Prior to being operated from Helmington House, the Post Office had been based on the opposite side of the road, run by Mrs Raine, in a shop towards the top of Cooperative Terrace [31]. When William Raine sold his shops to Willington Cooperative Society, it is possible that they retained the Post Office and Drapery business for a number of years.

Later the Post Office moved to 20 Wear View [30] where it was run by Les and Doreen Barker, then by Pat and Harry and finally by Kathryn and Peter Kay. In 2018 the Post Office was robbed by two armed men. Shortly after, the Post Office closed and was converted into a house.

The last shop standing, 'Jean's' [32], was originally the second house in Primrose Terrace. It became Wear View in 1961 when the street names were rationalised.

Jean and Maurice Little, as a young couple, bought the shop in 1961. In the early days customers were entertained by their Parrot who enjoyed talking. Anyone knocking on the shop door would be welcomed by a well-spoken "Hello". Jean has kept the village in newspapers and provisions for the past 62 years!

Tom Lumley, Hunwick Postmaster, 1938

Image 0372

Jean Little

Image 0166 – by kind permission of Robert Cunningham

Previously the shop had been owned by Tom Shaw (1940), Mr Mann (1950) and Mr Buxton (1955).

Stephen Whitfield operated a Chemist's shop [33] from the front room of the house at the southern end of Primrose Terrace, just before the gap that allowed access to West View.

The other side of this gap was the Church Institute Reading Room [34]. When the institute closed in 1935, it was run by Bishop Auckland Cooperative Society as a Grocery Store. Later it was used as surgery by the Crook Doctor's Practice. Before moving to this surgery, they had operated a surgery on Mondays, Wednesday & Friday mornings every week, in a room above Mason's Café at Norman's Buildings. The house to the rear of the Church Institute Reading Room was used by the Church Army Captain and later by the shop keeper of the Cooperative store. There was a large hut in the garden behind that was used for dances and meetings of the allotment's association etc. In Kelly's Directory, 1925, it was described as the Church Army Social Centre.

Moving south along what is now Wear View, was Highbury House [36] which was the police house for the village. The village had its own policeman from the 1860s. The 1861 census lists William Hopps as a police constable and the 1871 census lists Mark Goodman as a constable. Villagers remember Sergeant Scott and two constables policing the village and remember P C Tommy White living at Number 8 Rough lea Colliery. A newspaper report in May 1939 recognises Constable Appleby's promotion and transfer to West Hartlepool, and that Constable Jobling was taking over his duties. Details of Hunwick's Police Station were included in the Police and Constabulary Almanacks for 1945, 1950 and 1955. The Police Station was manned until late 1950s.

On the opposite side of the road was Meadow View, now Wear View. Hunwick Working Men's Club [37] purchased the first two houses in Meadow View in 1908. The ground floor of these houses was believed to be the workshop of Joseph Turnbull who was a Joiner and coffin maker.

In the 1960s, Teddy Bowes, a 'Bookies Runner', took bets using an outbuilding in the front yard of the Working men's Club. For one night a week, during 1969 and 1970, Dave Calcutt operated his barber's shop from this outbuilding which was where the ladies' toilets are today.

The single storey house next door to the Working men's Club [39] was a butcher's shop with slaughter house behind. It was not shown on the 1856 map. However, the 1861 Census records that William Wetherall, a butcher, lived in Kate's Close.

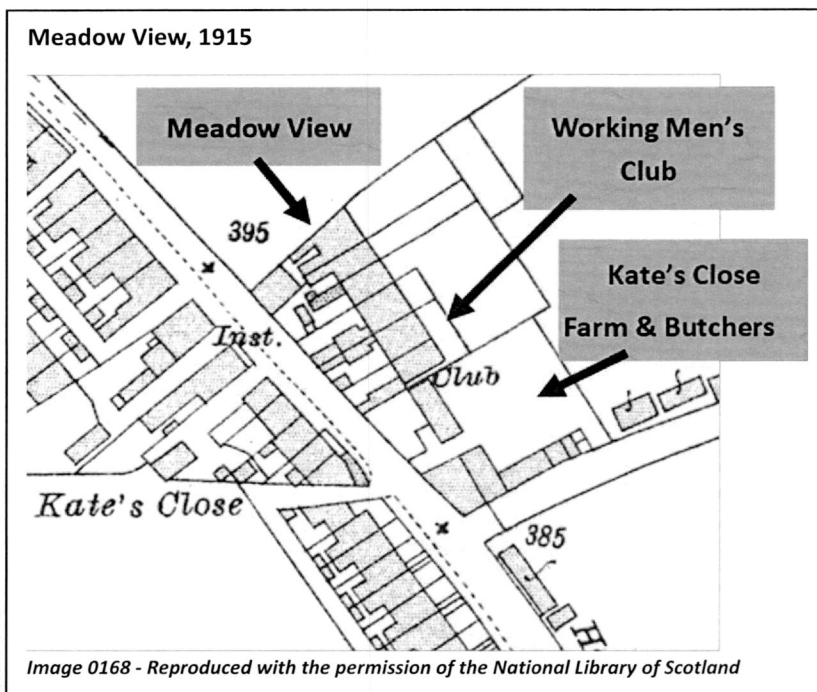

Image 0168 - Reproduced with the permission of the National Library of Scotland

Bishop Auckland Coop Butchers

Image 0167

The shop belonged to Kate's Close farm (the Poplars). The farm and shop were bought, in 1887, by William Raine who owned a shop at Lane Ends. The shop and farm were bought by Bishop Auckland Cooperative Society in 1897.

The Coop operated it as butchers until the early 1970s, when Norman Swann bought it and operated it as Grocers and General

Dealers until the 1980s when Wilf and Marjorie Sanderson took over shop and later converted into a house.

Moving along towards the Church, on the left-hand side of the road, opposite Belle Vue Terrace, was Church Lane. A sweet shop is listed in Kelly's 1938 Trade Directory, being run by Mrs Emma Sidgewick [40] in Number 8 Church Lane. Later it was run by Elizabeth Mary Pratt who Villagers remember sold single cigarettes. In 1860 George Ward, a Fried Fish Dealer, was listed at Number 12 Church Lane.

Joe Wood and his daughter Lilly Wood lived at Number 11 Belle Vue Terrace and then Belgrade House that was between Heseldene Terrace and Belle Vue Terrace.

At the southern end of Belle Vue Terrace, towards the rear of a large garden, there was a brown tin single storey shed from which Lily Wood operated a very popular hairdressing business [42].

On the opposite side of the road, at the end of Church Lane, her father, Joe Wood, operated a motor haulage business [41] from his garage. He fuelled his waggons from a petrol tank and pump that was in the garden at the end of Belle Vue. (Kelly's Directory, 1938)

Continuing up through the village, past the Church, North View is on the left-hand side of the road with Lilac House standing in an elevated position on the right-hand side.

During the 1950s and 60s, Harry Newby [43] operated his painting and decorating business from the Number 1 North View which started off as small single storey cottage before being converted to a garage and later to a house.

Above Lilac House was the Two Bay Horses Public House [45] that was the first house in South View. The Heslop family, who at one time owned Lilac House, operated a Butcher's shop [44] from a building that was attached to the eastern side of The Two Bay Horses. In the 1950s, Whites operated a general dealer and grocery shop in the front room of Number 2 South View.

Lily Wood and her Hairdressers Hut

Image 0169

On the opposite side of the road, Thomas Hedley [47] operated an egg, butter and cheese merchants' business from Raby House. During the Second World War when eggs were rationed, local farmers were not allowed to sell directly to the public. They had to sell to a buyer who was licenced by the Egg Marketing Board.

Thomas Hedley bought eggs, butter and cheese from the farmers and sold them to local shops who would then sell them to the general public. He travelled to farms across Durham, North Yorkshire and into Cumbria and in addition to his storehouse in Raby House Quarry, also had a warehouse in Bishop Auckland.

Further up, on the opposite side of the road, Hazel Robson and Bernie ran a General Dealers from Number 7 South View [48]. In the 1980s Lesley Richardson took over the shop. In the late 1980s David Cannon set up and ran his Dentist's Surgery on the first floor and had a waiting room on the ground floor of the house.

Opposite the Joiner's Arms, in Number 24 North View, was Agnes Jane Taylor's general dealers and grocery shop [50]. Agnes Jane Buxton, Agnes Smith's grandmother, was the eldest of 12 children who moved into the village from Swaledale. She married Samuel Taylor and the family including Agnes and her mother, Lizzy Bourne ran the shop until it closed in 1974.

This was quite a large store with store house to the side and rear. It sold a vast array of goods including: bacon, casks of vinegar, greaseproof paper, tinned stuff, fireworks, bread, cream cakes, cheese, eggs, cigarettes, sewing essentials etc.

Villagers remember the Beechnut and Wrigley chewing gum machines dispensing 4 tablets for a penny; ice lolly's being made in the shop; the jars of sweets lining the walls sold in paper cones; being tasked to return glass pop bottles and soda siphons in order to collect the bottle deposit and the wide range of self-help medicines including liver salts etc that were stocked. Audra Turner Golightly considered it to be *"the best shop in the village"* and the *"Beamish sweet shop reminds me of Lizzy's"*.

A J Taylor – General Dealers - 1963

Image 0172 – (Wally Smith, Digital Village Project 2006)

Higher up in the village, above the Joiners Arms, Richard Wood operated a Grocers and Drapery store [53] in what is now Woodbine House. Originally it was two properties, a house and a shop. The 1881 census shows Richard Wood running a Grocery store with a 1906 Trade Directory listing him as running a Grocery and Drapery store.

The window display in the photograph below confirms that the shop sold: underwear, clothes, household items, brushes, cleaners, packets of dry food, flour, sugar, bottled drinks, confectionery in addition to fruit and vegetables.

Richard Wood was the only one to trade from the shop and when he retired the shop was converted to a house.

There was a stable behind the house suggesting that he might have run a delivery service.

Woodbine House, R Wood Grocers and Drapery store

Image 0171 – by kind permission of Verna Rutter

In 1979, Ted and Barbera Steele opened a Convenience Store and Off Licence in Number 4 The Green [52]. The shop traded until 1984.

During the late 1950s and 1960s, Tommy and Jenny James, who also had a shop and cafe in Willington, ran a general dealers shop in Holme Dene. The shop was converted to a Community Centre in 1973.

Hunwick Green Store, 1983

Image 0400 - by kind permission of Dave Calcutt

Chapter 7 - Brewing and the Public Houses

We know from the Parsons and White Trade Directory, that in 1828, the Two Hunters Inn, that later became the Two Bay Horses, was the only Public House in the village and that Nicholas Welsh was the landlord. The same source confirms that a Brewery was operating at Quarry Burn and that Thomas Graham was the brewer. (William Parson, 1828)

Public Houses, as well as supplying alcoholic drinks and a place to socialise away from cramped and unsanitary housing, were also used for political and social gatherings, auctions and inquests. Dorothy Bromley (nee Brown) still remembers seeing, as a young girl, the dead body of a man who had drowned in the reservoir at West Hunwick Colliery, being wheeled through the village on an open-cart and left in the backyard of the Helmington Inn.

As the Temperance and Tea-Total Movements became influential in the village, they encouraged the community to hold all meetings and events away from the public houses. Harold Heslop explains that *"for any special non-religious occasions, such as a concert or a political meeting, the Temperance Hall was used."*. (Heslop, 1987)

Quarry Burn Brewery

Greenwood's 1818 map shows a building on what we know was the site of the brewery at Quarry Burn. An 1818 advertisement described the Quarry Burn Brewery as: *"most desirable and complete"* and *"the only brewery between the market towns of Bishop Auckland, Durham and Wolsingham"*. (Benninson)

The population of the village in 1831, before the collieries opened, was 164. For it to be viable to operate a Brewery at Quarry Burn in the early 1800s, there must have been something special about its location.

The brewing process starts when barley is soaked in water allowing germination to begin. The grains are then spread on the 'malting' floor, and turned occasionally as germination takes place. After a week or so, the part-germinated grains are dried in a kiln and mixed with hot water in a large, cylindrical vessel. It is then boiled with hops, allowed to cool before yeast is added and the mixture left to ferment.

In addition to large quantities of water, this process requires some way of heating, cooling, moving and storing large volumes of liquids. It would require a lot of space for the storage of the grain and the beer that had been brewed (barrels/bottles). It

Quarry Burn Brewery Site - 1857

Reproduced with the permission of the National Library of Scotland

would need a large space for the 'malting floor' and for all the large vessels required. The design of the buildings would need to allow the rooms to be ventilated and the temperature controlled.

Perhaps it was the quality and availability of the water and that coal could be found near the surface, that made the Brewery viable.

The 1761 enclosure map identifies the fields that were adjacent to the Brewery as *"Thomas Graham's enclosures"*. This suggests that before he opened the Brewery, he had run a farm on the site. Thomas Graham, in his will written in 1801. (Durham Probate Records DPR 1/1/1801/gb/1) left his estate to his grandson, Thomas Graham. An 1806 Map confirms that Thomas Graham owned the land at Quarry Burn and that there was a substantial property on the site of the Brewery. (The_Common_Room, NEIMME/WAT/32/30, 1806) (The_Common_Room, NEIMME/WAT/32/31, 1843)

The 1841 census list Thomas Graham, probably the grandson, living at the Brewery. Blackett explains that he had *"imported a traditional brewer of fine ales from Scotland".* (Blackett, 1980) Thomas Graham died in 1849 leaving the Brewery and farm to his son Robert Graham.

The 1871 census records Bertram Bulmer as a Brewer and a farmer. By 1879 he is just listed as a Brewer. (Ref Post Office Directory, 1879)

The Brewery was for sale again in 1894 when it included *"a malthouse, two cottages, stables, Inn and 25 acres".* (Benninson) An advertisement in Durham Advertiser 6th April 1894, offered, to let, a desirable farm, buildings and stack yard comprising 25 acres divided into 4 fields and a garth, offered by Bertram Bulmer. It describes the house as having 4 bedrooms, servants' rooms and an excellent cellar. Bertram Bulmer was retiring and leaving the district. Interestingly, in March 1897, the brewery fittings including coppers, vats, pumps and a 3HP steam engine, were auctioned by Mr J Pallister, an Auctioneer from Crook. This confirms that the Brewery had ceased trading by 1897.

The 1897 OS map identifies the Brewery as 'Quarry Burn House'.

Harold Heslop, when writing of his experience of living in Hunwick from his birth in 1898, until he left the village in 1911, mentions a relative who had moved to; *'a beautiful old house that had once belonged to the owner of Quarry Burn Brewery.'*

The front of the Old Brewery - 1983

Image 0304 - by kind permission of Dave Calcutt

The rear of the Old Brewery – 1983

Image 0302 - by kind permission of Dave Calcutt

Villagers reminisce about visiting the Heslop sisters, Mary, Margaret and Elizabeth, at Quarry Burn House in the 1950s,

The Public Houses

By 1861, when the population of the village had increased to 1203, there were seven public houses in the village:

- The Miners Arms [New Hunwick];

- The Helmington Inn [Front Street, Lane Ends];

- The Wheat Sheaf (the Quarry Tea Room) [Wear View];

- The Two Hunters (The Two Bay Horses) [South View];

- The Joiners Arms [South View];

- The Station Hotel (the Monkey) [Hunwick Station].

- The Brewer's Inn [Brewery Inn] (not listed in the 1861 directory but known to exist from 1848)

(Morris_Harriso_and_Co_Commercial_Directory, 1861)

There were other Public Houses within easy walking distance of the village. These included: The Drovers' Inn (Pixley Hill), the Hare and Hounds (Rumby Hill), the Red Lion (North Bitchburn), the Joiner's Arms (Sunny brow) and the Fox and Hounds Inn at Newfield.

In 1985, when only the Wheatsheaf, the Joiner's Arms and the Working Men's Club were still operating in the village, Brabban Bellerby, converted the Ginn Mill at Hunwick Hall Farm into a Public House.

It was a popular pub and restaurant until it closed in 2005 after which it was converted into a private house. In 1992, Brabban applied for planning permission for an 18-hole Golf course with a club house on Station Road just before the road that leads to the Equestrian Centre.

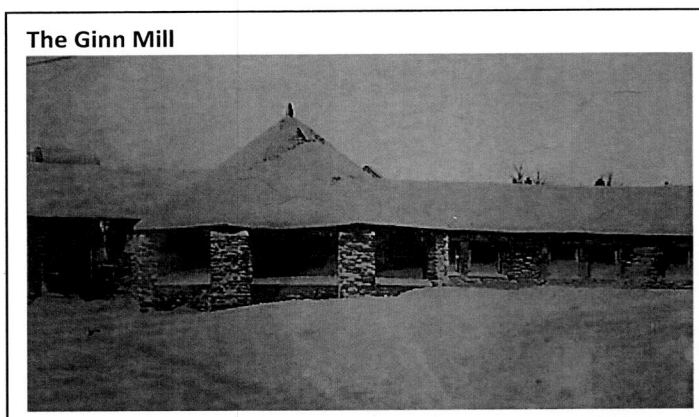

The Ginn Mill

The Brewer's Inn (The Brewery Inn)

The 1857 OS Map identifies the Brewery Inn, not on the site of the Brewery, but on the site of the Public House that was known locally, as the 'Quarry Burn'

In 1848, the Brewer's Inn was owned by Robert Graham. The 1873 Post Office Directory, lists the landlord as Benjamin Crack.

By 1911 its name had been changed to the Brewery Inn. It closed as a public house and was bought for conversion to a private house in 1961.

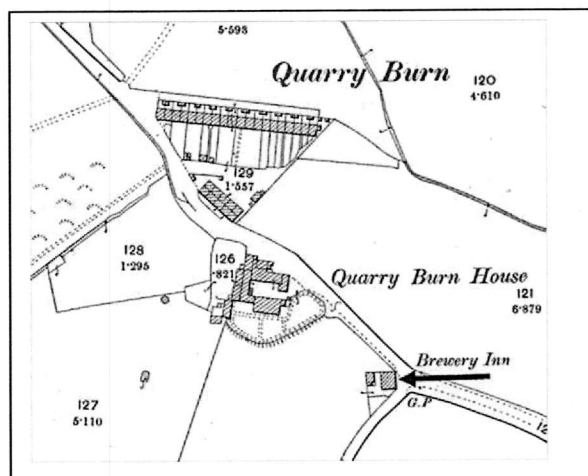

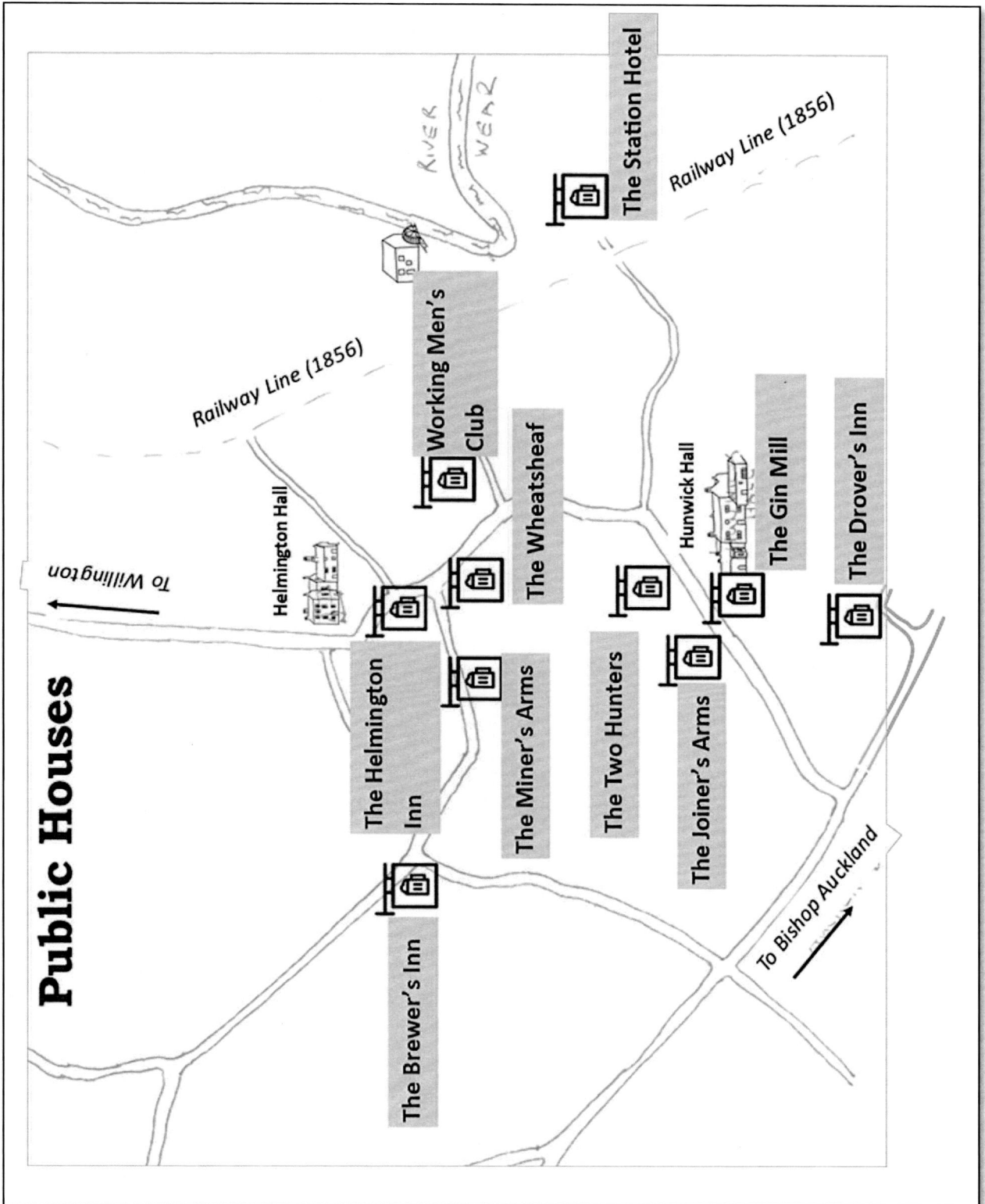

Public Houses

Railway Line (1856)

Railway Line (1856)

The Station Hotel

Working Men's Club

The Wheatsheaf

The Gin Mill

The Drover's Inn

Helmington Hall

Hunwick Hall

To Willington

The Helmington Inn

The Miner's Arms

The Two Hunters

The Joiner's Arms

The Brewer's Inn

To Bishop Auckland

RIVER WEAR

Looking towards The Brewery Inn and Quarry Burn Row

Image 0343 - the Herbert Coates Collection

The Brewery Inn -circa 1900

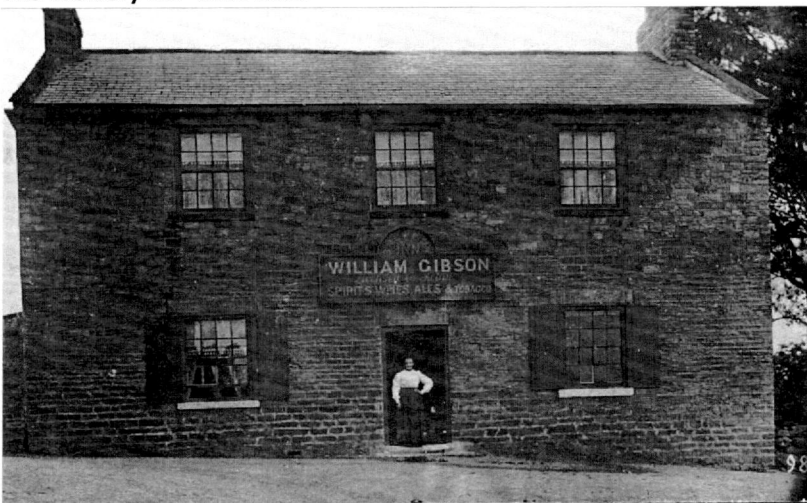

Image 0405- by kind permission of John Hughes

Landlords

1848 - owned Robert Graham	1900 - Robert Bowes owned by North Eastern Brewery	1921 - William Gibson - Kelly's
1856 - Charlton Morgan		1925 - Mary Ann Gibson
1864 – Ann Graham, Whellan's	1902 - George Dawson- Kelly's	1929 - John Edgar
1867 - Richard Bowser - owned by Ann Graham	1910 - William Gibson	1934 - James Rowell
1872 - Benjamin Crack - owned William Farrow	1911 - William Gibson - Census,	1935 - S J Slade – Kelly's
1875 - Robert Berkeley	1914 - William Gibson- Kelly's	1938 - S Slade – Kelly's
1890 - Robert Bowes	1921 - William Gibson	1961 - Marley Cotterel - Closed

The Two Hunters (Two Bay Horses)

In Pearson & White's, 1828 trade directory The Two Hunters is listed as a public house. It is shown on the 1856 OS map. It was built in the style of a Coaching Inn with a cellar. and stables to the rear

In July 1899, we know that the Two Bay Horses Inn was undergoing *'extensive alterations'* as that was given, by the landlord, Robert Crawford, as the reason that he had *"by mistake, mixed a quantity of brandy and whiskey together and then added water to the measure required for whiskey"*. (Journal)

The three cottages, now Numbers 1a -5 South View, above the Two Hunters Public House, had been built by 1856. The Public House had a cellar, stabling for two horses and a hay loft, confirming that it had been purpose built as an Inn. It was owned by Plew's Brewery from 1860 until 1923 when the brewery was bought by Cameron's Brewery.

At some point it was renamed as the Two Bay Horses.

The Two Hunters

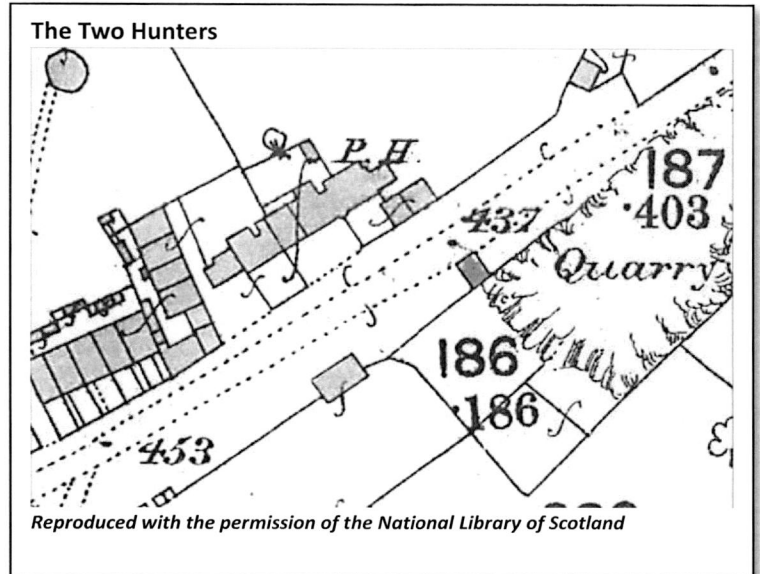

Reproduced with the permission of the National Library of Scotland

The Two Bay Horses

Image 0176 – by kind permission of Dave Calcutt

Landlords		
1828 - Nicholas Welsh - Pearson & White directory	1861 - Margaret Robson 67yrs – Victualler + Margaret Robson 25	1899 - Robert Crawford
1851 - Margaret Robson (Bay Horses) – Haggar's directory	1871 - Thomas Buckley, quarryman and Inn keeper - census	1902 - Michael Tennick - Kelly's
1860 - To Let by Plews and Co, a Darlington based brewery	1873 - Thomas Buckley - PO Dir	1923 - sold by Plews and son to Camerons Brewery
1864 – Joseph Robson, Victualler and builder	1894 - J G Richardson of the Two Hunters as a manufacturer of bricks and all kinds of tiles at Hunwick Station Brick Works – Kelly's	1925 - Joseph Griffiths
		1938 - Chas Higgins - Kelly's
		Early 1950s - Alan Johnson
		1960s - closed

Alan Johnson, a village builder, ran the Two Bay Horses in the early 1950s, moving out of the pub in 1956. Shortly after, it closed as a public house and stood empty for a number of years. Alan bought it in 1965 and converted it into two private houses.

The Wheatsheaf Inn

The Wheatsheaf Inn is shown on the 1856 Ordnance Survey Map.

On the 4th November 1853, the Public House, out-houses, offices and the yard in the occupation of Mary Etherington, were advertised for sale, in the Durham Chronicle.

A second Lot, comprised of a dwelling house and shop with yard, out offices adjoining the Public House and a third Lot comprised of four dwelling houses, out offices adjoining the second lot.

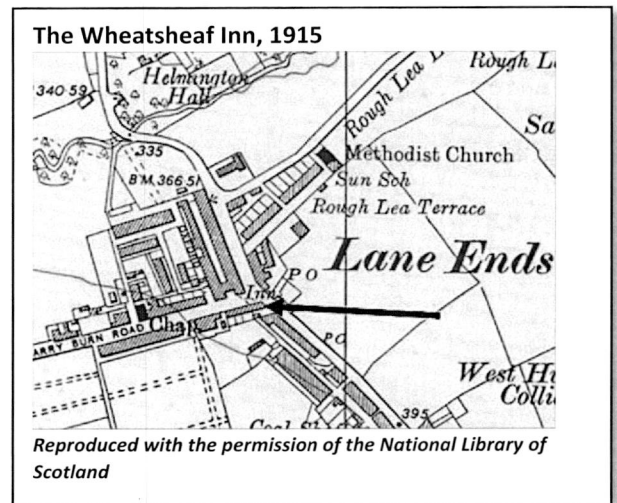

The Wheatsheaf Inn, 1915

Reproduced with the permission of the National Library of Scotland

The Wheatsheaf Inn, 1983

Image 0175 - by kind permission of Dave Calcutt

Harold Heslop explains that: *'liquid refreshments could be obtained at the Wheatsheaf Inn, where Jack Richardson rehearsed his brass band'* (Heslop, 1987)

Landlords		
1851 - John Heatherington – Haggar's	1894 - Isabella Mary Scurrah – Kelly's	1970s – Bobby & Margarita Dodds
1853 - Mary Etherington	1902 - Robert Vickers – Kelly's	1976-86 Dick and Margaret Watson
1856 - James Gibbons – Whellan's	1906 - Robert Vickers – Kelly's	Cliffy owens
1864 – James Gibson	1914 - William Robson – Kelly's	1985 -1987 Keith & Glynis Butler
1861 - Edward Race – Kelly's	1921 - William Robson – Kelly's	- Keith and Shirley Dufton
1864 - Edward Race – Slater's	1924 - William Robson – Kelly's	1994 Elaine -
1871 - Henry Storey	1938 - John R Woodward – Kelly's	1995 - Judith & Geoff Sains
1873 - Henry Storey - PO Dir	1939 – Jack Parkinson	2002 - Jill Fullerton
1879 - George Fell – PO Dir	1950 -60s - Winnie & Tucker Brown (Hunter)	2003 - Martin and Julie Bell

The Wheatsheaf was listed in the Good Beer Guide in 1984 and was recognised for "keeping a good pint of Cameron's Strongarm".

David Bennett recalled: *"one night a bus load came for Tuesday night CIU. You could tell by their fine sportsman-like physiques that they were no strangers to a pint or two…. They ordered a round and were 'wor, this is nice like'. There were maybe six or seven in the round. They didn't finish the round before the last one fell over. They had to be hoovered up and poured back on to the bus."*

In 1995 Judith and Geoff Sains took over and renamed it the Quarry Burn, it was then taken over by Keith and Shirley Dufton who in, 1999, removed the 'Burn' and renamed it The Quarry. Jill Fullerton ran it for a brief period in 2002 before Martin and Julie Bell took it over in 2003 and created the Quarry Tea House in 2021.

The Joiner's Arms

The house which became the Joiner's Arms, is shown on the 1856 OS map but it is not identified as a Public House. However, in a Trade Directory published in 1856, James Gibbons is identified as the Landlord of the Joiner's Arms. (Whellan, 1856) In 1864, John Robson was listed as the Landlord of the Joiner's Arms. (Slaters)

At this time, John Robson also owned Quarry Farm.

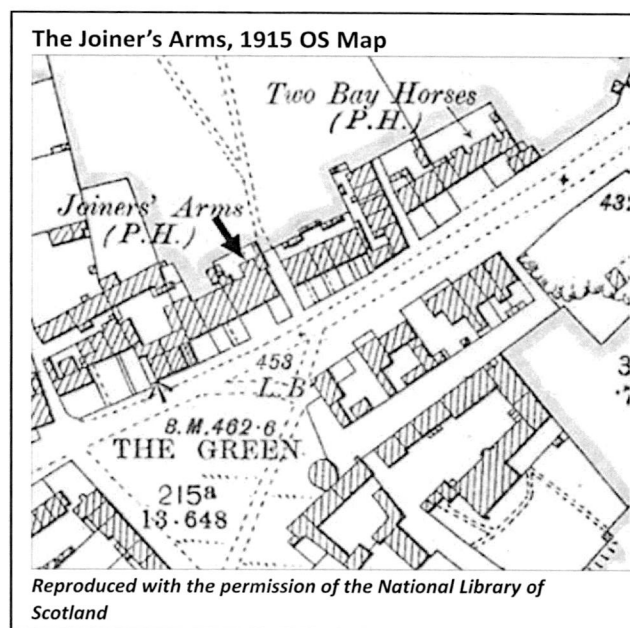

The Joiner's Arms, 1915 OS Map

Reproduced with the permission of the National Library of Scotland

The Joiner's Arms 1911

Image 0178 – by kind permission of Mo Butler

Records of the Licenced Victuallers show Samuel Goy as the Licensee in 1879. However, the 1873 Post Office directory lists him, six years earlier, against the Joiner's Arms. The 1871 census, records him as a coke drawer with no mention of being an Inn Keeper. The 1881 census lists him as a colliery labourer and by 1891 he is listed as a coke drawer aged 55 yrs.

David Smith is recorded as the Licensee in 1890 and Kelly's Trade Directory shows that he was still the landlord in 1894.

The 1902 directory lists Edward Nicholson as the landlord. On the 20 September 1894, The North Star (Darlington), reported that the Joiner's Arms had been sold

The Joiner's Arms, South View and Cross Row, circa 1900

Image 0090 - the Herbert Coates Collection

The Joiner's Arms, 1940s

Image 0406 - (Wally Smith, Digital Village Project 2006)

to Mr Murray of Blackhill, a Spirit Merchant, for £480. Moor's Brewery of Blackhill, under the control of Richard Murray was included in the amalgamation between the North Eastern Breweries and Vaux that took place in 1927. (Benninson)

John Henry Watson took over the Licence in 1908 when the building was owned by North Eastern Breweries.

The Census lists him as the Innkeeper at the Joiner's Arms in 1911 with the Licence being taken over by Mathew Dickinson Edgar in 1914.

The Licence was held by John Edmund Fawcett in 1920, by Janet Mackenzie Dowson in 1922 and Joseph Miller in 1923.

Henry Wright took over the License of Joiners Arms on the 7th of July 1924. In May 1935, he was convicted of drunkenness and fined 20 shillings or 14 months imprisonment. His wife Mary Anne Wright, known locally as 'Ma Wright', took over the licence and held it until 1948. Betty Thompson remembered that it was only after 'Ma' Wright's son, Alan, had begun courting, that women were allowed in to the back room of the pub. Previously it had been a male only Public House.

Edward (Tiddler) Temby was married to Hilda, who was the daughter of Henry and Mary Anne Wright. He took on the licence in 1948.

Until the 1940s, Albert Temby, Tiddler's father, had farmed 'South View' Farm, which was directly behind the Joiner's and included the fields upon which Quarry Farm Close is now built and those running up behind

Garden View. Tiddler's brother, Richard Temby took over the farm and also ran a milk and grocery delivery business.

Ian Richardson (Snr) took over the Vaux tenancy of the Joiner's Arms on decimalisation day, 15th February 1971. The Joiner's became a free-house in 1988 when Ian and Anne bought the business and building. Ian Richardson (Jnr) took over the Licence in 2002. (Ref John Cunningham, Joiner's Arms Licensees)

The Station Hotel

The Station Hotel, sometimes referred to as the Railway Hotel, was close to Hunwick Colliery and Hunwick Brick Works, at Hunwick Station. It was better known as the 'Monkey'. It was not marked on the 1856 map but the 1871 census records John Richardson as the landlord.

An article in the Northern Echo 27 Feb 1900, reporting on a Licencing Prosecution, explains that the *"Hunwick Station Hotel is known locally as the 'Monkey' "*.

There are many theories as to how it got its name, ranging from being named after a nearby drift mine that required miners to be as agile as a monkey, to being named after a 'hod' that workers in the adjacent brickyard used to carry bricks.

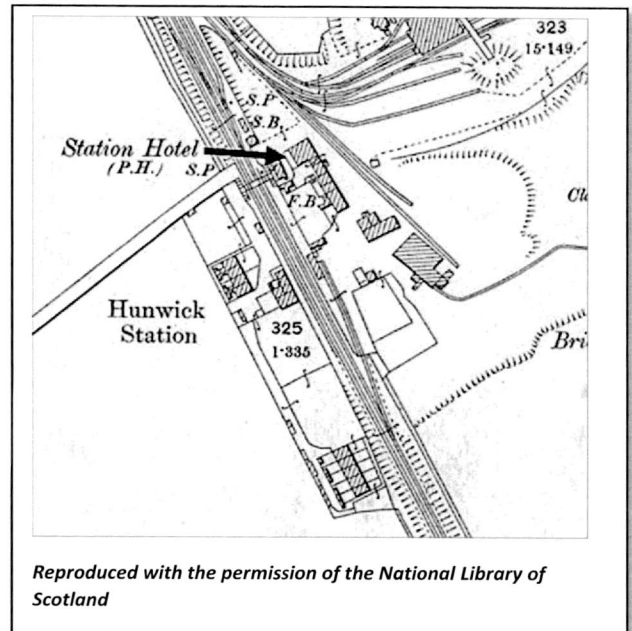

Reproduced with the permission of the National Library of Scotland

> *"Outside at the back was a crescent-shaped stairwell, about ten feet high," said Val. "When my mother was two, and her mother was pregnant with her sister, she got out onto the stairwell. Her mother panicked, ran out to grab her but fell down the steps herself, and James told my mother she was 'a little monkey'."*
>
> *James was so proud of his little monkey grand-daughter that he renamed his pub after her. "*
>
> (Echo, Oct 2021)

The Station Hotel Garden

Image 0181– (Catherine Finlinson, Digital Village Project 2006)

The Northern Echo thought that it had solved the mystery when a reader wrote to them on the topic in 2021. The reader's great-grandparents, James and Hannah Etherington, had run the Station Hotel in the 1880s:

In 1954, Harry Callow who had previously run the Big Jug Public House in Durham, along with his 80-year-old Mother who always dressed in the manner of Queen Victoria, took over the Station Hotel. It developed a reputation as an open-all-hours establishment.

Villagers talk fondly of the pub and are always ready to share stories of lock-ins and the large brass cash register that you were expected to operate yourself if Harry had gone to bed or had gone to Darlington.

> *"I came to Hunwick station and the inn. It was now after eight o'clock. I knocked at the door of the inn, but nobody came. Then I looked at the sign, and read " The Station Hotel. " But where was the Monkey?"* (Mothersole, 1927)

It was renamed the 'New Monkey' after it had been sold via a public auction in September 1972.

It was a very popular public house, that, pre-breathalyser, people were prepared drive to from all over the county. It had a dance floor in the cellar and a beer garden.

Villagers remember a fire at the pub in 1984. It was classed as a minor fire but two fire engines racing down Station Road attracted a lot of attention! It closed in 2002

The Station Hotel - 1983

Image 0180 – (Catherine Finlinson, Digital Village Project 2006)

Landlords		
1871 - John Richardson - census 1873 - John Richardson (Railway Hotel) - PO Dir, 1879 - John Richardson (Railway Hotel) & brick and tile maker, 1882 - (Feb) Liquidation – George Hall – station hotel, and brick manufacturer, Mary Hall, Hunwick Station Brick Works 1887 - James and Hannah Etherington	1894 - Mary Hall – Kelly's, 1900 - Mary Hall – owned by Cameron's Brewery 1902 - John Richardson - Kelly's, 1906 - John Richardson – Kelly's 1921 - John Parkinson – Kelly's 1929 - Joseph Miller, (reported in 1934, on his death, that he had owned for 5 years - killed by passenger train)	1938 – Joseph Wood - Kelly's 1954 - Harry Callow 1972 - Public Auction 1972 – Gordon Williamson? 1970s - Joyce Nicholson and Jack Davison 1980s - Lindsay 1987- Richie and Chris Lambert (

Miner's Arms

The 1857 OS Map shows the Miner's Arms but does not identify it as a Public House.

The 1841 census shows John English, a fifty-year-old coal miner, living at New Hunwick with his forty-year-old wife Mary

Whellan's 1856 Directory lists, Mary English, running a beer-house. The 1858 Post Office Directory lists her as a beer retailer. By 1864, Whellan's Directory lists her as the victualler of the Miner's Arms.

This would suggest that the Miner's Arms began trading in 1857.

The 1871 Census records Mary English(71yrs) as running a public house and being a farmer of 3 acres of grass.

The last mention, that I can find, of the Miner's Arms was in Kelly's, 1938 Trade Directory.

The Miner's Arms – 1898 Map

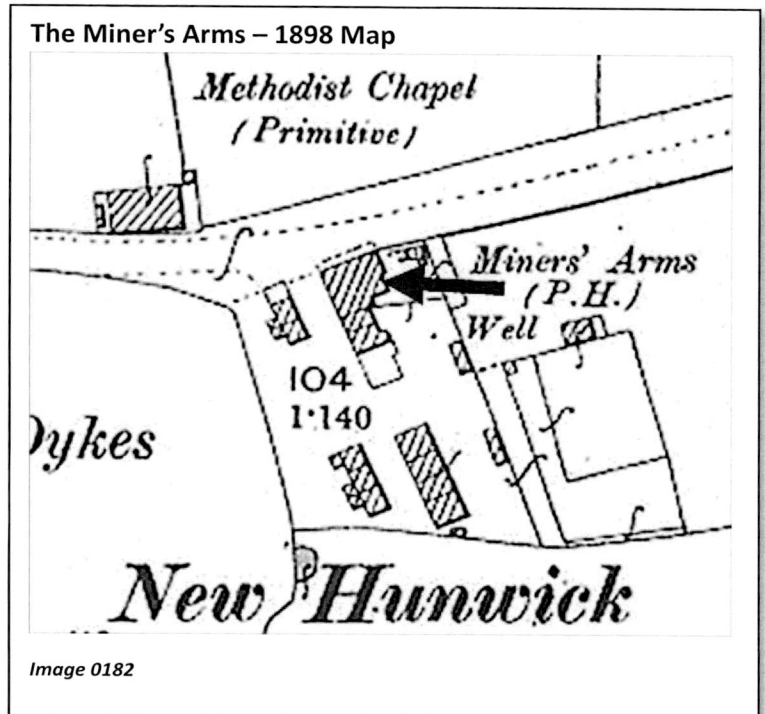

Image 0182

The Miner's Arms - *Miners parading the Rough Lea banner early 1900s*

Image 0183 – (Betty Dunn, Digital Village Project 2006)

Landlords		
1864 – Mary English	1902 - Jerimiah Bland – Kelly's,	1914 - Daniel Yates - Kelly's
1871 - Mary English public house and 3 acres	1902 - Edward English – Kelly's	1921 - Daniel Yates – Kelly's
1873 - Mary English - PO Directory	1906 - Joe Pearson - Kelly's	1924 – Daniel Yates - Kelly's
1879 - John Alderson - PO Directory	1910 - John Hewitson – Kelly's	1938 – Daniel Yates - Kelly's
1901 - Jerimiah Bland – coal hewer and Inn keeper	1911 - Mr Stephenson	

The Helmington Inn

The Helmington Inn is not shown on the 1856 OS map, however, Parliamentary records for a society which was established in 1856, Richard's Benevolent Lodge, lists the Helmington Inn as its registered office.

This would suggest that it was built after the survey but before the map was printed in 1856. The 1858 Post Office Trade Directory list Edward Waugh as the Landlord.

It was known locally as the 'Corner End' and was reputedly the first pub in the village to sell toasted sandwiches.

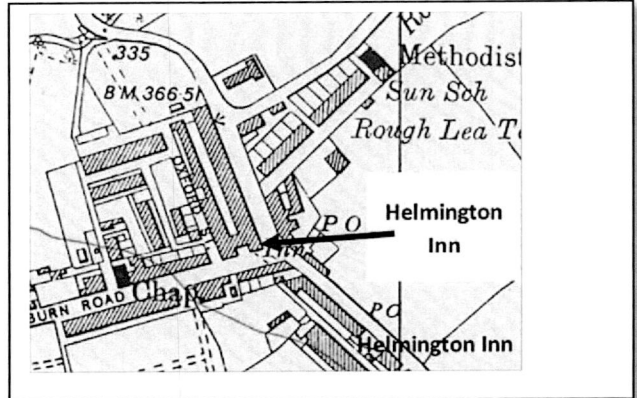

The Helmington Inn – *Chapel Street*

Image 0161 – by kind permission of Robert Cunningham

The Roman Well was, reputedly, in its back yard and the cellar was cold enough to use as fridge.

After it closed as a public house in 1965, Dave Calcutt ran a Barber's Shop from the premises until 1966 when Margaret Bruce took over and manufactured perfume in the building.

The Helmington Inn, *Front Street*

Image 0134 – The Herbert Coates Collection

Landlords		
1858 – Edward Waugh - PO Dir	1894 - William Thomas Thompson	1921 - Joseph Dowson
1864 – Edward Waugh – Whellan's, Joiner and Victualler	1890 - Arthur Bowman	1925 - John Parkinson
	1902 - Isabell White - Kelly's	1938 - Gamaliel Savage - Kelly's
1873 - Mary Waugh - PO Dir	1906 - Treddenick Raine	1951 - Gamaliel Savage - Kelly's
1879 - Mrs Mary Waugh	1914 - John Parkinson - Kelly's	

The Drover's Inn – Pixley Hill

The Drover's Inn is shown on the 1857 OS Map alongside the main road at Pixley Hill.

In an 1898 newspaper article it was reported that the public house was owned by Plews and Company Brewery and it was described as "very old". (Ref Middlesbrough Gazette)

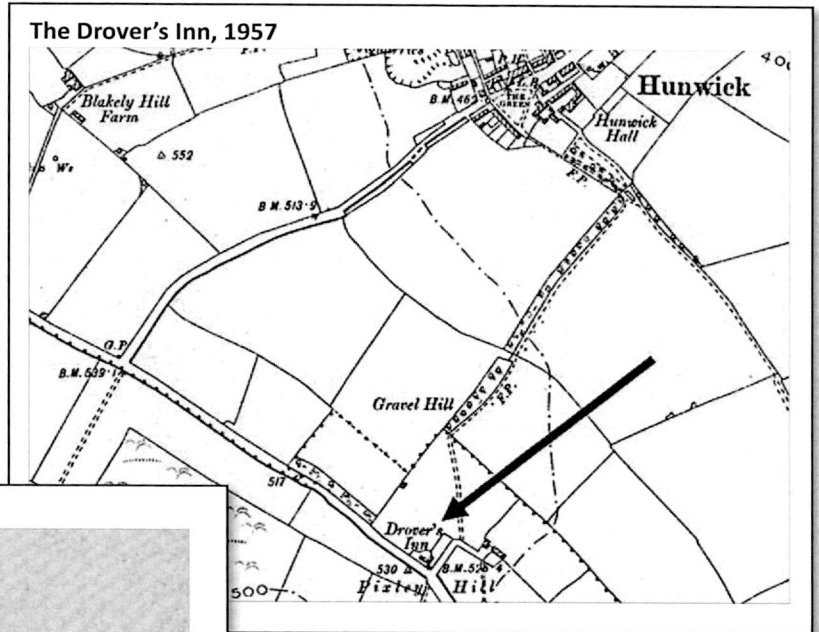

The Drover's Inn, 1957

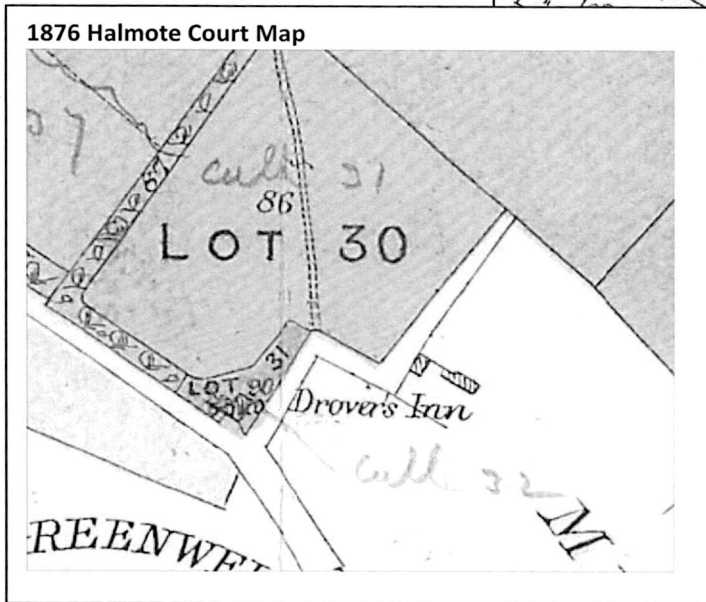

1876 Halmote Court Map

Land Lords		
1858 - Charles Cumming - PO directory 1856 - Charles Cumming - William Wellan	1871 - Charles Cummings - occupation a Publican 1879 - Peter Naylor - Post Office directory 1890 - Fredrick Mangles – Kelly's	1891 - Fredrick Mangles (44) wife Maria – coal hewer and beer house keeper with a servant 1898 - owned by Plews and Co

Hunwick Working Men's Club

Following a meeting in the Miner's Arms, a group of Villagers decided that they would set up a club for working men.

The Club opened in February 1908 when 25 members each borrowed £25 and purchased the premises, formerly a joiner's shop and a coffin-makers. The house next door was eventually purchased in 1950 with various extensions including the steward's accommodation, lounge and a concert hall in 1973. When the Club first opened it had a lending library that members could use.

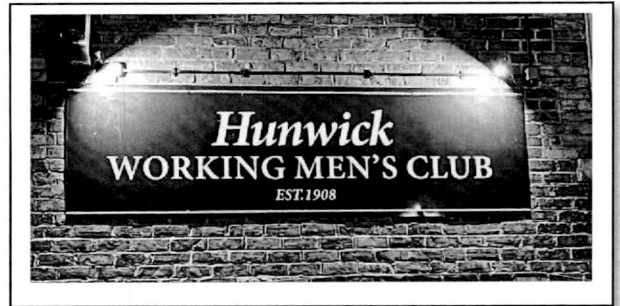

The extract below, written in Neville Blenkinsopp in February 2010, has been taken from the Club Historians website. (Historian, 2010)

"The club officially opened in February 1908 when 25 members each borrowed £25 and purchased the premises, formerly a joiner's shop and a coffin maker. The house next door was eventually purchased in 1950 with various extensions including the steward's accommodation, lounge and concert hall.

Between 1946-1954, the billiard team were Durham County CIU champions for 6 successive years. The shield is still proudly on display to this day. In the 1950s, the club organised an annual carnival for 4 years which included a fancy-dress procession through the village with 8 silver bands. There was then a silver band contest in the recreation ground behind the club with side shows, fun rides and a village queen beauty contest. The festivities lasted a whole week!

There were also summer trips to neighbouring seaside resorts where members could take their children for free and they were given some pocket money. This continued to the 1980s but by then, sadly, finances were difficult and there was less interest. Then a serious fire in 1984 almost destroyed the club but some members got together and kept the club open whilst the damage was cleared. True club and community spirit!

The snooker table survived but a lot of work had to be done by dedicated members to make the club usable again.

The club reached its all-time low in 1994, and was in serious danger of closing. New officials were installed who remain to this day. They were given just 3 days to pay ageing VAT debts otherwise the bailiffs would be sent in to shut the premises down- sadly, an all too familiar story. The secretary arranged an emergency meeting with the then Federation Brewery and a cheque was handed over to keep the club going. But things got worse with more debts uncovered until there was a staggering £98,000 totted up!

After many years of sheer hard work and effort, the corner was turned and the current debt is only £4500 for the mortgage which will be paid off in two years' time. Then, the club will finally belong to the members who have worked so hard to keep it going.

Apart from anything else, they have 'an amazing secretary', Thomas Ward, who is 87 years young. The club now has a small profit margin, an unusual thing in this day and age and Neville plans to put the full balance sheet onto the website when finalised. This should make some interesting reading for other clubs.... They survive on takings of between £1000-2000 a week. Neville's message to other clubs is simple - 'it can be done!'"

Beer Houses

The Beer Act of 1830 introduced the concept of the beer house, in effect a new type of public house created by allowing any rate-paying householder to apply for a license to sell (and brew) beer on the premises.

The 1856, Whellan's Directory lists Ralph Curry as an 'ale and porter seller' and Mary English and John Robson as operating 'beer houses'. (Whellan, 1856) Porter was a dark, weak beer that was designed to allow workers to drink and still work.

Chapter 8 - Utilities

Water Supply and Sewerage

There are many references to the quality of the water available in Hunwick. In 1820, Peter Fair, compared the quality of water of Furnace Spring to that of Harrogate. (A Description of Bishop Auckland, including the castle and park and Gentlemen's Seats - 1820, Peter Fair)

'Along the banks of the river, where the scenery is most romantic, you come to a corn - mill, near which is a spring bursting from the side of the hill, (close by the river side) strongly impregnated with sulphur, & c. little inferior to the Harrowgate waters. H. U, Reay, Esq. the proprietor, has lately inclosed it with a building, and made a good road to it down the hill, by an easy descent of a flight of stairs'. (Fair, 1820)

'There is a cold spring near Hunwick, Durham where parents and nurses bathed their children, with good effect, for rickets.' (Oulton, 1805)

'Hunwick ...It occupies a romantic situation on the north side of the Wear, and contains a spring of water, called Furnival well, which is said to possess some medicinal virtues.' (William Parson, 1828)

'A fine mineral spring, much resorted to in cases of indigestion, became dry in 1842, owing to the sinking of a coal-pit.' (Hurleston, 1858)

Before 'piped' water came to the village in 1897, households used communal wells and springs.

The sketch map highlights the wells shown on OS Maps surveyed between 1856 and 1897 and the estate version of the 1761 Enclosure Map, a copy of which is on display in the Joiner's Arms.

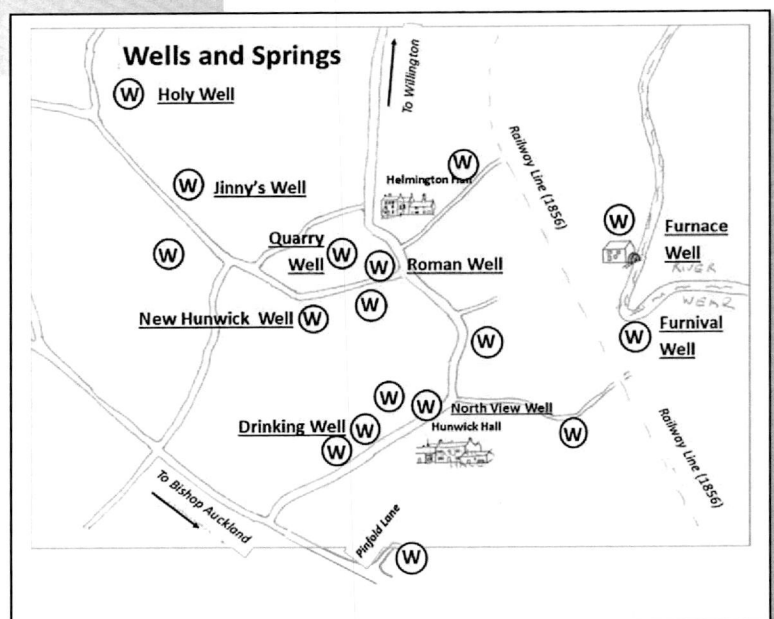

Wells and Springs

- (W) Holy Well
- (W) Jinny's Well
- Helmington Hall
- (W)
- (W) Quarry Well
- (W) (W) Roman Well
- New Hunwick Well (W)
- (W)
- (W) Furnace Well
- (W) Furnival Well
- (W)
- (W) (W) North View Well
- Drinking Well (W) Hunwick Hall
- (W)
- (W)
- To Willington
- Railway Line (1856)
- WEAR RIVER
- Railway Line (1856)
- To Bishop Auckland
- Pinfold Lane
- (W)

North View Well (fountain)

The well or horse trough, in front of Number 9 North View, is marked on both the 1856 and the 1896 OS maps. It is a Grade 2 Listed Building described as a 'fountain in wall'.

It is positioned just before the road begins to climb up from the Church towards the Village Green. Villagers remember the Rington's Tea and Coop Delivery cart horses stopping to drink from the well, before they tackled the hill.

When North View was being built, between 1892 and 1896, the well or trough was repositioned. Donald White, who represented the village on Crook & Willington Council from 1970 until 1991, remembers:

The North View Well

Image 0408 - (Wally Smith, 2006 Digital Village Project)

"The Well, although not a well but a trough, was a water supply. Strangely enough, when work was being done on the footpath in the later part of the 1970s or 1980s, I cannot remember exactly which year, there was revealed a similar looking trough, with arch like the well, in the bankside just to the right of the well. It is now earthed over. Also the pavement inner edge where the road goes through to the rear of North View there was revealed a channel, stone lined about a foot deep and stone capped, with clear looking water running a few inches deep".)

Furnival Well

Two wells were identified in an agreement for the sale of Hunwick Hall in 1635/36. The 'New Spring Fearnley' and 'ye Old Spring'
(Durham_University_Special_Collections, D/CG 33/14)

It is likely that the 'New Spring Fearnley', was the Furnival Well that is marked on the 1857 OS Map.

The choice of name is quite interesting. Perhaps it was linked to the Neville family that, between 1425 and 1569, held the Helmington Hall estate?

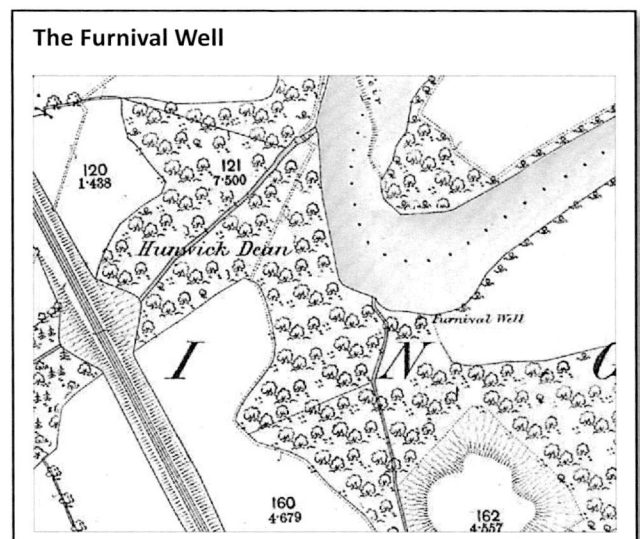

The Furnival Well

There are reports of a *"fine mineral spring, much resorted to in cases of indigestion"*, that *"became dry in 1842"*, owing to the sinking of a coal shaft. (Lewis, 1848)

The shaft for Hunwick Colliery was sunk in 1839. The Furnival Well was on the river side, below the spoil heap that can be seen on the left-hand side of the photograph.

The Furnival Well was probably covered over by the spoil heap that was created by Hunwick Colliery.

The only reference to the name 'Furnival', that I can find, is to 'Barron Furnival'.

The Mill Dam at Furnace Mill

Image 0349 - The Herbert Coates Collection

'Baron Furnivall is an ancient title in the Peerage of England …. The barony eventually passed to Thomas Neville (1362? – 1407), who had married the first baron's descendant Joan de Furnivall, and he was summoned to parliament in her right. Their daughter, Maud de Neville (1392-1423), married John Talbot, who was also summoned to parliament in her right.' (Wikipedia).

Furnace Well

In 1820, the location of a spring that was *'bursting from the side of the hill'*, was described as being, *'Along the banks of the river'*, beside *'a corn – mill'*. This suggests that the Spring was beside Furnace Mill, however, the Furnival Well, is also on the riverside, only a short distance from Furnace Mill.

Surtees explains that *'Mr Reay the subsequent occupier, enclosed the spring and constructed an approach to it by a flight of steps from the hill above.'* (Surtees, The History of the Parishes of Hunwick, Helmington, Witton Park and Etherley, 1923)

Joseph Reay held The Hunwick Hall Estate between 1750 and 1821. An 1876 Estate map confirms that the Furnival Well was on land held by Hunwick Hall.

The 1843 Tithe Map confirms that Furnace Mill was held by the Helmington Estate. This would suggest that the description was for the location of the Furnival Well.

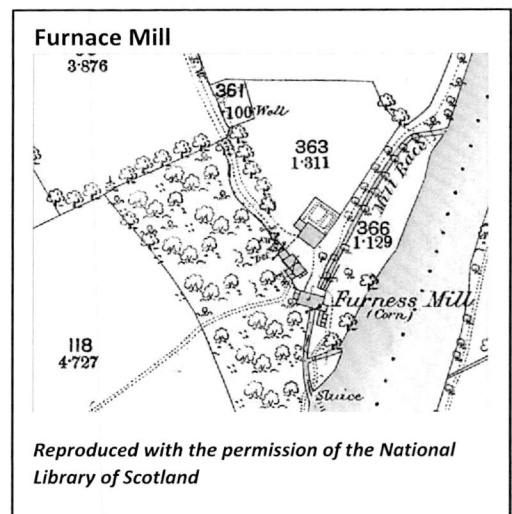

Furnace Mill

Reproduced with the permission of the National Library of Scotland

The description that it was enclosed in *'a building'*, and was accessed by *'a flight of stairs'* from the hill above, does not help us as the Furnival Well was also at the bottom of a hill and would need steps or a stairway to enable it to be accessed. (Fair, 1820)

It was reported in 1857, that, as a result of the *'cuttings for the Auckland and Durham railway'*, the supply of water for the Furnace Well, had been lost. (History and Antiquities of the County Palatine of Durham – W Fordyce 1857)

The Holy Well

The Holy Well, and Holy Well Beck are shown on the 1857 OS Map. Jayne Gilmore shared a story that the Well had been used by the Monks from Durham Priory, to Christen people who had no other religious input. Reputedly, Helmington Grange Farm was used to accommodate the Monks.

The 1957 OS Map, provides a location for the Well, but unfortunately, there is very little evidence, in the fields, to allow the location of the Holy Well to be pin-pointed.

'a small stream that flows into the River Wear south of Willington. Its source lies near the poorly defined footpath that links Annapoorna [Annapoorna was the name chosen by Doctors Sanik, in the 1970s, for what had been West Farm] and Rumby Hill. The spring would appear to lie in a corner of a field near this path where there are a few stones lying in the hedge and under some trees, but these are probably the remains of a field boundary.' (Ref - insearchofHolywellsandhealingsprings.com)

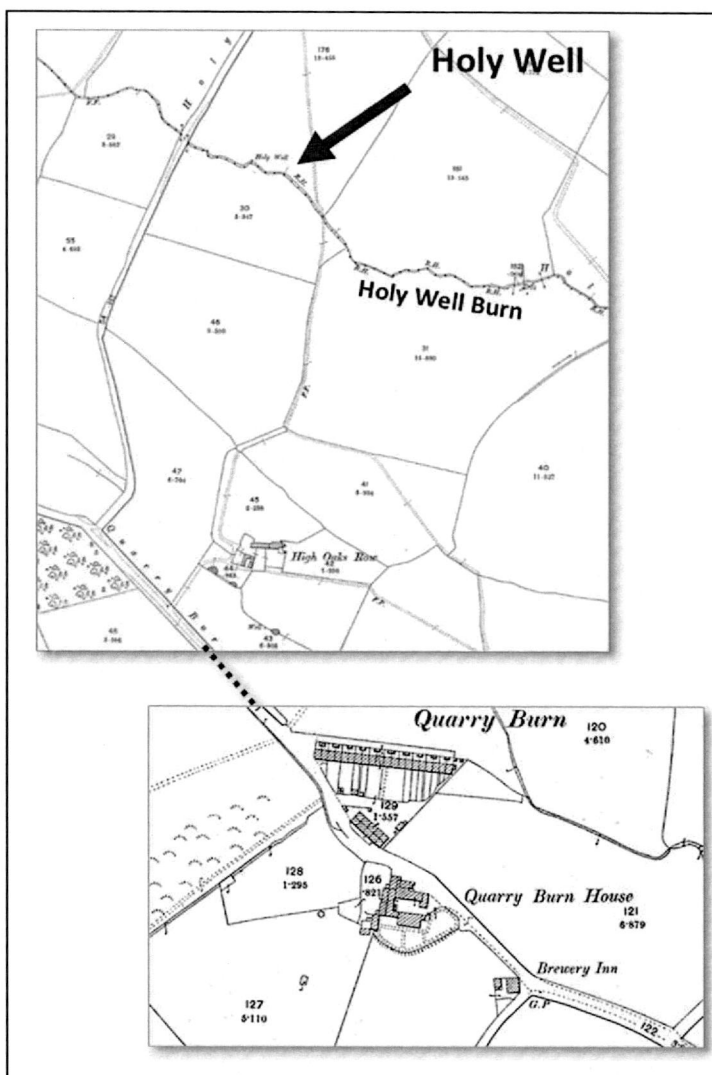

Holy Well

Holy Well Burn

Quarry Burn

Quarry Burn House

Brewery Inn

The Roman Well

The Roman Well is identified on the 1857 OS Map.

Donald White narrows down its location: *'There was Well in approximately the back yard of Mrs Sleath's shop behind the yard of the Helmington Inn about 10 or 20 yards west of the Roman Road, at the top of Oxford Street locally reputed to be a Roman Well.'*

John Cunningham reported that, after a land collapse in the 1970s or 1980s, Wear Valley Council excavated the site and confirmed that there was a Well. Its location was confirmed as either on, or close to the site of what had been, the Helmington Inn.

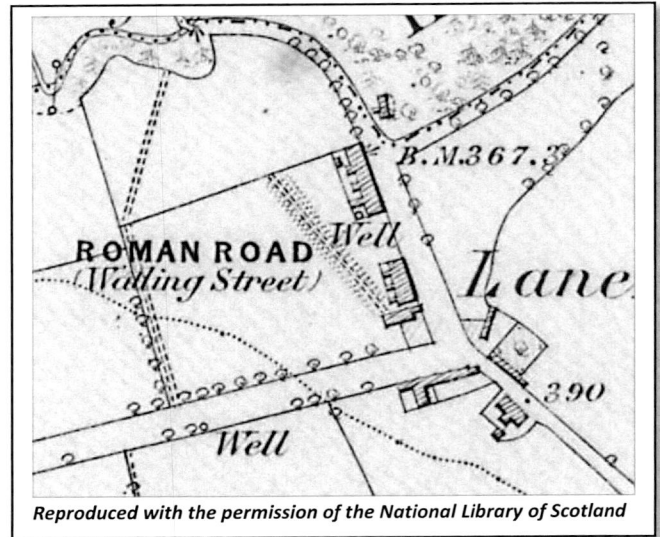

Reproduced with the permission of the National Library of Scotland

The Quarry Well

The 1761 Enclosure Map Identifies Quarry Well, close to Quarry Burn Beck, with a footpath leading to it from New Hunwick. The 1857 OS map shows the same footpath which helps us to locate the well.

Interestingly, Quarry Burn Beck changes its name to Helmington Beck, as it passes by Helmington Hall.

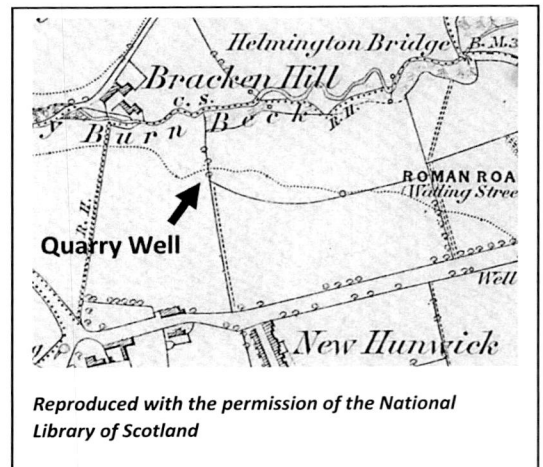

Reproduced with the permission of the National Library of Scotland

Water Supply

Before water companies were established, water supply and disposal of sewage and grey water was organised on a local basis, with the family being responsible for the provision of its own water. Households would use communal wells and simply dispose of sewage and grey water anywhere outside of their living space.

With low density of population, this would not be too much of a concern. However, when the population ballooned, and collieries, Coke Works and Brick Works simply dumped waste water into watercourses, pollution became a significant health risk.

In 1884, it was reported at a meeting of the Auckland Rural Sanitary Authority, that the water in a Hunwick Well had been analysed and it might be *' a channel for the conveyance of disease, and was, therefore unsafe'.* (The_Sanitary_World, 1884)

The importance of a safe water supply was recognised and began to be organised on a regional basis. Water was moved from water catchment areas, to the village where it was needed. The Weardale and Shildon District Water Works Company (a company created in 1866) piped water, from Waskerley Reservoir into Hunwick. Sometime around 1897 a reservoir was built at the top of High Grange Bank.

Receipts show that the Weardale and Shildon District Water Works Company, were supplying houses at Lane Ends in 1902. Water was supplied at ¼ pence for each £ of a house's rateable value. In 1904, Mrs Indigo Dixon, who lived at Lane Ends and had a house with a rateable value of £8 – 10 shillings, paid 11 shillings and 4 pence per year for her water supply]

'I was told in the 1960s by an old man who had worked for the water authority, (he had lived in the reservoir cottage until retired) that it came in the 1870s in lengths of cast iron pipes dropped into trenches from Waskerley reservoir down the valley and up the bank from Grange to the old high walled reservoir, by gravity. The cottage has a stone slab above the door. with 1897 carved on it. The water flowed day and night at less than the 2ft diameter of the pipe, usually less than half, and could be controlled by a valve manually. It supplied Hunwick, Sunnybrow, Newfield and possibly Spennymoor originally. The pipes could be seen coming down the bank at Furness Mill Farm before going under the river near the dam. The reservoir replenished itself to some degree overnight. It was open to the skies so when a council member I instigated the building of a new reservoir diagonally opposite at the top of High Grange Bank on the left and this was roofed in concrete and grassed over." (Donald White's notes)

When water was supplied to the back-to-back, terraced housing, at Lane Ends and New Hunwick, it was connected to an outside tap that was shared by several families.

Sanitary systems consisted of outside earth closets that were often shared by a number of families. *"These closets consisted of a large board with a hole in it"*. (Blackett, 1980) Below the board was a chamber that could be accessed by the dustman/night soil man who would empty the contents onto a cart and remove it to sites away from the village.

In an 1880 document there is a reference to *'Sewering Private streets'* with Helmington Square and Oxford Street being mentioned. The reference, in an 1877 Public Health report, to a small-pox outbreak that had been stamped out, would suggest that progress had been made with Village's sewage by that time. (Municipal Engineering, 1877)

Donald White believes that the sewage system was built in the 1870s.

'sewerage is drained in salt glazed fireclay pipes, about 2 ft. in diameter, from Old Hunwick all the way down to Rough Lea and on to the former Hunwick sewerage works which used to be half way down the steep bank of the road to Furness Mill, now not used.' (Donald White's notes)

An 1877 report of the Auckland Union Rural Sanitary Authority, includes a reference to a *'new sewerage works'* for Hunwick. Perhaps this was a 'sewage farm' as the minutes of an Auckland Rural District Council, Health Committee meeting in 1894 included a reference to a petition made by Hunwick and Helmington Row Parish Council, to the District Council in 1894, that they should not be placed under a Rivers Pollution Order as *'the sewage farm method of disposal is both costly and unsatisfactory'*. (Royal Commission on River Pollution, 1870)

Although a 1915 map shows that a sewerage works had been built at Rough Lea, some earth closets would continue to be in use, in some properties, until the mid-1960s.

Electricity

The London Gazette, November 25th 1902, includes a report that electric Lighting had been connected to Primrose Terrace, Thompson Terrace, Quarry Row, Oxford Street, Rough Lea Terrace, and The Green.

Reputedly, the lights were ceremoniously switched on, in 1928, by Mr R Holt, headmaster of the Secondary School using a switch, on a pole next to Tom Watson's Cobbler's shop.

Chapter 9 - Community, Religion and The Churches

The Chapels and the Church

The religious reforms introduced by Henry VIII saw the establishment of the Church of England. Many northern families, including the Nevilles' of Brancepth Castle, remained loyal to the Catholic Church. The Kennett family, who acquired the Hunwick Hall Estate in 1637, were Roman Catholics in a time when, although it was not an offence to be a catholic, refusal to attend Church of England services was. Initially those who refused would be fined, later fines were increased and prison sentences were introduced.

Before 1845, the village was part of the huge parish of St Andrew's, Bishop Auckland. Villagers had to walk to St Andrew's Church in South Church (4 miles). The footpath that starts at Hunwick Hall and passes through fields towards Newton Cap, was known as the Church Path and is still recognised today as a public right of way. In 1672, Margaret Wright, a widow from Hunwick and Jerimiah Head were fined for non-attendance at St Andrew's church. (Richley, 1872) (Durham_University_Special_Collections, The Kennett family papers (BRA 1297), GB-0033-BRA-1297, 1297)

The shaft for Hunwick Colliery was sunk in 1839, West Hunwick Colliery opened in 1854 and Rough Lea Colliery in 1858. The population of the village in 1831, before the collieries opened, was 164. By 1881, the population had increased to 2086.

Richard Ashby argues that the Church of England was not prepared for the growth of the mining communities and that the Church lacked the *'evangelistic zeal'* of Methodism (Ashby, 2005) The 'Chapelry' of Hunwick and Helmington was created in 1845 to look after the rapidly expanding population.

To house the mine workers, small terraced houses or cottages were built. For the miners who worked at Hunwick Colliery, at Hunwick Station, the houses were built on the other side of the river at Newfield. As more collieries were opened, more were built at Lane Ends, New Hunwick and at Quarry Burn. The majority of the houses were, back-to-back, one-up, one-down with communal earth closets.

Living conditions were poor. Harold Heslop describes the houses that had been built:

'Few of the houses had more than two bedrooms. All had a kitchen, and some a "front room". In the kitchen all the chores were performed, despite the fact that most held a double bed always occupied by the father and mother of the family. Here the miners reproduced themselves. Here the progeny crawled and dunged until they picked up and sent off to school.' (Heslop, 1987)

The Wesleyan Methodist Jubilee Souvenir document, printed in 1924, describes the need that existed in 1874, for a chapel to be built in Hunwick:

'The moral condition of the village of Hunwick when Methodism first planted her seeds was corrupt and anything but conducive to moral welfare of the young life in the village. Cock-fighting was a prominent sport and often on a Sunday. Rabbit Coursing was another cruel sport and these and many other vices are often fostered where drunkenness is prevalent and Hunwick in point of size at that time was very small compared with what it is today and possessed few if any attractions, but its surroundings are acknowledged to be both beautiful and picturesque.' (Wesleyan Methodist Jubilee Souvenir document)

Methodism evolved from within the Church of England and by the end of the 18th century had become a separate entity. Methodism concentrated on the individuals and sections of the community that the Church of England had not traditionally embraced.

Richard Ashby explains that *'Methodist enthusiasm soon gained a hold on the neglected mining communities where there was a spate of chapel building. Eventually there were three chapels in Hunwick.* (Ashby, 2005)

The New Connections Chapel opened in 1862, the Primitive Methodist Chapel opened in 1875 and the Wesleyan Chapel opened in 1881. Before these chapels opened, visiting preachers operated in the village.

While the church was closer to the old houses around the Village Green, the chapels were clustered around the high-density housing at Lane Ends.

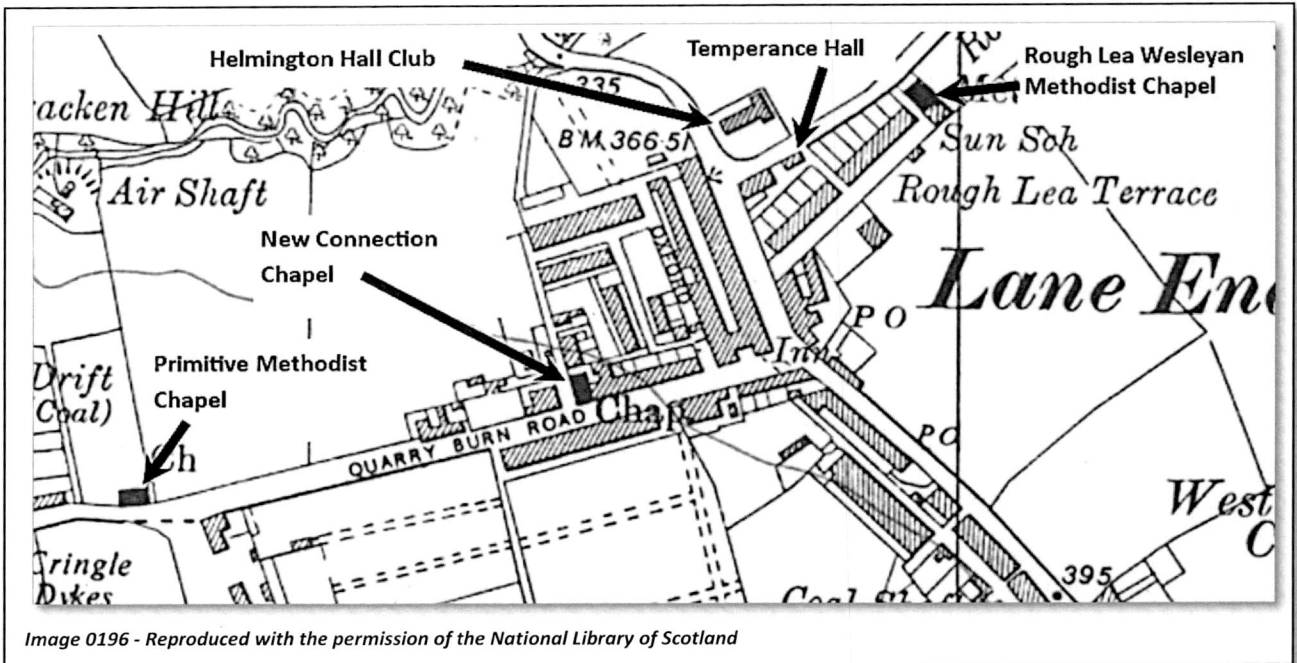

Image 0196 - Reproduced with the permission of the National Library of Scotland

Methodism was very strong in the village and engaged a greater share of population than the Church of England. The congregations of the different chapels had their own identities and were very close-knit. When asked to explain the differences between the different chapels, Villagers explained that the Primitive Methodist Chapel was for the *'get-your-hands-dirty'* workers and that the Wesleyan Chapel was for the managers and overseers.

In 1932 the different branches of Methodism were united to create the 'The Methodist Church'. It took a long time for the congregations to unite.

Methodism provided a sense of community and solidarity among coal miners, which was important in times full of danger and risk. Methodism, helped miners to find their 'voice' and encouraged them to improve their lives though learning and working with others. It provided opportunities for them to study and develop the confidence to talk and to organise other workers. By encouraging communication and by promoting the meaninglessness, in God's eyes, of 'social class', Methodism can be credited with promoting the rise of miners' unions.

St. Paul's Church

Matthew and Elizabeth Bell owned a lot of land in Hunwick and in Northumberland. They provided the land onto which the church, the national school, the vicarage and school master's house were built. It is not clear whether the land was given free of charge (Richard Ashby) or sold to the Church Commissioners (at £19 per acre- Donald White's notes). It was constructed using stone from the village quarries.

The Church designed by William Cory, built in 1844 and consecrated in 1845.

St Paul's Church circa 1900

Image 0104 – The Herbert Coates Collection

St Paul's Church, circa 1910

Image 0392- The Herbert Coates Collection

In 1886 the church was remodelled and enlarged following the designs of the architect J.P. Pritchett. The Chancel was enlarged with vestry and organ chamber added.

The North transept and two bays were added to the west nave. The Lady Chapel and a coke fired central heating system was installed. (Ashby, 2005)

The Vicarage, circa 1900

Image 0339 - The Herbert Coates Collection

Most windows are of early English style and are fitted with Victorian stained glass. The East Window that is above the altar, was donated by Mrs. Spencer of Helmington Hall in memory of her late husband the Rev. Robert Spencer. The window is said to have been copied from glass in Salisbury Cathedral.

A stained-glass window was donated in 1989, in memory of Denise Metcalf. It was designed by S Beattie who specialised in the re-interpreting Christian Symbolism.

Stained-Glass Window in memory of Denise Metcalfe, 1989

Image 0434 – by kind permission of Steve Musgrove

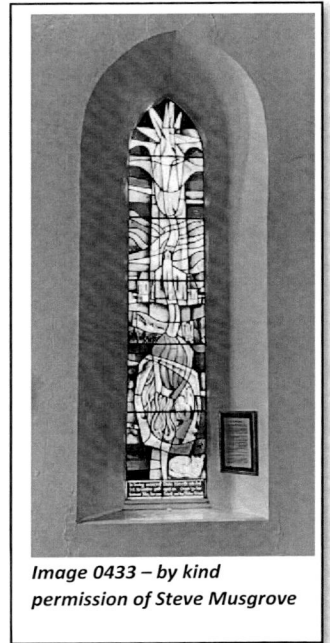

Image 0433 – by kind permission of Steve Musgrove

"At the base of the window is a kneeling figure, enclosed in a womb-like shape representing the 'Garden of the soul'.... Symbols in the centre of the window evoke the life and history of the village. The Roman past of Hunwick is represented by the distorted SPQR of a legion's standard. More contemporary aspects of the village's life are shown by the miner's lamp and the plough."

New Connection Chapel

The New Connection Chapel was built in 1862 and was run by the controversial Pit Owner Joseph Love.

"He was the national President of the Methodist New Connection movement and was said to only promote men who worship in his chapel." (Blackett, 1980)

Straker and Love owned the Helmington Hall Estate and ran Collieries in Willington and Sunnybrow.

The Chapel could seat two-hundred people.

The New Connections Chapel

Image 0198 - The Herbert Coates Collection

New Hunwick Chapel

The Primitive Methodist Chapel was built at New Hunwick in 1875, reputedly built on the site of a former Chapel, using reclaimed stone from High Oaks Farm.

The Chapel, with Wallace Terrace in the background

Image 0361 – the Herbert Coates Collection

School Choir at the Rededication of the Banner, 1994

Image 0418 – (Betty Dunn, 2006 Digital Village Project)

Arthur Scargill and Laurie Pratt

The Chapel had seating for three-hundred people. It hosted the rededication ceremony Rough Lea Colliery banner in 1994. The ceremony was attended by Arthur Scargill, President of the NUM. The school choir sang at the ceremony and were addressed by NUM Officials.

Rough Lea, Wesleyan Methodist Chapel

Hunwick, appears for the first time on the programme for the Wesleyan preachers of Bishop Auckland, in 1839. In 1854 Services were held at a dwelling in Oaks Row owned by a Thomas Hedley. Services were later transferred to a dwelling in Quarry Burn until it became too small for the number of people who wanted to attend the services.

In 1871 the Methodist Pioneer, Simpson Heslop, was appointed manager at Rough Lea Colliery. He allocated the colliery reading room at Number 19 Rough Lea Colliery, as a meeting place free of rent and coal.

In 1880 Simpson Heslop and George Wright, a local landowner, championed the cause for a new chapel. In 1880 they acquired the land at Rough Lea from William Elliott and built the chapel in the following year.

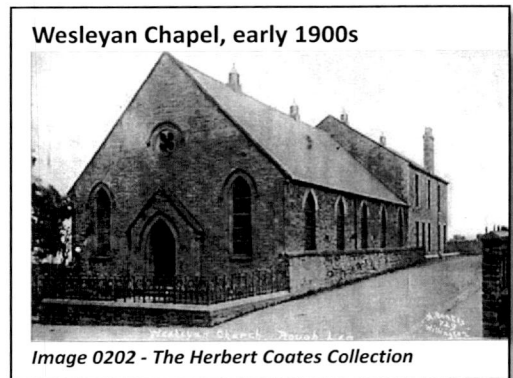

Wesleyan Chapel, early 1900s

Image 0202 - The Herbert Coates Collection

Parade assembling, 1900

Image 0410 - By kind permission of John Cunningham

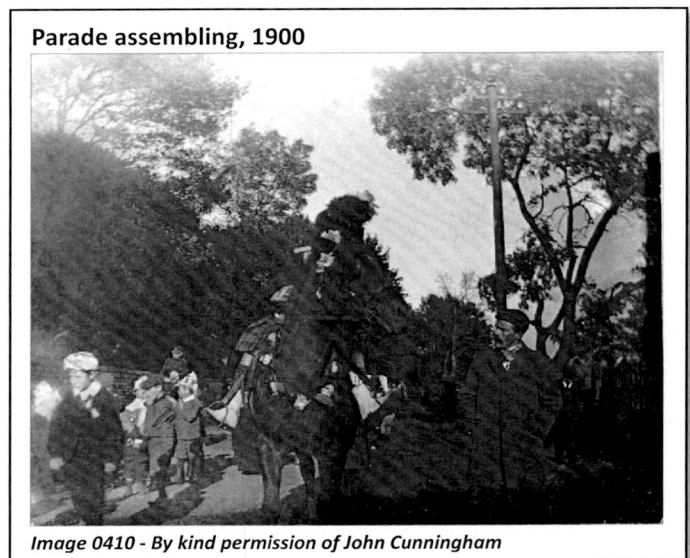

Looking towards Rough Lea

Image 0201- The Herbert Coates Collection

In 1889 the chapel was enlarged by the addition of a 'commodious vestry', with the school rooms being built in 1903 and a pipe organ installed in 1910. It could seat a congregation of two-hundred and fifty.

In 1920, the National School, which was run by the Church of England, was unable to accommodate the number of children that were required to attend. The Church of England, between 1920 and 1924, rented the school rooms at the Chapel, to use as an annex to school.

After the Methodist union in 1932, the chapel lost the name 'Wesleyan' from its title. Central heating was installed in the chapel in 1955

Trade Unions

Working conditions in the mines were dangerous and unregulated. Mine owners attempted to derive the maximum profit from their mines while taking very little responsibility for the safety or well-being of the men and boys that they employed. Miners, while suffering physical, social and economic hardship, found that they had to look after themselves and those who worked around them.

A developing feeling of social injustice resulted in workers coming together in an attempt to improve their lot. Colliery Lodges were established and were funded through membership fees. As well as a group 'voice', they provided welfare, recreational and educational support and facilities.

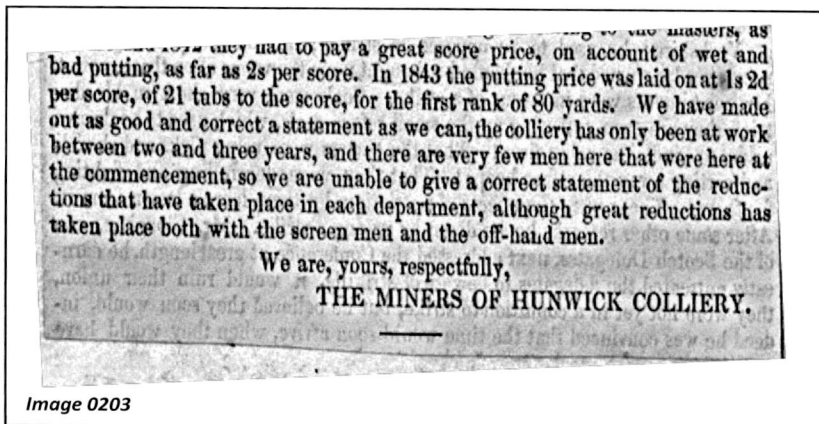

Image 0203

The Miners' Welfare Fund was established by the Mining Industry Act 1920, to improve the social conditions of colliery workers.

The fund was administered by the Miners' Welfare Committee and was dependent on a levy on each ton of coal that the country produced.

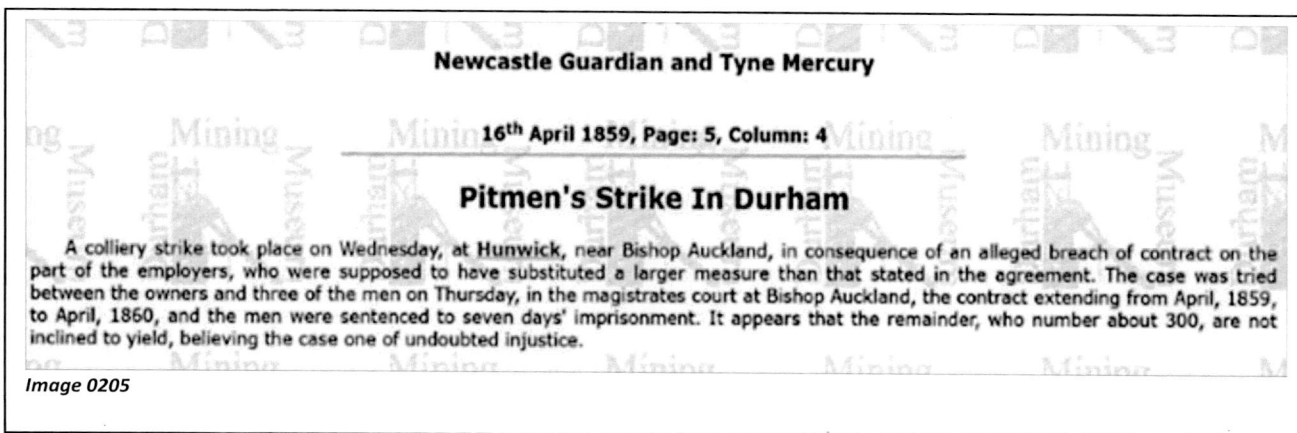

Newcastle Guardian and Tyne Mercury

16th April 1859, Page: 5, Column: 4

Pitmen's Strike In Durham

A colliery strike took place on Wednesday, at Hunwick, near Bishop Auckland, in consequence of an alleged breach of contract on the part of the employers, who were supposed to have substituted a larger measure than that stated in the agreement. The case was tried between the owners and three of the men on Thursday, in the magistrates court at Bishop Auckland, the contract extending from April, 1859, to April, 1860, and the men were sentenced to seven days' imprisonment. It appears that the remainder, who number about 300, are not inclined to yield, believing the case one of undoubted injustice.

Image 0205

Hunwick Colliery, West Hunwick and Rough Lea Collieries had their own 'lodges' and were represented at the 'Pitman's Parliament' based at the headquarters of the Durham Miners Association at RedHills, Durham.

Hunwick Lodge

Image 0204 - (by kind permision of Michael Wilson)

In 1872, Hunwick Lodge had two-hundred and ten members and Rough Lea Lodge had one-hundred members. (Moyes, 1974)

In 1915 West Hunwick Lodge had seat number 188 with one vote and Rough Lea Lodge had seat number 104 with 2 votes at the Parliament. Hunwick Colliery closed in 1921 and did not have a seat at the Parliament in 1915.

West Hunwick Lodge

Image 0386 -By kind permission of Sarah Lewis of East Durham Detectors

'Redhills is a shining example of what people can collectively achieve. From here, the miners in effect created and ran their own welfare state in the first part of the 20th century. They built hospitals, homes, recreation halls. There was no state to do it for them so they did it for themselves and that was a tremendous source of pride and satisfaction.' (Guardian, March 2020)

The 1950, seating plan for Redhills, shows West Hunwick taking seat number 162 and having one vote and Rough Lea taking seat number 95 and having one vote. (Information kindly provided by Durham Miners Association)

Hunwick Colliery and Rough Lea Colliery had their own bands. Both bands marched with their respective Lodge banners, at the 1872 Durham Miners Gala.

Hunwick Colliery band, known as Hunwick Silver Band, was formed in the 1890s. It competed in Crystal Palace Championships in the 1930s, and at some point, merged with Evenwood Colliery Band.

Rough Lea Colliery band was also formed in the 1890s and competed in the Crystal Palace Championships in 1936

Hunwick Silver Band, 1920

Image 0207 – (Linda Paley, 2006 Digital Village Project)

Rough Lea Band, 1936

Image 0417, Beamish Museum - Peoples Collection

"The union leadership up until the early 1920s consisted largely of 'respectable' Liberal Methodists who felt that they commanded the respect of the owners." (Sagar)

Colliery workers and their families recognised the importance of and were proud of their Lodge. At picnics, Galas and events they would congregate around their Lodge's Banner which were symbols of community identity, spirit and pride.

A banner was a large square of woven silk that would be decorated on both sides. The centre piece was painted with a picture, different on each side, designed to represent the identity and values of the Lodge. A Lodge would commission a banner from a specialist flag and banner maker. The 1873 Rough Lea Banner was made by J. Tuthill's of London. Manufacturers would have a pattern book and Lodges would be able to select and develop their design based on these patterns/templates. The choice of imagery and motto was often the subject of a long and bitter debate amongst Lodge members. In the early days of the Durham Miners Association, the Lodge Officials were often Methodist Preachers.

The Temperance Movement

The Temperance Hall

Image 0317 - By kind permission of Donald White

Maps show that the Temperance Hall, a pink or red corrugated iron shed, at the top of Rough Lea Lane just before Normans Buildings, had been built by 1915.

Harold Heslop, when talking about the Temperance Hall, describes it as *"a grim structure, mainly of galvanised iron, which stood under the rookery".*

He also explains that *'The Temperance and Tea-Total Movements pressed the community to hold all meetings away from the public house'* and that --- *'for any special non-religious occasions, such as a concert or a political meeting, the Temperance Hall was used'.* (Heslop, 1987)

Rough Lea Methodist Youth Club used the Hall until 1956 when they relocated to the Helmington Hall Club

Anthony Pratt, Superintendent of The Independent Order of Rechabites.

Image 0210

Colliery Banners

Hunwick Colliery and Rough Lea Colliery Lodges had their own banners.

Hunwick Colliery Banner

The banner for the Hunwick Colliery Lodge, is 'lost'. However, we know something about its design from an article written in the Durham County Advertiser on 20th June 1873. The banner that was in use in 1873 showed Labour and Capital, with three men on each side, and two in the centre shaking hands: *'Come let us reason together.'* The reverse bore a scene of a hand holding scales, and the words *'A just weight is His delight'* above a picture of Christ pointing to a cherub holding a scroll inscribed *'Whatsoever ye would those men do unto you, do ye unto them'* (Matthew 7.12) The illustration also bore Christ's command *'See that ye love one another'* – (Emery, 1998)

We do not know when the banner was made. If it was made before 1869, when the DMA was formed, a scroll on the banner will include 'Hunwick Lodge'. If it was made after 1869, a scroll, in addition to identifying the lodge, will include 'Durham Miners' Association'. (Wray, 2009)

Rough Lea Banner

Workmen, removing the slates during the demolition of Sunnybrow Welfare Hall, discovered the nineteenth-century Rough Lea Banner. The contents of the Welfare were offered for sale by auction at Edkins Sale Rooms in Bishop Auckland. Fortunately, Betty Dunn (nee Pratt), a villager, recognised it and informed Durham Miners' Union who stopped the auction and took possession of the banner.

The banner was restored and then rededicated by Arthur Scargill, at New Hunwick Methodist Church in 1994. After that it was stored by Durham Miners' Association at their Redhills headquarters, where it deteriorated to such an extent that it had to be remade again in 2022.

The banner that was carried at the 1873 had been made by the London banner maker, George Tutill and carried the portrait of Home Secretary Bruce, with MacDonald and Crawford. The reverse bore the 41st Psalm: 'the lord will deliver him in time of trouble'.

The 1890 banner carries the title 'Durham Miners' Association Rough Lea Lodge' on a blue ribbon, over a large roundel showing a child holding stalks of corn, sitting on the back of a lion and feeding a garlanded lamb. The sky is painted with a loop of cloud around sunlight illuminating a heart and hand design.

Rough Lea Colliery Banner, 1994

Image 0208

Within the scene is a scroll bearing the motto, 'Peace and Friendship'. The reverse carries a large roundel with a Good Samaritan scene: the inscriptions around the border read 'Bear ye one another's burden' and 'Blessed is he that considereth the poor'. (Emery, 1998)

In 2022, the Hunwick Community Social and Environmental Group raised the funds, and worked with Mandy Foster of AA Flags Ltd, to re-manufacture the banner based on the 1890 design. The re-manufactured banner was paraded by proud Villagers at the 2022 Durham Miners' Gala and is on display in Hunwick Working men's Club.

Helmington Hall Community Club

Following a public meeting in 1935, the Social Services Movement, who had a presence in surrounding villages including, Bishop Auckland, Howden, Crook and Helmington Row, decided that a Community Club should be built in Hunwick.

A plot in the rookery of Helmington Hall was acquired from Strakers and Love who were the owners of Helmington Hall and Willington and Sunnybrow Collieries.

Building work began in December 1935 when forty volunteers from the village dug the foundations. The Social Service Centre, was officially called Helmington Hall Club but was affectionately referred to by Villagers as 'the Green Hut' although there were really two buildings at ninety degrees to each other.

One of the buildings was used as a cookhouse during the 1939 – 45 war, to feed the soldiers that were based at Rough Lea. The left hand hut housed two billiard tables and a reading room. There was a large hall with a stage and a changing rooms in the right hand hut.

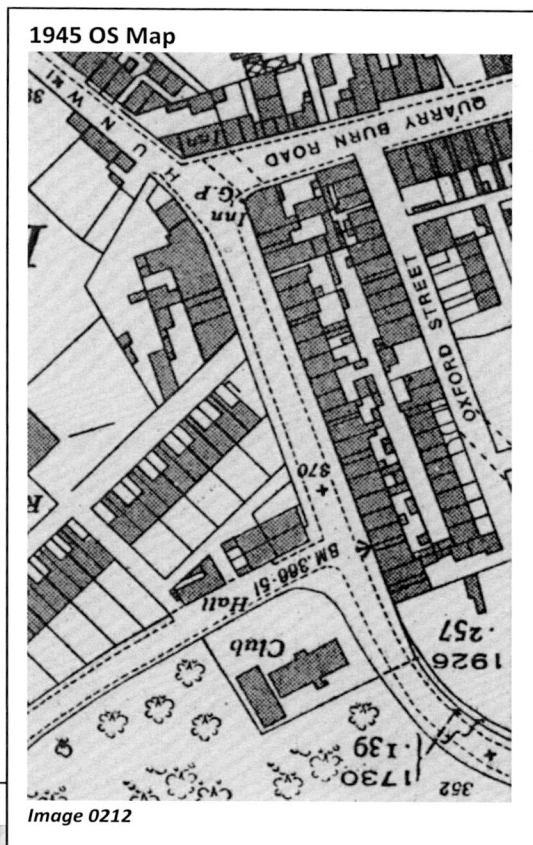

1945 OS Map

Image 0212

Helmington Hall Community Centre, Hall Bank

Image 0211 - The Herbert Coates Collection

In November 1937 the 'Rookery Nook', the monthly magazine produced by Helmington Hall Club, describes a very active centre with 350 members. It lists the classes in the Adult School: Woodwork Class (open every week day), Boot Repair Class (operating Mondays and Wednesday), a Physical Training group (Monday and Wednesday evenings); a Drama Section that staged frequent productions and a Lending Library with 615 books and 64 borrowers. The Women's Section had 65 members. At their AGM in 1940, it was reported that the boot repair class had repaired 320 pairs of shoes during the year.

The two Social Service Huts at the turn into Rough Lea Lane.

Image 0313 - By kind permission of Donald White

In 1956, Rough Lea Methodist Youth Club moved to the Hall. They ran a very active cinema club that used two 35mm cinema projectors to show films. They also organised dances, football matches and many other activities for the 'youth'. Villages still speak very fondly of their time at the Youth Club. Harry Gowland remembers the Rough Lee youth club commenting that

"it was for me a wonderful social outlet. There were regular dances with live music for only a 20 pence entry fee in today's money. The dances were from 9 pm until 1 am in the morning. The youth club programme was very varied including theatre visits in Stockton and Newcastle, bus trips to where ever we decided to go and a good number of interesting speakers."

Villagers admit that their involvement with the club did not stop when they got married. They remember fondly the youth club holidays that were organised every other year to either Scarborough or Blackpool.

Palm Court Hotel Blackpool, 1950

Image 0213

Methodist Youth Club Pantomime of Cinderella 1963

Image 0214

Church Institute

1894 Kelly's directory identifies Rev J G Ryles as the president of the Church Institute & Library.

An article in the Newcastle Journal, on 24th March 1894, describes a billiards handicap that had been run at the Church Institute.

However, a date stone exists that recorded that Hunwick Church Institute had opened in 1900 and records exist showing that, in May 1901, St Paul's Church Wardens bought the land at Kate's Close, now 31 Wear View, to build a Church Institute. It is not clear where the Institute operated before 1900.

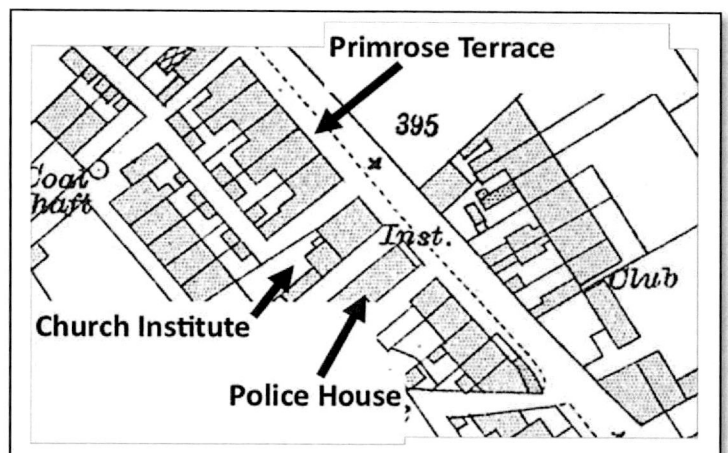

The Church Army Captain lived in the house behind the Church Institute. The Reading Room was upstairs and there was a large hut in the garden behind in which dances were held.

In the 1925 Kelly's Directory it was described as the Church Army Social Centre. The Institute had closed by 1935.

Women's Institute (WI)

A report in the Darlington and Stockton times in 1994, explained that the Hunwick branch of the Women's Institute had closed after 58 years, because the members were too old. The rules of the Women's Institute would not allow a Treasurer to be more that seventy-years old.

The WI had been established 1935. When Evelyn Gallon joined the WI in 1935 it had 70 members. In the report she was explained that *"we did not go out to work. We were just ready for the WI as our one night out"*.

Mrs Rachel Smith, aged eighty-four, had been present at the first meeting and also at the last meeting of the WI. During the War

Women's Institute, date unknown

Image 0421-(Irene Pickerskill, 2006 Digital Village Project)

years the WI supported many fundraising activities and knitted socks and vest for children and socks and gloves for soldiers.

Chapter 10 - Sports and Recreation

The reminiscences of Villagers and contemporary newspaper reports, confirm that Hunwick, as a village, has always had a strong interest sport. In addition to football, cricket and tennis, village teams have a strong track record in a range of pub games, including darts, billiards, quoits and ball.

Villagers who grew up in the 1940s and 1950s, put this down to their childhood being vastly different from that of today's youngsters. Apart from card games, and for some, reading, there was nothing to entertain them in their homes. They looked for adventure on the pit heaps, the pit ponds, the quarries, the river and the back streets. They lived to play sports, either down the Recreation Ground or on the Village Green, even with a slope and a stream running across it. Alan Edmundson explains that *"Football was played for two thirds of the year and then, in the summer the cricket gear came out. This inspired us when we were older to set up teams and, in some cases, join a league. This rubbed off on pub games with snooker, pool and darts teams representing the Village in local leagues"*

The 1939 OS map shows a recreation ground at Gigg Lane, Brecken Hill. The field was rented by Simpson Heslop, a local butcher with an enthusiasm for sports, from the North Bitchburn Coal Company. Two converted railway carriages were used as pavilions. Cricket, football and tennis were played on this ground until the early 1950s when Simpson Heslop sold his business. The field behind the Working Men's Club was acquired by the Crook and Willington Urban District Council who maintained it as a Recreation Ground for the village.

'Gigg Lane' Recreation Ground, Brecken Hill – 1939

Image 0218 - Reproduced with the permission of the National Library of Scotland

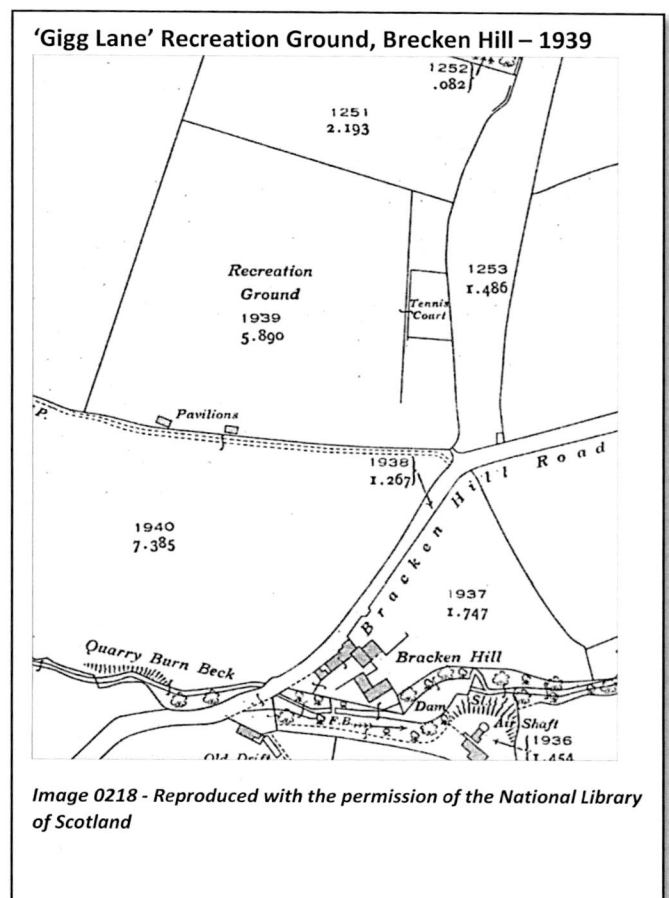

Recreation Field, 1950s

Image - Reproduced with the permission of the National Library of Scotland

In the 1960s, there were swings and a 'teapot-lid' in the 'Rec'. Village football and cricket teams used the 'Rec' for their matches although. Being in the shadow of the pit heap and being on a slope, did present the players with additional challenges!

In the 1950s, the Working Men's Club organised an annual carnival, a silver band contest and fancy-dress parade that was based in the Rec. The side shows, fun rides and village beauty queen contest were enjoyed by Villagers.

In the 1960s, Turners Travelling Shows, visited the village and set up in the Recreation Field for one week each year. They brought excitement and noise to the village with their small fairground rides and side-stalls with games including hook a duck, coconut shy, and tin-can alley, where a sand-bag (mop) is thrown at a pyramid of tin cans.

Ozzy Rae's Side Show Sign

Cricket

Hunwick Cricket Club was founded in 1894. The team has played at various locations within the village. An early account of a competitive game against a team from Coundon, reported that the game was played at Hunwick Station. Other games, reputedly, being played at 'Daniel's Riggs', a field running alongside a narrow wood stretching from Hunwick Hall Farm Plantation towards Pixley Hill.

Their home from the early 1900s until 1964 was in a field at Brecken Hill on the righthand side of the Bracken Hill Road, the road that runs from Helmington Hall towards what used to be the Quarry Burn public house. The field was rented from Bitchburn Fire and Clay Company by Simpson Heslop, who ran the Butcher's shop in Helmington Square. The Simpson family were heavily involved with the Cricket Club and are pictured in a 1925 photograph of the team having just won the Coxhoe and District Cricket League.

The field at Brecken Hill had two 'pavilions', two very basic railway carriages. One was used a changing room and the other for teas. There was also a lawn tennis grass court in the same field that was very popular with Villagers.

In the early sixties the club moved to the recreation field behind the Working Men's Club. The field had a very steep slope running from top to bottom. The cricket square was re-laid to level up the playing surface but this was not successful. Interest waned and the club disbanded.

In 1974 interest resurfaced and a committee was formed. Many residents, who share their stories in Chapter 11, talk of the Cricket Club Teas, fundraising events and coach trips.

The committee approached Durham County Council who gave permission for the school field to be used. Friendly games were played until 1977 when they joined the Mid Durham

Cricket Club Fund Raiser at the Monkey, 1980s

Image 0371 – by kind permission of Harold Newton

Senior League. The Club was very well supported both on and off the pitch presenting both a first and second team as well as a junior side. 1987 brought membership to the North East Durham League.

In 1995 the club moved on to its current site that was developed on the reclaimed colliery spoil heaps. In 1995 the field had no facilities at all. Since that time, a small band of volunteers have worked to improve the facilities such that it now runs 3 senior teams and several junior sides. A new pavilion was built in 2021.

Hunwick Cricket Club, 1978

Image 0352 – (Alma Edmundson, 2006 Digital Village Project)

Hunwick Cricket Club, 1950s

Image 0219 – (Mavis Alderson, 2006 Digital Village Project)

Football

Alan Edmundson lists some of the football teams that have been associated with the village: Hunwick Rooks (1931 – 1936), Hunwick St Paul's (Juniors and Seniors), Hunwick West End (1968 - 1984), Rough Lea Methodist Youth Club (1960s), The Monkey/Joiners Arms, Hunwick Rough Lea Pipe Works and Hunwick Villa. Between 1994 and 2001, Hunwick's Junior Football team enjoyed success in the Russell Foster Junior League.

An article in the Daily Gazette for Middlesbrough, 11th March 1898, reported that an accusation had been made that Willington had poached a Hunwick player. The article confirms that Hunwick's football team was playing in the Wear Valley League in the late 1890s.

Betty Dunn has kept a newspaper clipping that includes a photograph of Hunwick's 1906 or 1907 football team, that her father, Anthony Pratt, had found.

He approached the Northern Echo and asked for the assistance of their readers, to identify the players shown on the photograph.

1906/1907 Football Team

Image 0435 - (Betty Dunn, Digital Village Project 2006)

Footbal team, date unknown

Image 0393

An article in the Durham County Advertiser on 27th November 1914, reports on a match played at Hunwick, between the village team and Willington United, confirms that Hunwick Juniors were playing in the Auckland District League in 1914.

Hunwick West End Football Team

A newspaper article explains *"Hunwick West End, with a goal scored in the 75th minute, beat Wearhead United 1 – 0 to win the Crook District League Cup last night at the Crook Town Ground. The goal was scored by centre forward Dave Craggs."*

George Dodds designed the team badge which can be seen on the managers blazer worn by George Daniel.

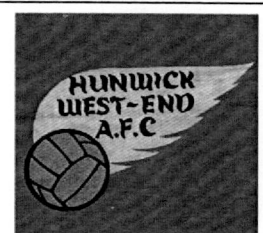

Image - by kind permission of Marian Brown

Crook and District League Cup Winners 1969/70.

Back Row L/R: Eric Richardson, William Foster, Barry Quarmby, Mel Hodgson, Gordon Pratt, Billy Goodridge, John Pratt, George Daniels (manager)

Front Row L/R: Barry Blackburn (Trainer), Frank Hudson, Colin Genner, Kenny Fish, David Craggs, Tony Robinson, Maurice Quarmby.

Image 0367 - by kind permission of Marian Brown

Hunwick Methodist Youth Club football team

Hunwick Methodist Youth Club Team 1950

Image – Alan Edmundson

Back L/R: Keith Higginbottom, Doug Watson, ??, Alan Moore, Wally Smith, Ray Humble, Dick Peacock.

Front L/R: Dereck Robinson, Alan Henry, Harry Dobinson, Wilf Bourne, Don Shoulder.

Hunwick Youth Club football team 1948.

Image m00088 – (Dorothy Turnbull, Digital Village Project 2006)

Back L/R: Doug Watson, Arnold Johnson, Wharton Peacock, Keith Higginbottom, Derek Robinson, Alan Moore, Ray Humble, Walter Turnbull.

Front L/R: Wilf Bourne, Wally Smith, Ronnie Wright, Dick Peacock, Harry Dobinson, Mick Pearson, Donald Shoulder.

Tennis

There was a tennis court at Helmington Hall and at Gigg Lane Recreation ground.

Thomas Hedley, a cheese merchant, allowed the Youth Club to develop a tennis court in the grounds of Raby House.

John Pratt has memories of rolling cheeses, wrapped in cheese-cloth, down into the quarry.

He also remembers the Youth Club having competitions to see how fast the cheese-cloth could be removed from a cheese.

Helmington Hall Tennis Club Pavilion, 1890

Image 0222 – by kind permission of John Cunningham

Hunwick Tennis Club, 1930s

Image 0221 – (Betty Dunn, 2006 Digital Village Project)

A Destination for Hunting and Horse Racing

Matthew Richley explains that *'the woods of Birtley, which adjoin Newton Cap, and extend along the northern banks of Wear as far as Hunwick and Helmington, were a few centuries ago a forest, and formed one of the hunting grounds of the Bishops of Durham'*. (Richley, 1872) By 1754, Birtley Woods had been *'grubbed up, and the park disparked'*. (Hutchinson, 1785)

Horse racing first took place on Hunwick Moor in March 1662. (Slusar, 2016) In 1770, J Fairfax-Blakeborough reported that there were only two recognised race meetings in County Durham. One at Durham City and the other at Bishop Auckland. Many of the races that were organised by Bishop Auckland, actually took place on Hunwick Moor. (Fairfax-Blakeborough, 1770) The races were run over a 4-mile course.

A note written in 1662 to the Bishop of Durham's land agent suggests a well-attended, high-profile event being staged on Hunwick Moor:

> *'Auckland, 3rd March. This day wee have horse races heare on Hunwicke Moore. Mr Davison has a little nag runs with the like of Capt. Darcy's. Mr Bricknell rides Mr Davison's nag. There will be much company there. Our Lady's goe in my Lord's coache from hence'*. (Fairfax-Blakeborough, 1770)

The races offering prizes of £50, attracted large crowds from quite a wide area. Diary entries in Surtees describe the journeys of titled people who were travelling from London in a coach, stopping in York for two nights, before attending the races on *'Hunwicke Moor'*. (Ref J Cunningham LARGE Surtees Bk).

Records exist of meetings in May 1721, September 1722, April 1724, May 1725, July 1728, September 1729, and 1739. What is interesting is that some of these four or five-day meetings were held on both Hunwick Moor and Auckland Edge, alternating between the two courses during the week. (Slusar, 2016) Chris Pitt in his book 'A long Time Gone' reports that the last Bishop Auckland race meeting was in May 1863. (Pitt, 1996)

A letter written in April 1731, between Walter Blackett of Newcastle, and his agent

> *"On the 12 of May will be run for in Hunwick near Auckland a purse of 15 guineas by aged Horses carrying 10 stone, …, I desire your directions whether to send him there, or keep him fresh for Newcastle Races, which will be about five weeks after."* (Dukesfield_Documents)

It has not been possible to determine the actual route that the races took. Villagers still refer to the field below the cemetery as the 'racing field'. If the races were 4 mile long and started and finished at the Flatts (Kynren), a **possible route** might have started at the Flatts, at Bishop Auckland and then along the riverside to Birtley Cottages. Along the Roman Road to Kate's Close [passing below the cemetery], up to Dixon's House (Blakeley Hill Farm), back down past the Riggs and back to the Flatts.

Pigeon Fancying

Rabbit coursing, horse racing and greyhound flapping also engaged Villagers.

Durham County Working Men's Club Fancy Pigeon Trophy Hunwick Winner 1950, 51 and 52

Hunwick Working Men's Club Homing Pigeon Society 1932

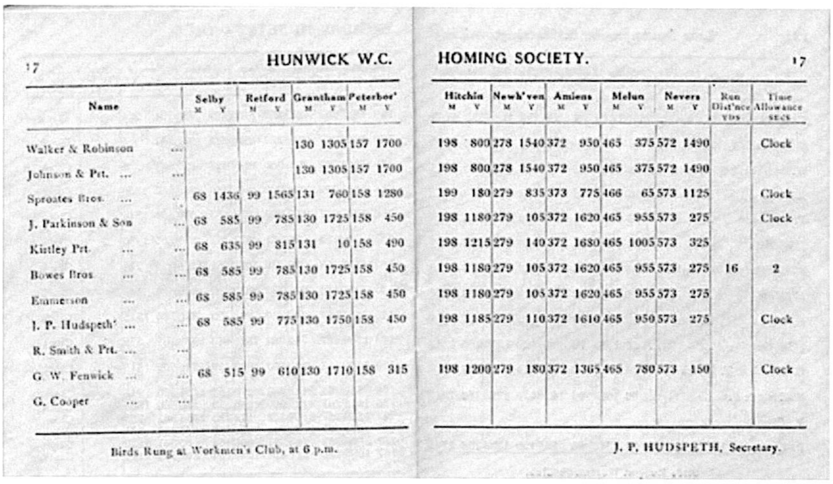

Name	Selby M	Selby V	Retford M	Retford V	Grantham M	Grantham V	Peterbor' M	Peterbor' V	Hitchin M	Hitchin V	Newh'ven M	Newh'ven V	Amiens M	Amiens V	Melun M	Melun V	Nevers M	Nevers V	Run Dist'nce YDS	Time Allowance SECS
Walker & Robinson ...					130	1305	157	1700	198	800	278	1540	372	950	465	375	572	1490		Clock
Johnson & Prt. ...					130	1305	157	1700	198	800	278	1540	372	950	465	375	572	1490		
Sproates Bros. ...	68	1436	99	1565	131	760	158	1280	199	180	279	835	373	775	466	65	573	1125		Clock
J. Parkinson & Son	68	585	99	785	130	1725	158	450	198	1180	279	105	372	1620	465	955	573	275		Clock
Kirtley Prt. ...	68	635	99	815	131	10	158	490	198	1215	279	140	372	1680	465	1005	573	325		
Bowes Bros. ...	68	585	99	785	130	1725	158	450	198	1180	279	105	372	1620	465	955	573	275	16	2
Emmerson ...	68	585	99	785	130	1725	158	450	198	1180	279	105	372	1620	465	955	573	275		
J. P. Hudspeth' ...	68	585	99	775	130	1750	158	450	198	1185	279	110	372	1610	465	950	573	275		Clock
R. Smith & Prt. ...																				
G. W. Fenwick ...	68	515	99	610	130	1710	158	315	198	1200	279	180	372	1365	465	780	573	150		Clock
G. Cooper ...																				

Birds Rung at Workmen's Club, at 6 p.m.

J. P. HUDSPETH, Secretary.

Image 0223 – (Edward Bowes, 2006 Digital Village Project)

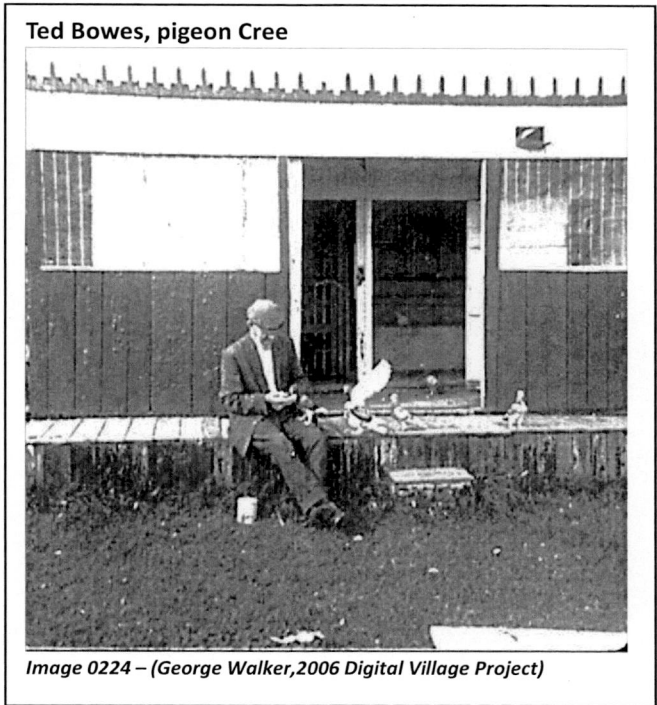

Working Men's Club Fancy Pigeon Trophy

Image 0384 – by kind permission of Kevin Dunnett

Ted Bowes, pigeon Cree

Image 0224 – (George Walker, 2006 Digital Village Project)

Darts

All of the village Pubs and Clubs had darts teams at one time or another.

Weight Lifting

In the early 1960s, a weight lifting club used the Temperance Hall as its base before moving up to the Church Hall in the early 1970s.

The club was popular, regularly attracting fifteen or more members, who trained and regularly competed.

Villagers remember the well-attended weight lifting and bodybuilding demonstrations that the club organised. Kenny Prest, a regular weightlifter, became the bodyguard for Bob Monkhouse

Joiner's Arms Darts Team, 2003

Image 0422 – (Ian Richardson, 2006 Digital Village Project)

Pub Games

Harold Heslop lists popular Pub games as being darts, ball, quiots, grass ends (for old men/boys), tipcat, knaurr and spell.

In Hunwick, the Miner's Arms and the Station Hotel both had Ball Alleys.

The Ball Alley at the Station Hotel, Hunwick

The Ball Alley at Hunwick station

Image 0184 – (Wally Smith, 2006 Digital Village Project)

Station can be seen in the background on photographs below.

The Public Houses were used for drinking, relaxation and pub games. The Miner's Arms and the Station Hotel both had 'Ball Alleys'.

Ball Alley at Hunwick Station in 1953. The Station Masters House can be seen in the background along with the wooden waiting room

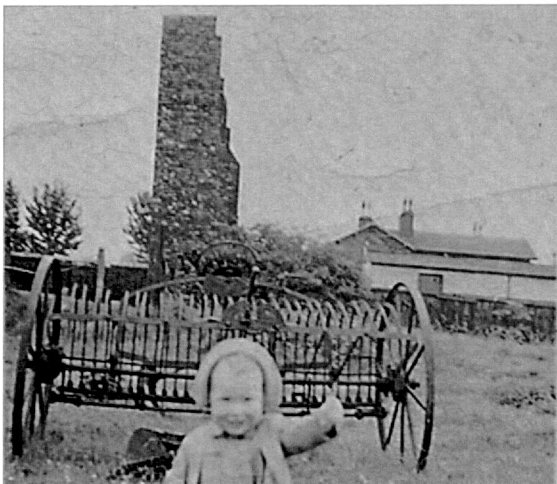

Image 0185

Harold Heslop describes the Masons Arms as being at the top end of the village opposite the Primitive Methodist Chapel. When he writes, he renames the Miner's Arms as the Mason's Arms. He explains

"Near the Mason's arms stood the Ball Alley, an imposing structure if its utter vulgarity was any measure of its aesthetic purpose. It towered to a great height, and was just a buttressed wall, faced smoothly on its playing surface with cement. It stood athwart a playing pitch of compounded clay upon which the two kinds of quoits- clay ends and grass ends – could be played. On this cemented wall face was played the game of handball. Such a game had fallen into disuse before the first world war". (Heslop, 1987)

The Newcastle Daily Chronicle advertises a match of 'fives, 33 up', with a £30 prize fund, that was to be played at the 'Star Ball Alley, New Hunwick', on 22 October 1892. The Newcastle Journal on 9 June 1893 reported that it had been agreed that a *"novel new match"* of fives would take place at Station Hotel, with each team contributing £15. *"Each player had a wooden leg, but nevertheless, they are clever exponents of the game, and a novel and keen contest is looked for".*

Billiards

Between 1946 and 1954, the Working Men's Club billiards team, were Durham County CIU champions. In 1950, they were selected to represent England in the National Shield, which they also went on to win, beating King's Cross in the final.

An article in the Newcastle Journal, on 24th March 1894, describes a billiards handicap that had been run at the Church Institute.

There were Billiard tables in Helmington Hall Social Club and the Working Men's Club.

Working Men's Club Billiards Team, 1950

Image 0354 – Northern Echo 18th November 2010

Hunwick Horticultural Show

The fourth annual show of the Hunwick Horticultural, Industrial and Livestock Society was held on Saturday 28th July 1906. An article in the Newcastle Daily Chronicle lists the prize-winners for categories including rabbits, cats, dogs and pigeons.

The Durham Chronical, on 14th August 1908, reports on the Hunwick Flower Show and Band contest that attracted seven bands from across the region.

Welly Throwing Competition at Lane Ends

Image 0420 - by kind permission of Robert Cunningham

Chapter 10 - Education and Schools

The first school was built in 1635 on the *"edge of the present Village Green, one of 37 built by the Bishop of Durham"*. (Gowland, 13 November 1980)

"the end house on the Green next to the road was double fronted, facing the road, with a small stone walled yard on the road side. This was thought to be a Dame school in the 18th or 19th century. These were usually run by an elderly woman who taught the local children how to read and write often using a horn alphabet ie a square horn with handle (like a hand mirror) on which was written the alphabet, and also aided by using the Bible." Donald White's notes)

In 1833, ten boys and six girls attended the school. The school was partly funded by Matthew and Elizabeth Bell of Hunwick Hall, and partly by payments made by parents. (Abstract of Education Returns, 1833)

The National School (St. Paul's Church School) was built in 1848.

The site, was donated by Elizabeth Bell, whose family had owned the Hunwick Hall Estate from 1759 until she married Matthew Bell in 1816.

Matthew and Elizabeth Bell also provided the land for the Church and the School House. As well as managing a large tract of agricultural land around the village, Matthew Bell opened Hunwick's first colliery on his land at Hunwick Station.

The National School

Image 0105 - the Herbert Coates Collection

Playground with Church in the background

Image 0370 – by kind permission of Harold Newton

In 1860 the National School was enlarged to create a large room and three classrooms.

"In the 1870s the large classroom to the back was always known as, the New Room, that was built as the school expanded. There was an open fire in most rooms around which children placed bottles of tea in the winter. As the school was too small for its needs, the upstairs Sunday school room of the Wesleyan Chapel was rented by the Church and my mother mentioned having to carry books up and down from the school." (Ref Donald White's notes)

From 1880, children who were aged between five and ten-years-old, had to attend school. To accommodate the additional pupils, in 1879, Helmington Infants School was built at Chapel Street.

Image 0226, shows that it was still operating on the site in 1921.

The school leaving age was raised to eleven in 1893, twelve in 1899 and fourteen in 1918

Helmington Infants School 1921

Image 0226 – (Sue Smith, 2006 Digital Village Project)

Hunwick Modern School and Hunwick County School

Image 0230 – (Sue Smith, 2006 Digital Village Project)

A Senior School, Hunwick Modern School and a Primary School, Hunwick County School were built on the site of the current Primary School. The schools, which took two years to build, were built as temporary structures with a design life of 25 years.

The schools were opened on the 1st of September 1924. The County School was for five, to seven-year-olds and the Modern School for eight, to fourteen-year-olds.

Donald White explains: '*Having identified the need for a larger school, the Local Education Authority went ahead, on a site opposite the old Church School with a field attached, to quickly build a new school. It was built on a timber frame covered with wire mesh and plastered and pebble dashed. A temporary building? But still it was in use until not so long ago and quite sound. Jack Straw the headmaster of the Church School was appointed head of the upper part of the new school and Miss Milne, a Scottish lady and a firm disciplinarian, who had come as head of the West End Infants School in 1919, was appointed headmistress of the new Infants School which eventually became 5yrs – 11 yrs. She retired the same year that I left, 1953. The desks in the top class were double tip-up seats on an iron frame with a shelf for books below the desk top at the back of which was a groove for pens and at each end an ink well. There were two slits at the back for slates. These must have come from the Church School, where, when grandmother was there (1870s) all writing was done on slates with a cloth to rub out. She said it was a serious offence to break your slate.*'

Parents were expected to contribute to the cost of running the school with parents in the 1920s paying four pence per week for each child that attended the school.

After the new schools were built, the National School was not required. It was used as the Church Hall until the mid-1980s when it was converted into two private houses.

In 1926 school dinners were introduced to abate some of the physical hardships children faced during the General Strike. This year also saw the worst attendance on record due to an epidemic of Small-pox, Chicken-pox and Scarlet Fever.

In 1932 the school was extended with a new hall and practical rooms being built. In 1936 the school playing field was drained and levelled.

The school became a Senior Mixed School for pupils aged eleven-plus. Previously it had taken them from seven-plus.

Donald White remembers that in 1952, the Junior School had five teachers, one for each class and a Headmistress.

In 1964, the Secondary School had nine Teachers and a Headmaster.

Sports Day 1947, cenotaph and School House in the background

Image 0229 – the Herbert Coates Collection

In June 1942, 12 pupils from the school were taken to Houghall College and featured in a Ministry of Information film, 'A Tale of Two Villages'. Unfortunately, I have not been able to find a copy of the film.

Hunwick School Sports Day, 1947 or 1948

Image 0366 – by kind permission of Joan Potts

From 1949 and because of the 1944 Education Act, Secondary Education in County Durham was remodelled to create a 'multi-lateral' system where a school specialised in particular curriculum areas and pupils were chosen to attend schools that offered the subjects that they were thought to be best suited. Hunwick children were either sent to King James or Bishop Auckland Girls Grammar School, Wolsingham Grammar School, Alderman Cape Secondary School in Crook, Willington Secondary School or Hunwick Secondary School.

Villagers remember how traumatic it was for them, as eleven-year-olds, to have to travel on their own to Bishop Auckland and then to find the school and sit in a large hall to take the examination. And then there was the wait for the result!

Pupils from the village who passed the two-part 11+ examination would continue their studies at King James Grammar School or later, Wolsingham Grammar School. The two Grammar Schools concentrated on preparing pupils for General Certificate of Education, 'O' Level and 'A' level qualifications with many progressing to study at university. Most pupils would travel by bus but some would use the train until Hunwick Station closed.

Dave Warner remembers his daily journey to Wolsingham in the 1960s: *'We caught the service bus at 7.30 to go to Willington where we were collected by a Baldwin and Barlow (Tow Law) bus which had collected pupils from Langley Moor, Meadowfield and Brancepeth. School finished at 3.50pm and the reverse occurred meaning us Hunwick kids didn't get home until after 5pm.'*

Three school buses brought pupils from Fir Tree, Witton le Wear, Howden and North Bitchburn to Hunwick every day. Pupils from Toronto travelled on the normal service bus, while those from Newfield, High Grange and Quarry Burn, walked to school. After the wooden trestle bridge that connected Hunwick Station to Newfield was demolished in the 1962, pupils from Newfield had to travel to school via bus.

From 1959, at the end of their 4th year in the school (now called Year 10), students could take the School Certificate examination set by local examination boards like the Northern Counties Examination board or they could leave without any qualifications.

When the CSE qualifications arrived in 1965, Hunwick School allowed pupils to work towards qualifications specialising in Office Studies. An out building was erected on the school field where Mr. Mole taught shorthand, typing and accounting. Willington Secondary Modern specialised in woodwork, metalwork and domestic science. Alderman Cape School in Crook had one class that studied for 'O' level and some pupils who had passed the first half of the 11+ examination were allocated places in this school. At this time students could leave school at the end of year 4 but would stay on an extra year to take these examinations. It wasn't until 1972 that pupils were required to stay at school until they were 16 years old.

Brenda Styles remembers that the secondary school introduced a school uniform in the mid-1960s that consisted of grey skirts or trousers, red jumpers and white shirts/blouses. The school had a badge that could be used on blazers but as most families couldn't afford to buy a blazer for their children, they were not compulsory. Joan Mason (nee Daniel) describes the school badge as *'a Phoenix rising through flames'* and remembers being told that the school motto was *'To win without meanness and to loose without regret'*.

Secondary School Badge

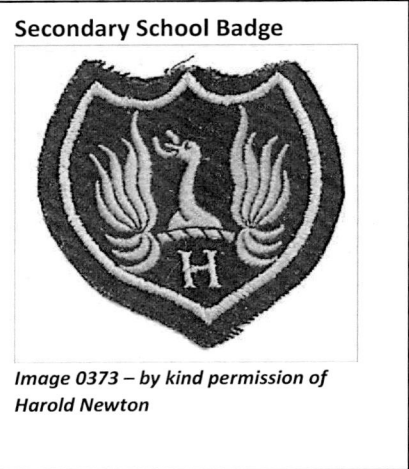

Image 0373 – by kind permission of Harold Newton

The school operated a house system for sports competitions. Inter house football, netball and hockey matches were held at the end of the Spring Term. In the 1920s the houses were named St Paul's (red), Helmington (Yellow), Manor (blue) and Rough Lea (green). Later the houses named after local castles, Raby, Brancepeth and Lambeth.

Mr Gregory and students, gardening in 1955

Image 0364 – (Jean Nicholson, 2006 Digital Village Project)

In 1976 when Comprehensive Secondary Education was introduced nationally, Hunwick Secondary Modern School was closed and existing pupils were transferred to Willington Comprehensive.

Plucking chickens in the school hall, 1932

Image 0365 – (Sue Smith, 2006 Digital Village Project)

Ronnie Thompson in the Science Lab, 1950s

Image – by kind permission of Judith Wills (nee Thompson)

The Primary school still operated on the site, but parts of the old School were condemned and boarded up. Parts were later reopened and used as a Community Centre until 2013 when the presence of asbestos meant that it was not economic to repair the building. The building was demolished in 2015.

In March 1980 the Primary School was burnt down in a fire and was completely rebuilt. During the rebuilding hardly any schooling was lost as parts of the old school were used to accommodate the displaced classes.

In 1989, Peter Nesom, involved his pupils with the design of a new badge for the Primary School. The Secondary School badge was based on the coat of arms of the Hoton family that had owned Hunwick Hall from 1418 until 1637. The coat of arms included a black ostrich head with blood red wings. The ostrich held a horseshoe in its mouth.

The Hoton Family Crest

Image 0230

A programme printed in 1968, for the annual Secondary School prize giving, uses the Hoton family crest with *"kindness and courage"* as the motto.

Primary School Crest - 1989

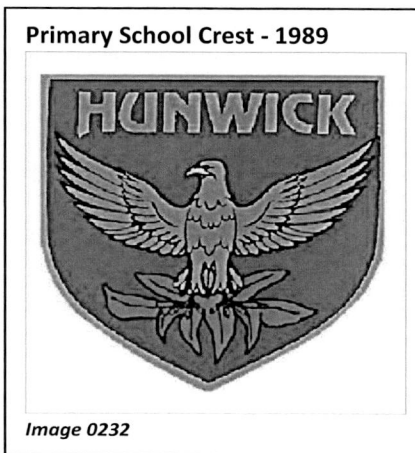

Image 0232

The new Primary School logo that was introduced in 1989, was based on the original secondary school badge but it used a phoenix rather than an ostrich to represent a school being raised from the ashes. The school adopted the badge and at the same time introduced a school uniform.

In 1974, as part of the school's 50th anniversary celebrations, Miss Milne was interviewed. She remembered that:

"the school had been designed to break away from the traditional school building and instead create a 'Garden School'. This would be a single storey school with plenty of large windows, almost to the ground and surrounded by gardens and playing fields."

When asked if any outside events had affected the school life, Miss Milne remembered that:

"the Great Strike of 1926 had very much upset the school and that a meal kitchen was opened to ensure that the children had at least one good meal a day."

She also remembered that:

"when Sunnybrow School had burnt down, Hunwick School gave up two of its classrooms to house the displaced students."

Chapter 11 - Stories from the Villagers

The stories which follow provide a flavour of village life. In December 2023, eleven Villagers volunteered to be interviewed and generously gave permission for their accounts to be shared here.

Tim Wellock spent time with each villager. He listened to, and wrote up their stories. Each adds a little to the overall picture of village life. Hopefully, these stories will inspire others to share their own stories of living or working in Hunwick.

The stories were gathered with the support of Northern Heartlands, who in turn were supported by funding provided by the National Lottery Heritage Fund and Durham County Councillors, Olwyn Gunn and Fraser Tinsley.

In addition to these eleven stories, Donald White's own short account of his life in the village and a transcript of a 2006 interview with Dorothy Turnbull, an evacuee, is included in this Chapter 11.

A poem "Only a Miner", which was written by George Henry Archer, is also included.

Agnes Smith

Born in 1931, Agnes has lived in Hunwick all her life and has clear and very fond memories of her childhood. She still lives in what she calls the Eternal Triangle, which links her house next to the Joiners Arms with the house next door, where she grew up, and what was the shop across the street. That was A J Taylor's general dealers, run by her grandmother then her mother with help from Agnes.

"There were about 30 shops in the village when I was young," she says. "We were one of six general dealers and we opened at 8am ready for three different bakers coming. People couldn't easily travel around so we had all kinds of shops in the village. My mum worked six days a week and I helped from leaving school at 14. It wasn't really what I wanted to do. I liked uniforms and would have loved to be a nurse, but my mother was my world and I wanted to help her. Dad used to say he wished he had a champion like me. He was a miner at Brancepeth Colliery and if he was on the back-shift he would cycle there at 1am. He was once buried for a few hours after a roof fall and the next time he didn't come home on his bike we found out he was in the surgery at Willington. He and a few others had been gassed and that's where they brought them round. Eventually we had enough money to buy a car and someone said miners must be getting well paid. But he regretted saying it when I pointed out it was because mum worked six days a week that we could afford a car."

Agnes went to school in the village and met her future husband, Wallace Smith, by chance at the age of 12 when returning across the school yard from the toilet. "He was with his mother, who asked me where the headmaster's office was. It gave me a chance to take a short-cut across the yard to his office, which we normally weren't allowed to take. Wallace told me years later that he told his mum that day he was going to marry the dark-haired little girl who had shown them the way. It was during the war and they had been bombed out of Sunderland. He had a sister who was engaged to a British Rail line inspector who had a house at Hunwick Station and they moved in there while he moved to Sunnybrow. Wallace said when he woke up to sunshine and saw trees and sheep, he thought he was in heaven.

"He was as bright as a button and got into King James's Grammar School at Bishop Auckland even though he missed the afternoon exam. They had all gone to Patterson's for pie and peas after the morning exam and he wasn't very well afterwards, but he had already done well enough to get through. He went on to be a teacher at Wolsingham Comp."

Agnes went to both junior and senior schools in Hunwick and remembers the air raid shelter outside the latter, as well as having to wear a gas mask during the war because of the proximity to the Durham Light Infantry camp at Brancepeth. "The mask was in a fancy black leather case, "she said". I only had to put it on a couple of times and I hated it. It was very claustrophobic and smelt of rubber."

Although they went to different schools, she and Wallace saw each other at the Wesleyan Methodist youth club, which Agnes had been attending from the age of six. "That was my favourite part of village life," she said. "The chapel people were wonderful. The chairman of the youth club was Mr Higginbottom and I remember him saying: 'Youth clubs may come and go but Rough Lea Methodist club will go on forever.' Kids came from all over and we were still going when we got married. We put on plays and pantomimes. The first play I remember doing was An Inspector Called. We also put on old people's treats and we had a fancy dress party every Boxing Day. Every other year we had a holiday. You had to be 12 to go, but they let me go just before my birthday to Scarborough, where we stayed in a Methodist guest house on the Esplanade. There was some religion involved but it was mainly about companionship. Next time we went to Blackpool on the service bus and stayed at the Palm Court just behind the miners' convalescent home. The club was our life and we were all great friends."

Agnes also developed a love of ice skating and went on the bus to Durham ice rink and remembers the famous Icy Smith, who launched the very successful Durham Wasps ice hockey team. *"We used to see Icy a lot in his funny little hat. He had two sons and a granddaughter who were very good players. On the way there we would call at the British Restaurant in Silver Street for corned beef pie and chips and if we had two pence to spare, we would go into Woolworths afterwards for a cup of tea and two crumpets."*

Agnes was married at 23 and they lived with her mother initially, knowing that the cottage next door would shortly be vacant. "We told them not to put it on the market, we would buy it," she said. And she's been there ever since.

Alan Edmundson

Alan first played for Hunwick West End football team at the age of 16 and a year later started an 18-year stint as secretary. He was powerless to stop its demise when other clubs started paying their players, but played a leading role in resurrecting the cricket club, which has gone from strength to strength.

Born in 1952 in Valley View (now West View), Alan's childhood memories are of playing outside with his friends. "We used to kick a football under the street lamps in front of Jean's shop," he said. "Or in the holidays we'd be out all day, playing cops and robbers or cowboys and Indians down by the pit heaps. We'd be climbing up and down them several times a day. I also remember being sent out with a shovel by my grandad to collect horse droppings for the allotment.

"The Co-op delivery man was Denzil Morland. He came round with his horse and cart and there would be a few of us competing for the horse muck. Another man with a barrow came round sharpening scissors and knives on a big stone wheel."

Alan went to the junior school in Hunwick but opted for the senior school in Willington because it offered him the chance to do metalwork. He became an engineer with a firm in Crook for ten years then worked for Rothmans in Darlington, while football dominated his leisure time.

"The Methodist Youth Club had a football team and so did the Pipe Works, but it was the West End team which really got me involved. The original pitch was down by the Brick Works but it deteriorated and after the move to the West End everybody used to go to the Wheatsheaf. Damaged knee ligaments stopped me playing seriously at 24 and I also discovered the delights of beer, but we won four cups during my time as secretary. We had a really good side, but then teams like Coundon Three Tuns, Crook Horse Shoe and Bishop Auckland Supporters' Club started paying money. The only income we had was from domino cards so we couldn't compete."

Alan's role in reviving the cricket club started over a drink in the New Monkey. There had been a club in the village from the 1890s but it had folded in the 1960s.

"Tommy Waggot said he had a cousin whose team at Thixendale in North Yorkshire wanted a friendly with us. They asked us to raise a team and go down there. Our bus struggled on Sutton Bank so we had to get out and push. After that we had more friendlies closer to home against Stapleton, Barton, East Cowton and Barningham. Interest grew and we formed a committee to raise money and buy equipment.

Among those involved were Ted Steele, Jack Davidson, John Sproats and Ken Penticost. Dave Crossan agreed to play and we raised £100 from a disco at the Elite Hall in Crook. We approached Harry Dobinson, who lived in Hunwick and played for Shildon BR. He got us some equipment and after a couple of seasons to establish ourselves became the mainstay of our team. We ran the club from the Monkey once we got established and we joined the Mid Durham Senior League in 1977, playing matches on the school field. The club has really moved on since then."

Betty Dunn (nee Pratt)

Scrapbooks and photo albums, lovingly compiled, provide Betty with a heart-warming record of her 94 years in Hunwick. For most of those she has attended the annual Durham Miners' Gala in Durham City and alongside her photos of the bands and banners are some of herself with luminaries such as Arthur Scargill and John Prescott. A 1920s photo of around 30 men assembled outside the Miner's Arms ready to leave for the Gala shows them all in their Sunday best, complete with trilbies. There's also a group photo from a 2005 reunion of Rough Lea Methodist's youth club members from the early 1940s.

Betty is a member of a stalwart village family, although her dad, Anthony Pratt, hailed from Gunnerside and came to Hunwick as a child when some Swaledale lead miners turned their attentions to coal. "He was a miner at 12," she said. "He worked at Rough Lea, but he said there was 'too much watter' and it had to close. He became a staunch Labour supporter and chairman of the local council. He was also a Rechabite, preaching 'Thou shalt not drink' and went to the Temperance Hall in the village.

Betty remembered that a lot of the ladies in the village were Aycliffe Angels, travelling on the train to work in the munitions factory at Newton Aycliffe during the war. During the War her mam had made her a tunic out of blackout curtains when she was captain of the youth club's netball team. "We played matches at the school and went round the other villages. The only time we lost was at Auckland Park because the referee was from there."

Betty was one of five children living in a two-bedroom house in Rough Lea Terrace. I went to the village school and remember the kids from Newfield walking there, coming over the old bridge, bringing their own jam sandwiches. The headmistress was very strict and you got caned just for talking in class. I remember when they ran leather-working and knitting classes there during the war. It was half a crown for ten lessons."

One of Betty's brothers, Laurie, played football for Durham County schoolboys and Willington during their glory years. Another brother, Raymond, played for the Hunwick cricket team during its early days at Brecken Hill and his son, John, became a driving force after the club rose from the ashes. Raymond also became a solicitor and registrar so he was the one Betty turned to when she spotted the long-lost Rough Lea Colliery banner at a preview for an Edkins sale at Bishop Auckland in 1975. "I often went along to the viewing just to see what was there," she said. "I rang Raymond and said I'd found dad's banner in the saleroom. It had a lion and a lamb on the front and I recognised it because I'd been dragged along to march behind it from an early age. I hated it then, but I grew to love the Gala and have only missed one. I got wrong off the family for going on the bus last year.

"The banner had been found by a builder from Crook called Arthur Lax. He said it was in a hotel at Crook but then changed his mind and said he found it when working at the Miners Welfare Hall in Sunnybrow. When I rang Raymond, he told me to go back and bid for the banner the next day, but then he rang the union people in Durham City and they got the sale stopped. They took it back to Redhills, but the roof came off there in a big storm and some banners got ruined."

John Cunningham's council influence resulted in the banner being restored by Caroline Rendell from Evenwood and it was re-dedicated by Arthur Scargill at Hunwick Methodist Chapel in 1994. That's how Betty came to be photographed with the NUM leader but she says the union bigwigs in Durham had fallen out with him so they weren't there.

Verna Rutter (nee Alderson)

Verna has spent most of her 79 years living alongside the Village Green, initially across the main road in Woodbine House. Until she was married, she was one of many Aldersons in Hunwick. "My mam and dad and both sets of grandparents were born in the village and dad had seven brothers and sisters," she said. "Dad worked at the Brick Works. He helped to feed us by fishing and hunting, bringing back rabbits, trout and salmon. Geoff Foster, the optician, once asked mam if she had ever had poached salmon and she jokingly said she'd never had any other kind. She was very sharp. Most people were quite poor, but we didn't feel poor."

Verna's earliest memory, at the age of three, is of having to go into Shotley Bridge Hospital for three weeks without any visits from parents. "I think they were told it would be too upsetting and in any case travelling there would have been difficult. I remember when my mam finally came my first thought as she approached was 'she looks a nice lady,' not realising at first it was her."

Once back home, Verna was soon playing out with her brother, Michael, in what they called the Back Hollows. "There was a field behind Woodbine House which had been deeply quarried and it was a wonderful place to go sledging or play cowboys and Indians. We had to go through an arch past a row of netties to get there. On other days we would climb into our stable loft. Among the things stored there was a cylinder for protecting us as babies from gas attacks when we were too small to wear masks.

"When I was 19 my other brother, Graeme, was born, bringing more great joy into our lives after growing up at a time when all the children were great friends. Apart from Michael, I was closest to Christine Hudspeth and John Shaw. We went to watch the village cricket team because it was quite a big thing on Saturday afternoons, and we took an interest in the farm by the Green. We watched them making cheese and went potato picking, but I don't think I ever filled a bucket because I was too small."

Part of Woodbine House had been a shop and that was the bit Verna's family lived in, while the property owners, her auntie, Grace Wood, and uncle Tom, lived in the other half. "Monday was wash day in both our houses and Auntie Grace had her own wash house in the yard. She lit a fire under a brick-based tub to heat the water, and she used a poss tub and a wooden mangle to wring out the water. In bad weather clothes lines would be strung across the living room. Uncle Tom was a great gardener and loved growing roses. To this day the smell of roses takes me back to happy days in the garden at Woodbine House."

Although they both retired before she left, Verna remembers Miss Milne as the headmistress and Miss Parkin as her deputy at the village primary school. "Lady teachers had to be single in those days," she said. Miss Milne was a strict, no-nonsense Scot and we were surprised to see her in tears when she assembled us to announce that the King had died. The Queen's coronation was an exciting time at the school. We were all given a coronation mug, which was special for us because we didn't have much. I loved my time at the school, especially books and drawing with coloured pencils. We took pleasure in things like paper chains and lanterns. When I became a primary school teacher 20 years later it was extraordinary what was available compared with what we had. The world was quite small for us, so everything we had was really precious."

Religion played a part and Verna went to what they called the Little Chapel and later became a Sunday School teacher. "My grandad, Tom Wardle, was a preacher at Rough Lea Chapel. He was a strict Methodist and if he came round on a Sunday mam had to hide her knitting. She made all my clothes. No work was allowed on a Sunday unless it was to provide dinner for the family. Everything was really Victorian. Grandad also had a barber's shop in a hut along from West View and there are still a few who can remember suffering his haircutting 'style.' Mam's mother died when she was 11 and grandad eventually married Doris. She was a midwife and many in the village can remember her delivering their babies. Mam's uncle, Hodgson Fletcher, had a carpenter's shop where he built coffins and mam sewed cushions for them as a girl. One day he picked her up and put her in a coffin. She thought it was great fun."

Verna remembers extra buses being laid on from Willington, through Hunwick, to Bishop Auckland on market days. "We used to go to the pictures there and to Doggarts. Their top floor was always turned into a magical Christmas department. But mostly we were in the village. Old Hunwick was quite small, so we knew everyone. We would go to the butcher's and the grocer's and to A J Taylor's opposite the pub to buy sweets. They were rationed until I was eight or nine, so you would only get two ounces if you were lucky. I had to share with my brother and if there was one left someone else had to have it.

"We had no indoor toilet or gas and you could be in the tin bath in front of the fire when the lights would go out and someone would have to scurry around to put a half crown in the meter. We had a crackly old radio, but no television until I was in my teens. Before that I can remember sitting on the wall at the Joiners Arms trying to watch the tele through the window. When we got one it was rented and always breaking down, so we had a terrible fear of it going off at Christmas."

Verna went to Crook Secondary Modern so she could do GCEs, saying: "I didn't know Crook at all until then so it was quite an adventure." They changed buses in Willington except when she and her friends decided to run down Station Road and catch the train just for the fun of it. After school Verna worked in the office of an electrical engineering company, Westool at Tindale Crescent, until she was married in 1966. She had two sons, Michael and John, then studied for a teaching certificate at Neville's Cross, followed by a final year at Durham University to gain a B.Ed. Starting in her early 30s, that led to a 30-year career at St Charles Roman Catholic School in Spennymoor.

Stephen Wragg

Memories of mischief feature prominently in the childhood recollections of a 75-year-old former HGV driver still known as "Wraggy" to his mates. Pinching apples and plums from Hunwick's orchards were minor misdemeanours, but he claims to have been caned regularly at school.

"I was always fighting," he said. "Usually, I accepted the caning from the headmaster, Mr Neesham, but one day I was falsely accused of something and told him I wouldn't have it because I'd done nothing wrong. I shoved him on his bottom and went home. My dad was always telling me to stick up for myself but he wasn't happy about that. Soon after that they wanted me to do a morning reading at assembly but I was too nervous. They said: 'You're frightened of nothing but you're too scared to get up and read'?"

Stephen was born at 13 Quarry Burn but a few years later the street was condemned and after living in Willington for two years the family returned to live in what had been the Miners Arms. Stephen's dad, John, set up a haulage business there in the mid-1950s and built a large garage on the side of the pub's ball alley. "He got an old ship's boiler to heat the garage and fed scrap wood into it and other odds and ends. We had a goat called Matilda and when it died, he chucked that on."

They were close to Quarry Burn Farm, which offered one of the fruit-stealing temptations. "Three sisters lived there," he said. "Me and my pal, Lesley Johnson, climbed on a wall to pinch plums and Elizabeth Heslop came out and chased us with a stick. Later she announced that she was giving away apples and plums. We went along but she said: 'You needn't have bothered coming.' We also used to go to the walled orchard at Hunwick Hall, where they had apples, plums and a huge pear tree."

Other early memories include digging bottles out of the ash in the disused quarry, 16-foot snow drifts in 1963, and the fairground people erecting a prefab, which served as a bingo hall next to their 'posh caravan.' His sense of humour was tickled by a tiny signal box at the Brick Works' railway sidings being christened Bantycock Hall, while a passageway off Church Lane used by courting couples was known as Tittlecock Alley.

"I went to the youth club in the Green Hut and there was another shed with a snooker table. They kept a good fire going in there so it was always lovely and warm. It was across the road from the Temperance Hall, but I didn't go there much."

His dad's haulage business got Stephen into lorry driving and he went to work in the Middle East for three years. "When I came back my teeth fell to bits and after the local dentist, Dave Cannon, fixed them I was told I wouldn't look out of place on the bridge of a Japanese battleship. So Dave re-fixed them."

Stephen met his wife, Lillian, in the Top Hat at Spennymoor in 1968 and they were married in 1974. "You used to get a tax rebate when you got married but that was the year they did away with it," he said. "The Wheatsheaf was my local but we used to come up to the Joiners when we were courting because that was the posh end of the village. Sometimes we would go to the Red Lion at North Bitchburn, where Lillian liked a 'gin and it'.

"The fish shop man, Phil Patterson, would cook his fish and chips then nip out to the Wheatsheaf. Sometimes he'd be playing the piano in there while his customers were helping themselves. He trusted them to leave their money on the counter.

"There was once a break-in at the Working Men's Club when the one-armed bandit was stolen. It was found the next day on the recreation ground but whoever took it hadn't been able to get it open. Back in the club the policeman who found it said: 'He must have been a bonny bugger if he couldn't get the money out.' The culprit was standing there and said: 'You should have been there, we couldn't get into it.' I think he did time."

Malcolm Fox

Born in 1941 at 3 Chapel Street, Malcolm continued in the family tradition of working at collieries and Brick Works. His grandad had been a miner at Eldon and his dad worked at Brancepeth Coke Works, but after tasting life in three local collieries Malcolm headed for Maltby in south Yorkshire. "I was 20 and went from earning £9 a week to £36. Maltby also had an open-air swimming pool. It was a deeper mine with a much higher coalface so you could stand up all the time. Round here you'd be working in 18 inches or two feet six at the most and they had to dig a bit of the floor out to move the tubs.

"I'd also worked in the drift mine at Sunnybrow, where you went in down some steps. It went under the river to Newfield. We took the coal out through a six-foot tunnel after digging it out using what they called the board and pillar method. We used to leave pillars of coal and in later years those pillars were mined from open cast sites."

Malcolm began life in a back-to-back house with one bedroom and a shared WC. He was one of three children and remembers his brother, Norman, being placed in one of the cylinders used to protect babies when a gas attack threatened. "It had a pump to press air in," he said. "I remember standing with my dad watching flashes over Coundon from bombing raids. Brancepeth Colliery had some imitation lights well away from the pit to act as a decoy.

"When I was seven we moved to a brand new council house in Willington, which was like a palace compared with what we had before. Sproat's waggon moved what little furniture we had. I had started school in Hunwick and there was a kiddie catcher called Jack Savage who went round the houses looking for those who weren't at school. He married one of the teachers, Miss Reeves, and we had to call her Mrs Savage after that. They later bought the Helmington Inn, which changed hands quite a lot."

When his mining days ended Malcolm worked for a motor spares company, Snowballs, in Bishop Auckland before two spells as a kiln burner at West Hunwick Brick Works either side of a stint at the Willington carpet factory. "I worked at the continuous kiln after the beehive kilns had gone. The firebricks went in one end and stayed in for a few days. We had to change the burners and clean them twice per shift. Oil went into the burner, which was inside a water jacket to keep it cool."

Malcolm took up weightlifting at one of the two recreation huts in Hunwick and also did a lot of jogging, which he blames for having to have both knees and a hip replaced.

John Pratt

John is the son of Raymond Pratt, brother of Betty, and has enjoyed a long association with Hunwick Cricket Club. His dad was a club stalwart and John started in the juniors at the age of eight in the late 1950s. After it folded in the 60s he got involved again following the resurrection in 1974. As well as playing he has served as secretary, treasurer and for the last 30 years he has been the groundsman. The club was in the Mid Durham Senior League from 1975 until the league folded 12 years later, then they were in the North East Durham League until they won it in 2017, since when they have competed against the likes of Durham City in the Durham and North-East League.

Other than the few moribund years, John believes the cricket club has always been at the heart of the village and the impressive facilities are a reflection of the community spirit. "We've done it all ourselves with about ten volunteers," he said. "We had been using the school field but there was a diesel spillage on the cricket pitch at the time when the Pipe Works land had been reclaimed and levelled. We got permission to use it, but there were no facilities in the early years. We got two wooden buildings from nearby schools and put in a septic tank, followed by a water supply and electricity in 2012. We built the current brick-built clubhouse with changing rooms, showers and a bar in 2022, with great efforts from his son Chris and daughter-in-law Lianne. We run two senior teams and juniors from under nines upwards. The players, committee and volunteers are all local lads and they all do it just for the enjoyment.

John is well versed in local history, partly through the writings of Harold Heslop, his mother's cousin. He also knows that butcher Simpson Heslop rented the original cricket field at Brecken Hill and they lost the use of it when he sold his business. "We tried to lay a square on the recreational field but it didn't work," he said. "It was also a football pitch, but it was on such a slope you needed to score three or four playing downhill to have a chance. There was a time when the youth club, the Joiners Arms, the Quarry Burn Inn and the Pipe Works all had football teams."

The best footballer among John's contemporaries to come out of Hunwick was David Crosson, who lived in Railway Terrace. He played six times for Newcastle's first team before new boss Gordon Lee released him and he spent five years with Darlington. "As boys we spent most of our spare time playing football or cricket on the Village Green," said John. "Later I used to travel with Dave to watch Newcastle training in the days of people like Malcolm Macdonald. After his time with Darlington Dave went to play in Tasmania and is still in Australia.

"There are hardly any local football teams now and it was a sad day when the cricket club also folded, but we started again on the school field. The school kids played on it every day and if you scored 30 on there it was worth 70 anywhere else. The club kept going because it was a big part of the community with wine and cheese parties, barbecues and quiz nights at the Joiners raising funds. We had meetings in all the pubs."

John Cunningham

Born in 1951 in Coronation Terrace, John rose from humble beginnings to become a national trade union figure and represent Hunwick with distinction on Wear Valley Council, where he was chairman of planning and finance. He also took charge of saving the Wear Valley railway, became managing director of the company and persuaded well-known record producer and railway enthusiast Pete Waterman to join the board.

"Hunwick stood still for a long time after it was designated a Category D village in the 1960s," he said. "But it has since gone from being a small mining village to a well-thought-of, prosperous village which everyone can be proud of. When I was first on the council there was a saying that Hunwick gets what Hunwick deserves – nowt. Much later it became 'Hunwick gets what Hunwick wants' and some council officers said it had become the centre of the universe."

Although Coronation Terrace survived, many of the adjacent streets of miners' houses were demolished under Category D. One benefit was that the surviving dwellings said goodbye to their outside WCs. "From a wooden seat everything went straight down into a pit, which was cleared by a man in a horse and cart," said John. "Then he would chuck in some pink powder disinfectant. I remember there was a tin on the bottom of his cart which was always swinging.

"We moved to Sunnybrow when I was eight, but I went to both junior and secondary schools in Hunwick until I was 15. I left on a Friday and started work on the Monday at Rough Lea Pipe Works. I was a mould maker, then I made garden gnomes, but there wasn't a big demand so it didn't last long. We sent pipes all over the world with big black ink stamps on them. One stamp I remember was to Dar-es-Salaam.

"After the Pipe Works closed, I worked at a carpet factory in Willington, where I became the full-time convenor for the Dyers, Bleachers and Textile Workers Union. They sent me to Newcastle Arts and Technology College for five years on day release and within two years I was on the national executive. The union became part of the Transport and General and after the carpet factory closed, they put me through Northern College in Barnsley, which was renowned for producing urban guerrillas. I used to hitch-hike there from home. The college's founding principal was Michael Barratt Brown, one of the cleverest men I ever met. He was also one of the founders of the Fair-Trade movement."

John continued his studies at Durham University, gaining a degree in sociology and social politics prior to being elected to Wear Valley Council. His contacts at the university enabled him to borrow a Geiger counter from the physics department to test for radioactivity at the former Rough Lea Pipe Works. "There was a saying: 'Work at West Hunwick and glow in the dark'. The waste material went into 48-gallon drums which got taken away in the middle of the night. The man who lent me the Geiger counter said the reading levels went from nought to three, but even if it went to one I should get out of there. It happened as soon as I got over the fence, so I did as he said. I'd torn my trousers and got a bad scratch on the fence so I went to the doctor. It turned out he was the Works' doctor so it went no further."

Despite his later involvement with the Weardale railway, as a boy John was not one of the many enthusiastic train-spotters at Hunwick Station. "There were loads of them," he said. "The beauty of it was that on Sundays when they were doing repairs on the main line engines like the Flying Scotsman and Mallard would come through Hunwick. Some lads would put copper pennies on the line and after the train passed over them, they would be more than twice the size."

As a union man, John is proud of his part in saving Rough Lea Colliery's banner, although he admits it was a stroke of luck that after being missing for years it was spotted at an Edkins sale in Bishop Auckland by Hunwick resident Betty Pratt. "She just happened to be there and stopped the sale," he said. " It was in a state of disrepair but I got the council to cover the cost of refurbishing it. We wanted to have it draped in Hunwick WMC but the NUM said it was their property and it spent 18 months standing in open sunlight at their Redhills headquarters. It was in a poor state again, so I got Arthur Scargill to come up and he re-dedicated the banner on a great day for the village. We now have our own replica which we take to the Durham Miners' Gala every year."

From the Big Meeting to the surreal meeting, John had the task of accompanying Bjorn Vernhardsson on his visit to the village. The Icelander hoped to prove that Rough Lea was the site of the Battle of Brunanburh in 937 AD and that Hunwick was the social centre for Anglo Saxon Northumbria.

"I went around with him for three days," said John. "One of his ancestors died in the battle and he had done a lot of research into it. He kept going on about Helwith, a hamlet on the moors above Marske in Swaledale. He said the Saxons were steered by the stars and at the summer solstice Hunwick lined up with Helwith. We went up there and he was disappointed that there wasn't a cross or a church denoting the significance of the place. We were taken to a mound on the moor, which was in the exact shape of an inverted Viking ship and Bjorn said the stern pointed directly to Hunwick and the prow to Iceland. If he thinks Hunwick is the centre of the universe, why should we disagree?"

Pub tales from John Cunningham

Although most of the local collieries had closed by the time John was 15 he remembers that there was still a big drinking culture. "The miners would drink until closing time and still be at work at 6am," he said. "For some, it didn't really stop. At the Wheatsheaf there was a group known as the four wise men – the fish shop owner Phil Patterson, Joe Noble-Eddy, Jimmy Finnegan (known as Fagin) and Freddie White, known as dyno-rod because he worked at the sewage works. Fagin could deal a hand of cards and knew every card that everybody had. He was a likeable rogue, but it caused a lot of bother. He walked with a stick and one night the landlord went upstairs and left them to it. Fagin took a needle out of his lapel, put it in the rubber on the end of his stick and leaned over the bar to stab a packet of cigarettes, which went into his pocket.

"A chap called Puffer Archer looked after the fish shop while Phil was at the pub and one night when Phil got back he told Puffer to get himself a fish and six and get away home. The next night Phil told his mates it had cost him a fortune because Puffer went and battered a whole cod.

"The four of them were still in the pub at 3pm one Sunday afternoon when the door burst open and Freddie's wife sent a full dinner plate with knife and fork spinning across the floor. She said: 'You've been here all day, so you might as well have your dinner here.' He didn't bat an eyelid, just set away and ate it.

"There was a regular at the Joiners called Jackie Hopkinson who had served in the war and was always telling a story about losing a military vehicle in the desert, forcing him to walk miles in the heat. They heard it so often that some of the lads in the pub put together a letter from the Ministry of Defence and sent him a bill for the cost of the vehicle."

Harold Newton

Harold moved to Hunwick after he was married to local girl Anne Johnson in 1956 and has lived in the village for 68 of his 93 years. He was born in Witton Park and after his own father was invalided out of the First World War in 1917 he was brought up with tales of the Fighting Bradfords, the four Witton Park brothers famous for their war exploits, which earned two of them Victoria Crosses. "Their house was converted into the police station. We had three PCs," he said.

He was also familiar with pitman painter Tom McGuinness, who was very friendly with Harold's elder brother, Jack. Harold has a drawing of himself aged 17 on his living room wall, sketched by Tom, who became a miner as a Bevin Boy, selected to boost coal production instead of going to war. "Jack married a Sussex girl and went to live in Chichester," said Harold. "But when he came up to visit he'd get in touch with Tom and they would come and have a meal with us.

"Tom was a Catholic and we were Protestant and normally we didn't mix. Even at the pictures they'd be on one side and we were on the other. But Tom and Jack got on really well. We lived just down the street from his family. Mum and dad had five kids in five years and we all slept in the same bed with the two girls at the top end and the boys at the other."

Harold met Anne at a King's Hall dance in Bishop Auckland and they were married at Hunwick Church, living first at Rough Lea before moving to No 5 The Green. "I was a welder at the Shildon railway works but it was under threat of closure when I was offered a job at Newton Cap brickyard, so I went there".

"A lot of people at Rough Lea worked at the Pipe Works, where Anne's dad was a manager. He made things like Belfast sinks. I remember when they did away with the beehive kilns in about 1960 and a German company built a continuous kiln.

"I used to walk up from Rough Lea to drink at the Joiner's and played cribbage and quiots on the Village Green. A lot of the old blokes drank whisky and Peter Laws put milk in it. He would pop across the Green to his farm to fetch it. Tiddler Temby was the landlord and if anybody complained about the Vaux beer he would say: 'Well I'm drinking it'. He went to Darlington every Monday, when the pubs were open all afternoon because it was market day. He'd bring some pies back to serve in the pub. When he died his wife had the pub, then Ian Richardson Snr took it over on decimalisation day."

Harold was one of the founder members of the cricket club when it was resurrected in the 1970s, although he hadn't been brought up with the game. "It was all football at Witton Park and some good players came out of there," he said. "I still pay my membership fees to the cricket club but I don't watch much now."

Betty Thompson (nee Nattrass)

At 91 Betty has vivid memories of being in the 100,000 crowd at Wembley in 1954 to see her husband, Ronnie, score one of the 117 goals which made him Crook Town's record scorer. "I'd just had my appendix out but went on the team bus with most of the other wives. I'd never been to London before," she said. "It was part of Ronnie's banter that if a friend talked about what he'd achieved he'd say: 'Yes, but you haven't scored a goal at Wembley'."

The match against Bishop Auckland became legendary for its record aggregate attendance of 200,000 because it took replays at Newcastle and Middlesbrough to settle it. Crook won 1-0 at Ayresome Park, but Betty missed that because of work. She still has a telephone directory which Ronnie's dad used as a scrap album, pasting in all the newspapers cuttings about his son's exploits.

Army service and injury cut short Ronnie's career, but he played cricket for Hunwick and golf at Bishop Auckland, where he was friendly with county player Lester Aisbitt. After gaining a B Sc degree he taught at Hunwick's senior school then Crook and finally Willington Parkside until he died at the tragically early age of 52.

Betty has never moved far from her birth home in Quarry Row and when it was condemned, she remembers being the first family to move into some new council houses. Her dad, Ernest Nattrass, was a miner from Weardale who came to work at Rough Lea, while her mum was from Hunwick.

"I remember being in the garden with my dad and watching planes go over during the war. My brother, Tom, was stationed at the DLI camp at Brancepeth, but we thought the planes were on bombing raids to Sunderland or Newcastle."

She knew Ronnie from their time together at the junior school in the village. "We had to behave because the headmistress was very strict and there was another teacher who would chuck the blackboard rubber at us. I also remember going with three cans on my arm every night to collect milk from the farm across the Green. It was a proper green then with a maypole next to two wooden seats, where we congregated and the boys would play Knocky Nine Doors.

"The Laws family had the farm and I spent a lot of time with their eldest daughter, Dopper. She had a sister, Bella, and two brothers, Thomas and Peter. My brother used to help them, looking after the cattle and hay-making. I enjoyed going to the youth club. It was great fun putting on pantomimes and going on trips. We stayed one year in the Methodist guest house at Bispham, just outside Blackpool. There was one day trip up Teesdale when a few of them caught typhoid, including my brother. He had to go into the hospital at Helmington Row."

Among Betty's other random recollections are the village band practising next to what is now the Quarry Tearoom, the barber Tommy Wardle putting a basin on gentlemen's heads, Jane Nick's shop supplying everything, including paraffin, and Heslops the butchers taking meat round in a van on Fridays.

Ronnie's family were transferred from their colliery house to Sunnybrow after his dad lost a leg in a mining accident. After junior school Ronnie went to King James's Grammar in Bishop, then got called into the army before studying to be a teacher at Bede College in Durham. Betty went to work at Doggart's store in Bishop, travelling by bus. "There were three bus companies, Bonds, Frankie Wilson and Elite, and they would pile the passengers on so sometimes they could hardly get up Newton Cap Bank. Then I decided to train to be a nurse and went to the county hospital in Durham. But it changed to specialise in orthopaedics so those of us doing general training had to move. I went to Bishop hospital, but in those days, it was just a hut and I didn't like it so I went to work at the Ramars clothing factory in Crook."

Betty married Ronnie when she was 23 and they had two children, Ian and Judith.

Ian Richardson

Ian inherited the Joiners Arms when his dad, also Ian, gave it up in 2002 after taking over the Vaux tenancy on decimalisation day in 1971. Ian junior still owns the village's last remaining pub. *"It's hard work mainly because of the energy costs but I'm sure it can survive,"* he said.

"Mum and dad live next door. They came to Hunwick from Willington and when dad lived in Co-operative Terrace he worked as a bag man for Cyril Parkinson, the village bookie. They used to go round all the flapping tracks. Dad always knew when his own dog was going to win. He fed it lots of Mars bars. There was a villager called John Nicholson who drove the bus on one trip to a greyhound meeting when they loaded up with beer and were almost at the track when they realised, they'd forgotten to bring the dog. Dad and his pal still have a couple of dogs, but the flapping tracks have gone so it's either Sunderland or further afield at Sheffield or Nottingham."

Ian was born shortly after his parents took over the pub and learned later that on the first day the till became obsolete. "Dad took out the wooden drawer and threw the rest of the till away. When I took over in 2002 the police came in just after closing time and the new inspector asked to see the till roll. My mother simply handed him the till and said: 'Check that son.' His training on what to do to check up on pubs serving after time was in tatters."

Ian remembers a story about a man named Geordie Maddison riding a pig round the Village Green. And Mel Calvert drank so much stout that he was known as Mel Guinness.

"There were also fishing trips from here. Once they went to Hartlepool and went out in a strong wind. Most of them were seasick and they caught nothing, but back on land they bought a load crabs and mussels to make it look as though they'd had a good day.

"A scaffolder called Billy Chicken challenged dad to see which of them could lose the most weight. Dad got on the scales with his fishing weights down his trousers and every time they were re-weighed, he left out one more of the weights. He carried on eating and drinking as much as usual and Billy couldn't understand how he was winning the contest.

"There was once a problem with flies in the pub and dad put up two of those sticky fly papers and took bets on which one could catch the most. He took the money then collected dead flies from the window sills and stuck them on the tape he wanted to win.

"My grandad, John, didn't drink much and didn't like dad taking the pub. He once won Santa Claus of the Year in a competition run by The Northern Echo. Drinkers in the pub would book him for Christmas Eve and once when my sister saw him coming across the Green she said: 'Why is Santa wearing grandad's boots?'

"I remember grandad going mad when dad had to be held up at the oche in a darts match after getting drunk at Wolsingham Show. But dad shot 180 to win the match. Things have changed, but most of the Villagers like a drink and there's always something going on. We still have the village show and the pub is a community asset. We need to keep it going."

Donald White

"I was born at 15, Rough Lea Colliery, then moved to number four and, aged ten, to number one. So, I'd moved up in the world and been about a bit! Number one was the colliery manager's house, quite a bit larger than the rest apart from number three, the engineer's house, and in 2024 I am still there, aged 82. The colliery manager, Michael Heslop JP, had moved to Quarry Burn House in the early 1900s, where his three daughters continued to live after him. Much later I talked to one of them who said she had been born at Roughy!"

"Roughy was a self-contained community of 19 houses. Grandmother and Aunt Amy lived at number 18 and my cousin Edna and family at number six. It is a glorious place surrounded by open country and woodland. The Rough Lea Works and the pit heaps were there, but it was still a wonderful place to explore as a child. Hunwick is an ancient, beautiful village. I love it."

"Father and my brother kept hens and pigs in an allotment opposite the houses. I had to feed them morning and night and collect the eggs. My brother spent time at Furnace Mill farm and Rough Lea farm. He ran two bullocks on Furnace Mill land and I had to go on a black dark winter morning and night to the open the building where they sheltered and climb into the loft to fork down hay for them. It was frightening."

"When World War Two was over there was a street party in the bottom field. It was a treat for me at three years old, with sandwiches, cakes, custard and jelly. The whole street was there. There was another party for the Coronation on the veranda of the old colliery offices with bunting and pictures of the Queen. Again, a treat. During the war and for a short while afterwards we children spotted many planes and the shout was always: 'Is it one of ours?' It invariably was."

"In 1947 winter snow fell very heavily. People had to dig a trench from their gate to get to the road. It was about 3 feet deep."

"Saturday shopping in Bishop Auckland was an experience. I had to go with my mother to carry the bags of groceries. You could hardly stay on the pavement for the hundreds of people shopping. The bus was packed for the journey back to Hunwick."

"From King James 1 Grammar School I went to Bede College, Durham, and became a teacher. At the age of 29 I was elected to the Crook & Willington Council from 1970 until 1991. In 1974 this was expanded to include Bishop Auckland, Weardale and Tow Law as Wear Valley Council. I instigated many improvements to the community -- a new reservoir as the old one was open to the skies, backstreets tarmacked, stone bus shelters, the removal of part of the field from Quarry Farm Close to the school to put in a footpath, the removal of four streets of mainly two-roomed houses without facilities, among other things. I also answered an incalculable number of other individual requests – helping all who asked. It was a privilege to be involved in the school, football clubs, social centre, recreation ground and the church as a church warden for 20 years. I served as an active magistrate from 1971 until 2005."

"Rowing was my sport from college to Durham Amateur Rowing Club and after many years of rowing and coaching in Durham I am a life member of the club."

"I daily thank my Maker for allowing me a useful and a beautiful life. Long may it continue in Hunwick!"

Dorothy Turnbull (nee Moore)- Recollections of an Evacuee

Dorothy Turnbull (nee Moore) was born in Bensham on 17th April 1932. In 1939 Dorothy and her sister Gladys were evacuated from Gateshead to Hunwick. They lived with Mr and Mrs Joe Heslop who ran the butcher's shop in Helmington Square.

In 1956 Dorothy married Jack Turnbull, an accountant from Sunnybrow, who worked at Brancepeth Colliery in the office and later as a driving instructor. They lived in the village, initially at 13 Helmington Terrace then from 1970 until 2011, at Number 7, The Green.

Dorothy also worked as a driving instructor, and she worked at Smith's garage at Willington for many years. In 1974 she got the job of school auxiliary at Hunwick Junior and Infant School where she remained until 1985 when she left to look after Mrs Heslop when she became ill.

Dorothy enjoyed village life and in July 2006, as part of the Digital Village project, she wrote down her story of being an evacuee during the Second World War. She volunteered to be recorded while she shared her story. A transcript of the recording is included below:

"The first picture that comes to mind of that traumatic day in 1939 is of myself hiding away in the bedroom of my home in Gateshead and literally being dragged to school by my older sister.

We gathered in the school yard, children from 5 to 11 years old, most of whom had never been further than the school itself, and were bewildered and frightened like myself. Some were excited by what they saw as a big adventure. We all carried a square cardboard box containing a gas mask and a small suitcase or a pillowcase tied at the top to hold a few belongings. We all had a label pinned to our coats with our personal details, name, age, home address, destination etc written on it. We walked in "crocodile" fashion to the train station where family and friends were waiting to wave goodbye as the train pulled away.

We arrived at Hunwick Station, after what seemed to us to be a very long journey. Again, we formed a long "crocodile" and walked from the station to the school where we were met by teachers and "billeting officers". Many village people had volunteered to take children into their homes. We sat on the floor in the school hall and were taken by the teachers and helpers to our new homes.

A teacher from the school, Mr Moore, took my sister and myself by car (a ride in a car was really exciting) to our new "foster parents", Mr and Mrs Joe Heslop who owned the village butchers' shop, where we were welcomed with open-arms, given a good hot meal and were really fussed over.

For the first few nights we slept on a "shake me down", a made-up bed on the floor of the bedroom. Eventually we had new beds and bedroom furniture. We were very lucky indeed!

Several of our teachers from Gateshead came for a few weeks so there were familiars faces when we came to lessons again. We settled in well and everyone was kind to us.

At the side of the school hall there were several air-raid shelters. In every classroom cupboard there was a large tin of barley sugar sticks. Each week we had air-raid practice, everyone was given half a stick of barley sugar and taken into the shelters. We had to put on our gas masks for ten minutes, not a pleasant experience as they were very uncomfortable to wear.

My sister went home two years later in 1941. I was fortunate in gaining a place at Bishop Auckland Grammar School and so stayed until I left school at seventeen when I was able to choose where I could live. I was very happy in Hunwick and decided to stay here. I am still here, the original evacuee, after 68 years in the village!

My life has cantered around this village with its many activities, School, Chapel, Youth Club, Cricket Club and Women's Institute and the Community Centre. Hunwick is very special to me, I recommend village life to everybody, I don't think that I will be leaving now!"

George Henry Archer- Only a Miner

The poem "Only a Miner", was written by George Henry Archer.

He was born in the village in 1894 and had been a miner for all of his life with the exception of his time in the army during the first World War.

During the Second World War he served as a member of the Home Guard.

The poem only came to light when his grandson, Alan Edmundson found it after his death in 1979.

Only a miner who works underground,
Toiling and striving all the year round,
Fretting and pining his poor life away,
Though he labours hard he receives little pay.

Shut up in the dreary, dismal, dark mine,
From the pure air of heaven, where the sun never shines,
Stripped to the waste like a Trojan of old,
As he breaks into fragments the hard solid coal.

Surrounded by darkness and dangers unseen,
As the sweat trickles down him in many ways a stream,
He braves death and dangers to earn a bit of bread,
While others stay snugly and warm in their bed.

The caller he comes close to 3 o'clock,
And wakens him up from his sleep with a knock,
"Call the men up" he cries out with a shout,
And from his warm bed he is forced to turn out.

He must then at once get to his feet,
Put on his pit clothes and get something to eat,
He barely has time his pipe to get lit,
Before he must hurry to get to the pit.

When he gets to the shaft where the men stand around,
Waiting their turn with the cage to go down,
As the heps are drawn back the banksman does say,
"Fairly on to the bottom lads; heave her away!"

As down in the earth he descends with a gloom,
While all is as silent as and dark as the tomb,
Far away from his home and those he loves dear,
The brave honest miner no danger does fear.

As soon as the cage at the bottom does land,
He must hurry in-by with his lamp in his hand,
For oft in the mine he has a long way to go,
And must travel half-double the roof is so low,

When they get to the kist the men have to stop,
While the deputy goes and examines the top,
He's to see all's right and no gas at the face,
Before he dare send a man to his place.

For a few minutes he has time for a rest,
Till the deputy comes back again to the kist,
As he looks at his watch , to the men he will say,
"Time up now lads you can all go away".

Each man from the flat then away takes his tub,
Sometimes it may happen he's in a loose jud,
Where the coal is canny he may get a good day,
To keep up his bit wage at the pay.

Perhaps it may be he's in a bad wall,
Where the coal is so hard he can't hew at all,
Tho' he works till he's silly and does all he can,
Yet the master tells him he's not an average man.

God help the poor miner, for hard is his lot,
Tho' he works every day he can scarce boil the pot'
As he toils on in slavery year after year,
Too proud a man to dare shed a tear.

So now my dear friends ere I finish my rhyme,
Take a word of advice from an old friend in time,
Let brotherly love be your motto through life,
And show love and respect to your dearest wife.

Let unity be a password to all,
United we stand divided we fall,
Then when to this earth we bid adieu,
Let our record prove we are faithful and true.
Amen.

Chapter 12 - Transport

The Industrial revolution created a massive demand for coal to generate steam and for coke to fire the furnaces needed to smelt iron. Much of the coal that was mined in the village was turned into coke. There were coke ovens at Hunwick, West Hunwick and Rough Lea Collieries.

Bricks and pipes were also in demand to build the factories and the houses for the workers. Hunwick, West Hunwick and Rough Lea Collieries all had their own Brick Works.

Not only did the coal have to be mined, the bricks and coke made, but they had to be transported to the sea ports and to the steel works on Teesside. This created the demand for railways.

West Durham Railway

Hunwick Colliery was sunk at Hunwick Station in 1839. In the same year, an extension of the Byers Green branch of the West Durham Railway was opened. (Bell, 1852)

From Hunwick Station, the line passed over the River Wear, on a wooden trestle bridge, to Newfield and on to Byers Green.

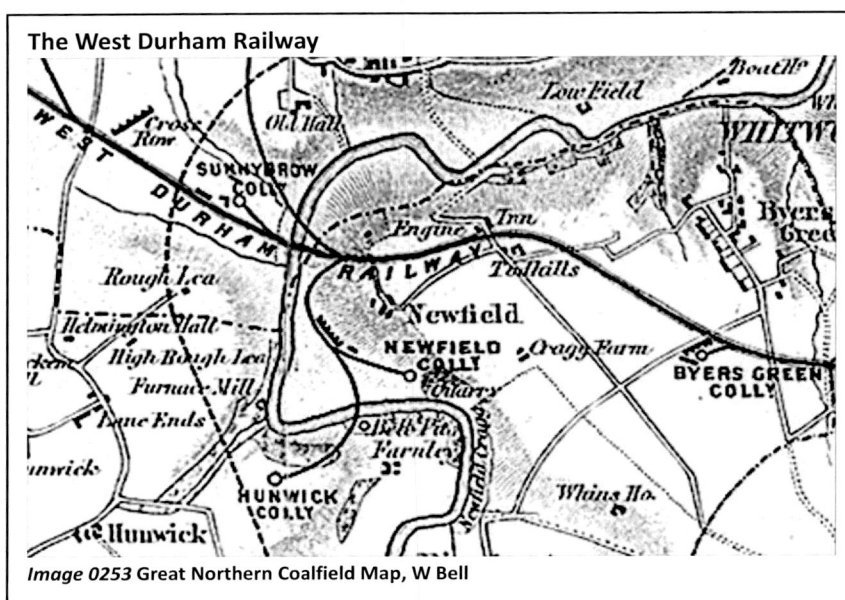

The West Durham Railway

Image 0253 Great Northern Coalfield Map, W Bell

The bridge was built in 1838, *"it consists of one stone pier and two abutments, with a timber platform trussed above the level of the roadway to form 4 lines of railway".* It was 200ft long and 39 ft wide and was 20 ft above the level of the river (The_Railway_Times_Volume_2, 1939)

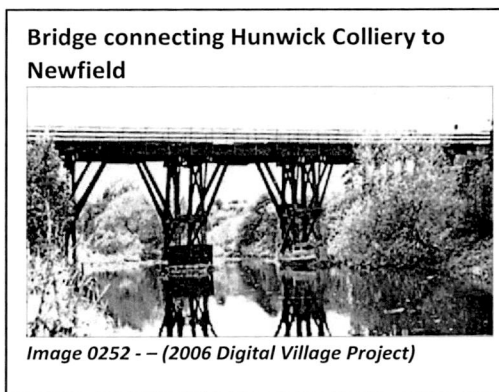

Bridge connecting Hunwick Colliery to Newfield

Image 0252 - – (2006 Digital Village Project)

A stationary steam engine powered a rope haulage system that lowered waggons, full of coal, down the inclined track and across the bridge to Newfield. Empty waggons were hauled back up to the colliery.

From Newfield, the full waggons were hauled, by rope up to the Engine House at Todhills. From there, the waggons were moved onto the Byers Green branch of the West Durham Railway line. Locomotives pulled the waggons to Port Clarence at Hartlepool where the coal was loaded onto Colliers and transported to the industrial centres in the south.

The North East Railway (LNER)

The national railway network developed very quickly after the Stockton to Darlington Railway opened in 1825. Railways encouraged trade and personal mobility as well as supporting the creation of the national postal and telegraph services. The main NER railway line that used to pass through Hunwick Station, now part of the Brandon to Bishop Auckland footpath, ran between Bishop Auckland and Durham and then onto Sunderland and South Shields.

The North Eastern Railway (NER), opened the line to carry freight in August 1856 and to carry passengers in April 1857. This railway line, as well as allowing coal to be shipped from the original Hunwick Colliery, also served West Hunwick and Rough Lea Collieries.

After the NER line opened, the mineral line that connected Hunwick Colliery to the West Durham Railway, via Newfield, was not used to take coal, coke and bricks from Hunwick. However, it was used to bring coal and bricks from Newfield to Hunwick Station and onto the NER line. It was also used to transport waste from Newfield to fill in the clay pit at the Brick Works at Hunwick Station.

Hunwick, West Hunwick and Rough Lea Collieries all had their own sidings and shunting locomotives. The shunting engines moved waggons around on the colliery sites and assembled the train of waggons in the railway sidings so that they could be collected by the main-line locomotives.

This was much easier as the mineral line link to the West Durham Railway was a hybrid system that used a standing steam engine and ropes to haul the trucks up the incline from Newfield to Todd Hills before they were connected to a locomotive.

Rough Lea Junction Signal Box

Image 0254 – A Alder, Willington

Hunwick Railway Station

Hunwick Station had two platforms, a station masters house, a signal box, a level crossing and a passenger bridge. Donald White explains:

"Hunwick station had two waiting rooms, one each side of the track. That on the east side consisted of two wooden buildings with a 10ft gap between but all covered by a single roof. The waiting room was on the Willington end and in the middle of it a freestanding iron stove and chimney pipe. It was sometimes lit in the winter mornings. The room at the Auckland end was storage. Myself and several other pupils attending King James 1st Grammar School for boys and those at the girl's grammar had to take the train, a steam engine, to Bishop Auckland every morning. It was quite a walk

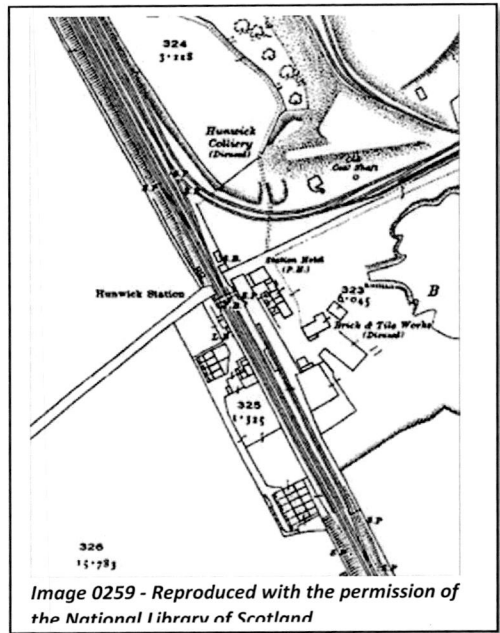

Image 0259 - Reproduced with the permission of the National Library of Scotland

On the village side of the NER railway line at Hunwick Station, there were sidings that connected West Hunwick and Rough Lea Collieries to the main line. On the river side of the line there were sidings that connected Hunwick Colliery and Brick Works to the main line as well as connecting the Bell Pit and Newfield Colliery and Brickworks.

Hunwick Station, looking towards Willington

Image 0258 - by kind permission of disused-station.org.uk

The signal-box controlled access to the goods yard, the colliery and Brick Works sidings as well as the opening and closing of the crossing gates.

Hunwick Station Signal Box, 1963

Image 0256 - by kind permission of disused-station.org.uk

It was a well-used passenger and freight station.

'In 1911 the station served a local population of 3143 with 40982 tickets being issued that year. In the same year, 14030 bricks, 11366 tons of clay/gannister and 4847 sanitary tubes were despatched from the Brick Works.' (Catford)

In addition to the scheduled services, there were rail excursions to destinations such as: Tynemouth, Whitley Bay, Ulverston, Newcastle Races and Oxenholme.

Platforms looking from the Pedestrian Bridge

Image 0260 – (Catherine Finlinson, 2006 Digital Village Project)

Supporters returning from 1951 Amateur Cup Final

Image 0257 - by kind permission of Dave Calcutt

By 1920 the Brick Works had closed and the sidings had been lifted. Hunwick Colliery closed on 20th August 1921 although the sidings were retained as part of the mineral line that served Newfield.

The Station Hotel Ball Alley

Image 0261 – (Wally Smith, 2006 Digital Village Project)

Looking down towards the bridge

Image 0409

The trestle bridge across the river connecting Newfield and Hunwick Station, was in use until it was demolished in 1962. Newfield residents walked across the bridge to get to the station and pupils used it as they walked to and from the school. After the bridge was demolished, Newfield residents had to use the Pay-bridge at Sunnybrow and walk along the riverside to get to Hunwick.

Railway Accident – October 1869

There was a fatal railway accident at Hunwick Station in 1869. Workmen, who were shunting railway waggons at Brancepeth Colliery (Willington), allowed twelve waggons to 'run wild' and run downhill, through Willington Station and onto to Hunwick Station. The waggons hit a passenger train that was unloading passengers at Hunwick Station.

The engine driver and firemen were killed and several passengers were seriously injured.

Bus Services

The rapid expansion of coal mining resulted in the expansion of Bishop Auckland as a market town with a wide range of shops and lots of Public Houses and entertainment opportunities.

It was a large bustling town to which people living in the surrounding small villages flocked on a Saturday. The highlight of the week for many Villagers' living in Hunwick, was a visit to Bishop Auckland. It was in walking distance across the fields, but anyone with money in their pockets could use the trains that ran from Hunwick Station.

Later, the Imperial Bus Service operated a service that ran through the village but terminated at Toronto, as their bus was not capable of climbing Newton Cap bank when it had a full load of passengers. In 1928 they bought UP 1678, a bus that was powerful enough to be able to carry passengers up Newton Cap Bank and into Bishop Auckland. Olive Linge, in her book, Willington in old picture postcards, includes a photo of this bus. Imperial Bus Service later became Bonds Bros Buses.

During the 1950s when both Bond Brothers of Willington and Wilson's of Hunwick were operating bus services, there were three buses per hour running through the village.

Imperial Bus Services

Image 0262 - by kind permission of Olive Linge

Wilson's Bus, LPT 382

Image 0450

Frank Wilson, trading as the Royal Bus Company, operated a fleet of five buses from a garage to the rear of Rough Lea Terrace.

Andrew Dolan identifies the buses as: *"two AEC Regals, from memory LPT382 and KTC455, a Maudsley Marathon, LPT15, a Crossley SD42, FDT804 and a Bedford OB either HDK337 or BCB169."*

In 1957 Bonds took over Wilson's which gave them the monopoly on the bus services through the village. They reduced the service to two buses per hour, with three buses per hour on Saturdays.

Residents recall that Newton Cap bank was still presenting challenges to buses in the 1960s when the service was run mainly using Bedford buses, which drivers considered were under-powered. Fully loaded buses often had to decant passenger in order to be able to climb the bank. The introduction of AEC buses in 1964-66 improved matters.

Villagers remember that during the winter, the buses carried bags of sand in case they got stuck on the banks. Many also remember the buses so busy on Saturdays, that they were often full by the time that they came through Hunwick so were unable to take extra passengers. Determined passengers, caught the bus from Hunwick to Willington and stayed on the bus as it came back through the village on its way to Bishop Auckland. Andrew Dolan remembered his experience of driving the buses *"I used to love driving on a Friday night when the last bus from Bishop (11pm) always carried a standing load making Toronto side of Newton Cap quite a challenge!"*

In 1963 Wilson's garage was taken over by John Nicholson, who, until 1978, operated Rough Lea Coaches. He built up a fleet of four buses that were used on private contracts. In addition to providing buses that carried pupils to Hunwick School, he also had a 'mucky bus', that was used to carry miners from the pit at Oakenshaw to the colliery baths at Brancepeth Colliery.

The first cars in Hunwick, belonged to James Johnson who was the manager of Rough Lea Pipe Works.

The Singer is pictured in 1925 with his son, Cesil Johnson in the foreground.

The Village Postmaster, Thomas Lumley, 1938

Image 0372

The first car in the village

Image 0250 - (Linda Paley, 2006 Digital Village Project)

Chapter 13 - Hunwick at War

During the Second World War, many of the men were away from the village serving in the forces. Life for those remaining in the village, who were working in agriculture or mining, and for all of the village families, was difficult. Before the war, the country had relied heavily on imported food and goods. During the War, the merchant ships, that had previously carried imported foodstuffs, were being sunk at an alarming rate. The supply of imported food and goods was cut off, or seriously reduced. Food rationing was introduced with an individual being allowed three pints of milk, one fresh egg, two ounces of butter and two ounces cheese per week. Meat, tea, jam, biscuits, cereals, cheese, lard, canned and dried fruit were all rationed until 1954. The Villagers who lived during the war years all remember sweets being rationed to something like two ounces!

Individuals had ration books that had to be presented to the shop-keeper before they could buy anything. Rationing and Government Policy encouraged Villagers to grow as much of their own food as they could. Villagers kept goats, pigs or hens in their gardens or allotments. Often pigs would be fattened in their backyards. The allotment gardens in the village became very important. Being surrounded by open country side provided opportunities for Villagers to forage for blackberries and fruit, to catch fish in the river and catch rabbits etc. Poaching became a problem.

'Make do and mend' became a necessity, with blackout curtains being repurposed as netball attire, parachute silk for clothing etc Villagers remember Heslop's the butchers, keeping apples from their trees, so that they could give them to village children on Christmas Day.

Air Raids

Brancepeth Colliery at Willington was a very large colliery with a Coke Works and gas plant. It was a target for German bombers so there were imitation lights positioned well away from the colliery to act as a decoy. Villagers remember watching flashes over Coundon from bombing raids. Some Villagers were appointed as fire watchers and were given responsibility for watching over the streets and Works in the village.

Villagers reminisce about an air-raid shelter in the 'back-hollows' (a quarry at Quarry Farm), another one in the allotments behind North View and the three air-raid shelters that ran along the southern boundary of the school site. They had corrugated iron roofs which were covered with a thick layer of soil with grass growing on top. They were mostly above ground but Villagers remember having to go down six steps and through a brick arched doorway to get into the dark, damp and musty shelters.

Dorothy Turnbull explained how uncomfortable the gas masks were and how, during their weekly air-raid practice, pupils had to wear a mask for ten minutes. Pupils were given half of a stick of barley sugar to suck during the practice sessions.

The school log book noted that although air-raid warnings at night were not frequent, they greatly affected attendance on the following days.

In the event of a gas attack, adults and children had gas masks. Babies had to placed inside of a sealed cylinder which had a couple of small windows in it. Malcolm Fox remembers his brother being placed in one of these cylinders and his father operating the pump that forced the air in through the filters.

Gas Mask for an Infant

Evacuees

An article in the Newcastle Evening Chronical, 12 December 1939 explains how children from Gateshead had been evacuated to Hunwick and had been looked after by foster-parents in the village. It explains that the Headmaster, Mr J R Holt, had merged the Gateshead children, in with village children and that senior Gateshead boys were taking part in gardening and poultry keeping lessons. The boys built hen runs and pigsties, and with their help, an extra half-acre of land had been cultivated to grow food.The school planned to raise four pigs.

The article describes how the young evacuees had been allocated *'idea billets'*:

> *'The house-proud pitman's wife at Hunwick as well as the clerical and business people of the village, have provided an ideal billet for the Gateshead children.*
>
> *Margaret Mason took me proudly to meet her aunty, Mrs Sanderson. There, in her gleaming home, Mrs Sanderson told me what a good girl Margaret was, and Margaret said how kind Mrs Sanderson was to her.*
>
> *The little girl was homesick a month after she went to Hunwick. Instead of writing to her mother, who has eight other children, Mr Sanderson took her to Gateshead and let her speak to her family for two hours by herself. Then he called back, and Margaret put her hat and coat on and took his hand'.*

Some recent detective work by Ashley Longhorne (nee Little) and Debbie Hibbitts has identified Mr & Mrs Ernie Sanderson as the couple, mentioned in the article, who fostered Margaret in 1939. Margaret lived with them, as a member of the family, in their two bedroomed house Number 1 Coronation Terrace.

Dorothy Turnbull (nee Moore) was born in Bensham on 17th April 1932. In 1939 Dorothy and her sister Gladys were evacuated from Gateshead to Hunwick. They lived with Mr and Mrs Joe Heslop who ran the butcher's shop in Helmington Square.

After marrying Jack Turnbull in 1956, Dorothy lived in Hunwick, initially at 13 Helmington Terrace then from 1970 until 2011, at Number 7, The Green.

Dorothy enjoyed village life and in July 2006, as part of the Digital Village project, she wrote down her story of being an evacuee. She volunteered to be recorded while she shared her story. A transcript of the recording is included in Chapter 11.

Dorothy & Gladys Moore

Image 0266 - by kind permission of Susan Liddell (nee Turnbull)

The Land Army

The drive to increase the productivity of the land during the Second World War meant that more land had to be brought into use. With many male agricultural workers joining the armed forces, women were needed to increase the agricultural workforce.

The Women's Land Army had originally been set up in 1917 but was disbanded at the end of the First World War. It was reformed in June 1939. Women, aged between 18 and 40, were initially asked to volunteer to serve in the Land Army but from December 1941, they could also be conscripted into land work.

The Women's Land Army were generally referred to as Land Girls. They were trained to do a wide variety of jobs on the land and could be directed to work on farms or in forests anywhere in the country, although they often worked in the county in which they were trained. They would either be billeted in farm houses or in hostels. By 1944, when the Women's Land Army was at its peak, there were more than 80,000 Land Girls with one quarter of them employed in some form of dairy work.

Land Girls worked on farms in and around Hunwick, with several marrying Villagers. Italian and later German Prisoners of War from Harperley also worked on local farms.

The Home Guard

The village had its own Home Guard that often trained and took part in mock battles in the woods and on the pit heaps at Hunwick Station.

This photograph shows Captain Hills and nine men of the Home Guard followed by The Church Boys Brigade. They are marching through the village on 14th June 1944 on as part of the village's 'Save the Soldier' campaign.

Deborah Wright's research into her family history uncovered a copy of an enrolment form for the Home Guard for John Whitton of 3 Coronation Terrace. John was born in 1887 and served in the Durham Light Infantry during the first World War and in February 1942, joined the 20th Battalion of the Home Guard. He served in the Home Guard until it until it was disbanded in December 1945.

'Save the Soldier' Parade 14th June 1944

Image 0391 – by kind permission Kathleen Johnson

Supporting the War Effort

Betty Dunn (nee Pratt) remembers walking around the village with her mother, collecting socks that Villagers had knitted for soldiers who were serving overseas. The leaflet and posters below confirm that the village was running events to raise money which would support soldiers, sailors and airmen.

The 1944, 'Salute the Soldier Campaign' target was to raise £2000. The poster suggests that the 1943, 'Wings for Victory Campaign' had raised £7000. A crashed, German Messerschmitt Fighter plane was taken around towns as part of the fund-raising campaign. Phill Patterson remembers being allowed to sit in it when it was on display in Bishop Auckland.

The 1944 campaign slogan was: *"not by the word of praise alone should you "Salute the Soldier" but rather save, lend AND invest*

Messerschmitt in Durham Market Place

Image 0368 – by kind permission of Phill Patterson

your every pound". It encouraged people to invest their money in national savings certificates, defence bonds post office savings bank. It included the option of investing with street group collector.

Hunwick Salute the Soldier Campaign 1944

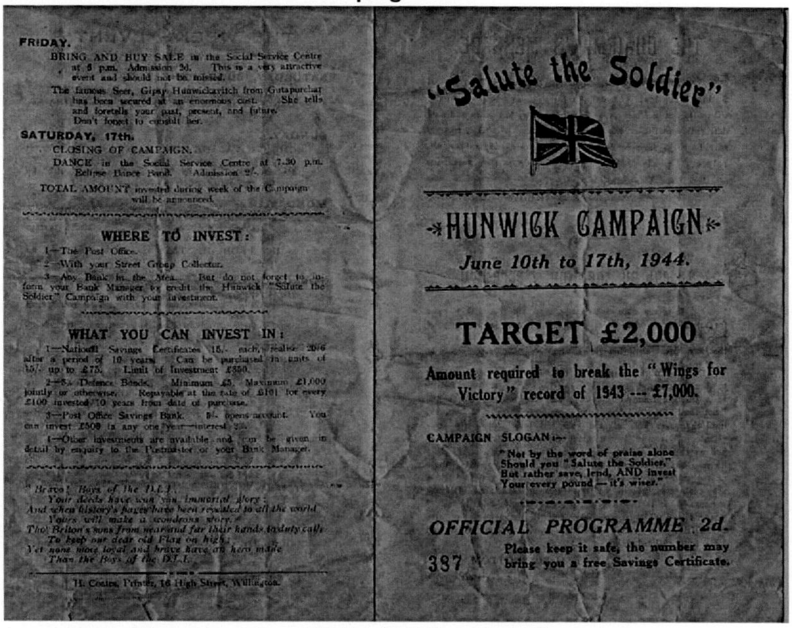

FRIDAY.

BRING AND BUY SALE in the Social Service Centre at 5 p.m. Admission 3d. This is a very attractive event and should not be missed.

The famous Seer, Gipsy Hunwickavitch from Gutapurchar has been secured at an enormous cost. She tells and foretells your past, present, and future. Don't forget to consult her.

SATURDAY, 17th.

CLOSING OF CAMPAIGN.

DANCE in the Social Service Centre at 7.30 p.m. Eclipse Dance Band. Admission 2/-.

TOTAL AMOUNT invested during week of the Campaign will be announced.

WHERE TO INVEST:

1—The Post Office.

2—With your Street Group Collector.

3—Any Bank in the Area. But do not forget to inform your Bank Manager to credit the Hunwick "Salute the Soldier" Campaign with your investment.

WHAT YOU CAN INVEST IN:

1—National Savings Certificates 15/- each, realise 20/6 after a period of 10 years. Can be purchased in units of 15/- up to £75. Limit of Investment £350.

2—3% Defence Bonds. Minimum £5. Maximum £1,000 jointly or otherwise. Repayable at the rate of £101 for every £100 invested 10 years from date of purchase.

3—Post Office Savings Bank. 5/- opens account. You can invest £500 in any one year—interest 2½%.

4—Other investments are available and can be given in detail by enquiry to the Postmaster or your Bank Manager.

"Bravo! Boys of the D.L.I.
Your deeds have won you immortal glory;
And when history's pages have been revealed to all the world
Yours will make a wondrous story.
Tho' Briton's sons from near and far their hands to duty calls
To keep our dear old Flag on high;
Yet none more loyal and brave have an hero made
Than the Boys of the D.L.I.

H. Coates, Printer, 16 High Street, Willington.

"Salute the Soldier"

HUNWICK CAMPAIGN

June 10th to 17th, 1944.

TARGET £2,000

Amount required to break the "Wings for Victory" record of 1943 --- £7,000.

CAMPAIGN SLOGAN:—

"Not by the word of praise alone
Should you "Salute the Soldier,"
But rather save, lend, AND invest
Your every pound — it's wiser."

OFFICIAL PROGRAMME 2d.

387 Please keep it safe, the number may bring you a free Savings Certificate.

Image 0265 – (Alma Edmundson, 2006 Digital Village Project)

Villagers had the opportunity to attend a Bring and Buy sale, a dance and an opportunity to consult the famous seer Gipsy Hunwickavitch from Gutapurchar, who *"tells and foretells your past, present and future".*

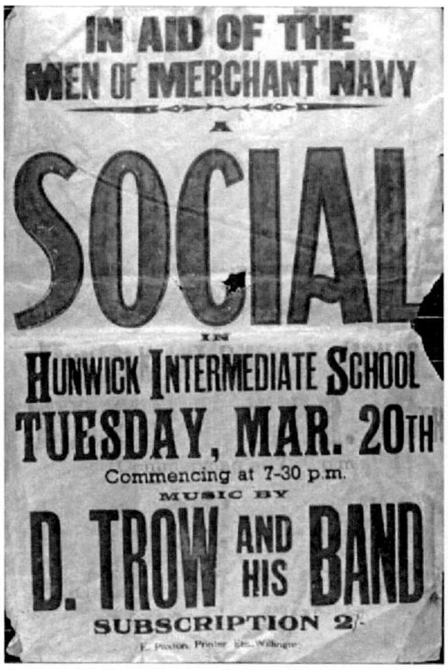

Image 0337 - Beamish Museum -Peoples Collection

The poster below advertises a dance that would raise money for men of the Merchant Navy. A second poster advertises VE Day celebrations with a grand procession from Quarry Burn, through the village and up to the Village Green with a grand dance in the Social Service Hut. The proceeds would go to the War Comforts and Welcome Home Funds.

Towards the end of World War 2, the Rookery, that belonged to Helmington Hall, and the wood that ran down towards Rough Lea, was felled to provide hardwood to support the War effort.

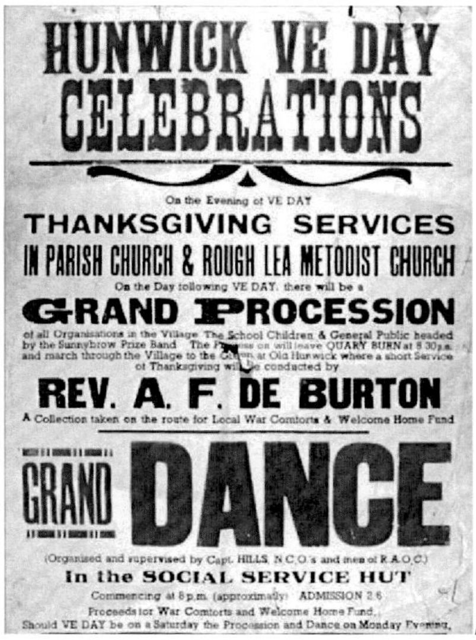

Image 0336 - Beamish Museum -Peoples Collection

The War Memorial

The war memorial for those lost in the First World War was unveiled and dedicated on 17th December 1922. A brass band marched through the village to the cenotaph. The memorial was updated with those lost in the Second World War and was dedicated on 31st October 1948.

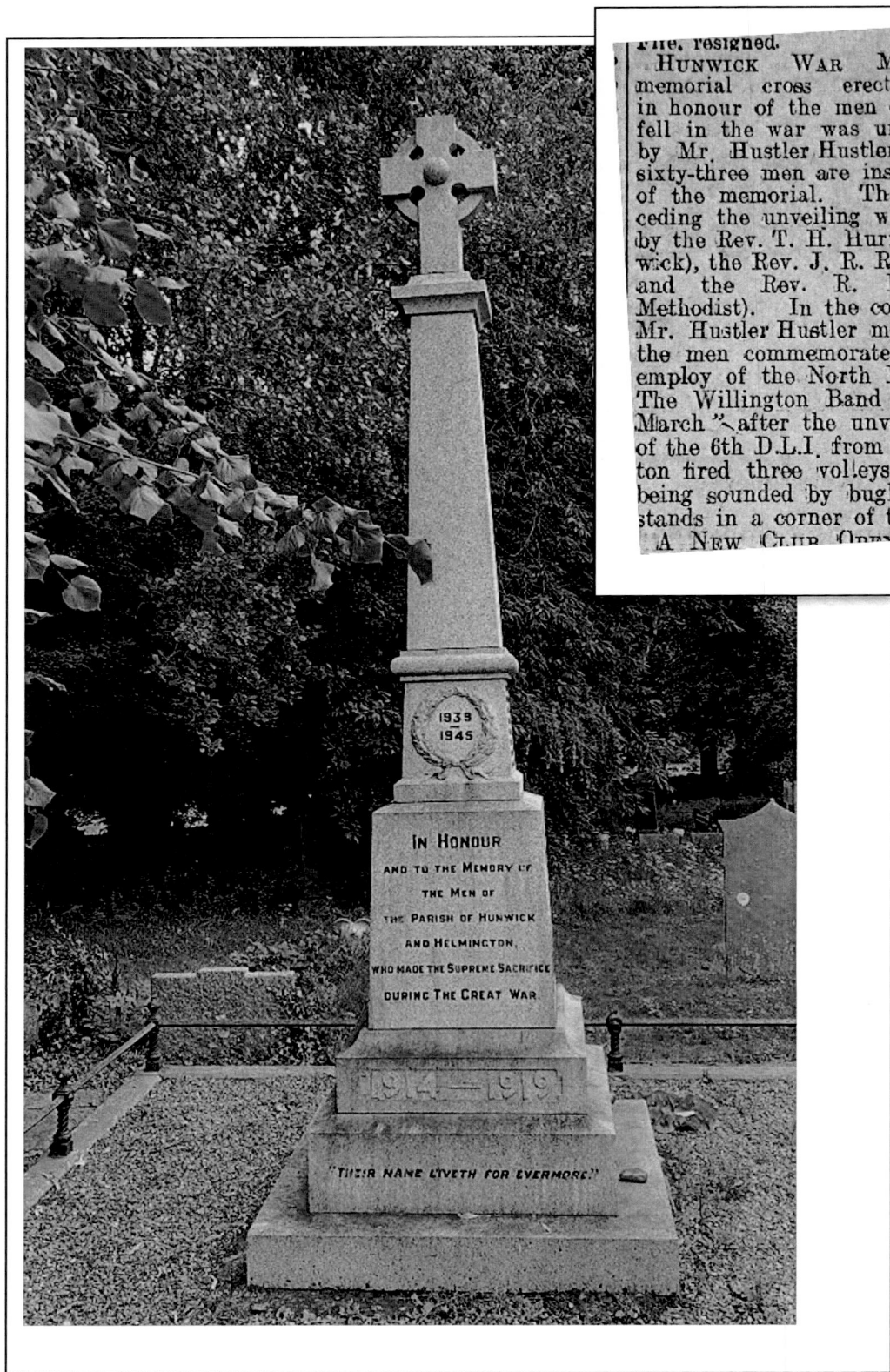

r're, resigned.

HUNWICK WAR MEMORIAL. — The memorial cross erected at Hunwick in honour of the men of the village who fell in the war was unveiled on Sunday by Mr. Hustler Hustler. The names of sixty-three men are inscribed on the face of the memorial. The proceedings preceding the unveiling were participated in by the Rev. T. H. Hurrell (Vicar of Hunwick), the Rev. J. R. Rushton (Wesleyan), and the Rev. R. Laidler (Primitive Methodist). In the course of his address Mr. Hustler Hustler mentioned that 24 of the men commemorated had been in the employ of the North Bitchburn Coal Co. The Willington Band played the "Dead March" after the unveiling, and a party of the 6th D.L.I. from Crook and Willington fired three volleys, the "Last Post" being sounded by buglers. The memorial stands in a corner of the churchyard.

A NEW CLUB OPENED. Th

Inscriptions on the Cenotaph

HUNWICK   East side of Church Lane

In honour
and to the memory of
the men of
the parish of Hunwick
and Helmington,
who made the supreme sacrifice
during the Great War.

1914-1919

On steps
Their name liveth for evermore.

Left face 1939-45
Scriven G.W.L.
Swann C.D.
Thompson J.C.
Thompson J.W.
Weighill R.
White F.
Wood H.
Wood J.

Left face 1914-18
Mangles F.
Mangles J.W.
McDougal A.
Mears A.
Metcalfe A.
Morgan W.
Morland F.
Newton C.
Richardson J.
Simpson W.S.
Nicholson J.
Simpson T.W.
Smith A.J.
Sunter T.
Tennick J.
Towse A.
Turnbull W.
Warner G.
Wearmouth G.
Wright W.
Jackson F.

Rear face 1939-45
Linton J.
Murray J.S.
Neil R.
Newton G.
Parker J.W.
Pipe W.
Rutter J.
Scorer J.

Rear face 1914-18
Ellis E.
English J.
English L.
English M.
Etherington J.W.
Graham T.
Groves R.L.
Hardy J.W.
Harland T.
Hedley G.N.
Heslop J.G.
Hird E.
Hodgson G.
Hudson E.
Hudspeth J.
Hudspeth R.
Husband A.
James H.
Johnson J.
Jones W.
Knight J.E.
Letby A.H.

Right face 1939-45
Burdon J.
Edmundson A.
Graham J.
Griffiths L.
Grimstone O.
Heron A.
Johnson F.
Kirkley J.

Right face 1914-18
Alderson P.
Barker J.
Barraclough T.
Bell H.D.
Bell R.
Bentley J.W.
Bolam J.
Brogdon J.
Brown J.A.
Carter J.G.
Cherry J.
Coates J.
Coatman G.H.
Curry H.
Dargue T.
Davis A.I.
Davison G.
Deighton R.
Dobinson H.
Dodson J.
Elliott J.C.
Elliott J.G.

Chapter 14 – The Village Farms

Hay Making

Image 0379 – by kind permission of Harold Newton

Harvesting Group

Image 0380 – Beamish Museum, Peoples Collection

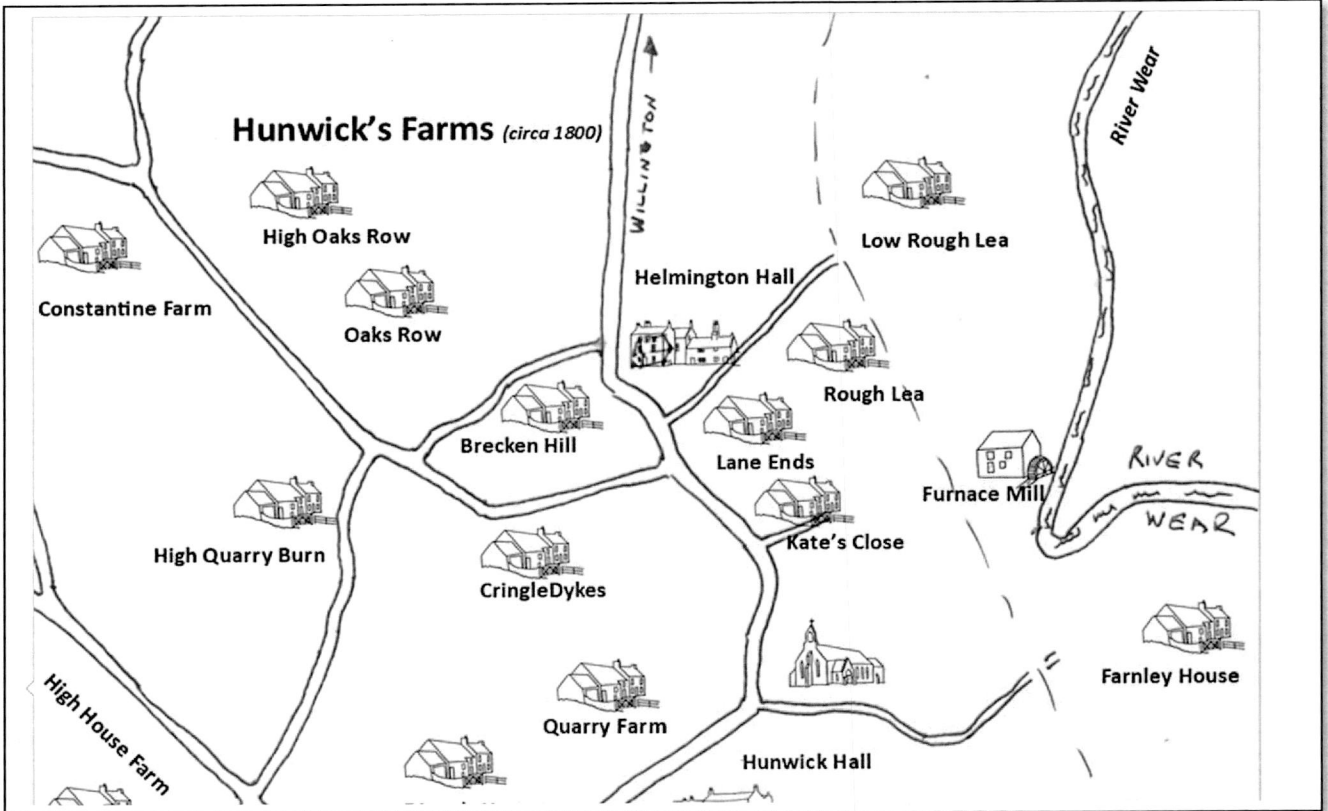

Hunwick's Farms *(circa 1800)*

High Oaks Row

Constantine Farm

Oaks Row

WILLINGTON

Helmington Hall

Low Rough Lea

River Wear

Rough Lea

Brecken Hill

Lane Ends

Furnace Mill

RIVER WEAR

High Quarry Burn

CringleDykes

Kate's Close

High House Farm

Quarry Farm

Hunwick Hall

Farnley House

Furnace Mill and Low Rough Lea Farm

In 1687, Sir William Bowes granted a House, a Fulling Mill and a 'close', to be built on a 'close' that had previously been known as 'Conyns Ryddings'. In 1690, Furnace Mill was acquired by Thomas Blackett of Helmington Hall and was held by the Helmington Hall Estate. (Surtees, The History of the Parishes of Hunwick, Helmington, Witton Park and Etherley, 1923)

William Sidgwick occupied the farm and mill in 1785. In 1827 William Dixon was recorded in the Parson and White Trade Directory, as working the farm. The 1841 Census lists Mary Dixon, aged 60 and James Dixon, aged 20, described as a miller. It also lists Robert Marr, aged 20, Mary Marr aged 20, John Marr aged 20 and Elizabeth Marr, aged one month. In 1871, the census lists Robert Marr as the Miller and farmer.

Furnace Mill Farm is identified on the 1843 Tithe Map as 'Farnley Mill'. It lists the landowner as 'Heirs of Spencer' confirming that the farm was part of the Helmington Hall Estate. The occupier was James Dixon and the area was listed as 17 acres.

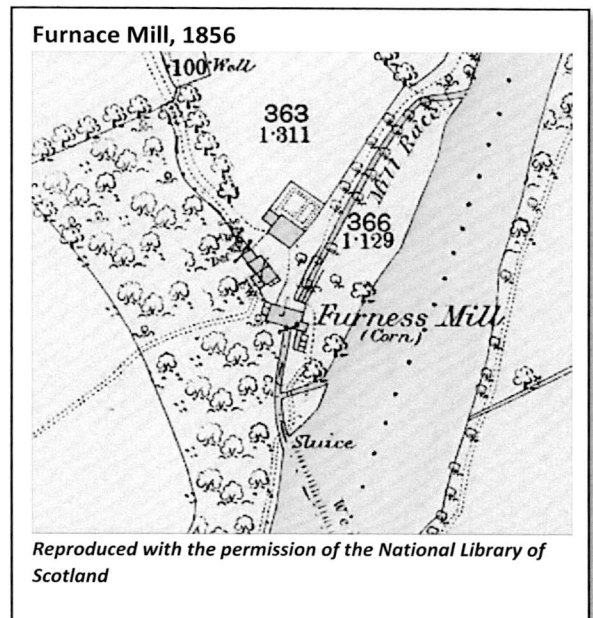

Furnace Mill, 1856

Reproduced with the permission of the National Library of Scotland

Furnace Mill

Image 0012 – by kind permission of Sally Moran

By 1870, the Helmington Hall Estate had been bought by Straker and Love and by 1922 it had been transferred to the National Coal Board (NCB). The NCB initially rented the farms to tenants with the 1921 Kelly's directory listing William Hanson as the farmer. Although early maps show many footpaths leading to the Mill, the cart track to it ran along the riverside from Sunnybrow. When the Village Sewerage works were demolished, the ancient footpath which led down from Rough Lea to the Mill, was made into a cart track using the rubble from the works.

By the mid-1950s, Norman Basey Snr had taken over the tenancy of both Furnace Mill Farm and Low Rough Lea Farm. Norman Basey Jnr, who had lived at Furnace Mill and had helped to run the farm, took on the tenancy in 1971. When he retired in the 1980s he built a bungalow at Quarry Farm. In the 1990s John Basey bought and ran both Furnace Mill Farm and Low Rough Lea Farm as well as Quarry Farm.

Surtees refers to Anthony Hodgson of *"Roughly"* who in 1656 conveyed 29 acres to Thomas Trotter of Helmington Hall. Low Rough Lea Farm was shown on the 1843 Tithe Map as being a farm of 200 acres. I suspect

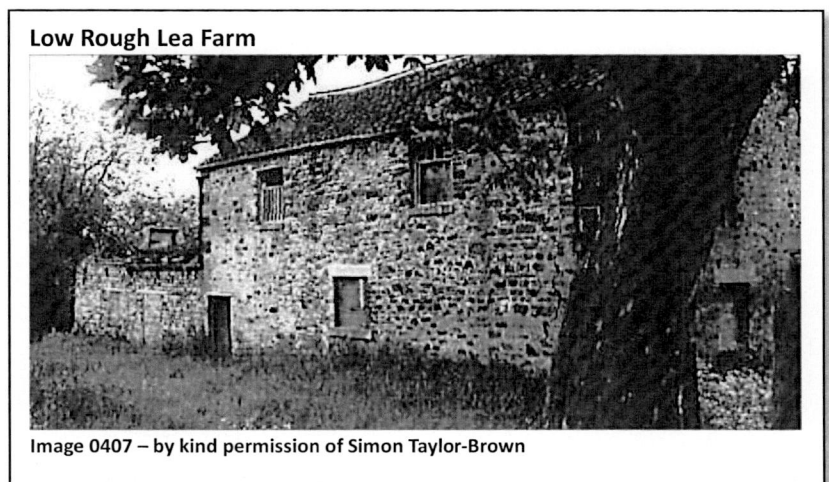

Low Rough Lea Farm

Image 0407 – by kind permission of Simon Taylor-Brown

that this acreage included other land which belonged to the Helmington Hall Estate.

The 1841 census identifies Charles Scurr, aged 40, as a farmer at Rough Lea. By 1851 the farm was described as 160 acres employing three Agricultural Labourers. By 1871 Charles Scurr, aged 83, in addition to three Agricultural Labourers, also employed a general servant.

Kelly's 1914, 1921 and 1938 Trade Directories list Matthew Horner and James Hird as the farmers. Mrs Horner delivered milk to the village.

Low Rough Lea Farmhouse and buildings were sold in 2011 converted to residential use.

Farnley House (Farm)

Farnley Farm was mentioned in 1796 when an inquisition after the death of John Rippon, described him as a *"gentleman, of Farnley in the township of Hunwick and Helmington"* (Records, 1796)

It was a large farm with the 1861 census describing it as a farm of 300 acres. Early maps show it having a Ginn Mill and extensive agricultural buildings. It was part of the Hunwick Hall Estate. It is shown on an 1861 Estate Map and is described in documents as consisting of 195 acres.

The 1828 Parson and White Directory recorded John Stobbs as working the farm. The 1871 census records that Hall Stobbs, aged 52, was farming 450 acres and living with his son, grandson, and 2 granddaughters. It also records that they employed four servants, one on the farm and three indoor servants.

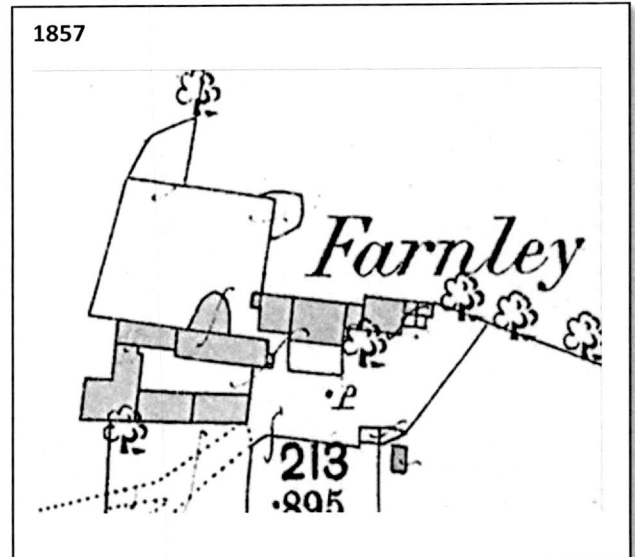
1857

Census records and Directories show that the Stobbs family were still working the farm in 1921. Kelly's 1938 Trade Directory lists William Appleby, bailiff to General Tarren, as working the farm.

Rough Lea Farm

Upper Rough Lea farm house still exists as a private residence with the agricultural buildings having been converted to residential use.

Upper Rough Lea Farm was described by Harold Heslop:

'Between the village and the pit head stood an ancient farm house, ringed with poplars …. As if reluctant to disturb the face of an ancient husbandry that was old before the Boldon Buke was fully compiled' (Heslop, 1987)

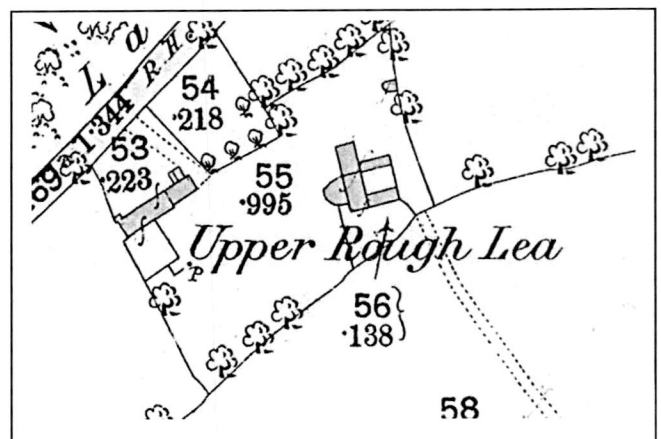

Rough Lea Farm

Image 0262 -by kind permission of Amanda Adamson

The 1828 Parson and White Directory lists Thomas Brass as the farmer.

A map drawn in 1861 shows the farm to be part of the Hunwick Hall Estate.

Early maps show a large farm house with extensive agricultural buildings including a Ginn Mill.

In 1948, Thomas Linsley took over the farm. Kathleen Race (nee Linsley) delivered milk from the farm until 1990s.

Farmers		
1828 - Thomas Brass as the farmer - Parson and White 1841 - Charles Lenn, aged 40 and his wife Jane, working the farm - census 1861 - Charles Lenn, Farmer of 150 acres - Census 1851 - Richard James, as a farmer of 128 Acre and employing three Agricultural Labourers - census	1864 - Richard James -Slaters Trade Directory 1871 - John James as being a Farmer of 150 acre, employing a Labourer, an indoor farm servant and a general servant – census 1873 - John Proud – Kelly's 1894 - John Proud – Kelly's 1902 - Elizabeth Proud – Kelly's	1906 - Elizabeth Proud – Kelly's 1914 - John Proud – Kelly's 1921 - John Proud – Kelly's 1938 - Robert Hart – Kelly's 1948 - Thomas Linsley

Kate's Close (House) Farm (The Poplars) (13 Acre)

Kate's House Farm was a working farm from the late eighteenth century until the 1950s when the last of its land was sold. It was mentioned in the will of Robert Cutter who died in 1811, and the will of his father who died in 1802. The farm house is still in use and is now known as 'The Poplars'.

The 1850s Coal Royalty map shows that Lowinger Hall, who died June 1835, owned three fields that ran down from Meadow View/Kates Close, past the railway line and down towards Furnace Mill. The field immediately behind the farm house was later used as the recreation ground. He also owned two fields on Hall Bank at Lane Ends. These two fields had been part of Hunwick Common until 1761, when the Enclosure Act allocated the fields to Joseph Hall. Hall Terrace, Thompson Terrace, Front Street, Chapel Street and Coronation Terrace were built on these fields.

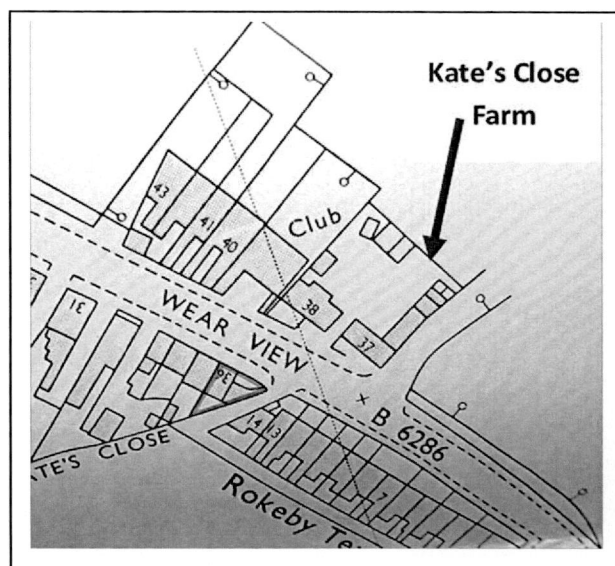

Kate's Close Farm

The 1828 Parson and White Trade Directory lists John Etherington as the farmer and the 1841 census lists Ralph Beck as the farmer. The 1843 Tithe Map records that Kate's Close Farm was occupied by Ralph Beck with the land being owned by the 'heirs of Hall'.

Ralph Beck died in 1848. The 1851 census tells us that his wife, Ann Beck had taken on the running of the farm and the 1858 Post Office Directory confirms that she was still running it in 1858. However, the census in 1861 tells us that William Wetherall, a butcher was running the farm. He continued to run the farm and butcher's shop until 1887, when the farm and butcher's shop, were bought by William Raine, who ran a shop at Lane Ends. In 1897 William Raine sold the farm house and butcher's shop to the Coop who continued to operate the butcher's shop and the farm. By this time some of the farm land had been sold to allow West Hunwick Colliery to develop.

The 1901 census lists Johnathan Walton as a farmer living at Kate's Close and the 1938 Kelly's Trade Directory, lists John Johnson as a farmer. John Johnson Jnr and his wife Jean, ran Quarry Farm in Old Hunwick. The cow byres for Kate's Close farm were more or less, where the Dyson sign is today, beside The Poplars.

The Poplars, 1954

In 1948, when John Johnson Snr was farming Kate's Close, George Heslop, the landowner, sold the field to the rear of the farmhouse. The field was bought by the Working Men's Club who retained a section of the field to improve access to the rear of the Club and to provide a car park. They sold the remainder to the Urban District Council who maintained it as a Recreation Ground for the village.

Donald White describes the chaos that was caused by John Johnson Snr, as he herded his cattle from the byers beside The Poplars, up to graze on his son's fields at Quarry Farm, and then back down to The Poplars to be milked.

> 'in the 1950s the farmer lived in the Poplars. The field below that house, before becoming a recreation ground, was used to graze their large Friesan bull. It was tethered to a plough and weights by a long rope and grazed in a circle until moved for another circle. In the large yard beside the house was a substantial wooden shed housing the bull and some calves. The cow byre was across the road leading to West Hunwick Works right by the main road. Cows were grazed on land in Old Hunwick and the cows, at one time long horned Ayrshires, were walked down the main road to be milked'

In 1953 the farm house and stables were bought by William Burdon who had moved from RyWell Grange, a small holding at Hunwick Station. The Coop continued to operate the butcher's shop until it was taken over by Norman Swann who ran it as a Grocers and General Dealers until the early 1970s when Wilf and Marjorie Sanderson took it over and later converted it in to a house.

Dixon's House [Blakeley Hill] (15 Acre)

The farm originally took its name from an early tenant, John Dixon, who in 1772 was a tenant of Lord Strathmore. We know from the Tithe Map, that in 1843, it was owned by *'heirs of Trotter'* which tells us that it was part of the Helmington Hall Estate. At some stage the farm was acquired by the North Bitchburn Fireclay Company who sold it to Frank Hedley in 1935.

The 1843 Tithe Map lists the Farm as comprising 15-acres and occupied by Hannah Mason.

Dixon's House Farm continues to operate as a working farm but is now known as Blakeley Hill Farm. A document written in 1596, mentions a *'pasture called Cringledyke and a meadow called Blinklyhill'* (Records_Office_Durham, 1596)

Perhaps that is how Blakeley Hill acquired its name? When observed from the Village Green, the sun sets behind 'Blinklyhill'.

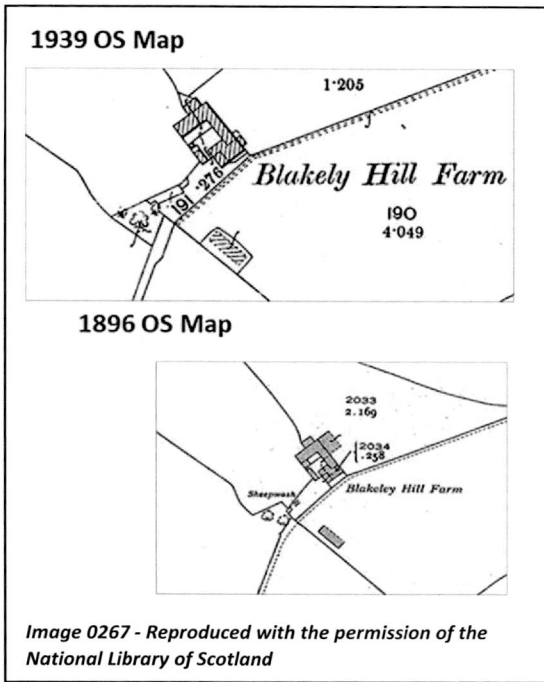

1939 OS Map

1896 OS Map

Image 0267 - Reproduced with the permission of the National Library of Scotland

It has a large farm house along with a range of barns and byres. It is thought that some rooms on the ground floor of the farmhouse had been used as stabling for animals. This style of 'byre house' was common until the early 1900s. The theory being that the heat from the animals that were kept below, heated the living accommodation above.

Interestingly, the 1939 OS Maps shows a 'sheep wash' at Blakeley Hill. On the 1761 Enclosure Map it is identified as a 'carr pond'. The sheep wash was fed by a natural spring. I cannot find another sheep wash marked at any of the other farms in the area, so perhaps it was something that was also used by other Farmers or maybe the Drovers?

Farmers		
1772 - John Dixon	1901 - Thomas Gibson	1935 - Frank Hedley – Kelly's
1841 - Cuthbert Mawson – census	1906 - George Gowland	195? - The Hedley sisters
1843 - Hannah Mason - Tithe Map	1911 - George Gowland - Census	1960 - Evelyn McClurg (nee Hedley)
1861 - Robert Grey (wife, daughter and 5 sons)	1914 - George Gowland – Kelly's	1974 - Michael McClurg
1890 - Thomas Gibson – Kelly's	1921 – Frank Hedley (also Cringle Dykes)	

Lane Ends Farm (18 Acre)

The farm is shown on Christopher Greenwood's 1818 map and on the 1856 OS map.

It also appears on the 1843 Tithe Map as an 18-acre farm, owned by John Booth and occupied by Ralph Hutchinson.

An 1861 Estate map identifies the farms three fields as belonging to, 'late Booth and afterwards Cutter, Nyle and North Bitchburn Coal Company'.

The last reference to the farm was in Kelly's 1921 Trade Directory, that listed William Thomas Thompson as the farmer. The farm also had a Slaughter House.

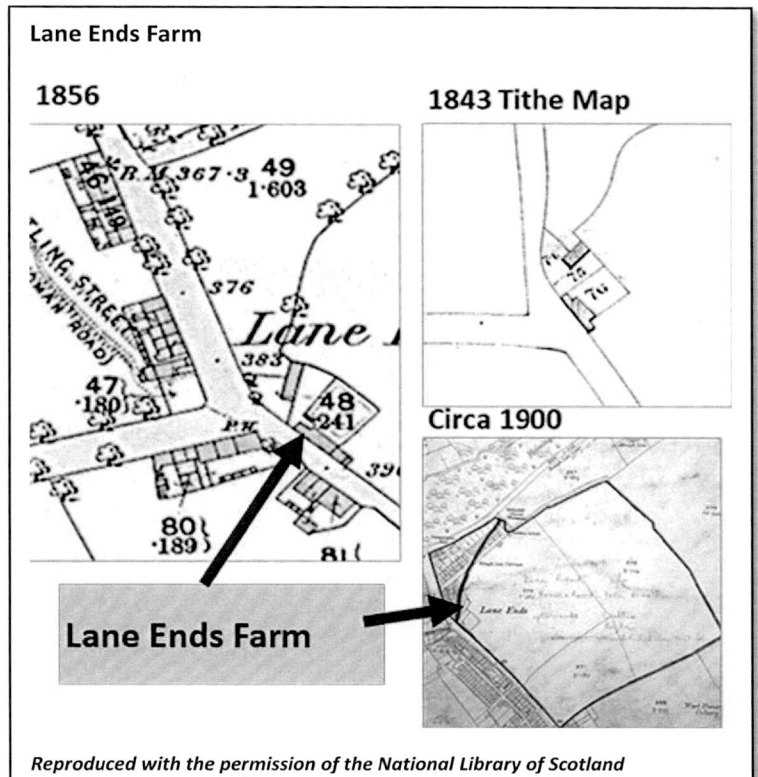

Lane Ends Farm

1856

1843 Tithe Map

Circa 1900

Lane Ends Farm

Reproduced with the permission of the National Library of Scotland

Quarry Farm (26 Acre)

Quarry Farm still operates as a working farm. It is likely that at one point, Quarry Farm and South View Farm were linked in some way. Number 18 South View, is the Farmhouse for Quarry Farm.

"Flagg Quarry", a flagstone quarry had operated on the farm from as early as 1663. Census returns and information provided by Trade Directories show that

Image 0428A -

Quarry Farm, 1876

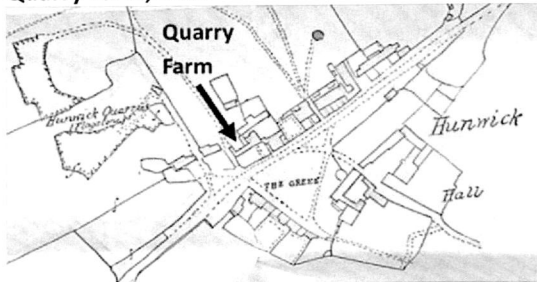

Quarry Farm

Image 21 - (Durham_University_Special_Collections, Hunwick Hall Estate Map, 1876)

the quarries were still working in 1856. Stone from this quarry and the neighbouring sandstone quarry was still being used in the 1890s to build houses in the village.

Some of the farm's land, including the Flagg Quarry, is identified on an 1861 map as belonging to Hunwick Hall Estate.

The 1841 census shows John Robson, aged 15 being an agricultural labourer and living in the household of John Young. The 1871 census records John Robson as a land owner, aged 46, farming 40 acres (possibly Quarry Farm). His wife Ellen, his son George Metcalfe, his three daughters and a servant also lived at the farm.

The Farm House for Quarry Farm, along with a collection of agricultural buildings are shown on the 1857 map. From the public footpath, you can see an old building with external steps that provided access to the upper floor and stabling on the ground floor.

The 1857 map shows the barns for Quarry Farm and South View Farm connected suggesting that at point, they were operated as one farm. The layout of the fields would support this theory

Deeds for the Joiner's Arms include an 1874 plan that shows that the land to the rear was owned by John Robson.

In 1894 the Joiner's Arms, along with the adjoining cottage, occupied by Thomas Sunter, and a 25-acre farm, including farmhouse and buildings, was offered for sale. This suggests that the Joiner's Arms, the two cottages above and South View Farm, were part of the same estate.

The 1891 Census records Thomas Sunter (56 yrs.), as a butter and cheese factor

Quarry Farm and South View Farm Fields

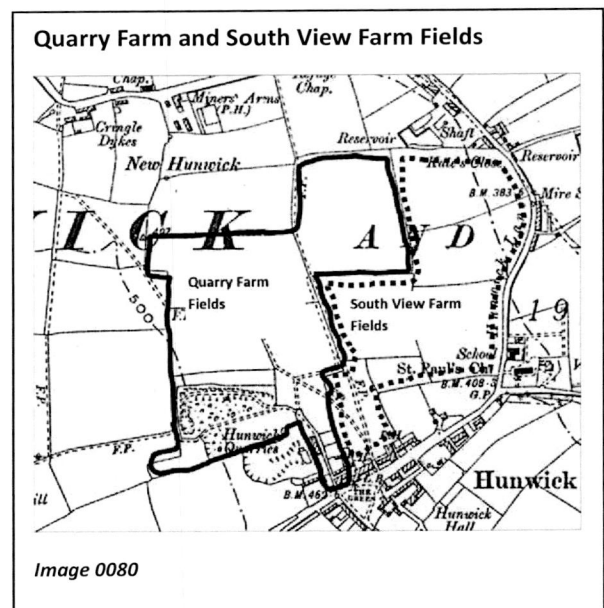

Image 0080

The 1901 and 1911 census record James Sunter, his wife Margaret and a servant, living on the farm. By 1925, Kelly's Trade Directory lists Margaret Sunter, as the farmer

Villagers remember, in the 1940s, Ann and Jayne Sunter, mother and daughter, living at Quarry Farm. Jayne had married John Raw in 1918. In the early 1930s, after John had returned having worked in the South African Gold mines, they built RyWell Grange, a bungalow at Hunwick Station. John died in 1939, and Jayne, known as 'Old Tighty' moved back to Quarry Farm

John Johnson Jnr and his wife Jean, farmed Quarry Farm until the late 1960s. John Johnson Snr farmed Kate's Close Farm lower down in the village, until 1953.

When Norman Basey retired from Furnace Mill Farm in the 1980s, he built a bungalow beside the derelict houses in Quarry Row. The houses were used to store agricultural equipment before being demolished in 2007

South View Farm

South View Farmhouse and some of its buildings still exist but it is no longer operated as a farm. Trade Directories list Albert Temby as a farmer and greengrocer running the farm from 1914 until the 1940s.

The fields for South View Farm, were directly behind the Joiner's Arms and included the fields upon which part of Quarry Farm Close is now built and those running up behind Garden View.

Richard and Jane Temby ran the farm until 1978, along with their son and daughter, Dickie and Valerie. They also ran a milk and grocery delivery business, which, as well as delivering milk in the village, also delivered to Sunnybrow and Toronto.

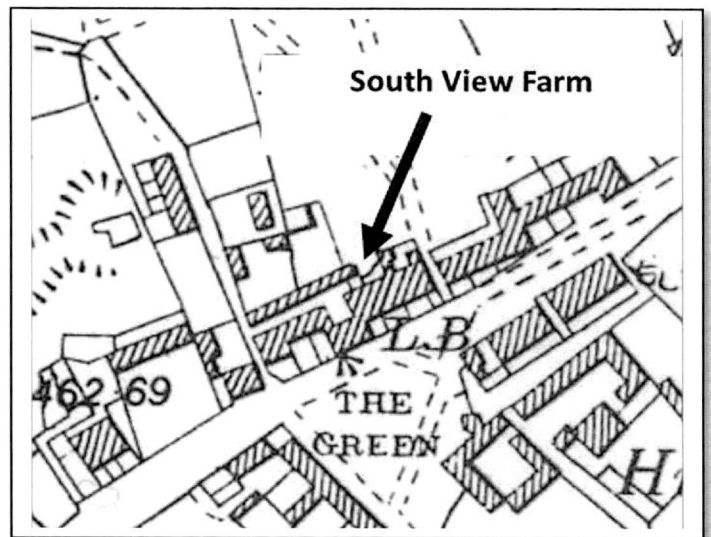

Richard's brother, Edward (Tidler) Temby and wife Hilda, ran the Joiner's Arms until Norman Temby, Tidler's son sold the pub to Ann and Ian Richardson Snr in 1971.

Cringle Dykes

Cringle Dykes is mentioned in 1596 when William Corneforth, was granted "a messuage, 2 bovates of land and close of pasture called Cringledyke". (Durham_Records_Office, Ref_D/X_235/1, 1596)

It is also mentioned in the will of Cuthbert Hodshon de Cringle Dykes in 1624. The Poll for Knights in 1761 listed John Fletcher who, as a landowner in Hunwick in 1761, was allocated land when the Common was enclosed.

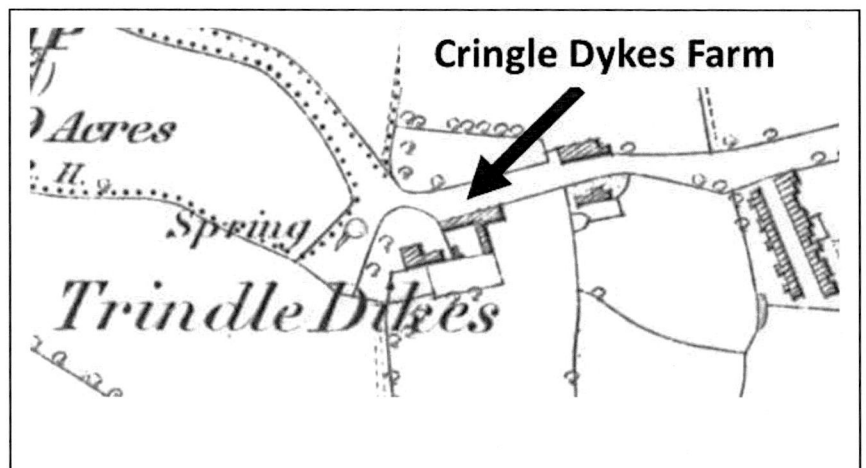

Cringle Dykes, 1983

Image 0275 - by kind permission of Dave Calcutt

Farmers		
1811 - Nicholas Welsh mentioned in Will of Robert Cutter -- Proud John 1825 – Thomas Blackmore – association fellons 1827 – 1848 Rev George Fielding, 1828 - Thomas Blackmore, Parson and White	1858 - William Hedley - P O Directory 1861 - William Hedley census 1879 - William Hedley - P O Directory 1871 - William Hedley, farmer of 125 acre employing I labourer	1873 - William Hedley – Kelly's 1894 - Frank Hedley 1914 - Frank Hedley – Kelly's 1921 - Frank Hedley – Kelly's Dir 1935 - Janet Hedley – Kelly's

New Hunwick Farm

Estate records show that, in the 1860s, Matthew Bell 'held' 3 acres at New Hunwick. The farm house is shown on maps until 1915.

It was to the south of Quarry Burn Road, between New Hunwick and Cringle Dykes, opposite, Number 14 to 17, West End. The garden wall for the farmhouse can still be seen just above Coppice Wood.

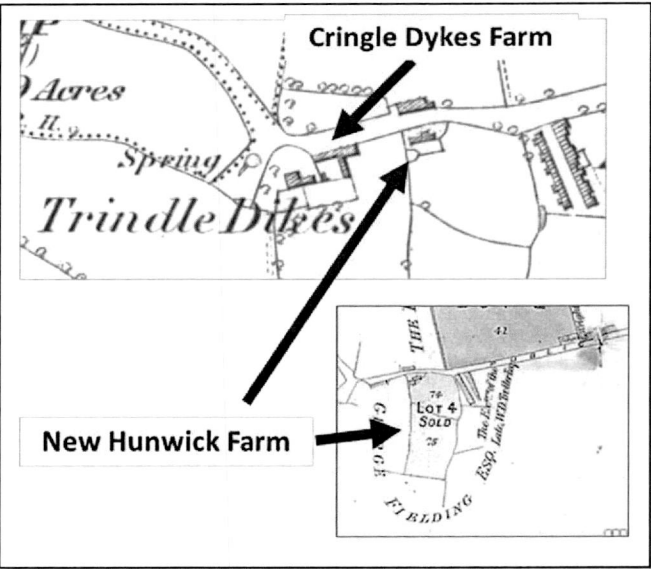

In 1828, the Parson and White Directory lists Hannah Liddle as the farmer. She is mentioned again, in an 1831 conveyance of a Farm of 3 Acre, occupied by Hannah Liddell

In 1841, Hannah Liddle was described as an Agricultural Labourer. In 1868, her daughter, Jane, married Robert Marr, of Furnace Mill, becoming his second wife. The 1843, Tithe Map, lists the farm as occupied by William Scott but owned by George Dixon. However, the 1861 census records Hannah Liddle still being at the farm.

Quarry Burn Farm

Quarry Burn Farm was advertised to let in the Durham Advertiser on 6th April 1894. It was advertised by Bertram Bulmer who was the Brewer at Quarry Burn Brewery. The farm included, a farm house, farm buildings, a stack yard and 25 acres comprising 4 fields and a garth of rich grass land. At that time, the farm was tenanted by John Pratt and son.

The 1841 census list Thomas Graham living at the Brewery. An 1843 Estate map shows a substantial property on the site. (The_Common_Room, NEIMME/WAT/32/31, 1843) An 1806 Estate map, confirms that Thomas Graham's grandfather, Thomas, owned the fields around the Brewery. (The_Common_Room, NEIMME/WAT/32/30, 1806).

The Graham family were certainly economic in their use of fore-names as the 1761 Enclosure map identifies enclosures at Quarry Burn, as belonging to Thomas Graham.

In the 1950s, the Heslop sisters Mary, Margaret and Elizabeth, lived in Quarry Burn House (the old Brewery) and ran the farm. Margaret and Elizabeth both taught in local schools.

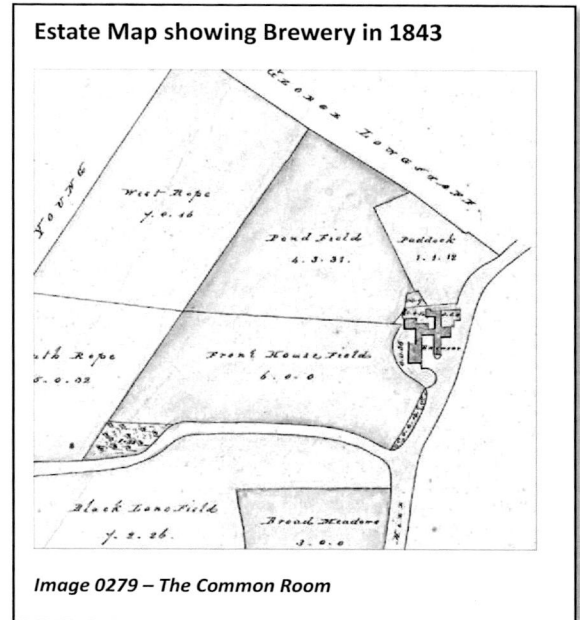

Estate Map showing Brewery in 1843

Image 0279 – The Common Room

Brecken Hill

Brecken Hill Farm was marked on the 1761 Enclosure Map.

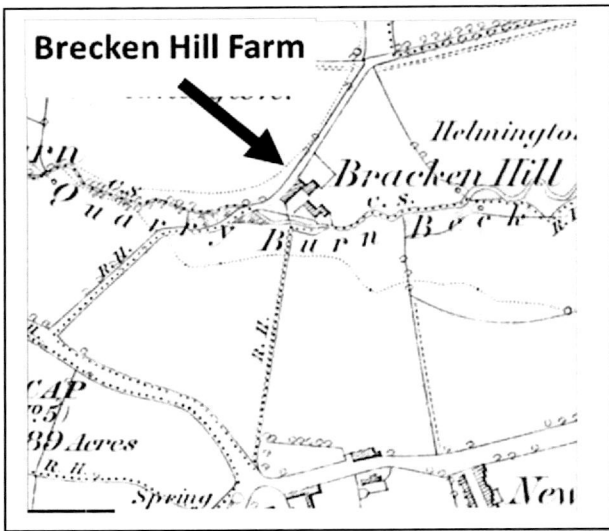

Brecken Hill Farm

In 1861, the forty-Acre farm, with coal royalties, was offered for sale in the Durham County Advertiser. It was occupied by John Fletcher and owned by Thomas Young.

Strangely, the trade directories that have helped to identify the farmers on the other village farms do not provide much information about Brecken Hill. However, we know that Emerson Adamson Hope was running the farm in 1928 and that between 1949 and 1992, Robert Tyreman ran the farm. His daughter, Nancy Tyreman, ran the farm from 1992 and 1999

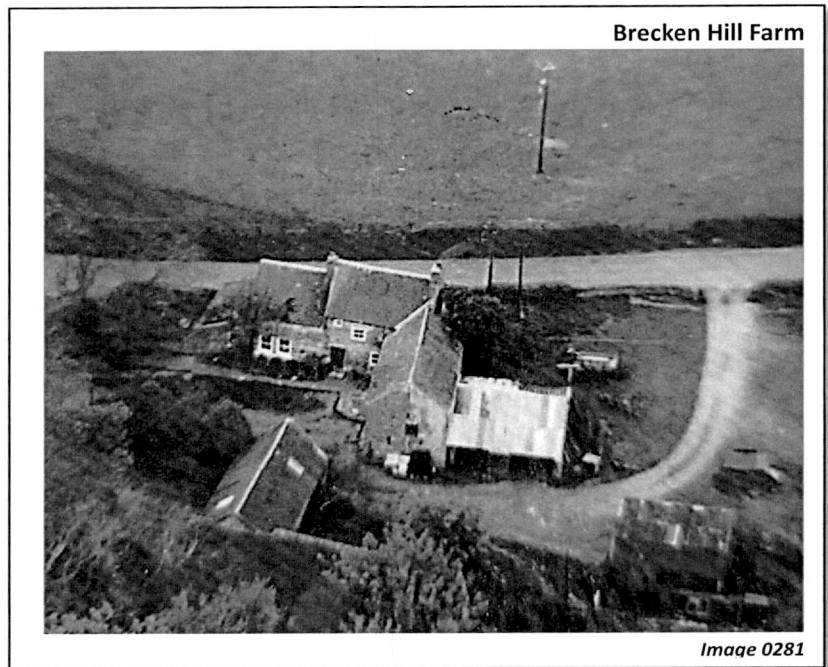

Brecken Hill Farm

Image 0281

Brecken Hill Farm

Image 0283 – by kind permission of Marjorie Tait

Chapter 15 – Hunwick Hall and Helmington Hall

Hunwick Hall

Hunwick Hall is a listed, late medieval, Manor-house. It is to the East of the Village Green, behind the octagonal Ginn mill that during the 1990s was used as a Public House.

The original house is still used as a Farm House but most of the agricultural buildings have been converted into houses.

Estate Map, 1876

Image 0290 - (Durham_University_Special_Collections, DHC11/VI/27)

Hunwick Hall, from the South, circa 1910

Image 0288 – the Herbert Coates Collection

Hunwick Hall, from the South, 1969

Image 0289 – Durham County Council, 1969

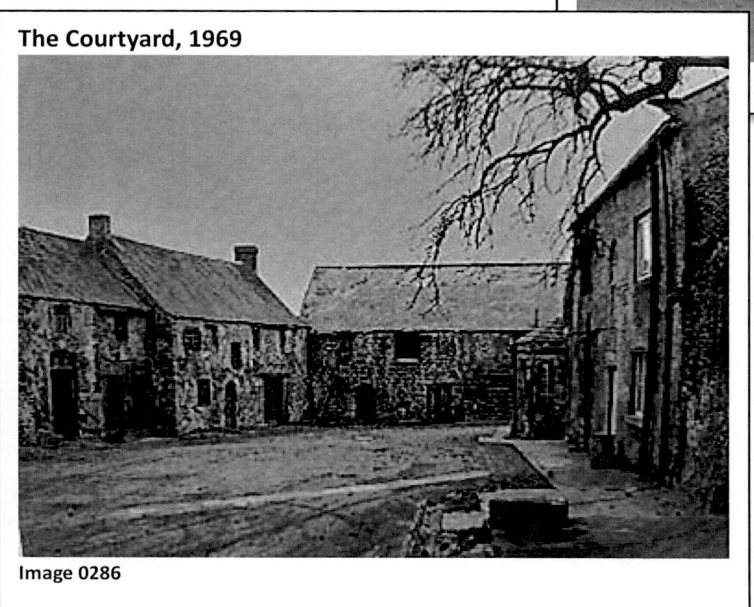

The Courtyard, 1969

Image 0286

In 2004, English Heritage commissioned a 'tree ring' analysis of some of the timbers in Hunwick Hall. The earliest timbers were dated as being felled between 1402 and 1497 with the roof timbers from the East Wing being dated between 1501 and 1526. (Arnold, 2004)

The Courtyard, circa 1910

Image 0345 - the Herbert Coates Collection

Bagnall provides a detailed commentary on the history of Hunwick Hall (Bagnall, 2003) He describes the major phases in the development of the Hall as:

Phase	Dates	
1	1300 – 1350	The East range, originally a single storey building
2	1500	Alterations to the East range and construction of the adjoining buildings in the North and South ranges
3	1615	Jacobean additions.

In 1418 John Hoton and his wife Joanne Whitworth purchased, from the Earl of Westmorland, *"the Manor of Hunwick-by-Binchester"*. At his death in 1420 John Hoton of Tudhoe was shown to be in *"possession of the manor of Hunwick, held of the bishop"*. He was succeeded by his son William, aged 22, who soon moved from Tudhoe to Hunwick. He inherited the manor Hunwick after his mother died in 1444. (Hampton, John Hoton of Hunwick and Tudhoe, County Durham, esquire to Richard III)

By 1450, William Hoton had died and his son Ralph had inherited his estates. Ralph died in 1468 and his son John inherited. In the spring of 1480, the Scots raided Bamburgh which belonged to the Bishopric of Durham. John Hoton was one of the commissioners who assembled and organised the men to fight for the Bishopric. He was also one of the trusted northern men who Richard III sent to take over the lands of the southern landowners whose lands had been forfeited because they would not support him. John Hoton was rewarded with considerable landholdings in Hampshire. It is probable that he fought and died at the battle of Bosworth in 1485.

The Estate continued to be held by the Hoton family until 1637 when it was acquired by William Kennett. The Kennett family were Roman Catholics in a time when, although it was not an offence to be a catholic, refusal to attend Church of England services was. Initially those who refused would be fined, later fines were increased and prison sentences were introduced. By 1586, the crown could claim two-thirds of an individual's estate. (University, GB-0033-BRA-1297 Title: Kennett family papers (BRA 1297) , 1297)

In 1672, Margaret Wright, a widow from Hunwick and Jerimiah Head were fined for non-attendance at the parish church, St Andrew's at Southchurch. (Richley, 1872)

The North Eastern Catholic History Society suggests that the Kennett's disappearance from County Durham *"resulted from a mixture of financial difficulties, involvement with Jacobitism and a lack of male heir's characteristic of the problems of the Northern Catholic gentry of the early eighteenth century. "* (Society, 1986) It appears that by 1698 they could no longer afford to keep the Estate and it was sold to the Stephenson family in either 1708 or 1716. (Durham_University_Special_Collections, https://reed.dur.ac.uk/xtf/view?docId=ark/32150_s1xp68kg20p.xml)

The Stephenson family held the Estate until 1744. In 1759 it was acquired by Joseph Reay, who had married Margaret Cuthbert, the granddaughter of John Stephenson of Hunwick. A 1772 *'Rental for allotments'* document, identified that George Walker was the tenant. Henry Utrick Reay was described as a lawyer, a landowner, a banker and philanthropist. He had two daughters, Elizabeth Ann and Georgina.

Matthew Bell was an MP for Northumberland from 1826 until 1852. The Bell family were identified as one of the six families that dominated the development of the coal trade in the North during the eighteenth century. (Eden, 1952)

Matthew's father, also Matthew, died in 1811 making Matthew Jnr, one of the *'Great Northern Coal Owners'*, before he was 20 years old. In 1816 he married Elizabeth Anne Reay, the eldest daughter of Henry Utrick Reay and inherited the Hunwick Hall Estate in 1821. In 1826, he took command of the Northumberland Hussars from his uncle, Charles Brandling. He commanded the yeomanry during the Tyne pitman's strike of 1830 – 1832. (The_History_of_Parliament, 1820-1832)

When Mathew Bell died in October 1871, he had mortgage debts of over £50,000. In his Will he left his estates, to his brother Henry, who died without issue in 1887, and then to his nephew, Charles Lorraine Bell.

A Halmote Court Plan, drawn in 1876, shows the Hunwick Estate *"divided into to lots for sale"*. (Durham_University_Special_Collections, DHC11/VI/27) The Estate was acquired by Thomas Edward York, a direct descendant of a previous owner, Joseph Reay. He was a joint owner, between 1902 and 1923, of the North Bitchburn Coal Company

The Bell's had engaged in mining speculation and development in the late 18th century and had owned Willington Colliery at Wallsend since 1808. When Matthew inherited Hunwick Hall in 1821/1828, he used his experience to open Hunwick Colliery at what became Hunwick Station.

The Stephenson's, Reay's, and Bell's were all well-connected families. They were 'Merchant Adventures' who had, in addition to Hunwick Hall, owned grand houses in Northumberland. Joseph Reay owned Killingworth Hall and had a house in Westgate Street, Newcastle. Matthew Bell owned Woolsington House in Northumberland. To them, Hunwick Hall and Estate was probably an investment that they hoped would generate some return, although family burials and donations to St Andrew's Church in Bishop Auckland might suggest that they had some affection for the village.

Records show that Hunwick Hall Farm, the farm belonging to the Hall, was tenanted by Thomas Sanderson, during the ownership of the Reay's. In January 1847, during the ownership of Matthew Bell, the tenancy was advertised in the Durham County Advertiser as a farm of 402 acres. A long lease was available for an *'improving Tenant'*.

In 1861, the Census records John Thompson as a 'Farmer living in Hunwick Hall' with three servants, two male and one female. During Thomas Yorke's ownership, it was tenanted by Robert and Elizabeth Marriner (1869 Voters List) and then by Robert C Lawes.

Farmers		
1772 - George Walker – tenant	1869 - Robert Marriner (died 1873) & Elizabeth)	1921 - Robert Cuthbert Lawes – Kelly's
1828 - John Emerson – Parson and White Dir	1879 – Elizabeth Mariner (died 1899– PO Dir	1923 - Robert Lawes (Surtees)
1833 - John Stonehouse – Poll for Knights	1894 - Robert Cuthbert Lawes – Kelly's	1938 - Thomas Lawes, Davison, John Peter –
1847 – John Hope - Farm advertised to Let	1901 - Robert C Lawes + Isabella (Martha, Thomas	1953 – for sale with vacant possession
1858 - John Thompson P O Directory	20, Mary 14, John Peter 13) - Census	- Eric Stephenson
1861 - John Thompson -Census	1914 - Robert Cuthbert Lawes – Kelly's	1969 - Brabban Bellerby

In the 1990s, a relative of the Marriner family visited the village from their home in America. They gave John Cunningham a copy of a photograph that was taken during the tenancy of Robert and Elizabeth Marriner (circa 1869 – 1894). The photo graph showed an elaborate carved oak panel above a fire place in Hunwick Hall.

In 2016 the panel, attributed to a Newcastle workshop of Dutch Carvers, circa 1630, was sold at auction for £30,000

Hunwick Hall Mantle Piece

Image 0429 – by kind permission of John Cunningham

Tennants Auction Listing, 2016

Lost oak panel at Tennants

📅 March 22, 2016   👤 admin   💬 0 Comments   🏷️ auction news, auctions

Tennants Auctioneers is selling a large carved oak overmantel which has previously been referenced in Anthony Wells-Cole's book *Art and Decoration in Elizabethan and Jacobean England*, as 'whereabouts officially unknown'.

The panel will be going under the hammer on Saturday 9th April, as part of the two day, Spring Fine Art Sale. The overmantel's pre-sale estimate is £8,000-10,000.

The panel once hung in Hunwick Hall in County Durham, but was inherited by the Yorke family circa 1900, when Hunwick was demolished. There was no record kept of who had inherited the panel, or whether it had been demolished with the property, hence 'whereabouts officially unknown' in Wells-Cole's book.

It is attributed to a Newcastle Workshop of Dutch Carvers, circa 1630, with a moulded cornice and vine-carved frieze. A central panel of Royal Arms is flanked by panels on each side depicting Orpheus and Orion, all between stiles with standing figures personifying the four parts of the world, each carved and named Africa, Asia, Evropa and America. The panel is 17th century and later, and measures 372cm by 124cm.

The two carved panels of Orpheus and Orion are similar to a set of prints designed and engraved in Cologne and dated 1602. This exact overmantel is referenced and illustrated in Anthony Wells-Cole's book. Photographed in situ at Hunwick Hall in County Durham and listed as "whereabouts unknown", the overmantel was inherited by the Yorke family c.1900, and thus by descent. The overmantel is similar to a carving formerly at Clervaux Castle, Croft-on-Tees, North Riding of Yorkshire.

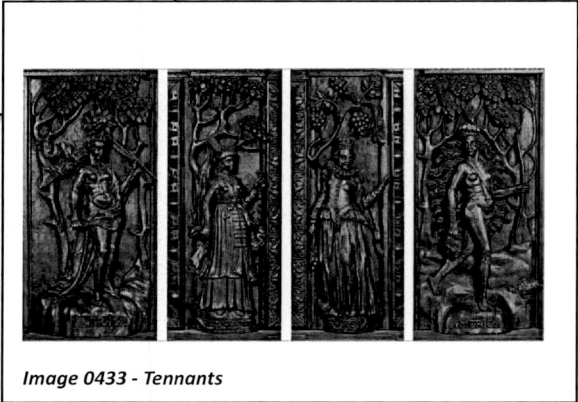

Image 0433 - Tennants

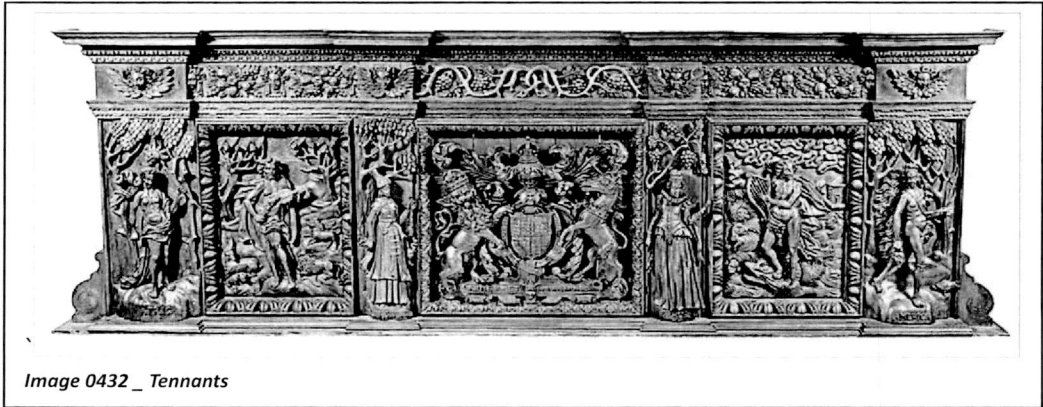

Image 0432 _ Tennants

Helmington Hall

Helmington Hall, 1983

Image 0314 - by kind permission of Dave Calcutt

> 'As Helmington was given over to the Northern Earls as a ville in late 900 AD or early 1000 AD, there must have been some sort of manor house on the site'. (Ref Donald Whites notes)

A survey, in 1183, of the land held by the Bishop of Durham was recorded in the Boldon Book. It records that 'Ralph of Binchester holds Hunwick' and that Roger Bernard, the son of Robert Bernard, held 48 acres in 'Helmygdene' of the Bishop of Durham. The estates held by the Cathedral Priory of Durham were not included in the Boldon Book. (Greenwell, 1852)

Sir Roger Bernard de Helmington was included in a list of the Knights of the Bishopric of Durham in 1264 (Hutchinson, 1785) and a reference, in a lease dated 1285, confirms that Sir Roger Bernard continued to hold Helmington Hall Estate twenty years later. (Durham_Records_Office, D/Gr 57 For Bernard's estate, see HS, P. 16)

At his death in 1425, Ralph de Neville was recorded as holding the *'manor of Helmeland with appurtenances'* and *'2 messuages and 2 bovates of land in Hunwick'* (Durham_University_Special_Collections, 126r-127v 19 November [1425], 1425)

The Neville Family owned Brancepeth Castle from early in the 14th century, until 1569, when it was confiscated following the family's involvement in the Rising of the North. Liddy explains that Ralph Neville had concentrated on acquiring land close to his estate at Brancepeth and that he had swapped land in Heighington for the estates of Binchester and Hunwick in the first decade of the 15th Century. (Christian Drummond Liddy, 2005)

In 1385, Thomas Neville of Brancepeth Castle, married Joan, the daughter of William Lord Furnivall and inherited the Furnivall title. Thomas sat in Parliament as Lord Furnivall in 1384. (Ref Wikipedia)

Surtees's interpretation of the Hatfield survey was that the only free tenant in Hunwick was John Burdon, who had probably taken the surname of his wife, Alice. Alice was the daughter of Roger de Burdon who had died in 1357. When he died, he had amongst his holdings a *'messuage and 48 acres in Helmington and lands and tenements in Hunewyk – held of the Bishop and also of the lord (dominus de) Bynchester'*. (Surtees, The History of the Parishes of Hunwick, Helmington, Witton Park and Etherley, 1923)

Helmington Hall was in Brancepeth Parish until St Stephen's Church was built at Willington, in 1857, while Hunwick was in St Andrew's Parish until St Paul's Church was built in 1844. Early documents relating to the Bridge of Hunwick Pit describe it as being in the Parish of Brancepeth although the Parish boundary was Helmington Beck.

So Helmington Hall, in some form, existed since the late 900s but certainly since 1183.

In 1398 John de Burdon (Byrden), died *"in possession of five houses, three tofts and one hundred and twenty four acres of land in Hunwyk , held of Ralph, Earl of Westmorland".* Also, *"a house, 70 acres of land and 10 acres of wood and the site of a water mill in Helmeden held of the Bishop of Durham in capite by military service".* His heir was his son Thomas de Burdon.

When Alice, the daughter of Roger de Burdon married, her husband adopted her surname and became John Burdon. When John Burdon died in 1397 he was *"seized .. of a messuage, 70 acres of land, 10 acres of wood, and the site of a water mill in Helmindon".* His son Thomas Burdon, who died in 1449, was recorded as *"seized of Helmdon Manor and Hunwyk".* His grandson John Burdon, who died in 1476, left *"his daughters Katherine and Johanna as his co heirs".*

Johanna married Thomas Harper and had a daughter Jane. Jane Harper inherited the Helmington Estate and sometime around 1572, married Christopher Trotter. A Heraldic College Visitation to County Durham in 1615 records William Trotter at Helmdon.

It looks probable that the Burdon's and the Trotter's leased the Helmington Estate from the Neville family who in turn 'held' the lands in Helmington from the Bishop of Durham.

The Trotter family held the estate until 1688 when Thomas Trotter sold the last of the Helmington Estate. His father, Anthony Trotter (1576 – 1639), had disposed of much of the property that they held at Helmington. (Richley, 1872)

Thomas Blackett bought Helmington Hall Estate in 1686, having previously leased it. The Blackett family, who owned land in Hamsterley forest, held the Helmington Estate until 1792. An announcement of the marriage of Jane Blackett in 1772, referred to her brother as Sir William Blackett Esq (1732 – 1799) of Helmington. William Stephenson Blackett was baptised in 1773 but by 1791 was being prosecuted for cutting down some trees at Hamsterley without permission.

In 1792, Mr Ralph Spencer, a merchant who had lived in India for 20 years, returned to this country and bought the Helmington estate. His son, Robert went into the church and was for a time a curate at Stockton Parish Church. In 1805, when his father died, Robert inherited the estate and lived in Helmington Hall.

In 1798 Robert married his first wife Maria. For a time, Maria's aunt, Lady Maxwell, the widow of Sir Robert Maxwell of Orchardton, Kirkcudbrightshire, lived with them. She died at the Hall 1807.

In 1805 alterations and additions were made to the house and gardens.

In 1820, Peter Fair, when describing the 'Gentlemen's seats of Hunwick Hall and

Helmington Hall Gardens, 1956

Image 0295 - Reproduced with the permission of the National Library of Scotland

Helmington Hall', recognised the potential of the improvements that had been made to Helmington Hall, to create a *'delightful place'*. He also recognised the 'romantic scenery' and considered that the quality of water of the Furnace Spring was not quite as good as the 'Harrowgate waters'. (A Description of Bishop Auckland, including the castle and park and Gentlemen's Seats - 1820, Peter Fair)

The Rev. Robert Spencer married his second wife Margaret, in 1829. He was a magistrate and deputy lieutenant for County Durham. He died in 1836. In 1842 his nephew, Henry Shield took on the Spencer surname and coat of arms. Census records show that between 1841 and 1871, Margaret Spencer lived at Helmington Hall.

The 1871 Census shows that she employed a ladies maid, a cook, two house maids, a kitchen maid, a footman and a gardener. Sometime before 1896, Helmington Hall cottages were built to accommodate servants.

An article in the Journal of Horticulture and Practical Gardening in 1870, when commenting on the mildness of the winter weather, reports:

Helmington Hall Cottages, circa 1910

Image 0003 – the Herbert Coates Collection

"At Helmington Hall there are now in flower, in the open air, a number of plants of the salvia fulgens, China roses, fuchia, sollya heterophylla, &c. They have bloomed well through the third season of the year, and continue, so far to produce flowers and foliage in the winter, if winter it be. Calceolarias, petunias, and myrtles are also flourishing, to the admiration of visitors"

Helmington Hall was in Brancepeth Parish. An article in the Newcastle Journal, 3rd July1869, reported that a Grand Bazaar had been held at Brancepeth Park to raise money for a peal of bells for St. Stephen the Martyr's Church at Willington.

It explained that the bazaar had enjoyed the patronage of Mrs Spencer, Helmington Hall. However, contemporary reports describe how Mrs Spencer travelled from the Hall up to the St Paul's church in Hunwick, in a coach drawn by two white horses.

She hosted the annual school fete at the Hall, and provided entertainment for children and residents.

An article in the Durham County Advertiser, 28th September 1855, reports on the *'annual treat to the children of Hunwick School"* explaining that the children *"amused themselves with various games. The day was most lovely, and it was a gratifying sight to witness such a number of merry faces, and to hear their joyous peals of laughter'.*

Sometime after 1871 Mrs Spencer went to live in Yarm. A "Return of Landowners" document in 1873 recorded that the Executors of Mrs Spencer administered 613 acres.

The Newcastle Courant on 4th December 1830 carried an advertisement for the tenancy of Helmington Farm. This confirms that the Hall and the Farm were being managed as two separate entities.

By 1870, Straker and Love, who owned and operated many collieries in neighbouring villages had become the owner of the estate and by 1922 it had transferred to the National Coal Board. In 1870 the Hall and Farm were tenanted by F Wood and then, more recently, by Frank Tinkler.

Maypole Dancing at Helmington Hall

Image 0299 – (Betty Dunn, 2006 Digital Village Project)

Kelly's Directory reports that in 1890 the Hall was 'unoccupied and in ruins'. In 1895, the south wing of the hall caught fire and was burnt out and stood roofless for a while until it was demolished, leaving the present building.

In 1923 it was reported that the Hall *'is now in a ruinous condition'.* (Surtees, The History of the Parishes of Hunwick, Helmington, Witton Park and Etherley, 1923)

Helmington Hall, circa 1900

Image 0297 – the Herbert Coates Collection

The South Wing of Helmington Hall

Image 0298 – by kind permission of John Cunningham

Helmington Hall, 1983

Image 0314 By kind permission of Dave Calcutt

Chapter 16 - Battle of Brunnanburh, 937 AD

Two Icelanders, Bjorn Vernhardsson and Stefán Björnsson, are so convinced of Hunwick's historic place as an important central hub that they have gone to astonishing lengths to prove it. None of the many factors they have unearthed provides concrete proof, but together they provide a convincing argument. They believe that the area on which football pitches and the cricket field stands was a regional hub in pre-Christian times and was the site of the Battle of Brunnanburh in 937AD. They paint a picture of an invading army moving south using the Roman roads and the meeting of King of England's forces in Hunwick where they engaged in a particularly bloody fierce battle.

There is no doubt that an important battle took place, but its location is the subject of various theories and it is interesting to outline how the Icelanders reached their conclusion.

Much of it stems from a 13th century Icelandic text called Egil's Saga, that is based on poems that are assumed to be contemporary to events. Egil fought in the battle alongside his brother, Thorolf, who was killed. The saga draws on contemporary poems, believed to have been written by Egil himself, in which he says it took place "in a field on Vinheith by Vinewood" and he buried his brother "near Vinu." The theory is that Vinu (or Veanu Flumen) is an old name for the River Wear from the Roman Times, hence the original name for the nearby Roman fort at Binchester being Vinovia, translating as road crossing the Wear.

The poem refers to the field as 'Ymbe Brunnanburh'. 'Ymbe' is like amphi in an amphitheatre and 'Brunnan' translates to fountains. Ymbe Brunnanburh means a field or an amphitheatre surrounded by springs or wells.

Icelanders are apparently very keen on genealogy and the two in question can trace their ancestry back to Egil. They believe that they lost an ancestor in the battle, hence their interest. In addition to a book about the battle, they have produced a booklet called 'Hunwick as a social centre of Anglo-Saxon Northumbria.' There is a theory, based on Early Medieval cosmology, that the border settlements were aligned in a circle 20.5 miles from the centre. The centre, in this case the cricket field area, is known by the authors as the Mithgard. The origins of this word are from the old Edda Poem Völuspá, but it seems to be the same concept as Tolkien's Middle Earth and Bjorn goes so far as to suggest that the Lord of the Rings author was searching for this site that was so important in the old Edda poems.

The distance of 20.5 miles represents how far someone could walk in a day. Although it hasn't been verified, Hunwick is said to be 20.5 miles from Gateshead, Jarrow, Sunderland, Hartlepool, Middlesbrough, Richmond and lesser sites of historic significance such as Helwith, Whitley Chapel near Hexham and Chapel Fell, which lies directly west. Helwith is a tiny hamlet on the edge of Barningham Moor and Bjorn claims it is where the sun can be seen setting from Hunwick at the winter solstice. He is so convinced of its significance that he insisted on being taken there during a visit to Hunwick.

The Mithgard was basically a field used for gatherings such as a court, sports events or a market. It would be an open area with good views, allowing sunrise and sunset to be measured at the solstices. The authors emphasise the centrality of Hunwick by saying it is the mid-point between the Tyne and Swale and the North Sea and the Pennines. It is also halfway between the northern tip of Scotland and England's south coast.

The 'field' in Hunwick

Bjorn teases out a description of the field from a number of different poems. In the Eddic poem Grímnismal the field was said to be 960 feet by 960 feet. Within this field there was an inner field, measuring 640 feet by 640 feet. In the very centre there was a circular, inner sanctuary, having a diameter of 216 feet. It was used by the highest court and the most important assemblies.

He compares the design on an Anglo-Saxon Sceatta coin, to layout of the field.

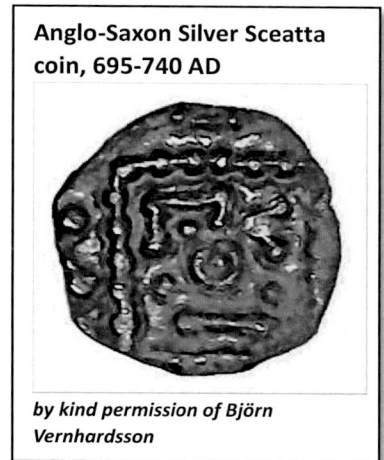
The area around the inner field but that was still inside the outer field, was used by anyone not involved with the actual activity that was taking place, and perhaps were just spectators or support workers This probably included slaves, children and people who did not own land.

The battle of Brunanburh was fought in 937 between King Athelstan of England and an alliance of the King of Dublin (Olaf), The King of Scotland (Constantine II) and the King of Strathclyde. There are many competing theories as to where the battle took place.

The Icelandic theory is that it was decided, at the suggestion of King Athelstan, that the battle would take place in the Field at Hunwick.

Egil, who fought in the battle, tells us in his saga, that King Athelstan's army arrived at the battlefield first and camped to the south of the field.

We will try to explain the battle as it might have taken place in Hunwick.

King Athelstan's army set up their camp at the top of the slope that ran down from the Roman Road towards what is now the Cricket field. Their camp would have run from the Working Men's Club, along to the Quarry Tea Room.

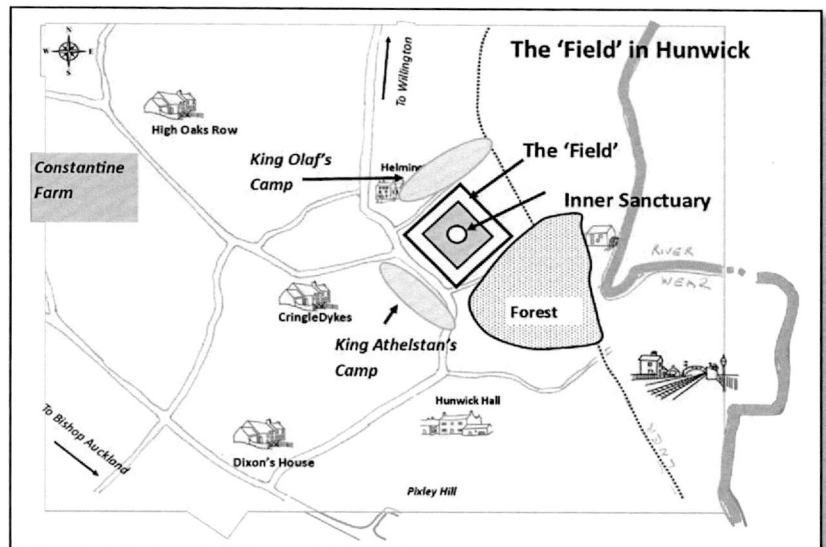

In an attempt to convince the Northern Alliance that his army was much larger than it actually was, King Athelstan's men erected at least three times as many tents than his army actually needed.

King Olaf's army, the northern Alliance, approached from the north and set up their camp upon what is now Rough Lea Lane.

Egill was fighting alongside King Athelstan. His saga tells of two battles. A small-scale battle on the day before the main battle and then a larger battle on the second day.

On the first day, some of King Olaf's men, the Picts and the Britons, fled into the forest to the east of the field and hid overnight.

On the second day, King Athelstan divided his army in two sections. He led one section onto the field, approaching from the south-west [from the Quarry Tea Room]. The other section, led by Thorolf and including the Vikings, approached from the forest in the south [from the Working Men's Club].

King Olaf also split the army of the Alliance into two sections. He led one section onto the field from the north [from Rough lea Colliery]. The other section entered the field, a little further to the south, but again, from the north [from Rough lea Colliery].

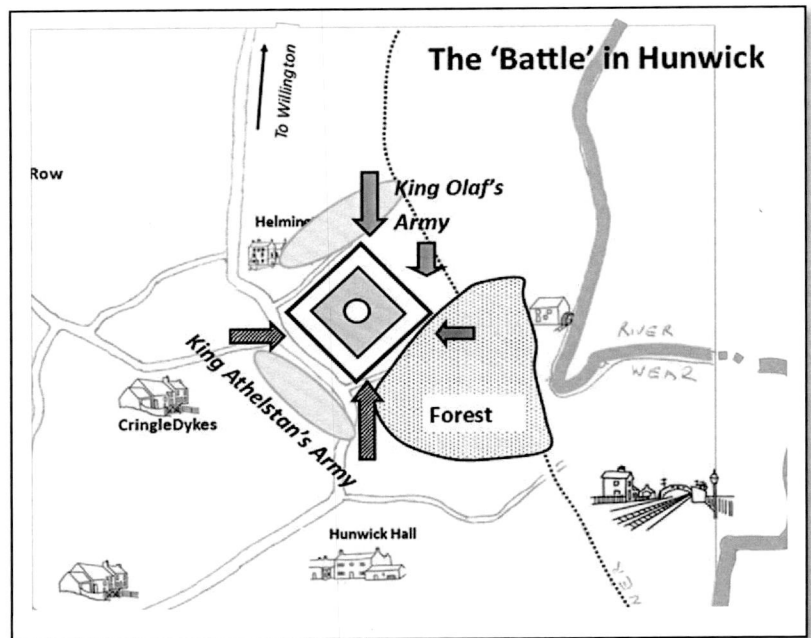

The 'Battle' in Hunwick

The Picts and the Britons, who, on the previous day, had fled and hid in the forest, came out of hiding and advanced onto the field from the forest [from Dyson's Brick works]. They engaged with the flank of Thorolf's advancing army cutting him off from his men.

Thorolf was killed. When Egill, who was fighting on the west flank with King Athelstan, realised that his brother had been killed, ran across the battlefield and took command of the Vikings. The Vikings advanced and killed the commander of the Picts.

There was chaos on the battle field with King Athelstan's army approaching from the south and Egill and the Vikings from the east. King Olafs army was in complete disarray. Men of the northern alliance, attempted to flee from the battle field following the only route open to them, towards the west. They were pursued, in a pincer movement, by Egill, leading the Vikings and King Athelstan leading his men.

The fleeing men had to negotiate the steep banks of the stream, that changes its name from the Quarry Burn to Helmington Beck as it passes under Helmington Hall bridge. While scrambling down the bankside to the stream and scaling the far bank, they were pursued by both King Athelstan's men and the Vikings.

The battle was particularly bloody with many lives lost, including five Kings, seven Earls of Ireland and the son of Constantine II, the King of Scotland. According to the Brunnanburh poem and the poems in Egil's saga, most of the men were killed fleeing to the west.

At that time, the west was seen as the 'land of the dead' as the sun sets in the west. Constantine Farm is due west of the battle field as is Howden-Le-Wear. Perhaps Constantine Farm took its name from the battle, perhaps Howden-Le-Wear. was a 'graveyard of the Danes'?

Bibliography

Durham eThesis. (n.d.).

Abstract of Education Returns. (1833).

Arnold, A. (2004). *Tree_Ring_Analysis_of_Timbers_from_Hunwick_Hall_Farm.* Centre for Archaeology Report 47/2004 and R E Howard and Dr C D Litton.

Ashby, R. (2005). *The Parish Church of St Paul, Hunwick, A Short History.*

Aspin, C. (2006). *The Woolen Industry.* Shire Books.

Atkinson, F. (1974). *Industrial Archaeology of North east England, Volume 2, DCC Ref D844).*

Bagnall, B. L. (2003). *Hunwick Hall, some historical and architectural notes.*

Bailey, J. (1810). *Agriculture in the County of Durham.* https://www.google.co.uk/books/edition/General_View_of_the_Agriculture_of_the_C/o53QCG8cieIC?hl=en&gbpv=1.

Bell, J. T. (1852). *Bell's Plan of the Auckland Coal District.* https://iiif.durham.ac.uk/index.html?manifest=https://iiif.durham.ac.uk/manifests/other/pip/pip-97.json.

Benninson, B. (n.d.). *Brewers and Breweries of North-Eastern England.*

Blackett, M. A. (1980). *Hunwick, un-published thesis.*

Blacketts (1688 – 1792). (1688).

Bowes_Museum. (R1_RPM_9_12_76). *Bowes_Museum.*

Boyle, J. R. (1892). *The County of Durham: Its Castles, Churches and Manor houses.*

C_Mountford, L. (1977). *Industrial_Locomotive_of_Durham_Handbook_L.*

Catford, N. (n.d.). *Disused Stations: Hunwick Station .* www.disused-stations.org.uk.

Census_Office. (1821). *Abstract of the Answers and Returns Made Pursuant to an Act, … Great Britain.*

Christian Drummond Liddy, . H. (2005). *North-east England in the Later Middle Ages, The Bishopric of Durham in the late Middle Ages.*

Clayworkers. (1901). directory_of_clayworkers1901.pdf .

Close, R. A. (n.d.). *Pack Hourse Routes U400a170.* Darlington Library.

Common Room Wat-32_32 . (n.d.).

Council, A. R. (1894). *Health Committee minutes.*

Davison, P. J. (2022). *Brickworks of the Northeast.* PathHead Press.

DCC_Archaeology. (D410). *D410.*

Directory, C. T. (November 1949). *Newcastle and Middlesbrough Areas.*

DRO. (n.d.). *D/X 235/1 .*

Dukesfield_Documents. (n.d.). http://www.dukesfield.org.uk/documents.

Durham City Railways, County archive reference book no. B 43 . (n.d.).

Durham Probate Records DPR 1/1/1801/gb/1. (n.d.).

Durham_Mining_Museum. (2024). *DMM.*

Durham_Records_Office. (1596). *Ref_D/X_235/1.*

Durham_Records_Office. (n.d.). *D/CG_33/14 .*

Durham_Records_Office. (n.d.). *D/Gr 57 For Bernard's estate, see HS, P. 16.*

Durham_Records_Office. (n.d.). *D/Gr_57 For Bernard's estate, see HS, P. 16).*

Durham_university_Special_Collections. (1297). *GB-0033-BRA-1297 Title: Kennett family papers BRA 1297.*

Durham_University_Special_Collections. (1297). *The Kennett family papers (BRA 1297), GB-0033-BRA-1297.*

Durham_University_Special_Collections. (1425). *126r-127v 19 November [1425].*

Durham_University_Special_Collections. (1596). *D/X235/1.*

Durham_University_Special_Collections. (1843). *Tithe Map, Hunwick and Helmington township (Auckland St Andrew parish) (DDR/EA/TTH/1/135) Award with plan.* https://iiif.durham.ac.uk/index.html?manifest=t1m6w924b83h.

Durham_University_Special_Collections. (1876). *Hunwick Hall Estate Map.* https://iiif.durham.ac.uk/index.html?manifest=t1m9c67wn332.

Durham_University_Special_Collections. (1956). *CCB/D/1956/12/32857.*

Durham_University_Special_Collections. (n.d.). *D/CG 33/14.* Durham Records Office.

Durham_University_Special_Collections. (n.d.). *D/CG 33/14.* Records Office.

Durham_University_Special_Collections. (n.d.). *DHC11/VI/27.*

Durham_University_Special_Collections. (n.d.). *DHC11/VI/27 .* https://iiif.durham.ac.uk/index.html?manifest=t1m9c67wn332.

Durham_University_Special_Collections. (n.d.). *https://reed.dur.ac.uk/xtf/view?docId=ark/32150_s1xp68kg20p.xml.*

Durham_University_Special+collections. (1761). *Enclosure of Hunwick Moor.*

Dymond, D. P. (1961). Roman Bridges on Dere Street, Country Durham With a General Appendix on the Evidence for Bridges in Roman Britain, Archaeological Journal,. *Archaeological Journal*, 118:1, 136-164, DOI: 10.1080/00665983.1961.10854190.

Echo, N. (Oct 2021). *Meet Pico the County Durham Pub Monkey who was kept on a lead.* https://www.thenorthernecho.co.uk/news/19620429.met-pico-pub-monkey-new-monkey/.

Eden, T. (1952). *The _County_Books,_Durham_Volume 2).* Robert Hale.

Emery, N. (1998). *Banners of the Durham Coalfield.*

Eneas Mackenzie, . R. (1834). *An Historical, Topographical, and Descriptive View of the Palantine of Durham.*

Engineering. (1879).

Extracts from 'correspondence of John Cosin'. (1663).

Fair, P. (1820). *A Description of Bishop Auckland, including the castle and park and GENTLEMENS SEATS.* https://play.google.com/books/reader?id=05OxwDSG70sC&pg=GBS.PA68&hl=en_GB.

Fairfax-Blakeborough, J. (1770). *Northern Turf History Vol 2, extinct race meetings.*

Fordyce, W. (1860). *A History of Coal, Coke, Coal Fields, Progress of Coal.*

Freemen, D. C. (n.d.). *Freemen, a brief history.* http://www.durhamcityfreemen.org/downloads/freemen-brief-history-booklet-1.pdf .

Gates, T. (2015). An early 17th-century blast furnace at Furness Mill Farm, Hunwick, Co Durham. *Historical Metallugy.*

Gowland. (13 November 1980). *The Auckland Chronical.*

Greenwell, W. (1852). *Boldon Buke: a Survey of the Possessions of the See of Durham Made by order of Bishop Hugh Pudsey, in the Year MCLXXXIII.* ISBN 978-0-543-97277-4.

Guardian, T. (March 2020). *redhills pitmans parliament durham saved.* https://www.theguardian.com/uk-news/2020/mar/15/redhills-pitmans-parliament-durham-saved.

Haggar's_Directory. (1851). *Haggar's Directory.*

Hampton, W. E. (1985). *John Hoton of Hunwick and Tudhoe, County Durham, esquire to Richard III.* The Richardian VII.

Hampton, W. E. (n.d.). *John Hoton of Hunwick and Tudhoe, County Durham, esquire to Richard III .*

Hartlepool. (n.d.). *SS_hunwick_a_general_history.* https://hhtandn.org/notes/879/hunwick-a-general-history.

Heslop, H. (1987). *From Tyne to Tone. A Journey.*

Heslop_Harold. (n.d.). *The Earth Beneath.*

Hildyard. (1952,1). .

Historia de Sancto Cuthberto. (n.d.). https://www.google.co.uk/books/edition/Historia_de_Sancto_Cuthberto/A9GT60kKqEsC?hl=en.

Historian, T. C. (2010). *http://www.clubhistorians.co.uk/html/hunwick.html.*

Hodgson, R. I. (1990). *Coalmining, population and enclosure in the Seasale colliery districts of Durham(northernDurham),1551-1810.* astudyinhistoricalgeography: Durham University http://etheses.dur.ac.uk/961.

Hurleston, H. a. (1858). *Transcribed from A Topographical Dictionary of England, by, seventh edition, Samuel Lewis.* British History Online (british-history.ac.uk).

Hutchinson, W. (1785). *The History and Antiquities of the County Palatine of Durham - Volume 1.*

Hutton, G. (2011). *Roads and Routeways in County Durham: 1530-1730, Durham.* : http://etheses.dur.ac.uk/853/.

Journal, T. P. (n.d.). *Food and Sanitation.*

Kelly's Directory . (1938).

Keys_to_the_Past. (D1788). *Keys_to_the_Past.* Council, Durham County.

keystothepast. (Ref_D1812). *keystothepast.info* . https://keystothepast.info/search-records/results-of-search/results-of-search-2/site-details/source-of-reference/?PRN=D1812.

Lewis, S. (1848). *A_Topographical_Dictionary_of_England.*

Lloyd, E. (1916). *Cooperation in Crook and Neighbourhood, 1865 – 1915* .

MacLauchlan, H. (1858). *Memoir Written During a Survey of the Roman Wall: Through the Counties of Northumberland and Cumberland.*

Magazine, T. G. (n.d.). 1883.

Midlands and Northern Coal and Iron Trade Gazette. (17 October 1877).

Morris, J. (1982). *Bolden Book, History from sources.* Phillimore.

Morris_Harriso_and_Co_Commercial_Directory. (1861).

Mothersole, J. (1927). *Agricola's Road into Scotland: The Great Roman Road from York to the Tweed* .

Moyes, W. A. (1974). *The Banner Book.*

Municipal Engineering, C. a. (1877). *Volume 7.* https://www.google.co.uk/books/edition/Municipal_Engineering_Cleansing_and_Publ/fvxQAAAAYAAJ?hl=en&gbpv=1&dq=sewerage+hunwick&pg=PA310&printsec=frontcover.

Murray, J. (1864). *Handbook fro Travellers in Durham and Northumberland.*

National_Library_of_Scotland_Maps. (n.d.). *National_Library_of_Scotland_Maps.*

NCB. (n.d.). *NCB 24/117.* .

Office, D. R. (n.d.). https://iiif.durham.ac.uk/index.html?manifest=t2mbn999679p&canvas=t2tkd17cw58m.

Oulton, W. C. (1805). *The Traveller's Guide; Or, English Itinerary.*

Parsons_and_White Trade Directory. (1828).

Pitt, C. (1996). *A long Time Gone: History of Defunct Race Courses Since 1900.* Portway Press.

Records, D. P. (1796). *DPR/I/1/1796/R5/1-4.*

Records_Office_Durham. (1596). *Ref: D/X 235/1.*

Richley, M. (1872). *History and characteristics of Bishop Auckland.*

Room, T. C. (n.d.). *Johnson material (John-9-429.*

Room, T. C. (n.d.). *WAT_3_50.*

Royal Commission on River Pollution, 1. -1. (1870). *oral examination re water quality at Durham, Volume 3 Issue 2* . https://www.google.co.uk/books/edition/Reports_of_the_the_Commissioners_Appoint/a24KAQAAMAAJ .

Sagar. (n.d.).

Saxon, C. (1576). *Christopher Saxon's map.* Durham University Special Collections.

Slusar, J. (2016). *Here Today, Gone Tomorrow, Bishop Auckland Racecourse.* www.greyhoundderby.com.

Society, N. E. (1986). *Northern Catholic History* . isbn 0307-4455.

Star, D. N. (n.d.). *20 April 1894.*

Star, D. N. (Friday 20 April 1894).

Surtees . (1931).

Surtees, B.-G. H. (1923). *The History of the Parishes of Hunwick, Helmington, Witton Park and Etherley.*

Surtees, B.-G. H. (n.d.). *The History of the Parishes of Helme Park etc.*

The_Common_Room. (1806). *NEIMME/WAT/32/30.* Newcastle upon tyne.

The_Common_Room. (1843). *NEIMME/WAT/32/31.* Newcastle upon Tyne.

The_Common_Room. (n.d.). *NEIMME/WAT/101/2/6.* Newcastle upon Tyne.

The_Common_Room. (n.d.). *NEIMME/WAT/3/50.* Newcastle upon tyne.

The_Common_Room. (n.d.). *NEIMME/WAT/3/50/008.* Newcastle upon Tyne.

The_Common_Room. (n.d.). *NEIMME/WAT/3/50/457.* Newcastle upon Tyne.

The_Common_Room. (n.d.). *NEIMME/Wat/32/33.* Newcastle upon Tyne.

The_History_of_Parliament. (1820-1832). *Matthew_Bell.*
https://www.historyofparliamentonline.org/volume/1820-1832/member/bell-matthew-1793-1871.

The_Railway_Times_Volume_2. (1939).

The_Sanitary_World. (1884). *The_Sanitary_world - Volume 2 - Page 583.*

Tyne, S. o. (n.d.). *Proceedings: 1855-1857, Volume 1.*
https://books.google.co.uk/books?id=KLxCAAAAYAAJ&pg=PA144&dq=bridge+of+Hunwick+&hl=en&ne
wbks=1&newbks_redir=0&source=gb_mobile_search&sa=X&ved=2ahUKEwir_L-ysr_9AhWNQcAKHS.

University, D. (1297). *GB-0033-BRA-1297 Title: Kennett family papers (BRA 1297) .*

University, D. (1761). *Enclosure Act.*
https://iiif.durham.ac.uk/index.html?manifest=t2mbn999679p&canvas=t2tkd17cw58m.

University, D. (1761). *Enclosure of Hunwicke Moor.*
http://iiif.durham.ac.uk/jalava/#index/t2c6h440s44b/t2crn301138p/t2cjm214p12g!t2m12579s92h/t2
m12579s92h_t2tx059cp97c.

Wesleyan Methodist Jubilee Souvenir document . (n.d.).

Whellan, W. (1856). *History Topography, and directory of the County Palantine of Durham.*

William Parson, . W. (1828). *History, Directory, and Gazetteer, of the Counties of Durham and Northumberland).*

Wray, D. (2009). The Place of Imagery in the Transmission of Culture: the Banners of the Durham Coalfield.

Young, R. (1984). *Aspects of the prehistoric archaeology of the Wear Valley, Co. Durham.* Durham theses,
Durham University. Available at Durham E-Theses Online: http://etheses.dur.ac.uk/1212; Young, R;.

Young, R. (1984). *Aspects of the prehistoric archaeology of the Wear Valley, Co. Durham.*
http://etheses.dur.ac.uk/1212/1/1212_v1.pdf.

1. MAPS - www.nls.uk
2. The Hunwickian | Facebook - https://www.facebook.com/hunwickian
3. Community links past and present together on website, The Northern Echo 5th July 2005
4. Huntingfield - Hurleston | British History Online – www.british-history.ac.uk)
5. Durham Mining Museum - Rough Lea Colliery www.dmm.org.uk
6. Brancepeth, Crook and Witton-le-Wear - England's North East www.englandsnortheast.co.uk
7. Kirby, D. A. (1968) Some physical and economic aspects of water use in the wear basin, Durham theses, Durham University. Available at Durham E-Theses Online: http://etheses.dur.ac.uk/9371/
8. https://insearchofholywellsandhealingsprings.com/source-first-series-contents/ancient-healing-and-holy-wells-of-county-durham/
9. https://books.google.co.uk/books?id=8dERAAAAIAAJ&pg=PA240&dq=quarry+hunwick&hl=en&newbks=1&newbks_redir=1&sa=X&ved=2ahUKEwjqjNyYp8f8AhUColwKHTtjDVo4FBDoAXoECAkQAg
10. (Abstract of Education Returns 1833) E Thesis Cloth seals https://core.ac.uk/download/pdf/76946276.pdf
11. http://www.colchestertreasurehunting.co.uk/clothseals.htm
12. (The Sanitary world - Volume 2 - Page 583 — 1884)
   https://www.google.com/search?q=sewerage+hunwick&client=firefox-b-d&tbm=bks&sxsrf=AJOqlzVr_BBEsznlrC5dRGJXunoZ9_ExEA:1674225836984&ei=rKjKY8fNO6iAhbIP5aWe2Ak&start=10&sa=N&ved=2ahUKEwjH06Wisdb8AhUoQEEAHeWSB5sQ8NMDegQIDxAW&biw=1280&bih=559&dpr=1.5
13. 1870—oral examination re water quality at Durham
   https://www.google.co.uk/books/edition/Reports_of_the_the_Commissioners_Appoint/a24KAQAAMAAJ
14. Abstract of the Answers and Returns Made Pursuant to an Act, … Great Britain. Census Office · 1821)
15. John Poulter, The Planning of Roman Roads and Walls in Northern Britain)
16. 1870—oral examination re water quality at Durham
   https://www.google.co.uk/books/edition/Reports_of_the_the_Commissioners_Appoint/a24KAQAAMAAJ
17. https://www.amazon.co.uk/Hunwick-social-Anglo-Saxon-Northumbria-Brunanburh-ebook/dp/B07XV63W8Y
18. "Reproduced with the permission of © The Coal Authority. All rights reserved"
19. Hodgson, RobertIan(1990)Coalmining,populationandenclosureintheSeasalecollierydistrictsof Durham(northernDurham),1551-1810:astudyinhistoricalgeography.,Durhamtheses,Durham University.AvailableatDurhamE-ThesesOnline:http://etheses.dur.ac.uk/961/
20. (northern catholic history, north eastern catholic history society 1986 isbn 0307-4455)
21. Digitised material for Copy of inclosure awards for Hamsterley, Hunwick Edge, Ushaw Moor and Evenwood - DHC1/M1 - page 152 – page 194
22. Wesleyan Methodist Jubilee Souvenir document
23. A J Arnold, R E Howard and Dr C D Litton, Centre for Archaeology Report 47/2004
24. Sir Timothy Eden, The County Books, Durham, Volume 2)
25. Hunwick Hall inventory 1635/6(Durham Records Office (D/CG 33/14)
26. E M Halcrow , The Decline of Demesne farming on the Estates of Durham Cathedral Priory theses, Durham University. Available at Durham E-Theses Online: http://etheses.dur.ac.uk/853/
27. DHC11/VI/27: https://iiif.durham.ac.uk/index.html?manifest=t1m9c67wn332
28. DHC11/VI/77: https://iiif.durham.ac.uk/index.html?manifest=t1mbc386j76w
29. CCB MP/100: https://iiif.durham.ac.uk/index.html?manifest=t1m9g54xh66v
30. Drove Roads of Northumberland, Ian Roberts, Richard Carlton, Alan Rushworth